Spying Blind

*

Spying Blind

The CIA, the FBI, and the Origins of 9/11

*

AMY B. ZEGART

PRINCETON UNIVERSITY PRESS

PRINCETON AND OXFORD

Copyright © 2007 by Princeton University Press
Published by Princeton University Press, 41 William Street,
Princeton, New Jersey 08540
In the United Kingdom: Princeton University Press, 3 Market Place,
Woodstock, Oxfordshire OX20 1SY

Library of Congress Cataloging-in-Publication Data

Zegart, Amy, 1967–
Spying blind : the CIA, the FBI, and the origins of 9/11 / Amy B. Zegart.
p. cm.
Includes bibliographical references and index.
ISBN: 978-0-691-12021-8

1. Intelligence service—United States. 2. United States. Central
Intelligence Agency. 3. United States. Federal Bureau of Investigation.
4. September 11 Terrorist Attacks, 2001. 5. Terrorism—Government
policy—United States. I. Title.

JK468.I6Z42 2007
973.931——dc22   2006103325

British Library Cataloging-in-Publication Data is available

This book has been composed in Palatino

Printed on acid-free paper. ∞

press.princeton.edu

Printed in the United States of America

1 3 5 7 9 10 8 6 4 2

For my children:

Alexander, Jack, and Kate

✳

✳ *Contents* ✳

* *Tables* *

* Figures *

* *Acknowledgments* *

FOR YEARS, I have been fascinated by the dark side of organizations,[1] and one puzzle in particular: why U.S. foreign policy agencies cannot adapt easily to new challenges. In 1999, my initial idea was to write a book comparing how well different agencies responded to the end of the Cold War. But two problems quickly stumped me. The first was the absence of much variation across agencies. When I asked a number of senior officials and experts which U.S. foreign policy agencies had adapted better than others, the response was universal: none had done particularly well. The second problem was that adaptation was too vague a concept. I needed a set of facts on the ground, a dramatic event that would enable me to pinpoint a major new threat and trace how well America's foreign policy machinery had responded to it.

Then came September 11th. Like most Americans, I can still vividly picture that day. I remember standing stunned in my kitchen as the World Trade Center towers collapsed on television. I remember watching my son, Jack, take his first steps and wondering how his world would differ from my own Cold War childhood. And I remember thinking that this was the event I had to examine.

The journey has been a long one, with many people to thank. Above all, I would like to express my deepest gratitude to the seventy-five current and former government officials who agreed to be interviewed for this book. Five of them spoke on the record and can be thanked by name: Senator John McCain (R-AZ), former Senator Gary Hart (D-CO), FBI Director Robert Mueller, FBI Intelligence Directorate Chief Wayne Murphy, and Robert Baer, who served as a CIA clandestine officer for twenty-one years. The rest spoke on the condition that they remain anonymous. Some battled their own bureaucracies at considerable professional risk to help an outsider gain an insider's view of the U.S. Intelligence Community. Others provided crucial assistance in obtaining government documents that were unclassified but unavailable to the public. Many were interviewed several times over a period of years. All deserve far more than my thanks and the free book I promised too long ago.

Academic studies are not always welcomed by the national security agencies they expose and examine. In the 1950s, the Pentagon classified and banned publication of Roberta Wohlstetter's award-winning book about intelligence failures at Pearl Harbor for five years, even though all of her sources were unclassified.[2] Half a century later, the battleground between security interests and First Amendment rights remains contentious and complex. I am eternally grateful to my lawyer, Richard Sauber, for helping me navigate this terrain.

A special thanks goes to Bill Duhnke, Senator Pat Roberts, (R-KS), Senator Jay Rockefeller (D-WV), and the other Members of the Senate Select Committee on Intelligence, who pressed me during the committee's reform hearings in 2004 to suggest ways of making the U.S. Intelligence Community work better rather than just criticizing it from the Ivory Tower.

I am deeply indebted to my doctoral advisor, Condi Rice. I am also grateful to Steve Krasner, Scott Sagan, Terry Moe, and David Brady. Ten years after I finished my Ph.D., they are all still challenging me to think harder and dig deeper. The Stanford Political Science Department has been the gift that keeps on giving.

I had the good fortune to land at UCLA shortly after Al Carnesale became chancellor. He made good on every promise, from reading my work, to playing the president for my foreign policy seminar simulation, to improving UCLA's basketball team. I would also like to thank Barbara Nelson, the Dean of UCLA's School of Public Affairs, and the Public Policy Department Chairman, Mark Peterson, for giving me the most precious gift of all: time. Without their support for a research sabbatical, I would still be toiling away.

Howard Aldrich, Charles Perrow, Diane Vaughan, and Lynne Zucker welcomed a wayward political scientist with open arms and provided a fascinating foray into sociology. Thanks also to Brian Balogh, Matt Baum, J. R. DeShazo, Richard Betts, Bruce Berkowitz, Dara Cohen, Lynn Eden, Geoffrey Garrett, Loch Johnson, Mel Leffler, Ernest May, Richard Posner, Richard Steinberg, and Greg Treverton for their suggestions and comments on earlier drafts; and to Graham Allison and Juliette Kayyem at Harvard, Eric Patashnik at the University of Virginia, Scott Sagan and Lynn Eden at Stanford, Dick Kohn and Dan Gitterman at the University of North Carolina, Adam Winkler and Russell Korobkin at UCLA Law School, and Richard Betts at Columbia University and the Council on Foreign Relations, who all invited me to present various parts of the book in progress.

I am forever indebted to my dynamic duo of research assistants, Josh Mukhopadhyay and Jean Schindler, for running the research marathon alongside me. Thanks also to Daren Schlecter and Jenny Miller, who hunted diligently for information at the beginning; to Chris Yeh, who provided first-rate summer research help when I needed it most; to Stacy Edgar, Amritha Subramanian, Jennifer Mishory, Mai Truong; and to all the students in my foreign policy crisis decision-making seminar, who remind me how lucky I am to teach.

I would like to thank the Smith Richardson Foundation for funding the lion's share of this project with great enthusiasm and minimal bureaucracy. Thanks also to the University of California's Institute on Global Conflict and Cooperation, the UCLA Center on American Politics and Public Policy, and the UCLA International Institute for providing seed funding.

Chuck Myers, my editor at Princeton University Press, believed in this project from its inception. His patience is surpassed only by his persistence in getting me to attempt the ultimate unnatural act for a professor: writing an academic book that is readable.

There's an old saying that guests are like fish: both smell after three days. I will always be grateful to five people who graciously endured my extended visits to Washington: Randall Kempner, Michael Fitzpatrick, Miriam Gonzales, Maya Fitzpatrick, and Janne Nolan. I also would like to thank Nora Bensahel, Meena Bose, Dan Drezner, Mark Kleiman, Richard Riordan, Andy Sabl, and Jack Weiss for their unflinching support and humor.

Thanks to my parents, Shelly and Kenny Zegart, who have single-handedly kept my last book in print all these years.

Archie Epps, dear mentor and friend, passed away before he could read this book. But I cannot let the manuscript go to print without thanking him. I suspect somehow he is still conducting surveillance of Harvard Yard, searching for undergraduates in need of a gentle nudge.

I owe more than any preface can convey to my husband, Craig Mallery, who kept our own household insurgency at bay whenever I made the trek east, avoided political science at all cost as an undergraduate only to get an earful of it every night at dinner, always got the raw end of our mutual editing deal, believed in this project so much he built me a home office to prove it, and convinced me to undertake the behemoth task of tracking five hundred reform recommendations with the soothing but misguided words, "Honey, I'm sure it won't take that long." He is still the best thing I have ever found in any library.

I could not have spent the past six years examining tragedy at the office without coming home to my three children, Alexander, Jack, and Kate. Their sense of wonder and possibility is the ultimate antidote to pessimism. Every time a fire engine passes, I naturally start pondering the organizational deficiencies of emergency response systems. They immediately begin waving at the firefighters. For that, and so much more, this book is dedicated to them.

Spying Blind

*

CHAPTER 1

An Organizational View of 9/11

I was not surprised. I was horrified.
—General Brent Scowcroft,
former national security advisor[1]

IN JANUARY 2000, al Qaeda operatives from around the world gathered secretly in Malaysia for a planning meeting. The Central Intelligence Agency (CIA) was watching. Among the participants was a man named Khalid al-Mihdhar, one of the September 11 hijackers who would later help to crash American Airlines Flight 77 into the Pentagon. By the time the meeting disbanded, the CIA had taken a photograph of al-Mihdhar, learned his full name, obtained his passport number, and uncovered one other critical piece of information: al-Mihdhar held a multiple-entry visa to the United States.[2] It was twenty months before the September 11, 2001, terrorist attacks on the World Trade Center and Pentagon. George Tenet, the director of central intelligence (DCI), later admitted that the CIA should have immediately placed al-Mihdhar on the State Department's watch list denying him entry into the United States, and it should have notified other government agencies such as the FBI.[3] But the CIA did not do so until August 23, 2001, just nineteen days before the attacks and months after al-Mihdhar had entered the country, obtained a California motor vehicle photo identification card—using his real name—and started taking flying lessons.

The case of Khalid al-Mihdhar provides a chilling example of the subtle yet powerful effects of organization—that is, the cultures, incentives, and structures that critically influence what government agencies do and how well they do it. Why did the CIA take so long to put this suspected al Qaeda operative on the State Department's watch list, especially given Director Tenet's earlier declaration that the United States was "at war" with al Qaeda,[4] his clear public warnings to Congress—for three consecutive years—that Osama bin Laden was determined to strike major blows against American targets,[5] and when intelligence chatter about preparations for a "spectacular" attack was spiking in the spring and summer of 2001?[6]

The simplest answer is that the agency had never been in the habit of watch listing al Qaeda operatives before. For more than forty years, the Central Intelligence Agency and the twelve other agencies of the U.S. Intelligence Community (IC) had operated with Cold War procedures, priorities, and thinking, all of which had little need for making sure foreign terrorists stayed out of the United States.[7] Before September 11, there was no formal training program, no well-honed process, and no sustained level of attention given to ensuring that intelligence officers would identify dangerous terrorists and warn other U.S. government agencies about them before they reached the United States.[8] As one CIA employee told congressional investigators after the September 11 attacks, he believed it was "not incumbent" even on the CIA's special Osama bin Laden unit to place people such as al-Mihdhar on the State Department's watch list.[9]

No one will ever know whether the World Trade Center and Pentagon attacks could have been prevented. Evidence suggests, however, that the right information did not get to the right places at the right time. Many of the agonizing missteps and missed clues have been widely publicized. There is the star Phoenix FBI agent who warned in a July 2001 memo that Osama bin Laden could be training terrorists in U.S. flight schools, a warning that never made it to the top of the FBI or a single other intelligence agency. There is the refusal by FBI headquarters to seek a search warrant for the computer files of Zacarias Moussaoui, a foreign flight school student who Minneapolis field agents were convinced was plotting a terrorist attack with a large aircraft and who later became the only person convicted in the United States for his connection to the 9/11 attacks.[10] And there is the president's August 6, 2001, CIA briefing entitled "Bin Laden Determined to Strike in U.S." which gave the impression the FBI had the threat covered, erroneously suggested that Yemeni tourists taking photographs were terrorists casing federal buildings in New York, and made no mention of crucial pieces of information that should have been pursued aggressively. These included the Phoenix memo, the al Qaeda summit in Malaysia, al-Mihdhar's U.S. visa, and the CIA's discovery that a second September 11 hijacker who had attended the summit, Nawaf al-Hazmi, had also entered the United States.[11] Thanks to the extraordinary work of the 9/11 Commission and the House and Senate Intelligence Committees' Joint Inquiry into the attacks, most Americans have a good idea of what went wrong in the weeks and months before September 11.[12] The challenge now is to explain *why* it went wrong.

This book argues that the answer lies in organizations, more specifically, in the deeply rooted organizational weaknesses that have afflicted U.S. intelligence agencies for decades and in the enduring impediments to fixing them. The single most important reason the United States remained so vulnerable on September 11 was not the McDonald's wages paid to airport security workers, the Clinton administration's inability to capture or kill Osama bin Laden, or the Bush administration's failure to place terrorism higher on its priority list. It was the stunning inability of U.S. intelligence agencies to adapt to the end of the Cold War.

During the 1990s, for example, intelligence officials repeatedly warned of a grave and growing terrorist threat even while they continued old funding patterns that favored electronic surveillance—ideal for counting Soviet warheads—over human intelligence efforts better suited for penetrating terrorist groups. Although details about U.S. intelligence spending are classified, conservative estimates based on the declassified 1997 intelligence budget put annual human intelligence spending at $1.6 billion, a little more than the cost of building and launching a single spy satellite.[13] The amount of money spent directly to support human intelligence operations in the field was even less. As one official with access to the CIA's human intelligence budget put it, once pensions, salaries, and other expenses were paid, the "The James Bond fund that people think we're doing came down to $500 million," or less than 2 percent of the annual intelligence budget at the time.[14]

Counterterrorism efforts were as scattered as they were underfunded, split among forty-six different agencies without a central strategy, budget, or coordinating mechanism. Director of Central Intelligence George Tenet declared war on Osama bin Laden in a December 1998 memo and urged that "no resources or people [be] spared" to fight him, but proved unable to mass his troops in the right places.[15] Although Tenet tried to increase dramatically the size of the Counterterrorist Center, he failed,[16] leaving only five analysts assigned to Osama bin Laden on September 11.[17]

The CIA was not alone. The FBI formally declared terrorism its number one priority as early as 1998.[18] Yet on September 11, 2001, only 6 percent of FBI personnel were working on counterterrorism issues,[19] new agents still received more time for vacation than counterterrorism training,[20] and the vast majority of the FBI's intelligence analysts—precisely the people who were charged with connecting the dots across different FBI cases—were found to be unqualified to perform their jobs.[21] Steeped in an eighty-year-old culture that prized searching houses more than searching databases, the agency lacked basic computer capabilities to see whether the words "flight training school" showed up in any of its case files and even the FBI Director, Louis Freeh, ordered the computer removed from his office because he never used it.[22] In the words of one FBI official, the prevailing attitude was, "real men don't type. The only thing a real agent needs is a notebook, a pen, and a gun, and with those three things you can conquer the world."[23] Just weeks before the attacks, a highly classified internal review of the bureau's counterterrorism capabilities gave failing grades to every one of the FBI's fifty-six U.S. field offices.[24]

These problems were not isolated mistakes, failures of foresight, or the result of poor decisions by individuals asleep at the switch. Instead, they were symptoms of three deeper and more intractable organizational deficiencies: (1) cultural pathologies that led intelligence agencies to resist new technologies, ideas, and tasks; (2) perverse promotion incentives that rewarded intelligence officials for all of the wrong things; and (3) structural weaknesses dating back decades that hindered the operation of the CIA and FBI and prevented the U.S. Intelligence Community from working as a coherent whole. It was these core weaknesses that caused U.S. intelligence agencies to blow key operational opportunities—such as watchlisting al-Mihdhar or searching Zacarias Moussaoui's computer files—that might have disrupted the September 11 plot. And it was these core weaknesses that kept U.S. intelligence agencies from getting more chances to defeat al Qaeda in the first place. With FBI agents keeping case files in shoe boxes rather than putting them into computers, with CIA operatives clinging to old systems designed for recruiting Soviet officials at cocktail parties rather than Jihadists in caves, with career incentives that rewarded intelligence officials for staying cloistered in their own agencies rather than working across agency lines, and with a forty-year-old intelligence structure that gave no person the power to match resources against priorities and knock bureaucratic heads together, the U.S. Intelligence Community did not have a fighting chance against al Qaeda.

The existence of these organizational deficiencies, and the urgent need to fix them, was no secret in Washington before the September 11 attacks. Between 1991 and 2001, intelligence problems and counterterrorism challenges were the subject of at least six classified reports[25] and a dozen major unclassified studies.[26] The unclassified studies alone issued more than 500 recommendations for reform across the U.S. government. Two-thirds of these recommendations, or 340 in total, targeted the CIA, FBI, and the rest of the U.S. Intelligence Community. Yet only 35 of these 340 intelligence recommendations were successfully implemented before September 11, and most—268 to be exact—resulted in no action whatsoever.[27] In January 2001, nine months before the attacks, the bipartisan blue-ribbon Hart-Rudman Commission offered the most comprehensive assessment of U.S. national security challenges and deficiencies since World War II. The commission issued stark conclusions: "the dramatic changes in the world since the end of the Cold War," it noted, "have not been accompanied by any major institutional changes in the Executive branch of the U.S. government."[28] The commission presciently predicted that institutional deficiencies left the United States homeland exceptionally vulnerable to catastrophic terrorist attack.

No system is failure-proof. As Richard Betts wrote in *Foreign Affairs* shortly after September 11, "The awful truth is that even the best intelligence systems will have big failures."[29] Evidence suggests, however, that U.S. intelligence agencies were nowhere close to being the best before 9/11, and that they could have been better. When the Soviet Union fell in 1991 and the principal threat to U.S. national security changed, the Intelligence Community was slow to change with it.

Why? What is it that prevented the CIA, the FBI, and other agencies from adapting to the rising terrorist threat during the 1990s? To date, no one has provided satisfying answers. Academics have avoided the subject, concentrating instead on research topics that have more readily available data, fit more squarely into existing theories, and do not require delving into the controversial business of spying. At the same time, politicians and journalists have preferred to point fingers, focusing on who failed to do what and when. The result is a prevailing wisdom that mistakenly attributes the failures of September 11 to individuals.

The Finger Pointing Fallacy

Everyone has someone to blame for 9/11. Democrats such as former Clinton National Security Advisor Samuel Berger and Secretary of State Madeleine Albright have faulted President Bush and his administration for giving terrorism short shrift compared to missile defense and other foreign policy issues.[30] Republicans, including Secretary of State Condoleezza Rice and Vice President Richard Cheney, have charged the Clinton administration with failing to develop an effective counterterrorism strategy and emboldening bin Laden by responding weakly to earlier terrorist attacks.[31] Some, such as former Senate Intelligence Committee Chairman Richard Shelby (R-AL), have laid responsibility squarely on the shoulders of George Tenet, who served as director of central intelligence from 1997 to 2004.[32] The most blistering criticism came in the spring of 2004, when Richard Clarke, the White House counterterrorism czar under both Presidents Clinton and George W. Bush, accused Bush and his top aides of dropping the ball on terrorism.[33] Although different accusers have found different culprits, their point is the same: individual leadership failures are the root cause of the World Trade Center and Pentagon attacks.

Attributing failure to individuals is both understandable and dangerous. Casting blame after moments of great tragedy is a natural human response. It also makes for good politics and great journalism. No one should be shocked that politicians from both parties rushed to accuse and defend, and the press rushed to cover them. Nor is it surprising that nearly all of the 9/11 books penned by journalists since the attacks have focused on the human causes of tragedy, dissecting the power plays and personality clashes between various intelligence officers in the field and policymakers in Washington.[34] It is the nature of the business: journalists usually place individuals at the heart of the story rather than examining the forces that transcend them and tend to rely on anecdotal evidence to meet tight deadlines rather than studying a single problem in systematic and gory detail over a number of years. The best of this genre—such as Steve Coll's *Ghost Wars* and Lawrence Wright's *The Looming Tower*—have much to offer, yet nevertheless emphasize individual failures more than systemic ones. The worst in the genre suffer from what Malcolm Gladwell calls "creeping determinism," a tendency to view pre-9/11 warnings through post-9/11 lenses.[35] In hindsight, of course, smoking guns are everywhere—a 1995 report sent to the CIA from Philippine authorities noting that a captured terrorist had plans to fly an airplane into CIA headquarters,[36] or an al Qaeda telephone call intercepted during the summer of 2001 that mentions a "terrifying" attack using an airplane.[37] But proving that intelligence officials could and should have seen these signals as ominous warnings beforehand is quite another matter.

As the above discussion indicates, highlighting the role of individuals is also dangerous because it suggests the wrong causes of failure and the wrong remedies to address them. We are left to think that if only the right people had been heard, if only a few important officials had connected a few obvious dots, if only more leaders inside the corridors of power had had their hair on fire, tragedy could have been averted. As Bob Woodward, the dean of journalist nonfiction, once wrote, "Decision making at the highest levels of national government is a complex human interaction. . . . This human story is the core."[38]

Actually, the human story is the problem. What is missing from these accounts is a sense of context, the underlying constraints and forces that make it likely talented people will make poor decisions. It is easy, for example, to blame intelligence officials for overlooking warnings about a terrorist attack in an intercepted telephone conversation. It is much harder when one considers that several million such conversations are intercepted by intelligence officials every day of every week of every year.[39] Journalists, the old saying goes, write the first draft of history. In the case of September 11, however, journalists have provided the *only* draft of history. The fault is not theirs, but ours in the academy: political scientists have devoted almost no attention to studying U.S. intelligence since 9/11.[40] The result is that the role of individuals in September 11 has been grossly overstated, while the organizational causes of failure have gone largely unexamined.

Consider the strongest case that has been made for the importance of individual leadership: the Clinton administration's successful prevention of terrorist attacks during the Millennium celebration. The 9/11 Commission found that from December 1999 to January 2000, things were clearly different. Told that there would be between five and fifteen terrorist attacks on domestic targets, senior Clinton officials were at battle stations.[41] The national security advisor, the FBI director, the director of central intelligence, the attorney general, the secretary of state, Pentagon officials, the NSC staff—all of the federal government's senior most officials were focused as never before on one goal: preventing a terrorist attack inside the United States. National Security Advisor Samuel Berger held White House meetings with top officials every day for a month.[42] Information was flowing, both across agencies and up the chains of command. The commission concluded that the weeks surrounding the Millennium constituted the "one period in which the government as a whole seemed to be acting in concert to deal with terrorism."[43] During the summer of 2001, by comparison, the commission found no corresponding senior level push inside the Bush administration to focus and shake up the bureaucracy.[44]

In the eyes of many, this sense of urgency and attention at the senior levels made all the difference: The presence of high-level leadership led to success in thwarting the Millennium attacks, while its absence in the summer of 2001 led to failure on September 11. As Berger put it, "Things happen when the number one person is in the room. . . . When the principal spends an hour a day at the White House or more, he goes back or she goes back to his agency or her agency and he or she shakes that agency for whatever it has."[45] Berger told the 9/11 Commission that he was "convinced that our sustained attention . . . prevented significant losses of life."[46] Former counterterrorism czar Richard Clarke was more blunt, suggesting that if only the Bush administration had urged senior officials to "shake the trees" in the summer of 2001, as Clinton officials had done during the Millennium period, they would have discovered what lower-level agents in the FBI already knew: that al Qaeda operatives were in the United States.[47] "If Condi Rice had been doing her job and holding those daily meetings, the way Sandy Berger did, if she had a hands-on attitude to being national security adviser, when she had information that there was a threat against the United States, that kind of information was shaken out in December 1999, it would have been shaken out in the summer of 2001," Clarke declared on CNN's *Larry King Live*.[48]

The problem here is not facts, but logic. It seems clear that senior Clinton officials devoted more attention to thwarting imminent terrorist attacks during the Millennium period than their Bush administration counterparts did in the summer of 2001. The question is, did that attention matter? It could be that individual leadership made all the difference, forcing the system to move information to the right places and preventing disaster. Or maybe not. When it comes to cause and effect relationships, looks are often deceiving. In public policy 101, this is called the "correlation versus causation" problem: two trends can coincide without strong causal connections between them. If I said, for example, that my hair length historically corresponded to the rise and fall of the U.S. stock market, surely no reader would start adjusting his investments according to my hair styles. Leadership is obviously more connected to counterterrorism than hair length is to the Dow. But the point is the same: causal relationships cannot be assumed. Instead, they must be determined through careful analysis of facts.

In this case, closer examination suggests the individual leadership argument is not so convincing. The Clinton administration's own after-action report of the Millennium attacks concluded that the crucial break stemmed from luck and the experience of a low-level customs agent, not planning and the leadership of high-level officials.[49] On December 14, 1999, an alert customs inspector named Diana Dean noticed a fidgety passenger driving his rental car off a ferry traveling from Canada to Port Angeles, Washington. Dean decided to detain the passenger for a secondary inspection. When she began patting him down, the passenger panicked and tried to flee. He turned out to be Ahmed Ressam, an Algerian Jihadist who was planning to blow up Los Angeles International Airport (LAX). When inspectors examined Ressam's car, they found hidden explosives and timing devices.[50] Counterterrorism Chief Richard Clarke wrote that "strings from Ressam" led to a sleeper cell of Algerian mujahadeen in Montreal, which in turn led officials to what looked like sleeper cells in Boston and New York.[51]

Dean testified at Ressam's trial that it was her "training and experience" that led her to notice and stop Ressam.[52] "I don't recall any specific threats," she later told reporters. "I don't recall anybody saying watch for terrorists."[53] Her recollections turned out to be accurate. U.S. customs records reveal that the agency was not under any heightened state of alert.[54] Senior officials in Washington, DC may have been at battle stations to stop a terrorist attack when Ressam's ferry crossed the Canadian-U.S. border, but Diana Dean and every other customs agent in the field were not. The 9/11 Commission concluded, "It appears that the heightened sense of alert at the national level played no role in Ressam's detention."[55] In this particular case, the leadership of senior officials contributed much less to the outcome than most people believe.

My point is not that individual leadership never matters, but that the harder-to-see aspects of organizational life—such as training, procedures, cultures, and agency structures—often matter more. This is important, both for our understanding of the past and our expectations of the future. Indeed, if individual leadership determined counterterrorism success and failure, then fixing U.S. intelligence agencies would be easy. One need only identify the few bad apples and toss, or vote, them out. The reality is much worse. Yes, individuals made mistakes, but it was the system that failed us.

The post-9/11 efforts by FBI Director Robert Mueller to modernize the bureau's information technology capabilities illustrate just how powerful these organizational forces can be. By all accounts, Mueller had everything he needed to succeed. He had been on the job just one week when the September 11 attacks occurred, so could not be held responsible for the bureau's past failings. A decorated ex-Marine and former federal prosecutor, Mueller had high internal credibility as a no-nonsense law enforcement advocate and charismatic leader.[56] At the same time, he was a savvy political operator who had the full support of both Congress and the White House, especially after the September 11 attacks. The new director also was well aware of the bureau's computer problems—as one member of Congress put it, everyone knew that the FBI "was communicating by smoke signal and calculating by abacus"[57]—and he was determined to fix them, declaring information technology one of his top reform priorities soon after 9/11.[58] Perhaps most important, Mueller had something that no other FBI director ever had: urgency. As Mueller himself later reflected, "9/11. . . was the catalyst for triggering the urgency in all of us to change immediately."[59] In short, Robert Mueller appeared to be the right leader at the right moment to lead the FBI out of the information Dark Ages.

But even he did not succeed. In February 2005, more than three years after the attacks, Mueller told a flabbergasted and furious Congress that the bureau's first major technology initiative, converting paper files to a new electronic case file system, was two years overdue, had cost $170 million, did not work, and had no prospect of succeeding any time soon.[60] The problem wasn't Mueller, it was the FBI: according to the Justice Department's own review, the bureau had never developed the management structures, standards, processes, capabilities, or talent to manage information technology well, and was completely ill-equipped to develop and oversee such a large-scale project.[61] "My greatest frustration," declared Mueller in 2007, "is the technology."[62] In the end, Mueller's information technology initiative was undone by his own organization.

The Enduring Impediments to Adaptation

In the pages that follow, I take a different approach, examining the systemic forces that prevented the CIA and FBI from responding to changes in the threat environment between the end of the Cold War and September 11. It is important to underscore that this book looks backward, not forward. It is a study of past adaptation failure, not a blueprint for future reform. Far too often, policymakers formulate solutions that fail to address the root causes of failure. But as Roberta Wohlstetter argued in her classic analysis of the Japanese attack at Pearl Harbor forty-five years ago, root causes are everything.[63] Understanding the origins of past failures is the first, most important, and most often overlooked step toward future success.

Chapter 2 begins by making the case for adaptation failure. I ask whether the U.S. Intelligence Community adapted as well as could be expected after the Cold War given the challenges and constraints that it faced. The heart of the chapter is an analysis of every major unclassified study of U.S. intelligence and counterterrorism efforts between 1991 and 2001. Examining what these studies found, and what happened to their recommendations, provides a window into what intelligence officials and policymakers knew *before* the September 11 attacks rather than afterward, in the glare of hindsight. It turns out there were many canaries in the coal mine: a dozen studies issued hundreds of recommendations to fix crucial intelligence shortcomings, yet almost none were implemented. What's more, we now know that these recommendations were right on target, focusing on precisely the same failings that the 9/11 Commission and the House and Senate Intelligence Committees' Joint Inquiry into September 11 found in their postmortems.

Chapter 3 delves into theory, examining a wide body of academic research and developing a general model to explain intelligence agency adaptation failure. Although the chapter is intended primarily for an academic audience, I encourage general readers to resist the urge to skip it. For those who must, however, let me make the most important point here: theory matters. Academics often make theory inaccessible, loading it with jargon, mathematical models, and abstract ideas. At its best, however, theory is not the indulgence of university professors, but a vital tool for understanding everyday life. The purpose of theory is to simplify complexity, to identify cause-and-effect relationships, and to suggest why and how some causes are more important than others. In the case of September 11, I attribute the adaptation failure of U.S. intelligence agencies to three enduring realities: (1) the nature of organizations, which makes internal reform exceedingly difficult; (2) the rational self-interest of presidents, legislators, and government bureaucrats, which works against executive branch reform; and (3) the fragmented structure of the federal government, which erects high barriers to legislative reform. These three underlying factors explain why different officials at different times all failed to fix critical intelligence deficiencies that had been well known for years.

Chapters 4, 5, 6, and 7 apply this general model to specifics. Chapter 4 presents a case study of the CIA's adaptation efforts between 1991 and the 2001 terrorist attacks and shows how the nature of organizations, rational self-interest, and the fragmented structure of the American political system kept them from succeeding. Chapter 5 traces the connection between the CIA's failure to adapt and its failure to perform. I argue that lingering deficiencies in the CIA's structure, culture, and personnel incentive systems crippled the agency's ability to capitalize on eleven different opportunities to penetrate and possibly disrupt the September 11 attacks.

Chapters 6 and 7 provide companion case studies of the FBI, examining the bureau's failed counterterrorism efforts from 1991 to 2001 and tracking how the persistence of organizational problems led the bureau to failure. FBI agents had twelve opportunities to try to derail al Qaeda inside the United States before September 11. Like the CIA, the bureau missed them all.

Finally, chapter 8 examines intelligence reform efforts since September 11. Although this book seeks to explain the adaptation failure of U.S. intelligence agencies *before* disaster struck, peering past the World Trade Center and Pentagon attacks offers a tough test of my model: If ever we would expect to find a catalyst to transform the U.S. Intelligence Community, the worst terrorist attacks in U.S. history should be it. I find, however, that intelligence reform has remained elusive. The same enduring realities that prevented adaptation before 9/11 have stymied adaptation even in the aftermath of tragedy. Although intelligence reform continues to be a work in progress, improvements to date have been slow in coming and painfully difficult to achieve. At the time of this writing in May 2007, nearly six years after 9/11, the Intelligence Community's worst deficiencies remain.

A Note about Sources

This book is based primarily on unclassified government documents and personal interviews with seventy-five current and former government officials. Senator John McCain (R-AZ), former Senator Gary Hart (D-CO), FBI Director Robert Mueller, FBI Intelligence Directorate Chief Wayne Murphy, and former CIA clandestine service officer Robert Baer agreed to be interviewed on the record and are therefore quoted by name. All other sources agreed to be interviewed on the condition that they remain anonymous. Many were interviewed more than once. I have omitted references to specific interview dates and locations in order to protect their identities.

Anonymity comes with benefits and drawbacks. Protecting a source's identity encourages candor and prompts some individuals to speak who otherwise would not. For research about the public failures of secret agencies, anonymity is a vital—and sometimes the only—route to information.

On the other hand, anonymous sources are protected from having to defend their assertions and confront their biases in the light of day. Readers must consider the message without knowing the identity of the messenger. This places an added responsibility on the researcher to select sources with care, consider the motives and perspectives anonymous sources bring to bear, and verify the information they provide.

I have endeavored to select a group of sources that, together, could provide a comprehensive and realistic view of the problems and politics of intelligence adaptation failure before the 2001 terrorist attacks. To do this, I sought sources with diverse positions and political perspectives but one common trait: extensive experience in the intelligence business between 1991 and 9/11. The current and former officials I interviewed include Democrats and Republicans, come from both the executive and legislative branches, and range from cabinet-level officials and congressional leaders to working level staff.

All interviews were either tape recorded or documented with written notes. Rather than accepting comments from sources at face value, I tried to consider them in light of the individual's likely motives and incentives and weighed interview material against the wealth of other information uncovered by the 9/11 Commission, the House and Senate Intelligence Committees, and other documentary sources.

Personal anecdotes provided by an anonymous source that are illustrative in nature are presented without additional verification. However, assertions of fact—such as the conclusions of the FBI's classified internal counterterrorism assessment before September 11 or the state of the CIA's clandestine service in the late 1990s—have been verified by at least two different sources or one source with additional documentary evidence.

CHAPTER 2

Canaries in the Coal Mine

THE CASE FOR FAILED ADAPTATION

The road to real intelligence reform is littered with the
carcasses of forgotten studies and ignored reports.
—Senator Richard Shelby (R-AL)[1]

No bill has been enacted that fundamentally acted on any
of these commission reports. So for God's sake stop
doing it. Just shoot us and put us out of our misery.
—Senior intelligence official[2]

D ID U.S. INTELLIGENCE AGENCIES fail to adapt to the rising
terrorist threat during the 1990s? After 9/11, the answer seems
obvious but the truth is nobody really knows. In the glare of
tragedy and the distortion of hindsight, public debate has
jumped to the conclusion that the CIA, the FBI, and other intelligence agencies should have performed better than they did.[3] To
date, no government agency, journalist, or academic has attempted to examine systematically the evidence of intelligence
adaptation failure before September 11. Instead, most accounts
of the attacks have substituted assumption for analysis, taking
intelligence failure as a given rather than something to be determined and explained.

This chapter seeks to fill the gap, reaching into history to determine whether U.S. intelligence agencies did, in fact, fail to adapt
to the rise of terrorism after the Cold War. The answer is yes.

I begin by developing a more precise definition of adaptation,
so that the reader is in a position to know successful or failed
adaptation when he sees it. Next I consider the most serious alternative argument to my own: that the U.S. Intelligence Community adapted as well as could be expected after the Cold War
given the challenges and constraints that it faced. The heart of

the chapter is an analysis of all the major studies of the U.S. Intelligence Community and counterterrorism efforts between 1991 and 2001. Examining what these studies found and what happened to their recommendations provides a window into what intelligence officials and policymakers knew before the September 11 attacks and what they did with that knowledge. It turns out there were many canaries in the coal mine: twelve different blue-ribbon commissions, think tank task forces, and governmental initiatives during the decade recommended 340 reforms for U.S. intelligence agencies. The vast majority of these recommendations focused on just a few key organizational deficiencies that hampered U.S. counterterrorism efforts—*the same weaknesses* that the 9/11 Commission and the House and Senate Intelligence Committees identified in their investigations after the World Trade Center and Pentagon attacks. Almost none of these recommendations were implemented beforehand.

DEFINING ADAPTATION

What exactly does it mean to say that an organization adapts or fails to adapt? Organization theorists do not have a clear answer, referring to organizational change, transformation, evolution and adaptation in various and inconsistent ways.[4]

For this book's purposes, the term "adaptation" carries three important ideas. The first is *change*. To say that a business or government agency has adapted is to suggest that it has changed. But change alone is an incomplete measure; in some sense, organizations are always changing.[5] Last year, my department changed its mailing labels. Every quarter I teach different students.

This suggests a second element of adaptation: *magnitude of change*. It is one thing to say that an organization changes, quite another to say that it adapts. More specifically, adaptation involves large changes, or the accumulation of many smaller ones that lead to a transformation in what an organization does or how it does it. When basic organizational boundaries shift, when organizations assume major, new, nonroutine tasks, or when they go about their old tasks with substantially different structures, processes, or beliefs, adaptation has occurred. Using different mailing labels is a change. Launching an entirely new graduate degree program is an adaptation.

Finally, for adaptation to occur, these major changes must result in an *improved fit* between the organization and its external environment.[6] Organizations are not hanging in suspended animation in some fixed market or government universe. They exist in an external environment filled with all sorts of moving parts—competitors, technologies, regulations, cultures, customs, politics, and individuals, to name a few. Often, shifts in an organization's external environment are incremental and slow to develop. At times, however, shifts can be large and sudden.[7] An organization seeking to improve or merely sustain its performance over time must do more than change. It must change in ways that keep pace with environmental demands, whatever those might be and however fast they might develop.

This definition has two implications for research on U.S. intelligence agencies. The first is to beware of embattled agency heads toting long lists of new initiatives. Organizational changes, however monumental, do not by themselves make a strong case for adaptation. Instead, adaptation must be judged relative to environmental demands.

The second implication is the importance of avoiding 20/20 hindsight. Organizational deficiencies often become widely known only after scandal or disaster. To make a strong case for adaptation failure, however, it is necessary to demonstrate that intelligence officials and policymakers were aware of organizational deficiencies *before* the September 11 terrorist attacks but failed to fix them.

THE CASE FOR ADAPTATION FAILURE

At first glance, it is not evident that U.S. intelligence agencies adapted poorly to the rise of terrorism after the Cold War ended. Some foreign policy leaders and intelligence officials argue that the dangers of the post–Cold War world were too opaque, too numerous, and too fluid for U.S. intelligence agencies to assess the terrorist threat more effectively than they did. According to this view, the danger posed by al Qaeda and other terrorist organizations may appear obvious in hindsight, but was not clear before the September 11th terrorist attacks. As Clinton National Security Advisor Samuel Berger put it, "History is written through a rear view mirror, but it unfolds through a foggy windshield."[8]

Others point to evidence that intelligence agencies did, in fact, zero in on terrorism early on, allocating resources and launching new programs to combat it well before 9/11. According to former Director of Central Intelligence (DCI) Robert Gates, the U.S. Intelligence Community began to shift resources away from Soviet-related missions and targets soon after the fall of the Soviet Union in 1991. Whereas in 1980, 58 percent of all intelligence resources were devoted to studying Soviet-related issues, by 1993, the figure had dropped to just 13 percent.[9] Although specific budget figures are classified, resources appear to have been redirected to combat terrorism. Despite tight intelligence budgets during the 1990s,[10] direct spending on counterterrorism roughly quintupled.[11] Cofer Black, former director of the DCI's Counterterrorist Center, noted that the center was "the first among equals, the entity not to be cut."[12]

In addition, the CIA, the FBI, and other intelligence agencies launched a number of new counterterrorism initiatives. These included the creation, in January 1996, of a special multiagency intelligence unit—nicknamed Alec Station—to track the activities of Osama bin Laden and his network;[13] dramatic increases in the number of FBI legal attaché offices overseas, with a focus on countries critical to fighting terrorism;[14] and a concerted effort to forge closer relationships with foreign intelligence services, which resulted in the disruption of terrorist cells in roughly twenty countries after 1997.[15] As Director Tenet concluded in February 2002, "This community has worked diligently over the last five years, and the American people need to understand that with the resources and authorities and priorities, the men and women of the FBI and the CIA performed heroically." Tenet, in fact, strongly objected to the idea that the September 11 terrorist attacks signified an intelligence failure, adding, "when people use the word 'failure'—'failure' means no focus, no attention, no discipline—and those were not present in what either we or the FBI did here and around the world."[16] Tenet was not the only senior intelligence official to resist accusations that the September 11 attacks represented failure.[17] When asked how well the Intelligence Community had adapted to meet the terrorist threat, for example, another senior intelligence official answered, "I think before September 11th, I would have said exceptionally well. . . . [now] I think we've done very, very well."[18]

Indeed, since 9/11, CIA and FBI officials have defended their agencies by cataloging in great detail just how many wide-ranging changes they instituted during the 1990s to combat terrorism. Tenet's first public appearance before the House and Senate Intelligence Committees' Joint Inquiry into the September 11 attacks is revealing. The director of central intelligence politely but firmly refused to curtail his remarks. "I'm not going to be able to get this done in ten minutes," he flatly declared to the committees. "What I want to do this morning, as explicitly as I can, is to describe the war we have waged for years against al Qaeda, the level of effort, the planning, the focus. . . ." When Senate Intelligence Committee Chairman Bob Graham (D-FL) interrupted Tenet twenty-one minutes into his remarks, the DCI shot back, "Well, sir, I just have to say I have been waiting a year. . . . It's important. It's contextual, it's factual, and I would like to proceed." Tenet went on to provide an exhaustive description of counterterrorism initiatives. These included: a 1998 memo in which Tenet declared war with Osama bin Laden and ordered that "no effort or resource be spared in prosecuting this war"; a 1999 new comprehensive strategy against al Qaeda called "The Plan"; the creation of a nationwide program to identify and hire qualified personnel for counterterrorism assignments in hostile environments; the creation of an eight-week advanced counterterrorism operations course; and measures taken to improve cooperation with the FBI such as the exchange of CIA and FBI senior officials.[19]

Former FBI Director Louis Freeh provided a similarly comprehensive account of the counterterrorism efforts he led in the 1990s when he testified before the 9/11 Commission. Freeh told the commission that the FBI "effectively and relentlessly did its job pursuing terrorists, always with the goal of preventing their attacks."[20] In 1998, the bureau's strategic plan placed counterterrorism in its top tier of priorities. In 1999, Freeh reorganized the FBI, creating a new FBI Counterterrorism Division and an Investigative Services Division to better support counterterrorism efforts. In July 2000 he instituted a program named MAXCAP 05 to upgrade the counterterrorist capabilities of all fifty-six U.S. field offices. During Freeh's tenure, which lasted from 1993 to 2001, the FBI tripled its counterterrorism budget, dramatically expanded the number of Joint Terrorism Task Forces to improve coordination with local law enforcement agencies, doubled the number of agents working counterterrorism cases, arrested a number of high-level foreign terrorists, and disrupted major plots, including a 1993 al Qaeda plan to blow up New York City tunnels, bridges, and landmarks. Freeh testified that he traveled to sixty-eight countries and met with 2,100 foreign leaders during that period, primarily to "pursue and enhance the FBI's counterterrorism program by forging an international network of cooperation."[21]

As these statements and examples indicate, U.S. intelligence agencies changed considerably in response to the end of the Cold War and the rise of the terrorist threat, and they achieved some important operational successes.

THE DIFFERENCE BETWEEN CHANGE AND ADAPTATION

The conceptual flaw in these arguments is their assumption that change and adaptation are the same. They aren't. As sociologists have long pointed out, organizations are constantly changing.[22] The key issue is whether those changes matter, or more precisely, whether the rate of change within an organization keeps pace (or lags behind) the rate of change in the external environment.[23] This is not academic nitpicking. Presenting only the litany of intelligence reforms gives the impression that America's intelligence system was succeeding when it was not. Laundry lists always look good in isolation.

The relationship between an organization's internal changes and its external challenges is more easily observed in the private sector, where responding to shifting market forces, consumer tastes, and competitive pressures can mean life or death for a firm. This relationship may be less obvious, but no less important, for evaluating public sector organizations. The question is not, "Are you doing anything differently today?" but "Are you doing *enough* differently today to meet the challenges you face?" One former intelligence official put it more colorfully: "There's no point in saying we're going at half the speed of

Moore's Law when the world is going at Moore's Law. Not enough people . . . ask the right question. It's not how fast we've changed. It's how fast we've changed compared to the world. The good news is that other countries have organizations that are more feckless than we are."[24]

In the case of U.S. intelligence agencies, determining adaptation failure requires answering three questions:

1. Did senior intelligence officials and policymakers recognize the gravity of the threat posed by al Qaeda before September 11, and, if so, when?

2. Did they understand the connection between the terrorist threat and the imperative for organizational change in U.S. intelligence agencies?

3. To what extent did they achieve the organizational changes they believed were necessary?

The answers appear to be yes, yes, and not very much. Many intelligence officials and policymakers recognized the threat, but were unable to get the intelligence reforms they believed were vital several years before 9/11.

Recognizing the Threat

The historical record provides a treasure trove of information about how intelligence officials and policymakers viewed terrorism in the context of other threats. Below I turn first to analyses and statements made by intelligence officials in the public record. I then examine how terrorism figured into major speeches given by policymakers and policy reviews.

WHAT INTELLIGENCE OFFICIALS KNEW AND SAID

In 1994, the director of central intelligence began delivering unclassified annual threat assessments to Congress. These assessments provide a useful gauge of how both intelligence officials and policymakers perceived the terrorist danger during the 1990s. Analysis of them reveals that threat priorities were highly stable and, in retrospect, on target. Terrorism was identified as a significant danger to U.S. national security every year from

1994 to 2001. By 1998, terrorism ranked in the top tier of threats, alongside other transnational dangers such as the proliferation of weapons of mass destruction. In February 2001, seven months before September 11, the DCI testified that terrorism was the single greatest threat to U.S. national security.[25]

Indeed, the U.S. Intelligence Community had become aware of Osama bin Laden in the early 1990s, soon after he founded al Qaeda, and was aggressively collecting intelligence on him by 1996.[26] A number of terrorist attacks and plots from 1991 to 2001 associated with Islamist groups also raised the profile of foreign terrorism within the U.S. Intelligence Community and indicated that targets included the U.S. homeland (see table 2.1). Among these were the first World Trade Center attack; a foiled 1993 plot to blow up several New York City landmarks; the Bojinka plot of 1995, which included plans to crash an airplane into CIA headquarters; and the disrupted Millennium plot to blow up Los Angeles International Airport (LAX). After September 11, Dale Watson, the FBI's former Executive Assistant Director for Counterterrorism and Counterintelligence, told Congress:

> The perception that we, the FBI, never briefed the administration that al Qaeda could attack us in the United States . . . is absolutely incorrect. If you looked just at the fact that we'd been attacked in the World Trade Center in '93, if you looked at . . . the Ressam individual who was going to set off a bomb in LAX, you understand clearly that we were vulnerable in the United States. Looking at the pattern before 9/11 . . . I was convinced we were going to be attacked.[27]

Watson's view was shared by others within the FBI and the CIA. Former FBI Director Louis Freeh told the 9/11 Commission that before the end of 1999, "the FBI and the Intelligence Community clearly understood the immediacy of the foreign-based al Qaeda threat regarding targets within the United States."[28] During the 1990s, in fact, Freeh had on several occasions presented congressional committees with a chart showing locations around the United States where radical fundamentalist cells were active.[29] J. Cofer Black, former director of the DCI's Counterterrorist Center, echoed Freeh's assessments, telling the 9/11 Commission, "I . . . want to emphasize that [the Counterterrorist Center] and the Intelligence Community produced significant strategic analysis that examined the growing threat from international jihadist

TABLE 2.1
Islamist Terrorist Attacks and Plots against Americans
Known to U.S. Intelligence Officials before September 11, 2001[1]

Date	Plot/Attack
December 1992	Bombs explode outside two hotels in Yemen that house U.S. servicemen en route to Somalia, killing 1 Australian tourist and no Americans. In 1996, U.S. intelligence learns that the attack was carried out by a Yemeni terrorist group with ties to bin Laden.
February 1993	Ramzi Yousef, a Sunni extremist who trained in bin Laden's Afghanistan camps, masterminds truck bomb attack in World Trade Center parking garage that kills 6 and wounds 1,000. Al Qaeda's precise role remains unclear.
October 1993	Somali warlords, aided by al Qaeda, shoot down two U.S. Black Hawk helicopters, killing 18 U.S. soldiers.
June 1993	FBI thwarts New York City Landmarks plot to bomb the United Nations and the Lincoln and Holland Tunnels and other targets. Al Qaeda's role remains unclear.
January 1995	Ramzi Yousef's bomb-making lab accidentally explodes in Manila. Inside, Philippine National police uncover plot to blow up 12 U.S. aircraft in Asia, crash a jet into CIA head-quarters, bomb U.S. and Israeli embassies in Manila, and assassinate the pope. Al Qaeda's precise role remains unclear.
November 1995	Car bomb explodes outside Saudi-U.S. joint facility in Riyadh, killing 5 Americans and 2 Indian officials. Al Qaeda's role remains unclear.
June 1996	A Saudi Shia Hezbollah group, with assistance from Iran and possibly al Qaeda, detonates truck bomb outside of Khobar Towers, a U.S. military residential complex in Saudi Arabia, killing 19 Americans, wounding 372 others.
August 1998	Al Qaeda terrorists detonate truck bombs simultaneously at U.S. Embassies in Nairobi, Kenya, and Dar es Salaam, Tanzania, killing 12 Americans, 212 others, and injuring more than 5,000.
December 1999	Ahmed Ressam's Millennium plot to blow up Los Angeles International Airport is disrupted by an alert U.S. Customs agent at U.S.-Canadian border. Ressam conceived and implemented the attack on his own, with training and other support from al Qaeda affiliates.

[1] Includes attacks associated with Islamist terrorist organizations, not just those known or believed to have been directed by al Qaeda.

TABLE 2.1 (*cont.*)
Islamist Terrorist Attacks and Plots against Americans
Known to U.S. Intelligence Officials before September 11, 2001

Date	Plot/Attack
December 1999	Jordanian officials disrupt Islamist plot to kill Americans by blowing up hotels and tourist sites in Amman, Jordan. The Jordanian terrorists operated independently, but received loose support from al Qaeda.
January 2000	Al Qaeda terrorists attempt to blow up a U.S. warship, USS *The Sullivans*, in Yemen by parking an explosive-laden boat beside it. The plot fails when the attack boat sinks.
October 2000	Al Qaeda's second attempt succeeds: terrorists attack USS *Cole* in Yemen, killing 17 U.S. sailors, wounding 39.

Source: *9/11 Commission Report*, pp. 59–70, 174–80, 190–91; Joint Inquiry Staff Statement, October 8, 2002; 9/11 Commission, *Staff Statement Number 15*, "Overview of the Enemy," June 16, 2004; *Joint Inquiry Report*, pp. 191–98.

networks and al-Qa'ida. I believe that the record shows that the U.S. [government] understood the nature of the threat."[30]

By 1998, concern for and warnings about an al Qaeda attack reached a heightened level inside the Intelligence Community. As Clinton National Security Advisor Samuel Berger put it, "in 1996 [Osama bin Laden] was on the radar screen; in 1998 he was the radar screen."[31] In February 1998, bin Laden issued a public *fatwa* encouraging attacks on Americans anywhere in the world.[32] In May he discussed "bringing the war home to America" in a public press conference.[33] And in August his terrorist network succeeded in carrying out two sophisticated, simultaneous, and devastating truck bomb attacks against U.S. embassies in Nairobi, Kenya, and Dar es Salaam, Tanzania, killing 224 people and injuring 5,000 more.[34] Over the course of the year, U.S. intelligence agencies also received a number of reports indicating possible al Qaeda terrorist plots inside the United States. Taken together, these events led DCI Tenet in December 1998 to issue a memo declaring war against Osama bin Laden. He wrote, "We must now enter a new phase in our effort against Bin Laden. . . . We are at war. . . . I want no resources or people spared in this effort, either inside CIA or the Community."[35] The House and Senate Intelligence Committees' Joint Inquiry into the September 11 attacks, a ten-month investigation that examined nearly 500,000 pages of documents and conducted 300 interviews, concluded that "Bin Laden's declaration . . . and intelligence reports indicating possible terrorist plots inside the United States did not go unnoticed by the Intelligence Community, which, in turn, advised senior officials in the U.S. Government of the serious nature of the threat."[36]

Tenet reiterated his concern in public addresses over the next three years. In 1999 he testified in open session before the Senate Armed Services Committee, "Looking out over the next year . . . there is not the slightest doubt that Usama Bin Ladin, his worldwide allies, and his sympathizers are planning further attacks against us. . . . I must tell you we are concerned that one or more of Bin Ladin's attacks could occur at any time." [37] In 2000 he told the Senate Select Intelligence Committee, again in open session, "Everything we have learned recently confirms our conviction that [bin Laden] wants to strike further blows against the United States. . . . we still believe he could strike without additional warning."[38] In his 2001 public threat assessment, the DCI bluntly warned, "The threat from terrorism is real, immediate, and evolving."[39] As one intelligence official lamented after September 11, "You know, we've been saying it forever, [bin Laden] wants to bring the fight here, he wants to bring the fight here."[40]

Although the FBI apparently never received Tenet's memo declaring war on bin Laden, the bureau reached similar conclusions at the same time.[41] In a dramatic shift, its May 1998 strategic plan elevated terrorism to the top tier of priorities, while downgrading traditional FBI crime-fighting missions.[42] That year, Osama bin Laden was indicted twice, for murdering U.S. soldiers in Yemen and for his role in the U.S. embassy bombings in Africa. In 1999 a public FBI report noted that "the FBI has no higher priority than to combat terrorism."[43] By the end of the year, the bureau had created a special bin Laden unit at FBI headquarters and had placed bin Laden on its Ten Most Wanted List.[44]

PUBLIC STATEMENTS AND ACTIONS BY POLICYMAKERS

Public statements and actions by elected officials and policymakers during the 1990s suggest that they received and shared the Intelligence Community's assessment of the growing terrorist threat long before September 11. In 1993, after Islamist terrorists detonated a bomb in the World Trade Center parking garage, killing six and wounding more than 1,000, Attorney General Janet Reno noted that terrorism had become a major threat to U.S. national security interests.[45] Beginning in 1994, President Bill Clinton mentioned terrorism in every one of his State of the Union addresses, the most important annual policy speech to the nation.[46] In 1995 Clinton became the first world leader to go before the United Nations and call for a global counterterrorist effort.[47] In 1996, when announcing his new national security team after the presidential election, Clinton placed terrorism first in a list of challenges facing the country.[48] In June 1997 the danger of an Islamist terrorist attack on U.S. soil was so well recognized that the FBI's chief of International Terrorism Operations warned about it in a public speech.[49] That same year, two different strategic assessments, the Pentagon's Quadrennial Defense Review and the National Defense Panel, included strong warnings about threats to the American homeland.[50] In June 1998 Clinton National Security Advisor Samuel Berger appeared on ABC *Nightline* and called Osama bin Laden "the most dangerous non-state terrorist in the world."[51] Three months later, Clinton delivered a major address at the opening session of the United Nations General Assembly that issued a forceful call to combat terrorism. Referring to terrorism as "a clear and present danger," the president said the issue ranked "at the top of the American agenda and should be at the top of the world's agenda."[52] In 1999 U.S. Secretary of Defense William Cohen wrote an op-ed in the *Washington Post* in which he explicitly predicted a terrorist attack on American soil. Cohen summed up, "Welcome to the grave New World of Terrorism."[53]

These were not off-the-cuff remarks or obscure presentations. State of the Union addresses, an op-ed to the *Washington Post* by a sitting secretary of defense, a presidential address before the United Nations General Assembly, and the Pentagon's major four-year review—these were among the most important, high profile outlets available to the president and his advisors. The fact that terrorism received such attention in so many of them provides strong evidence that senior members of the Clinton administration understood the seriousness of the threat.

Evidence also suggests that the Bush administration was well aware of the terrorist danger. Bush's two major foreign policy addresses during the 2000 presidential campaign both mentioned terrorism.[54] In one, Bush noted "even in this time of pride and promise, America has determined enemies, who hate our values and resent our success—terrorists and crime syndicates and drug cartels and unbalanced dictators. The Empire has passed, but evil remains. We must protect our homeland and our allies against missiles and terror and blackmail."[55] The 9/11 Commission found that intelligence briefings that included a substantial focus on terrorism occurred throughout the presidential campaign and transition. During one four-hour intelligence briefing at Bush's Texas ranch, for example, Ben Bonk, then deputy chief of the DCI's Counterterrorist Center, spent one hour on terrorism, bringing a mock suitcase to show how the Japanese cult Aum Shinrikyo had released sarin nerve gas in the Tokyo subway in 1995, killing twelve people and wounding thousands. Bonk recalled that he told Bush Americans would die from terrorism during the next four years.[56]

Whether the Bush administration gave terrorism sufficient attention and priority has been vigorously debated. For our purposes, however, the point is that the U.S. Intelligence Community's assessments of a growing terrorist threat did not go unnoticed. Both the Congressional Intelligence Committees' Joint Inquiry into the September 11 attacks and the 9/11 Commission found that Presidents Bill Clinton and George W. Bush, along with their top advisors, were repeatedly warned about al Qaeda by U.S. intelligence agencies.[57] Policymakers "told us they got the picture," the 9/11 Commission concluded, "they understood bin Laden was a danger."[58]

Understanding the Imperative for Organizational Change

The next question is whether intelligence officials and policymakers also understood the need for organizational changes to combat a new terrorist enemy. It appears that they did. Between the fall of the Soviet Union in 1991 and September 11, 2001, no fewer than twelve major bipartisan commissions, governmental studies, and think tank task forces examined the U.S. Intelligence Community and U.S. counterterrorism efforts. All of their reports urged reform within intelligence agencies, across the Intelligence Community, and between the Intelligence Community and other parts of the U.S. government (see table 2.2.).[59]

These were not throwaway reports, but detailed, serious examinations of a variety of intelligence and counterterrorism issues. Six of the twelve studies were high profile, bipartisan blue-ribbon commissions chaired by well-respected leaders such as former Senators Gary Hart (D-CO) and Warren Rudman (R-NH), former Defense Secretaries Les Aspin and Harold Brown, and William Webster, the only person ever to head both the CIA and FBI.[60] Three studies came from leading nonpartisan think tanks: the Council on Foreign Relations, the National Institute for Public Policy, and the 20th Century Fund.[61] The remaining three reports were issued by governmental initiatives: President Clinton's interagency National Performance Review (the reinventing government initiative), the FBI's 1998 Strategic Plan, and a House Intelligence Committee staff study that was the most comprehensive congressional review of the Intelligence Community since the 1970s, when the Church Committee investigated CIA abuses.[62]

All twelve reports offered not only extensive discussion of key problems, but specific recommendations to fix them. The studies issued a total of 514 recommendations; two-thirds of them, or 340, focused specifically on improving U.S. intelligence capabilities (see figure 2.1).

It is worth noting that these studies addressed a wide range of topics and covered vastly different ground; not all of them gave the Intelligence Community the same level of attention. Six of the twelve—the National Performance Review, the Aspin-Brown Commission on the Roles and Capabilities of the United States Intelligence Community, the House Intelligence Committee Staff Study, the Council on Foreign Relations Intelligence Task Force, the 20th Century Fund Task Force on the Future of U.S. Intelligence, and the National Institute for Public Policy—focused exclusively on intelligence issues. The other six did not. The Gilmore and Bremer Commissions examined U.S. counterterrorism efforts and challenges across the board, from local level emergency response capabilities to U.S. policy toward Afghanistan and other state sponsors of terrorism. The Deutch Commission was charged with assessing organizational problems related to combating the spread of weapons of mass destruction. The Webster Commission's mandate was to review and recommend action to Congress about "Federal law enforce-

TABLE 2.2

Unclassified U.S. Intelligence and Counterterrorism Studies, 1991–2001[1]

Date Issued	Study Name	Number of Recommendations
1993, 1995	National Performance Review (Phases I and II)	35
1996	Commission on the Roles and Capabilities of the United States Intelligence Community (Aspin-Brown Commission)	39
1996	Council on Foreign Relations Intelligence Task Force	29
1996	House Permanent Select Committee on Intelligence Staff Study (IC21)	75
1996	20th Century Fund Task Force on the Future of U.S. Intelligence	18
1997	National Institute on Public Policy Report on Modernizing Intelligence (Odom Report)	34
1998	FBI Strategic Plan 1998–2003	60
1999	Commission to Assess the Organization of the Federal Government to Combat the Proliferation of Weapons of Mass Destruction (Deutch Commission)	57
1999, 2000	Advisory Panel to Assess Domestic Response Capabilities for Terrorism Involving Weapons of Mass Destruction (Gilmore Commission), Reports 1 and 2	60
2000	Commission on the Advancement of Federal Law Enforcement (Webster Commission)	21
2000	National Commission on Terrorism (Bremer Commission)	36
2001	U.S. Commission on National Security in the 21st Century (Hart-Rudman Commission), Phase III Report	50
	Total	514

[1] See appendix for a discussion of reform catalog methodology.

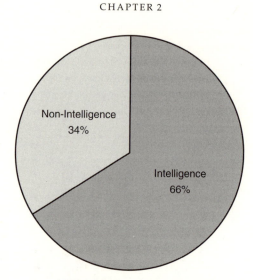

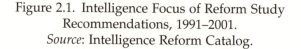

100% = 514 Recommendations

Figure 2.1. Intelligence Focus of Reform Study
Recommendations, 1991–2001.
Source: Intelligence Reform Catalog.

ment priorities for the 21st century, including . . . terrorism," as
well as criminal law enforcement operations and coordination
across Federal law enforcement agencies.[63] The FBI's strategic
plan aimed to set priorities for the entire organization. The U.S.
Commission on National Security in the 21st Century, better
known as the Hart-Rudman Commission, covered the broadest
territory, identifying emerging twenty-first-century threats to
U.S. security—including terrorism—and the strategic and organizational changes needed to combat those threats effectively.

As one would expect, the intelligence studies devoted a substantially higher share of their recommendations to fixing intelligence issues compared to the counterterrorism or law enforcement reports (see table 2.3). What is surprising, however, is just
how much attention even the counterterrorism and law enforcement studies—whose mandates directed them to consider a
wider range of issues—paid to fixing the U.S. Intelligence Community. The National Commission on Terrorism (the Bremer
Commission), for example, issued twelve intelligence reform
recommendations out of a total of thirty-six. Among them were
proposals for reinvigorating human intelligence efforts, clarify-

ing the confusing regulations for FBI terrorist investigations, and dramatically enhancing information sharing within the FBI and between the bureau and the rest of the Intelligence Community. The Gilmore Commission found many of the same problems and even suggested some of the same solutions in its fourteen intelligence recommendations.

The Deutch Commission, which sought to remedy organizational problems in nonproliferation policy across the federal government, issued seventeen intelligence recommendations out of fifty-seven, or 30 percent of its total. Here, too, commissioners saw direct links between weaknesses in intelligence organizations and the U.S. government's broader efforts to combat terrorism and the spread of weapons of mass destruction. Deutch, who served as director of central intelligence from 1995 to 1996, and the twelve other commissioners issued specific recommendations to improve coordination between the FBI and other intelligence agencies, enhance information sharing, revamp the FBI's computer capabilities, and integrate activities across the Community.

Even the Hart-Rudman Commission, with its sweeping scope of twenty-first-century national security challenges and organizational problems, devoted six of its fifty recommendations to the U.S. Intelligence Community, focusing particularly on the need to improve prioritization of intelligence efforts, analysis of asymmetric threats, and "greatly strengthening U.S. human intelligence."[64]

Tellingly, every study during the period included discussion of major intelligence deficiencies and every study issued recommendations to fix them. Together, the counterterrorism and law enforcement studies contributed one-third of all intelligence reform recommendations (see table 2.4).

Although the reports addressed a variety of intelligence issues and problems, the common theme was the need for major change. The Council on Foreign Relations task force noted in 1996 that "the intelligence community has been adjusting to the changed demands of the post–Cold War world for several years . . .[but] additional reform is necessary."[65] The report went on to list nearly forty recommendations that ranged from significant structural reforms to changes in personnel recruiting, training, and assignments. The 1996 House Intelligence Committee staff

TABLE 2.3
Intelligence Focus of All Reform Studies, 1991–2001

Study Name	Primary Topic	Number of Intelligence Recommendations	Number of non-Intelligence Recommendations	Total	Intelligence Percent of Study Total
Council on Foreign Relations	Intelligence	29	0	29	100%
National Performance Review	Intelligence	35	0	35	100%
National Institute for Public Policy	Intelligence	34	0	34	100%
House Intelligence Comm. Staff	Intelligence	74	1	75	99%
Aspin-Brown Commission	Intelligence	38	1	39	97%
20th Century Fund	Intelligence	17	1	18	94%
FBI Strategic Plan	Law Enforcement	54	6	60	90%
Webster Commission	Law Enforcement	10	11	21	48%
Bremer Commission	Counterterrorism	12	24	36	33%
Deutch Commission	Counterterrorism (WMD)	17	40	57	30%
Gilmore Commission	Counterterrorism	14	46	60	23%
Hart-Rudman Commission	Counterterrorism (national strategy, organization)	6	44	50	12%
Total All Studies		340	174	514	66%

Source: Intelligence Reform Catalog.

TABLE 2.4

Intelligence Focus of Counterterrorism and Law Enforcement Studies versus Others, 1991–2001

Study Name	Primary Topic	Number of Intelligence Recommendations	Number of non-Intelligence Recommendations	Total Number of Recommendations	Study Share of Total Intelligence Recommendations
Bremer Commission	Counterterrorism	12	24	36	3%
Deutch Commission	Counterterrorism (WMD)	17	40	57	5%
FBI Strategic Plan	Law Enforcement	54	6	60	16%
Gilmore Commission	Counterterrorism	14	46	60	4%
Hart-Rudman Commission	Counterterrorism (national security strategy, organization)	6	44	50	2%
Webster Commission	Law Enforcement	10	11	21	3%
Counterterrorism/Law Enforcement Study Subtotal		113	171	284	33%
Aspin-Brown Commission	Intelligence	38	1	39	11%
Council on Foreign Relations	Intelligence	29	0	29	9%
House Intelligence Committee Staff	Intelligence	74	1	75	22%
National Performance Review	Intelligence	35	0	35	10%
National Institute for Public Policy	Intelligence	34	0	34	10%
20th Century Fund	Intelligence	17	1	18	5%
Intelligence Study Subtotal		227	3	230	67%
Total		340	174	514	100%

Source: Intelligence Reform Catalog.

study found the Intelligence Community suffered from a lack of "corporateness," or integration between individual agencies. The report noted that "only intelligence, of all major government functions, is carried out by a very disparate number of agencies and organizations that are either independent of one another or housed in separate departments by officials whose main concerns are policy, not intelligence."[66] In particular, the report criticized what it saw as "the glaring gap" between the DCI's responsibilities and his authorities,[67] the "fundamental and urgent" need to improve the intelligence requirements process that sets agency priorities,[68] and the "internecine competition" between the various intelligence collection disciplines such as signals intelligence, human intelligence, and open source intelligence.[69] It issued eighty-two recommended reforms. Four years later, the Bremer Commission warned that "international terrorism poses an increasingly dangerous and difficult threat to America." It urged the government to take immediate "steps to reinvigorate the collection of intelligence about terrorists' plans. . . . "[70] The commission's key recommendations included clarifying existing authorities for the FBI to investigate suspected terrorist groups; rescinding CIA guidelines that hindered the recruitment of terrorist informants; giving higher funding priority to counterterrorism efforts in the CIA, FBI, and National Security Agency; and establishing a new cadre of reports officers to distill and disseminate terrorism-related information quickly once it is collected. Indeed, the commission noted with concern that "U.S. intelligence and law enforcement communities lack the ability to prioritize, translate, and understand in a timely fashion all of the information to which they have access."[71] Together, the twelve reports issued 340 recommendations to improve U.S. intelligence capabilities.[72] The imperative for organizational change was clear.

Failing to Change

To what extent were the studies' recommendations implemented? To be sure, gauging adaptation failure by examining the adoption of study recommendations has its limitations. Commissions may be created for the sole purpose of deflecting blame or delaying action rather than generating change, though this is far less often the case in national security affairs than most believe.[73] Even earnest efforts at reform often take a variety of forms, with some focusing on "the art of the possible," and others proposing more ideal and unlikely solutions. Some suggestions, moreover, appear shortsighted with the benefit of history. Examining the totality of study recommendations and their success, however, has the advantage of providing a macro view of adaptation that does not rely on hindsight or impose personal judgments of which reforms were better ideas than others. Asking only what recommendations were made and whether these were implemented provides a useful, systematic first cut at the problem that goes beyond anecdotal evidence of failure.

The data indicate a widespread inability of U.S. intelligence agencies to adapt to the terrorist threat before 9/11. Of the 340 recommendations for changes in the Intelligence Community, only thirty-five—just 10 percent of the total—were fully implemented. Notably, these implemented reforms included several minor recommendations that urged continued study of a problem rather than adoption of a particular solution.[74] Thirty recommendations were partially implemented, and seven were implemented to an unknown extent. The vast majority, 268 recommendations, or 79 percent of the total, resulted in no action at all (see figure 2.2).

COMMON FINDINGS

Although the reports covered a variety of issues, they reached a stunning degree of consensus about four major problems afflicting the U.S. Intelligence Community. The first was its lack of coherence or "corporateness." Of 340 intelligence recommendations issued by the reports, ninety-four, or 28 percent of the total, focused on the need to improve coordination across U.S. intelligence agencies and between these agencies and the rest of the U.S. government (see table 2.5).

As the Council on Foreign Relations study noted, the organization and leadership of the Intelligence Community was a "structural oddity," with more than a dozen major agencies and no one in charge of them all.[75] Technically the director of central intelligence was supposed to set broad strategies and coordinate efforts across these agencies (as well as run the CIA). In reality, however, the DCI controlled less than 20 percent of the intelli-

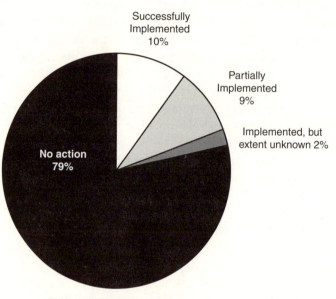

Figure 2.2. Implementation of Intelligence Reform
Recommendations, 1991–2001.

gence budget (the secretary of defense controlled the rest) and
had weak management authority for allocating money, people,
and programs to every agency outside the CIA.[76] The reports'
specific recommendations varied, but all of them offered ways to
enhance Intelligence Community integration and coordination.

Second, ten out of twelve of these studies found that intelligence officials and policymakers did not devote enough attention
to setting intelligence priorities.[77] To provide useful information,
intelligence agencies require guidance from policymakers about
what puzzles, people, and places rank higher on the priority list
than others, about which surprises U.S. policymakers can live
with and which ones they cannot. A robust mechanism for establishing and updating intelligence priorities, however, had
never developed during the Cold War. The Soviet Union's collapse, along with the emergence of new transnational threats,
only exacerbated these weaknesses. As a result, during the 1990s
intelligence agencies had to cover more issues with fewer resources and little guidance about where to focus their efforts.

In 1993 the President's National Performance Review found the system for establishing intelligence collection and analysis priorities to be a "jumble of loosely connected processes" that did not satisfy the needs of policymakers.[78] The House Intelligence Committee's staff study agreed, calling the prioritization process "one of the most vexing aspects of intelligence management" and the need for fixing it "fundamental and urgent."[79] Five years later the Hart-Rudman Commission warned that the continued absence of an effective process for setting intelligence priorities was creating "dangerous tradeoffs between coverage of important countries, regions, and functional challenges."[80] In total, fifty-six out of the 340 intelligence recommendations, or 16 percent, suggested improvements in the prioritization process.

A third finding was the need to revitalize human intelligence capabilities. Nine of the twelve reports called for more aggressive human intelligence efforts to combat terrorism, two did not address the issue,[81] and only one, the 20th Century Fund report, advocated downgrading collection from human sources. Most frequently mentioned was the need to revise the CIA's 1995 guidelines that required prior approval from CIA headquarters before an individual suspected of human rights violations could be recruited as an asset—guidelines that had come to be known as the "scrub order" because they had led to the removal of hundreds of assets from the CIA's payroll.[82] Many reports also advocated improving the intelligence budgeting process so that resources could be more effectively matched against priorities; these improvements would have had the likely effect of redistributing some of the vast resources dedicated to technical intelligence systems to human intelligence activities.[83] In addition, the Aspin-Brown Commission and the House Intelligence Committee staff report recommended revising personnel incentives and restructuring the Intelligence Community to ensure that human intelligence efforts could be more effectively and efficiently deployed against hard targets such as rogue states and transnational terrorist groups that are difficult to penetrate by other means.[84] Perhaps most radical, the National Institute for Public Policy report recommended stripping analysis functions from the CIA so that the agency could focus exclusively on human intelligence collection and even raised the possibility of disbanding the CIA's clandestine Directorate of Operations and replacing it with an entirely new clandestine service in order to address the directorate's longstanding cultural and management problems.[85] In all, the reports from 1991 to 2001 issued thirty-one recommendations to improve human intelligence efforts.

Finally, the reports ranked personnel issues high on the list of concerns. More than a hundred recommendations, or nearly a third of all intelligence reforms issued by the reports, addressed personnel and information sharing issues. As the House Intelligence Committee staff study bluntly concluded, "[The Intelligence Community] continues to face a major personnel crisis that it has, thus far, not addressed in any coherent way."[86] Although the specifics varied widely, two common themes emerged. First, the Intelligence Community lacked employees with the requisite skills to confront growing threats such as foreign terrorism.[87] Despite being technically exempt from a number of Civil Service regulations, intelligence agencies rarely fired poor performers. In addition, the Aspin-Brown Commission noted that even when confronted with mandatory reductions in personnel in the early 1990s, intelligence agencies reached targets through attrition and voluntary retirement rather than through strategically focused cuts to keep the best talent and those with the most needed areas of expertise for a post–Cold War threat environment.[88] Second, intelligence officers too often stayed in their home agencies rather than building institutional bridges to other policymaking and intelligence agencies through temporary rotations, and these practices impeded information sharing. Three studies—the Aspin-Brown Commission, the Council on Foreign Relations task force, and the House Intelligence Committee staff study—recommended that rotations to other agencies be required for intelligence officers to be promoted to senior ranks, and another three—the 20th Century Fund task force, the National Performance Review, and the FBI's 1998 Strategic Plan—urged the establishment of vigorous rotational assignments without requiring them for promotion. The need to realign the personnel skill mix and improve coordination through temporary tours of duty in other agencies received major attention in all but two of the reports.[89]

As table 2.5 illustrates, these four categories of organizational problems constituted 84 percent of the reports' intelligence recommendations.

TABLE 2.5

Commonly Identified Organizational Problems in Intelligence, 1991–2001

Organizational Problem	Number of Recommendations	Percent of Total
Personnel/Information Sharing	106	31%
Corporateness	94	28%
Strategic Mission and Priorities	56	16%
Human Intelligence	31	9%
Total Commonly Identified Problems	287	84%
Other Recommendations	53	16%
Grand Total All Intelligence Recommendations	340	100%

Source: Intelligence Reform Catalog.

CRUCIAL FAILINGS

Almost none of the recommendations to improve these four problems were successfully implemented before the September 11 terrorist attacks. Investigations since 9/11, moreover, reveal that the organizational deficiencies highlighted by reports in the 1990s turned out to be the crucial ones. The 9/11 Commission and the House and Senate Intelligence Committees' Joint Inquiry found that the Intelligence Community's fragmentation, inability to set priorities, poor human intelligence capabilities, and information sharing deficiencies created a dysfunctional intelligence apparatus that was incapable of penetrating the al Qaeda plot or capitalizing on opportunities to disrupt it.

The lack of integration across U.S. intelligence agencies topped the list of concerns for both the 9/11 Commission and the Congressional Joint Inquiry. In 2001 the Intelligence Community was 50 percent bigger than it was when the CIA was created in 1947, but the director of central intelligence had only slightly more power to oversee it. As the Congressional Joint Inquiry into the September 11 attacks darkly concluded, "The inability to realign Intelligence Community resources to combat the threat posed by Usama Bin Ladin is a relatively direct consequence of the limited authority of the DCI over major portions of the Intelligence Community."[90] The 9/11 Commission agreed, noting that the Intelligence Community "struggle[d] to collect on and analyze ... transnational terrorism in the mid-to-late

1990s" in large part because the Community was a set of "loosely associated agencies and departmental offices that lacked the incentives to cooperate, collaborate, and share information."[91] The Intelligence Community was so fragmented before September 11 that even Tenet's 1998 declaration of war against bin Laden and al Qaeda did not seem to have gotten much beyond the CIA's walls.[92]

The Congressional Joint Inquiry and 9/11 Commission also found major deficiencies in the Intelligence Community's system for prioritizing collection and analysis. The Joint Inquiry noted that intelligence officials found the process "confusing" and "so broad as to be meaningless," with more than 1,500 formal priorities for the National Security Agency alone by September 11.[93] The 9/11 Commission concluded that the setting of clear intelligence collection priorities "did not occur" before the September 11 attacks.[94] Even some of those responsible for setting priorities agreed. Former National Counterterrorism Coordinator Richard Clarke noted that the White House "never really gave good systematic, timely guidance to the Intelligence Community about what priorities were at the national level."[95]

Despite calls to vastly upgrade human intelligence efforts, the CIA's clandestine Directorate of Operations continued to languish. After the Cold War, money was in short supply for all intelligence needs, and the clandestine service was particularly hard hit. In 1995, the low point for recruitment, only twenty-five trainees became clandestine officers.[96] By the late 1990s, the Directorate of Operations had cut by nearly one-third the number of its personnel deployed overseas.[97] Although details about U.S. intelligence spending remain classified, available evidence suggests that between 1991 and 2001, more than 90 percent of the U.S. intelligence budget continued to be spent on hardware rather than recruiting spies.[98] As one former senior CIA official put it, "I'm cynical, but I think the reason people wanted to keep the [intelligence] budget secret was not to protect spies in Moscow, but because they didn't want people to know that 99 percent [of the budget] was stuck in some satellite."[99] In addition, the 1995 guidelines restricting recruitment of foreign assets remained in place until after September 11.

Personnel problems also continued. In 2001, only 20 percent of the graduating class of clandestine case officers were fluent in non-Romance languages.[100] Robert Baer, a veteran CIA clandestine case officer, noted that even after the 1998 U.S. embassy bombings, the CIA did not have a single case officer who spoke Pashto, the dialect of the major ethnic group in Afghanistan, and still had none as of 2002.[101] The Joint Inquiry's findings are consistent with these assessments. The congressional panel concluded that before September 11, the Intelligence Community "was not prepared to handle the challenge it faced in translating the volumes of foreign language counterterrorism intelligence it collected. Agencies . . . experienced backlogs in material awaiting translation . . . and a readiness level of only 30 percent in the most critical terrorism-related languages used by terrorists."[102]

Nor were temporary rotations commonly practiced. Although Director Tenet declared in the late 1990s that all intelligence officials were required to do a tour of duty in another intelligence agency before being promoted to the senior ranks, every agency, including the CIA, ignored him. When agencies did fill these rotational positions, moreover, they often sent mediocre employees. As one senior intelligence official grumbled, "I often think of writing a vacancy notice [for temporary transferees to his agency] that says, 'only stupid people doing unimportant work need apply,' or 'send us your tired, your sluggish, your marginally brain dead.' "[103]

SUMMARY

Between 1991 and 2001, U.S. intelligence agencies instituted a number of new programs and devoted new resources to counterterrorism. They did not, however, adjust to this emerging threat as fast or as fully as they could have before the September 11, 2001, attacks. Intelligence threat assessments reveal that years before 9/11, intelligence officials recognized the danger al Qaeda and other terrorist organizations posed to U.S. national security and warned elected officials. Policymakers, for their part, appear to have shared these assessments, issuing a crescendo of warnings about the grave new threat of terrorism in major public addresses, particularly after the 1998 embassy bombings. Senior foreign policy leaders in both the Clinton and Bush administrations also were aware that combating terrorism required a fundamental transformation of the U.S. Intelligence Community. A dozen unclassified studies, and a number of classified reports, highlighted a common set of critical deficiencies and suggested an array of potential remedies. Yet as dangers gathered, the U.S. Intelligence Community remained largely unchanged. The House and Senate Intelligence Committees' postmortem found that before 9/11, "the Intelligence Community was neither well organized nor equipped, and did not adequately adapt, to meet the challenge posed by global terrorists focused on targets within the domestic United States."[104] The question is why.

CHAPTER 3

Crossing an Academic No-Man's Land

EXPLAINING FAILED ADAPTATION

E XISTING RESEARCH does not offer a ready-made explanation for intelligence agency adaptation failure. This is because the CIA, FBI, and other national security agencies live in an academic no-man's land, overlooked both by scholars who study organizations as well as those who examine national security affairs. On the one hand, organization theorists (who usually come from sociology, economics, and business schools) investigate organizational problems but focus almost exclusively on understanding private sector firms. On the other hand, political scientists examine national security affairs but treat intelligence agencies as inputs to policy decisions, not as phenomena to be studied in their own right. The burning theoretical questions of both fields have directed scholarly attention elsewhere, leaving U.S. intelligence agencies and their organizational deficiencies on the sidelines.[1]

This chapter uses building blocks from both organization theory and political science to develop a general model of agency adaptation failure.[2] As we shall see, organization theory provides useful insights about the barriers to adaptation lurking deep within organizations such as the persistence of organizational habits, the unwillingness of agencies to veer from established routines, and adherence to old cultures, forces that political scientists prefer to avoid.[3] At the same time, political scientists focus on the role of political interests, incentives, and institutions that shape agencies from the outside, precisely the factors that many organization theorists ignore.[4] Working across these fields, I argue that agency adaptation failure can be attributed to three enduring realities: (1) the nature of organizations, which makes internal reform exceedingly difficult; (2) the rational self-interests of political officials, which work against executive branch reform; and (3) the fragmented structure of the federal government, which erects high barriers to legislative reform.

Although scholars prefer explanations that are simple and powerful rather than longer and more complicated, in the case of intelligence adaptation failure simplicity does not get us far. Considering only the forces operating within U.S. intelligence agencies cannot explain why legislators and presidents failed to overhaul the U.S. Intelligence Community during the 1990s, despite an awareness of the terrorist threat and repeated calls for reform. Conversely, examining only the political interests, incentives, and institutions operating outside U.S. intelligence agencies sheds little light on crucial internal adaptation failures— such as why so many FBI agents preferred to keep case files in shoeboxes under their desks rather than entering them into computer databases; why Director Tenet's efforts to revamp the CIA's own clandestine service and strategic analysis languished; or why, for a year and a half, intelligence officials neglected to watchlist a suspected al Qaeda operative with a multiple-entry U.S. visa in his passport. Organization theory and political science each illuminate different pieces of adaptation failure in the CIA and FBI. It is only by combining both approaches, however, that observers can understand the entire puzzle.

That said, nuance has its limits. My aim is not to discuss every reason the CIA and FBI failed to adapt to the rising terrorist threat; it is to highlight the most important reasons, the impediments that have persisted across presidential administrations, congressional sessions, individual leaders, and events. The enduring realities that I identify provide insight into the past as well as the future, explaining not only why the CIA and FBI failed to adapt before 9/11, but why effective intelligence is unlikely even now, years after the terrorist attacks. The nature of organizations, rational self-interest, and the structure of the American government are not going anywhere anytime soon.

I begin by surveying the terrain, highlighting key insights and limitations of both organization theory and political science. This review is critical for developing the intellectual underpinnings of the model. For general readers, I have tried to include only the bare essentials in the hopes that you will consider the ideas behind my ideas instead of jumping ahead to the CIA and FBI case study chapters that follow. For academic readers, I have sought to provide a glimpse of relevant work in different fields that can enrich our understanding of agency adaptation failure.

Such reviews never do justice to the literature. I encourage those who are interested in learning more to see the notes for more detailed discussions and suggestions of additional reading.

THE BOTTOM LINE OF ORGANIZATION THEORY

Organization theory is more a set of common interests than common ideas. The field has long drawn a multidisciplinary crowd seeking to understand what organizations do, how they do it, and how well.[5] Questions of organizational inertia,[6] evolution,[7] and learning[8] have generated rich and dynamic research programs over the past thirty years.

For our purposes, organization theory provides two main insights. The first is that adaptation is difficult even for private sector firms. This idea is more important than it sounds. Political scientists and politicians often lament the fact that government is not run more like a business.[9] But leading sociologists remind us that businesses also frequently fail to adapt for a host of reasons.[10] Consider the most basic test: whether firms adapt enough to survive. Of the 5.5 million businesses tracked by the U.S. Census Bureau in 1990, 1.7 million, or 31 percent, were no longer in business four years later.[11] In New York City, more than 60 percent of all restaurants surveyed in the *Zagat* guide between 1979 and 1999 folded.[12] Between 2000 and 2003, more than 400 public companies went bankrupt, including Enron, which rose to 7th on the *Fortune* 500 list; and Bethlehem Steel, one of the great industrial giants of the twentieth century.[13] Each year, more than 500,000 businesses fail in the United States. That's more than 1,500 per day, or about one every minute.[14] As these examples suggest, success today does not guarantee success tomorrow. Adaptation is fraught with peril.

The second insight is that the internal barriers to organizational change are powerful and deeply entrenched. While the organization theory literature is vast and filled with vigorous debate, much of it examines what most people know intuitively to be true: employees inside organizations become wedded to habits, thinking, routines, values, norms, ideas, and identities, and these attachments make change difficult.[15] As the saying goes, old habits die hard.

The most serious limitation of this work is that it cannot be applied easily to the political realm. This is understandable. The field emerged with firms in mind and has remained focused on the private sector ever since. As Richard Cyert and James March noted in the introduction to their 1963 classic, *A Behavioral Theory of the Firm*, "We had an agenda. . . . We thought that research on economics and research on organizations should have something to say to each other."[16] More than forty years later, the focus on business organizations continues.[17] The result is that organization theory has developed without paying much attention to political incentives, interests, institutions, or power, forces that turn out to be crucial for understanding the development of government agencies.[18]

Consider, for example, the literature that appears most centrally related to the question of agency adaptation failure: population ecology. Initially developed in the 1970s, population ecology quickly caught fire and has become a major intellectual current in the field. Simply put, population ecologists argue that most business innovation occurs *between* organizations, not within them. The competitive environment, technology, and consumer preferences all shift over time, but individual firms are rarely good at shifting with them. Instead, improvements more often occur at the population level, through the birth of new organizations and the death of others. In other words, individual organizations do not adapt; populations do, with newer, fitter firms constantly replacing older, outdated, ones through a process of natural selection.[19]

This approach is helpful in explaining the private sector, where firms routinely come and go. However, it is much less helpful in understanding the public sector, where there is substantially less organizational churn. As many scholars have observed, government agencies are notoriously hard to eliminate because there are always interest groups and elected officials who have vested interests at stake.[20] In his pilot study comparing agencies between 1923 and 1973, for example, Herbert Kaufman found that 85 percent of those in the 1923 sample were still in existence fifty years later.[21] By contrast, Howard Aldrich found that in 1957, 398,000 businesses were created in the United States, about the same number were transferred to new owners, and almost as many simply failed.[22] More recently, in 2003 David

Lewis found in his exhaustive study that Congress and the president established 438 new agencies between 1946 and 1997.[23] More businesses are born in a single day before lunch.[24]

Population ecology also assumes organizational resistance to change rather than treating it as something to be explained.[25] This is a serious weakness. If population ecologists are correct, and innovations are generated primarily through the replacement of old organizations by new ones, then the imperative to understand what keeps any single agency from adapting to environmental demands is even greater in the public sector: the government is likely to be riddled with poorly performing agencies that persist because they are unchallenged by the threat of new entrants.

Finally, most research in population ecology consists of large quantitative studies of entire organizational populations, with little attention given to the role of individual choice, decision-making processes, or politics. The result is a strangely antiseptic theory of natural selection that seems to ignore the role of real people exercising real power. As Charles Perrow notes, "It is almost as if God does the negative and positive selecting."[26]

THE TALLY FOR POLITICAL SCIENCE

The political science literature has different insights and limitations. On the positive side, this work makes two vital contributions. First, political scientists explain outcomes by examining what makes individuals alike rather than what makes them unique. The field's dominant approach, rational choice analysis, argues that all officials are driven by the incentives of office to behave in certain ways: namely, to take positions, select policies, and devote their energies to activities that maximize their political benefits and minimize their political costs. The desire to win reelection, for example, encourages all members of Congress, Democrats and Republicans alike, to secure pork barrel projects and choose committee assignments that further their districts' interests. It is no coincidence that the agricultural committees are stacked with representatives from places like Des Moines and Sioux Falls and not Los Angeles or New York City. Similarly, although no two presidents are alike, all wield the same formal

powers, confront the same institutional players, and seek to secure their place in history within the same short time horizon.
For political scientists, politics is all about interests, incentives,
and institutional power and constraints—about how individuals
are both motivated and limited by the positions they occupy in
government.

Second, this work emphasizes that bad results often come
from individually rational decisions. Nobody likes wasteful
government spending, but every member of Congress has
strong incentives to draft legislative earmarks to fund his dis-
trict's pet projects. The same logic explains why intelligence
agencies in the Pentagon and other parts of the U.S. government
have always fiercely protected their own turf and budgets from
centralized control by the CIA and its post-9/11 successor, the
Office of the Director of National Intelligence. Reform opponents in these other intelligence agencies are not bad people
with evil intentions. They are employees of organizations who
see benefits in autonomy and costs in ceding it. For each agency,
resistance to centralized management is rational. For the entire
intelligence system, it is disastrous.

The most serious limitation of political science is that it rarely
peers inside the black box of government agencies to examine
internal forces like norms, routines, and cultures that make the
bureaucracy resistant to change.[27] Indeed, most political science
research assumes that government agencies can and do adapt;
major work over the past twenty years argues that Congress
controls the bureaucracy, and in surprisingly efficient ways.[28]
Congressional dominance scholars such as Mathew McCubbins
and Barry Weingast contend that evidence usually thought to
suggest poor oversight, such as sparsely attended congressional
committee hearings, actually reveals oversight hard at work.
How can this be? The answer, they argue, is that legislators hard-
wire the system to respond to their demands from the start, so
that they do not have to expend much time identifying or fixing
problems later. Much of the literature examines how lawmakers
craftily ensure their preferences are heeded by building control
mechanisms into the very design of government agencies, or by
using (or threatening to use) existing controls such as withholding appropriations, or both.[29] The mechanisms vary but the logic
is the same: government bureaucrats usually respond to legisla-

tors' demands. Agency officials are not stupid. They know, as McCubbins puts it, that "Congress holds the power of life or death in the most elemental terms" for their existence.[30] The mere anticipation of possible congressional punishment makes bureaucrats fall into line from the start. The overall picture is one in which government agencies are savvy and responsive, adjusting their priorities and activities to satisfy congressional desires.

Notably, even critics of the congressional dominance literature agree that government agencies can adapt. Terry Moe, for example, argues that Congress is not alone in determining agency behavior; many factors, including presidents, interests groups, and courts, influence what agencies do.[31] According to Moe, agencies are not stuck in their ways; they are swayed by more forces than the congressional dominance school admits. Others argue that congressional dominance does not capture the degree of bureaucratic shirking, when agencies opt to pursue their own organizational interests instead of the interests of their congressional overseers. As David Epstein and Sharyn O'Halloran conclude, the literature on congressional-bureaucratic relations has reached something of an impasse in recent years: "The general consensus has been reached that legislators have more effective means of control than was previously realized, but bureaucrats still retain significant amounts of discretion in setting policy."[32]

This is strange. All of this work suggests that agencies are out there, on the move, doing things. Usually agencies respond to congressional wishes; sometimes they pursue the interests of presidents and others in the political system; and sometimes they shirk to serve their own interests. Nowhere, however, is there a sense that government agencies may be *unable* to change. According to this literature, the challenge is to keep agencies from running amok. But as September 11 suggests, the greater danger may be that agencies are stuck running in place.

A General Model of Agency Adaptation Failure

Although neither organization theory nor political science rational choice theory offers an off-the-shelf explanation of adaptation failure, together they provide useful foundations for a general model. Organization theory offers insights about internal impediments to agency reform, while rational choice theories in political science explain external impediments to reform.

Rather than viewing government agencies from without (i.e., as more limited public sector versions of firms or as objects of congressional control), I begin by assuming the bureaucracy's perspective. Any agency leader confronting a changing environment must answer two questions: "How can I get the necessary reforms so my agency can keep pace with the challenges it faces?" and "What obstacles are likely to stand in my way?"[33]

Answering these questions reveals three major sources of bureaucratic reform: internal reforms made by the agency itself, whether in memos, speeches, revised guidelines, or sanctions of undesired behavior; executive branch action, for example, executive orders, presidential directives, or efforts by executive branch officials outside the agency in question such as the National Security Council; and statutory reforms that require the involvement of both Congress and the executive branch. These paths suggest that impediments to adaptation are likely to emerge from both inside and outside the agency. Some changes may fail because they challenge deeply held organizational values and threaten to alter established routines. Others may trigger opposition from competing government agencies that stand to gain or lose depending on the outcome. Proposed statutory changes that require the consent of multiple congressional majorities and the president bring institutional forces more centrally into play. Thus, developing a better understanding of agency adaptation failure requires combining the enduring realities operating within organizations with those operating outside them. More specifically, these are: (1) the nature of organizations; (2) the rational self-interest of political officials; and (3) the fragmented structure of the U.S. federal government. Taken together, these three forces raise exceptionally high obstacles to agency adaptation.

The Nature of Organizations

The first route to agency reform is through the adoption of internal changes. Yet much of the work in organization theory argues that organizations do not change easily by themselves.[34] Examples abound. The U.S. Army kept a horse cavalry until World

War II. Until the mid-1990s, U.S. customs forms asked ships entering American ports to list the number of cannons on board, and federal law required the U.S. Agriculture Department to keep field offices within a day's horseback ride to everyplace in the United States. As noted above, even private firms, which have considerably more leeway over personnel decisions, more access to capital, and fewer management constraints than government agencies, do not fare well when changing circumstances require adjustment. Three reasons explain why. I turn to each of them below.

BOUNDED RATIONALITY

The first reason organizations adapt poorly on their own has to do with individuals and their cognitive limits. Even the smartest and most powerful organizational leaders are not omniscient. Instead, they operate in a world of tremendous uncertainty about the future, imperfect information about alternatives, and only limited ability and time to consider their options. These facts of life make fully rational decision making within organizations impossible.[35] Instead, decision-makers operate in a world where rationality is limited or bounded. Confronted with an unknown future, incomplete information, and cognitive constraints, organizational leaders do the best they can, settling for options that appear "good enough" but may in fact be nowhere close.[36]

When it comes to adaptation, bounded rationality suggests real limits at work: because organizations are filled with imperfect decision-makers, changes that could improve organizational performance often are not identified or implemented, and changes that are selected may be the wrong ones, making matters worse. As we shall see, both the CIA and FBI encountered tremendous bounded rationality problems when the Cold War ended. Confronted with the Soviet Union's sudden collapse, the Central Intelligence Agency spent the early 1990s cutting costs without much of an eye toward emerging threats or needs, while the FBI simply clung to its old crime-fighting mission. The responses were different but the problem was the same: in the days immediately following the Soviet Union's collapse, leaders in both agencies, as well as their congressional and executive branch overseers, struggled with profound uncertainties about the changing nature of the world and made choices that ultimately led both organizations in the wrong direction.

STRUCTURAL SECRECY

The very structure of organizations also impedes their ability to adapt. In their quest for efficiency, organizations specialize, dividing work into subunits that become proficient at specific tasks. Specialization, however, also prevents the transfer of knowledge within an organization in some powerful and often unforeseen ways. The deepening of specialized knowledge means that people in one part of the organization often lack the expertise to understand the work of people in other parts of the organization. Over time, the performance of individuals and even entire divisions can become unobservable to senior managers, leaving them in the dark about what is working well and what isn't. Employees, meanwhile, grow increasingly disconnected from the organization's goals, unsure of where they fit into the picture or what improvements they could be making. Solutions to these problems often exacerbate adaptation failure: managing across subunits often takes the form of routine reporting processes and automated information technology systems. But these measures weed out ideas and stifle innovations that do not fit easily into existing forms or channels. As a result, managers often find it even more difficult to ascertain what an organization is doing or what it needs to be doing differently. The very structures, rules, and technologies designed to improve efficiency sabotage an organization's ability to learn.[37]

As we shall see, these abstract ideas can have very real consequences. In the FBI's case, for example, structural secrecy proved devastating; the bureau's decentralized organization ensured that different FBI offices operated in isolation, unaware of what agents in other offices or headquarters were thinking or doing or finding. The bureau's inability to transfer information was a major concern years before the September 11 terrorist attacks. Former U.S. Attorney General Janet Reno told the 9/11 Commission that during her tenure in the Clinton administration, she "lacked confidence" in the FBI's ability to "know what it had" and "share what it had."[38] She was right. In the summer of 2001, three different FBI field offices uncovered clues to the 9/11 plot: an agent in the Phoenix office wrote a memo warning that bin Laden might be sending terrorists to train in U.S. flight schools; in Minneapolis, agents detained a suspicious foreign flight school student named Zacarias Moussaoui, the only person subsequently convicted in the United States in connection with 9/11; and the FBI's New York office began searching for Khalid al-Mihdhar and Nawaf al-Hazmi, two of the hijackers who ultimately crashed American Airlines Flight 77 into the Pentagon. But because the bureau was divided into fifty-six relatively independent and specialized field offices, none of the agents working these cases knew about the others.[39] As a result, these clues led nowhere. The FBI's field office structure enhanced specialization—enabling individual field offices to address local law enforcement priorities—but prevented officials in one part of the organization from learning what others in the organization already knew.

THE LIABILITY OF TIME

Finally, time is almost never on the side of government agencies that must adapt. All organizations become more resistant to change as routines, norms, and relationships become firmly established.[40]

Part of the problem comes from deliberate policy choices. Managers often go to great lengths to develop training programs, issue policies, create standardized ways of doing things, and instill values that motivate employees.[41] These measures often provide substantial benefits, enhancing an organization's reliability and stability. Standard operating procedures, for example, ensure that financial reports are prepared in the same way each quarter and guarantee that every military pilot operates with the same rules of engagement in wartime. However, these measures can also lock in ways of doing things that become maladaptive over time.[42] As Charles Perrow writes, "most bad rules were once good, designed for a situation that no longer exists."[43]

Natural social pressures also fuel resistance to change. The longer people work together, the more homogeneous their outlooks usually become and the more hostile they feel toward behavior or views that deviate from the norm.[44] Over time, people inside an organization also develop vested interests and fight to maintain them.[45] Organizational norms, relationships, and behaviors take hold. Employees become increasingly comfortable doing things the way they have been done before and expect newcomers to do the same. While these internal social pressures can reinforce positive aspects of organizational culture, creating an esprit de corps and a shared belief in "the way things are done," they also provide strong natural resistance to change.

Why Government Agencies Have the Hardest Time of All

For government agencies, bounded rationality, structural secrecy, and the liability of time are only the beginning. While all organizations have difficulty adapting to changing environmental demands, government agencies have the hardest time of all because they lack three key advantages that businesses enjoy.

The first is the imperative of markets to adapt or suffer the consequences. In the private sector, organizational survival is never guaranteed and everyone knows it. As Enron, Tyco, Kmart, Global Crossing, WorldCom, Polaroid, and United Airlines executives can attest, even industry leaders can fairly rapidly go from profitability to insolvency. Markets create the ultimate incentive to adapt. There is nothing quite like the prospect of unemployment to focus the mind.

Government agencies live in an altogether different world. Although congressional scholars have made much of Congress's oversight powers, the fact is that government agencies almost never fear that poor performance will lead to their death and replacement by newer, fitter organizations.[46] More than twenty-five million small businesses operate in the United States. There is only one Internal Revenue Service, it has been in business since the Civil War, and nobody is about to let it go under. The House Intelligence Committee's Report authorizing the 2005 intelligence budget makes clear just how weak Congress's oversight powers can be. The committee wrote: "After years of trying to convince, suggest, urge, entice, cajole, and pressure [the] CIA to make wide-reaching changes to the way it conducts its HUMINT [human intelligence] mission ... [the] CIA, in the committee's view, continues down a road leading over a proverbial cliff."[47] This sounds more like a plea for help than an iron-fisted demand for change.

The truth is that government agencies are not built to adapt. They are designed to be reliable and fair, performing tasks consistently and predictably and ensuring that all citizens receive the same level of service, regardless of their wealth or connections. Every state has a Department of Motor Vehicles and every neighborhood has a post office, no matter how small or remote. The mail may be slow, but everyone in the United States can get it. The lines at the DMV may be long, but detailed rules and procedures guarantee that everyone must stand in them. Reliability and fairness have their benefits. But these benefits come with a price: The more often things are done in the same way, the harder it is to alter them.

The second advantage that firms possess in the adaptation struggle is that their creators and employees want them to succeed. No one foists a new company on reluctant owners. No employee cheers silently for the day when company profits tumble and layoffs are announced. Instead, businesses are filled with organizational well-wishers who have vested interests in the company's continued success. Competitors may be plentiful and powerful, but they must do battle from the outside.

By contrast, government agencies are created by many who want them to fail. In politics, new agencies are forged by winning political coalitions who must compromise to succeed. The important point is not that winners win but that losers have a say in the organization's design and operation. The fragmented structure of the American political system ensures that political opponents have plenty of opportunities to sabotage the creation of any new agency at the outset—hobbling it with all sorts of rules and requirements—and possess the interests and capabilities to dog the agency forever after.[48]

Third and finally, business leaders have far more freedom to run their organizations than public sector managers do. Business executives can determine the organization's mission; hire and fire personnel with relatively few restraints; institute the policies, procedures, and customs they believe necessary; and attract capital from a multitude of sources. Government officials can only dream about this kind of freedom.[49] Any manager working for Coca Cola knows that his mission is to sell soda. But conflicting goals are built into the very mission of public sector agencies. The U.S. Forest Service, for example, is supposed to help harvest timber and protect national park lands at the same time. In addition, although intelligence agencies are technically exempt from a number of Civil Service regulations, the process of hiring and firing personnel is still riddled with bureaucratic red tape. As we shall see in chapter 4, managers in the CIA's clandestine service found personnel procedures so cumbersome, they often retained and even promoted poor performers instead of firing them. As one intelligence official complained, the Intelligence Community "is the Commerce Department with secrets. Fifty percent of every manager's time is spent managing the three percent of the people in the office who shouldn't be there. . . . Up or out? Survival of the fittest? We can't go there."[50] Finally, intelligence agency leaders must answer to many but have few places to turn to for help. The CEO of Intel can acquire needed resources from any number of financial institutions and investors around the world. The head of the U.S. Intelligence Community cannot.

Together, these forces suggest that prospects for internal reforms are not promising. What is a difficult challenge for businesses is a Herculean feat for government agencies. To adapt, all organizations must contend with bounded rationality, structural secrecy, and the liability of time. But firms are relatively lucky. They are fueled by market competition (and its shadow of death), focused by a unified mission, filled with stakeholders seeking success, armed with broad managerial discretion to match resources against organizational needs, and built to adjust as conditions change. Government agencies lack all of these adaptation advantages from birth.

Agencies that do not adapt on their own may be subjected to change from the outside, either through executive branch action or through legislation. In such cases, the rational self-interest of political actors and the fragmented structure of the federal government work to block success.

Rational Self-Interest of Presidents, Legislators, and National Security Bureaucrats

Government officials are constrained by the incentives and capabilities that come with their positions. Although individuals have their own ideas, skills, and policy preferences, institutional incentives and capabilities exert a powerful influence, making some courses of action easier and less costly than others. These incentives and capabilities explain why, before the September 11 attacks, no president championed intelligence reform, why legislators largely avoided and blocked it, and why national security agency bureaucrats opposed it.

All presidents have strong incentives to improve organizational effectiveness. To make their mark on history, they must make the bureaucracy work well for them. Perhaps even more important, presidents are also driven to enhance organizational effectiveness by the electorate, which expects far more of them than they can possibly deliver. Held responsible for everything from inflation to Iraqi democratization, presidents have good reason to ensure that government agencies adapt to changing demands as much and as fast as possible.[51]

The problem is that presidents are weak.[52] With little time, limited political capital, few formal powers, and packed political agendas, presidents lack the capabilities to make the changes they desire. Instead, they almost always prefer to focus their efforts on policy issues that directly concern (and benefit) voters rather than on the arcane details of organizational design and operation. And who can blame them? Tax cuts and social security lock boxes win votes, but no president ever won a landslide election by changing the CIA's personnel system. Moreover, presidents are especially reluctant to push for agency reforms in the absence of a crisis or in the presence of anticipated resistance. Presidents are thus loath to reform existing agencies through executive action or legislation. Although dozens of investigations, commissions, and experts identified shortcomings in the U.S. Intelligence Community between 1947, when the CIA was created, and the September 11, 2001, terrorist attacks, no president attempted major intelligence reform.[53] Rational self-interest explains why.

LEGISLATORS

Self-interest leads most legislators to avoid tackling intelligence reform altogether or seek to block it. Like presidents, legislators have little incentive to delve into the messy inner workings of intelligence agency design because doing so does not provide tangible benefits to voters back home.[54] Indeed, the weak electoral connection is one of the reasons congressional intelligence oversight committees continued imposing term limits for their members throughout the 1990s, long after it became clear that these regulations severely weakened the development of congressional expertise and after numerous commissions recommended abolishing them.[55] When crises do arise, intelligence committee members are rewarded more for airing dirty laundry than cleaning it. They frequently hold hearings but only rarely take corrective action. The Bay of Pigs, the congressional investigations into CIA abuses during the 1970s, the Iran-Contra scandal, and the Aldrich Ames spy case all triggered major investigations but none produced fundamental change in the Intelligence Community. In addition, members of Congress care about maintaining the power of the institution. Generally, this means that legislators prefer executive arrangements that diffuse authorities and capabilities; the more agencies in the executive branch, the more power bases can accrue in Congress to oversee them.

NATIONAL SECURITY AGENCY BUREAUCRATS

Finally, national security agency bureaucrats have their own interests at stake and powerful means to pursue them. Whereas most domestic policy agencies operate in relatively autonomous policy domains—the Environmental Protection Agency (EPA), for example, has no reason to think about the design or operation of the Social Security Administration—U.S. national security agencies are more tightly connected. Policymaking inevitably crosses bureaucratic boundaries, involving diplomacy, the use of force, economic policy, and intelligence. In such a complex web, national security bureaucrats see reform as a zero-sum battle for agency autonomy and power. EPA officials may not be conjuring up ways to gain advantage over another government agency, but national security bureaucrats are. In the interdependent world of national security affairs, no agency wants to yield authority or discretion to another.[56]

The Problems of Decentralized Democracy

Rational self-interest makes reform difficult; self-interest coupled with the decentralized structure of the U.S. federal government makes it more so. Paradoxically, some of the cherished features of American democracy impede effective agency design and raise obstacles to reform. Separation of powers, the congressional committee system, and majority rule have created a system that invites compromise and makes legislation hard to pass. This has two consequences for government agencies. First, political compromise allows opponents to cripple any new agency from the start. As Terry Moe writes, "In the political system, public bureaucracies are designed . . . by participants who explicitly want them to fail."[57] Political compromise unavoidably leads to suboptimal initial agency design, even for critical national security agencies such as the Central Intelligence Agency.[58] Indeed, critics who contend that the CIA is poorly suited to meeting the needs of the post–Cold War world are only partially right: the agency was not particularly well designed to meet the United States' Cold War needs, either. In 1947, existing intelligence agencies in the FBI, State Department, and military services succeeded in stripping the CIA of any strong centralization powers. When the CIA was created, it was flawed by design.[59]

The decentralized structure of American democracy also means that the worst agency problems usually are the hardest to fix. Although agencies can make some changes on their own and can also be altered by unilateral presidential action, the most far-reaching reforms almost always require new legislation. But legislative success is difficult even under the best of circumstances because it demands multiple majorities in both houses of Congress. As Philip Zelikow, executive director of the 9/11 Commission put it, "the most powerful interest group in Washington is the status quo."[60]

SUMMARY

Taken together, these three enduring realities—the nature of organizations, rational self-interest, and the fragmented federal government—provide a basic model for understanding why U.S. intelligence agencies failed to adapt to the terrorist threat before September 11, why they have not done much better since then, and why they are unlikely to improve substantially in the future. Government agencies are not built to change with the times. Because reform does not generally arise from within, it must be imposed from the outside. But even this rarely happens because all organizational changes, even the best reforms, create winners and losers, and because the political system allows losers multiple opportunities to keep winners from winning completely. Indeed, the greater the proposed change, the stronger the resistance will be. As a result, organizational adaptation almost always meets with defeat, becomes watered down, or gets shelved for another day, when the next crisis erupts.

CHAPTER 4

Fighting Osama One Bureaucrat at a Time

ADAPTATION FAILURE IN THE CIA

Somebody should have been shot for blocking this.
—Former senior intelligence official[1]

W<small>HEN THE</small> 1990s began, the Cold War was ending and the CIA was fighting for its life. When the decade ended, the war on terror was in full swing and the CIA was on the front lines. Within just ten years, talk of peace dividends turned to terrorism, budget cuts were hailed and then criticized, and an agency that had spent forty years mastering the intricacies of Soviet nuclear warhead designs was suddenly hunting Islamist operatives armed with truck bombs and box cutters. How the CIA tried, and failed, to transform itself to combat a new enemy is the story of this chapter.

Although the chapter can be read as a standalone case study of the CIA's adaptation efforts from 1991 to 2001, it builds on earlier discussions. In chapter 2, I made the case that the U.S. Intelligence Community as a whole failed to adapt to the rise of terrorism after the Cold War ended. Using evidence from intelligence threat assessments, policymaker speeches, and quantitative analysis of the recommendations made by every major unclassified intelligence and counterterrorism study of the decade, I showed that intelligence officials and policymakers recognized the terrorist danger and understood the need for major intelligence reform, but failed to achieve the changes they sought. Between 1991 and 2001, twelve different studies issued a total of 340 intelligence recommendations. The vast majority of them, 84 percent, focused on the same shortcomings that the 9/11 Commission and the Congressional Joint Inquiry found to be crucial in their September 11 postmortems. Yet almost none of these recommendations were implemented beforehand. Chapter

3 turned to explaining adaptation failure, reviewing a wide range of academic literature on the subject and developing a general explanation of why U.S. intelligence agencies failed to adapt to changing environmental demands. Here I apply that general explanation to specifics. This chapter seeks to develop a more nuanced understanding of the CIA's adaptation efforts during the 1990s and shows how the nature of organizations, rational self-interest, and the fragmented structure of the federal government kept them from succeeding.

It is important to underscore that the CIA and FBI case study chapters are designed to do more than just tell an interesting story. They are included to strengthen my argument about the causes and consequences of adaptation failure. The statistics in chapter 2 provide some compelling evidence that the U.S. Intelligence Community overall adjusted poorly to the rise of terrorism before September 11. However, this data does not provide a complete picture of adaptation efforts inside the CIA and FBI (a closer look, for example, reveals that agency officials undertook some important reform initiatives that no reform study specifically recommended). Nor does it explain why adaptation failure occurred or say anything about the relationship between nagging organizational deficiencies and agency performance. In short, quantitative analysis of intelligence adaptation failure provides a useful start, but getting a better handle on adaptation failure requires delving into the details of history.

The CIA's Organizational Deficiencies

The CIA's post–Cold War adaptation story actually begins in 1947, when the agency was established. From the beginning, the newly minted Central Intelligence Agency was hobbled by three types of organizational deficiencies that grew progressively worse with time: structural problems, cultural pathologies, and perverse incentive systems that encouraged and rewarded the wrong behavior.

Organizational structure is often more criticized than understood, derided as the meaningless location of boxes on an organization chart. In truth, however, organizational structure is not about boxes, but power: structure defines jurisdictions and creates capabilities, determines who performs which tasks by what authority, who answers to whom, and what formal powers organizational leaders have. Although good structure is not a cure-all, bad structure can have devastating effects on organizational performance.

Culture, by contrast, involves the ideas, values, and beliefs that color how agency employees view the world and what they hold dear. All organizations have cultures, some more ingrained than others. When cultures correspond to organizational missions, they can serve as a powerful positive force, emphasizing "the way things are done around here." But culture can also foster attitudes that sap innovation, block change, and degrade agency performance over time.

Incentives, finally, determine which types of activities are rewarded—by things like performance evaluations, promotions, and awards—and which are not. Like culture, incentives exert a powerful and silent influence, encouraging employees to devote their energies to certain tasks instead of others.

In the CIA's case, weaknesses in structure, culture, and incentives festered throughout the Cold War and became debilitating in the 1990s, when the Soviet threat was replaced by an entirely new breed of terrorist enemy. As we shall see, ultimately these organizational problems prevented the agency from developing more opportunities to disrupt the September 11 plot and limited its ability to capitalize on the few opportunities that it had (see figure 4.1). Failures of adaptation led to failures of performance.

Structural Deficiencies: "Too Broke to Be Fixed"

The CIA's structural problems can be summed up in one word: fragmentation. Originally, the Central Intelligence Agency was supposed to be one component of a sweeping legislative overhaul of the nation's national security apparatus following World War II; the CIA's charter legislation, the National Security Act of 1947, also established the National Security Council and consolidated the Departments of War and Navy into a single Department of Defense.[2] Nearly every provision of the law, however, was bitterly contested and ultimately watered down. When President Truman signed the bill on July 26, 1947, he ended four years of some of the most intensive, protracted public military

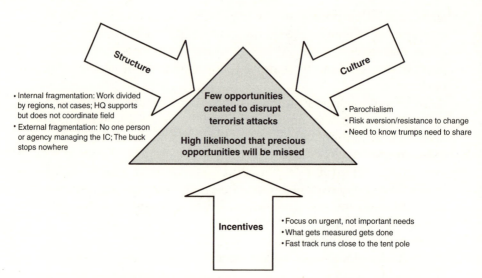

Figure 4.1. The CIA and 9/11: The Organizational Roots of Failure.

debates in U.S. history. The *New York Times* described the battle to pass the law as "a brass-knuckle fight to the finish."[3]

The Central Intelligence Agency became a casualty of the policymaking process. In principle, the CIA was supposed to integrate intelligence efforts across the U.S. government. In practice, however, the agency was never designed to work well. This was no accident. As Thomas Troy writes in his classic history of the CIA, the idea of a permanent and powerful central intelligence organization generated "intense hostility" from "old-line" intelligence agencies, particularly the FBI and existing military intelligence units, who were "determined" to prevent the new agency from controlling their activities.[4] The departments of State, Justice, War, and Navy joined forces to strip the proposed new CIA of its coordinating powers.[5]

They succeeded. The National Security Act of 1947 assigned the director of central intelligence two jobs, running the CIA and "coordinating the intelligence activities of the several Government departments and agencies in the interest of national security."[6] Yet the act gave the DCI strong budgetary and personnel authorities over the CIA only. The law also hamstrung the agency by placing it underneath the National Security Council, which included the heads of the very intelligence organizations the CIA was supposed to coordinate. Finally, the National Security Act of 1947 included language that explicitly protected existing intelligence components, making clear that they should "continue to collect, evaluate, correlate, and disseminate" their own intelligence.[7] Of particular importance, the CIA was legally barred from gathering intelligence about American citizens on American soil, from conducting any law enforcement or police activities, or performing any other internal security functions. These legal restrictions arose partly from fears of creating an American Gestapo, but also from intense lobbying by the FBI to protect its domestic turf. The effect over time was to create a structural split between domestic and foreign intelligence, with the CIA responsible for tracking enemies abroad and the FBI charged with finding them at home.

During the Cold War the number of intelligence agencies increased, but the CIA's authorities to manage them did not. By 1992, a year after the Soviet Union's collapse, the Intelligence Community had grown to thirteen major agencies.[8] Eight of them—the National Security Agency, which intercepts signals intelligence; the National Reconnaissance Office, which builds and maintains spy satellites; the Pentagon's imagery office, which processed maps and other images and eventually became the National Geospatial-Intelligence Agency;[9] the Defense Intelligence Agency; and intelligence units in the Army, Navy, Air Force, and Marine Corps—were housed in the Defense Department and effectively controlled by the defense secretary, not the director of central intelligence. Indeed, the DCI faced the worst of all worlds, holding responsibility for these agencies as well as the four others outside the CIA, but possessing almost no formal powers over them.[10] The DCI controlled less than 20 percent of the total intelligence budget (the secretary of defense controlled nearly all of the rest), could not transfer funds between agencies without their approval, and exercised no line authority over personnel anywhere except in the Central Intelligence Agency.

The existence of so many separate agencies and the absence of formal mechanisms to integrate them became reinforced by bureaucratic procedures over time. Throughout the Cold War, different intelligence agencies developed their own budgets and set their own priorities, hired their own staffs and trained them in separate programs, communicated by separate e-mail systems and kept intelligence in incompatible databases. By the 1990s, every intelligence agency had its own security badge, making it impossible even for officials with the highest level of security clearance to walk through the turnstile of any intelligence office building except their own. The CIA, in short, was supposed to manage a U.S. intelligence system that was all spokes and no hub.

This fragmented structural arrangement became even more problematic when the principal threat shifted from superpower conflict to transnational terrorism. For decades, the Soviet Union had been a monolithic, visible, and static threat. As one veteran clandestine officer put it, "the Soviet Union was constrained by borders [and] . . . it was on a, God bless them, a five year program. Everything was predictable."[11] Transnational terrorism was a different story. Multifaceted, dynamic, hidden from view, the terrorist threat that emerged in the 1990s demanded an unprecedented degree of joint action across U.S. intelligence agencies—precisely the kind of integration the intelligence structure was incapable of providing. In particular, the strict separation between the CIA and FBI proved devastating. As former National Security Advisor Brent Scowcroft noted after the September 11 attacks, "The borders, as far as the terrorists are concerned, have gone. There is no distinction for terrorists between inside and outside the United States and I think that makes much more serious the division that we have between the CIA and the FBI."[12] Another official was more blunt, describing the intelligence structure in the 1990s as "too broke to be fixed."[13]

To make matters worse, the CIA also had to contend with a highly fragmented internal structure. The Central Intelligence Agency was really two agencies in one: the Directorate of Operations (DO), which was the legendary clandestine service that stole secrets and ran covert operations; and the Directorate of Intelligence (DI), which was filled with Ph.D.s who were trained to put secrets together from across the Intelligence Community, fuse them with information gleaned from open sources such as foreign newspapers, and draft analytic reports for policymakers or "customers." Housed in the same building, the DO and the DI were worlds apart, with vastly different missions, capabilities, and personnel. The DO was powerful, glamorous, and engaged in activities that naturally dominated policymaker attention in both good times and bad, when operations went awry.

For clandestine case officers in the DO, being called a "cowboy" was a compliment, suggesting someone who was unafraid of running to the sound of gunfire and who stood in the grand tradition of the CIA's World War II predecessor, the Office of Strategic Services.[14] The DI, by contrast, was filled with Ivy League analysts who preferred to sit in cubicles studying information and who struggled to coordinate and synthesize various elements of the Intelligence Community in the background.

During the Cold War, moreover, the CIA further divided activities between headquarters and the field, creating a highly decentralized structure that gave field offices primacy and relegated headquarters to a supporting role. Each field office had responsibility for covering a specific geographic region, calling its own shots, and running its own operations. This arrangement made sense when the Soviet enemy was clear and its mobility limited. The structure was poorly suited, however, for tracking terrorists who were difficult to identify and moved more freely across national borders and field office jurisdictions.[15]

Cultural Pathologies

The CIA also faced a number of cultural pathologies. Chief among them were a debilitating sense of agency parochialism, resistance to change, and a belief in the overriding importance of security captured by the phrase, "need to know."

Structural divisions forged at the CIA's birth fueled the growth of parochial agency attitudes. Because officials were hired, promoted, and cloistered inside separate agencies and performed classified work that could not be revealed even to their own families, they naturally developed strong internal bonds of loyalty and identified with their home agencies rather than the Intelligence Community as a whole. One defense intelligence official described the problem this way: "We don't have much of a sense of loyalty to the Community. We see ourselves as employees of agencies. . . . When agencies get together . . . each agency tells their person, 'we're competitors. . . . Make sure those bastards from CIA don't run you over.' "[16] These attitudes persisted throughout the Cold War, but their costs rose dramatically in the 1990s, when cross-cutting issues such as the proliferation of weapons of mass destruction and terrorism demanded new levels of interagency collaboration.

Resistance to change also took hold during the Cold War. This should not be surprising: as noted in chapter 3, all organizations find it difficult to assume new tasks and behave in new ways as time passes. And the CIA had been confronting the same over-arching threat for more than forty years.

Finally, Cold War security demands bred a deep belief in the importance of protecting information, sharing it only with those who demonstrated a compelling "need to know." As one CIA official observed, "the hardest things to change are things that change fundamental underlying principles or beliefs about how to do your job differently . . . and the most deeply held principle [in intelligence] is the need to know. We believed in it for a long time. This principle is obviously now rubbing up against a new principle: the need to share. But what people believe and hold dear is very, very hard to let go of, even in the face of the need for change."[17]

Counterproductive Incentives

Career incentives, finally, reinforced cultural problems and encouraged intelligence officials to focus their energies on many of the wrong things. Evaluations for both CIA analysts and clandestine case officers emphasized activities that could be measured more easily and objectively, such as the number of spies recruited or the number of analytic reports produced. Quantity usually counted more than quality. As one intelligence official noted, "Your career as an analyst is determined by how many products you produce. It's about how many items you have in the PDB [the President's Daily Brief, the highly classified intelligence report that is given to the president each day and considered prestigious for career analysts], more than whether what you said was particularly smart."[18] What's more, CIA employees were not rewarded or even evaluated for working across agency lines. As one intelligence official wryly noted, incentives and cultures fostered an us-versus-them attitude between other agencies and the CIA. "For other agencies," the official noted, "a good year is when their own budget goes up 8 percent. An even better year is when their budget goes up 8 percent and CIA's goes up only 6 percent."[19]

Finally, in what one former National Intelligence Council official describes as the "tyranny of current intelligence," CIA analysts and their managers after the Cold War were increasingly preoccupied with, and rewarded for, how well they dealt with immediate needs and news, not how well they performed on longer-term, strategic analysis of patterns and puzzles looming over the horizon.[20] Whereas the Soviet threat had bred and rewarded patience—it made sense to think of long-term analysis for a predictable and slowly changing long-term danger—the proliferation of post–Cold War threats and the rise of the twenty-four-hour news cycle eroded the CIA's strategic analysis capabilities.[21] Focusing on longer-term needs rather than shorter-term priorities was a constant struggle, and one that intelligence officials and policymakers often lost. Brent Scowcroft described the pressure to "put out fires" as one of the most vexing problems in intelligence and foreign policymaking. He told the Congressional Joint Inquiry, "If you start to look for and anticipate contingencies and bring those to the decision-makers, they say don't bother me with something [in] 10 years, I've got something 10 minutes away."[22]

Summary

In sum, when the Cold War ended, the CIA did not emerge a blank slate. Its legislative origins had lasting effects, crippling the agency's ability to manage an expanding set of intelligence agencies, and erecting jurisdictional boundaries, particularly between domestic and foreign intelligence, that hardened with time. By 1991, the CIA had also become a middle-aged organization with deeply ingrained cultures, entrenched ways of operating, and counterproductive incentives that had developed over forty years of facing down the same enemy.

ADAPTATION AFTER THE COLD WAR

The CIA's adaptation to terrorism after the Cold War can be divided into three phases. Phase One, which lasted from 1991 to 1994, was a time of deep intellectual confusion, both about the nature of the post–Cold War world and the agency's mission in it. Phase Two began with a series of scandals in 1994 that triggered efforts to impose reform on the CIA from the outside. The moment, however, soon passed and reform died almost as quickly as it arose. Phase Three began at 10:30 a.m. on the morning of August 7, 1998, when al Qaeda operatives detonated two truck bombs outside the U.S. embassies in Nairobi, Kenya, and Dar es Salaam, Tanzania. These attacks were a wakeup call both for CIA officials and policymakers throughout the U.S. government. Again, however, internal and external reforms faltered. As al Qaeda gained strength and Osama bin Laden began formulating the 9/11 "planes operation," the Central Intelligence Agency fell farther and farther behind.

Phase One: Peace Dividend Confusion, 1991–1994

We weren't trying to reorganize the Intelligence Community. The country was trying to kill it.

—Senior intelligence official[23]

On December 31, 1991, as the Soviet flag flew over the Kremlin for the last time, the Central Intelligence Agency was fighting for its own survival. The collapse of the United States' principal enemy led many to question the role and relevance of intelligence in a post–Cold War world. Longtime intelligence supporters such as Senate Intelligence Committee Chairman David Boren (D-OK) and former CIA Director Stansfield Turner believed the CIA had to undertake new missions to survive.[24] Most urged dramatic cutbacks, believing the "peace dividend" could be better spent on pressing domestic concerns. William Hyland, one of the deans of U.S. foreign policy circles, noted in May of 1991 that, "The United States has never been less threatened by foreign forces than it is today. . . . [and] never since the Great Depression has the threat to domestic well-being been greater."[25] Peter Peterson, the chairman of the prestigious Council on Foreign Relations, issued a similar call in a speech at Columbia University, arguing that domestic problems in education and poverty "now threaten . . . America's long-term national security more than the traditional preoccupations of security and foreign policy such as the menace of Soviet nuclear bombs or conventional attacks on our territory. . . ."[26] Some went even further.

Former National Security Agency chief Lt. General William Odom and Daniel Patrick Moynihan (D-NY), one of the most powerful members of the Senate, recommended that the CIA be abolished altogether. Domestic policy concerns so dominated the 1992 presidential campaign that Governor Bill Clinton devoted just 218 words to foreign affairs in his notoriously lengthy, 54-minute,[27] 4,434-word acceptance speech at the Democratic National Convention.[28] For the CIA, the message was clear: the time had come to end business as usual.

Business as usual did end in many respects. The result, however, was not a more effective intelligence agency, but an organization hobbled by dwindling resources, internal turbulence, and strategic confusion. Determined to produce a peace dividend, Congress and the president slashed intelligence budgets every year from 1991 to 1996,[29] resulting in a whopping 25 percent work force reduction at the CIA.[30] R. James Woolsey, who served as director of central intelligence from 1993 to 1995, noted that he "spent a very great deal of time trying to hold onto enough money to keep a decent personnel system operating and to hold things together."[31] Woolsey warned in his confirmation hearings that "we have slain a large dragon" by defeating the Soviet Union, "but we live now in a jungle filled with a bewildering variety of poisonous snakes, and in many ways the dragon was easier to keep track of."[32] But he failed to gain an audience at the White House, meeting with Clinton only a handful of times during his two years as CIA chief.[33] When a mentally unstable pilot crashed a Cessna airplane onto the White House lawn in the fall of 1994, aides joked that it was Woolsey trying to get the president's attention.[34] Distanced from the president and disliked by many inside the CIA, Woolsey did not last long. His short tenure was not unusual; the CIA's top post became a revolving door, with five different intelligence chiefs between 1991 and 1994. With shrinking resources and unstable leadership, the CIA struggled to define its post–Cold War role.

The president and Congress did not help much. In 1991, President George H. W. Bush ordered a "top to bottom examination of the mission, role, and priorities of the Intelligence Community."[35] Rather than clarifying priorities, however, the review expanded them, producing a laundry list of possible intelligence requirements that ranged from environmental issues to global

71

health problems to international economics.[36] The review, along with the threat of possible reform legislation, prompted DCI Robert Gates to appoint fourteen internal task forces on intelligence reform. They produced only modest changes that languished over time. Intelligence warning, for example, was considered one of the most important intelligence issues after the Gulf War, and was the subject of one of Gates's task forces. Although the study issued several recommendations to improve warning capabilities, the 9/11 Commission found that these measures did not last over time, nor did they adapt well to develop useful warning indicators of a catastrophic terrorist attack.[37] One senior intelligence official who served during this period reflected, "I don't recall a whole lot from Gates, frankly."[38]

In Congress, meanwhile, the House and Senate Intelligence Committee chairmen, Representative David McCurdy (D-OK) and Senator David Boren (D-OK), introduced intelligence reform bills that would have radically restructured the Intelligence Community and placed it under a powerful new director of national intelligence.[39] Their proposals, however, were swiftly scuttled by opposition from the Pentagon and the Congressional Armed Services Committees. In March 1992, then-Secretary of Defense Richard Cheney wrote a letter to House Armed Services Committee Chairman Les Aspin (D-WI) that delivered a blistering attack. Calling the bills "severely flawed," Cheney threatened that he would recommend a presidential veto if necessary. "Of major concern," he wrote, "the reorganization bills hold the prospect of reducing the effectiveness of intelligence support to our warfighting commanders."[40] This battlefield effectiveness argument had little substantive merit but proved a savvy political move; pro-reform legislators were suddenly put in the position of supporting changes that promised abstract benefits in intelligence coordination at the expense of American lives on the front lines. And they were faced with the unattractive prospect of debating the Pentagon's claims with military leaders who were considered far more expert. So effective was this argument that the Pentagon repeated it in 1996 and 2004, when reform proposals again gained momentum in Congress.

Then in 1993, with intelligence reform dead and the agency struggling to make sense of a radically new threat environment with dramatically reduced resources, President Clinton launched a new program to revolutionize public management across the federal government, The National Performance Review. More popularly known as reinventing government, the initiative sought to apply business practices to make government work better and cost less. The timing could not have been worse. Although the National Performance Review issued a number of thoughtful recommendations to improve the effectiveness of the Intelligence Community, the program came to be viewed inside the CIA as a cost-cutting mandate. In the agency's strategic vacuum, management became the new mission, and meeting the bottom line, not meeting new threats, became an overriding focus. In 1996, three years after the National Performance Review published its first report, Director of Central Intelligence John Deutch proudly declared that "the intelligence community continues to be on schedule in its goal of downsizing personnel by 23 percent in this decade."[41] Deutch, meanwhile, had taken none of the specific steps suggested by the National Performance Review to implement its lead recommendation: enhancing Intelligence Community integration.[42]

Indeed, cutting costs so eclipsed big picture thinking inside the CIA's top ranks that personnel reductions were conducted without any strategic plan to retain the agency's best and brightest or to realign its skill mix. Rather than weeding out poor performers and those with outdated areas of expertise, the agency cut its work force solely through voluntary retirement and attrition.[43] Deutch's tactics infuriated many inside the CIA, who saw him as a flame thrower who was interested more in firing people and becoming secretary of defense than reforming the agency to tackle unconventional targets. As one former CIA official reflected, Deutch and his colleagues "just got rid of people . . . they really didn't know what they were doing."[44] Deutch's untargeted approach to cost cutting also drew the ire of the House Intelligence Committee. "Four years after the dismantling of the Berlin Wall," the committee complained in June of 1994, "the CIA is without a strategic plan for HUMINT [human intelligence] collection, one which defines essential roles and missions, maps a course for organizational restructuring and streamlining, and allocates scarce resources."[45] In 1995, the CIA's clandestine service trained only twenty-five new case officers, the lowest number in years.[46] By 1996, the Washington Post was reporting that young and midcareer spies were leaving in record numbers, and that morale inside the CIA was worse than it had been even during the agency's darkest days in the 1970s.[47] Personal accounts paint a similar picture. According to former Osama bin Laden Unit head Michael Scheuer, the CIA lost an entire generation of rising leaders during this period, "the age 40-to-48 group of very strong potential senior officers, those people who couldn't stand the bureaucracy anymore."[48] Veteran clandestine operative Milt Bearden described his personal reaction to the CIA's management-as-mission approach more bluntly: "Here I am, at age 54. . . . Am I going to put up with this shit from some bozo like John Deutch for one more fucking minute?"[49] By the time George Tenet became DCI in 1997, the clandestine service was in total disarray.[50]

Phase Two: Failed Reforms from Without, 1994–1998

Phase Two of the CIA's adaptation efforts began on February 21, 1994, when a CIA employee named Aldrich H. Ames was arrested in his Jaguar outside his Virginia home. It would become one of the worst spy scandals in U.S. history. Investigators discovered that Ames had been promoted up the agency's ranks and given access to highly classified information for thirty-one years, despite a history of alcohol abuse, security violations, and poor job performance evaluations. And for nearly a decade, he had sold vital secrets to Moscow, spending lavishly on new homes and luxury cars without detection.[51] Around the same time, reports surfaced that the National Reconnaissance Office, the agency that builds and maintains spy satellites, had mismanaged more than a billion dollars in congressionally authorized funds. Coming on the heels of the Soviet Union's collapse, these two scandals led to a new push for intelligence reform. During the next four years, three think tanks, a presidential commission, and the House Intelligence Committee all conducted comprehensive studies and issued major reports urging changes to the CIA and the rest of the U.S. Intelligence Community. The Congressional Intelligence Committees rose to the challenge, attempting to pass the most significant intelligence overhaul since the CIA's creation. Their efforts, however, were again torpedoed by the Pentagon and prodefense legislators on the defense oversight committees. The CIA managed to create some important and innovative counterterrorism programs in the absence of wholesale intelligence overhaul, but they were nowhere near enough.

FROM SCANDAL TO STUDY

In the fall of 1994, in the wake of the Ames and NRO scandals, the president and Congress created a bipartisan blue-ribbon commission to conduct a comprehensive review of the U.S. Intelligence Community. Chaired by former defense secretaries Les Aspin and then Harold Brown, the U.S. Commission on the Roles and Capabilities of the U.S. Intelligence Community—better known as the Aspin-Brown Commission—was given a broad mandate to examine "the efficacy and appropriateness" of U.S. intelligence activities in the post–Cold War era.[52] Aspin-Brown was soon joined by four other intelligence reform studies: a lengthy review conducted by the House Permanent Select Committee on Intelligence, a task force study at the Council on Foreign Relations, a report commissioned by the 20th Century Fund, and a review by the National Institute for Public Policy. As noted in chapter 2, these studies covered different issues but came to similar conclusions: the U.S. Intelligence Community, and the CIA in particular, needed help. All five reports urged greater integration across U.S. intelligence agencies, improvements in setting intelligence priorities, and personnel policy reforms to enhance information sharing. In addition, four of the five recommended revitalizing the CIA's clandestine human intelligence capabilities. Of the 192 specific intelligence reform recommendations they issued, 153, or 80 percent of the total, focused on these key problems.

FROM DISAPPOINTMENT TO FAILURE

On March 1, 1996, the Aspin-Brown Commission released its final report. Public reaction could only be described as disappointment. Many believed the commission had identified major problems but had recommended relatively minor changes. For example, while the commission saw the need for enhancing Intelligence Community integration, it suggested adding some deputy positions to assist the director of central intelligence rather than fundamentally reshaping the DCI's role or granting him greater budgetary and personnel authority over the twelve intelligence agencies outside the CIA. As Commission Staff Director L. Britt Snider admitted, the blue-ribbon panel concluded that, "major surgery was not the solution."[53]

Just four days later, House Intelligence Committee Chairman Larry Combest (R-TX) took a different approach, demanding bold change. Declaring that "everything is on the table,"[54] Combest released his committee's year-long study and unveiled a series of recommendations that were by his own admission "radical."[55] Among them were spinning off the CIA's clandestine human intelligence service into a new organization, concentrating the CIA's energies on analysis, particularly longer-term strategic analysis, and greatly expanding the DCI's budgetary and personnel power over the entire Intelligence Community. Senate Intelligence Committee Chairman Arlen Specter (R-PA) soon followed suit, introducing a reform bill that differed in specifics but offered a similarly ambitious vision of intelligence overhaul. Both bills went much further than either Aspin-Brown or the Clinton administration's proposed changes. Both were also short-lived.

Although Combest and the rest of the House Intelligence Committee softened provisions of the bill to make it more palatable to the defense establishment, the bill never made it out of the House National Security Committee: at the Pentagon's behest, the committee insisted on eliminating virtually every provision that would have bolstered the DCI's power. In the end, the bill was so watered down that Combest decided against sending it to the House floor.[56] The Senate bill suffered a similar fate. In a replay of Cheney's 1992 letter, Deputy Secretary of Defense John White sent a letter to Senate Armed Services Committee Chairman Strom Thurmond (R-SC) on April 29, 1996, warning that the Senate bill threatened to create a "monolithic intelligence community" that would hurt the warfighter and produce no offsetting benefits.[57] The sympathetic Senate Armed Services Committee at first stalled for time, asking the Intelligence Committee to delay consideration of intelligence reform for a year. When Intelligence Committee Chairman Specter refused, the Armed Services panel took the teeth out of his bill. What began as a sweeping proposal ended with only minor changes: the Intelligence Authorization Act, which was signed by President Clinton in October 1996, established four new Senate-confirmed positions to help the DCI run the Intelligence Community. Gone were measures that sought to improve CIA analysis and enhance the DCI's budgetary and personnel control over the entire Intelligence Community. Even the meager provisions that survived were never fully implemented. Resistance in the White House and the CIA proved so strong that between 1996 and 2004, only two of four new Intelligence Community management positions were ever filled.[58]

INSIDE THE CIA: MOVING FORWARD AND FALLING SHORT

With intelligence reform legislation languishing in congress and the president staying conspicuously out of the fray, the CIA had to make do, adjusting to the terrorist threat without the help of a realigned intelligence structure, new statutory powers for the DCI, or legislative mandates to improve deficiencies in information sharing. Despite these constraints, between 1994 and 1998 the agency made some notable improvements in its counterterrorism efforts. Chief among them were creating a special unit to track the activities of Osama bin Laden, launching a program to exchange senior counterterrorism officials between the FBI and CIA, and developing better relationships with foreign intelligence services. None of these efforts were envisioned or recommended by any of the intelligence reform studies of the period. All were important steps in the right direction. And all of them fell short.

In 1996, the CIA established a special unit of about a dozen people inside its Counterterrorist Center—mostly junior grade intelligence officers drawn from the CIA and FBI—to learn more about Osama bin Laden's activities and develop counterterrorism operations.[59] It was the first time a CIA station had targeted a person rather than a country,[60] and it was the first "virtual station," an office based at headquarters that collected and operated against targets in the field just as CIA stations in foreign countries do.[61] The unit quickly discovered that Osama bin Laden was more than just a terrorist financier.[62] By 1997 intelligence officers there knew that al Qaeda had a military committee that was planning attacks against U.S. interests across the world and was actively trying to obtain weapons of mass destruction.[63] According to the House and Senate Intelligence

77

Committees' Joint Inquiry into September 11, the bin Laden unit became "the U.S. Government's focal point for expertise on and operations" against bin Laden and his al Qaeda network.[64]

Around the same time, Director of Central Intelligence John Deutch and FBI Director Louis Freeh launched an effort to improve their agencies' cooperation on terrorism cases. They began by holding "Gang of 8 meetings," monthly sessions between the top four CIA and FBI officials engaged in counterterrorism to explore new ways of working together. Soon the two agencies agreed to swap deputy directors at the CIA and FBI counterterrorist centers. Although staunchly resisted by counterterrorism officials in both agencies, these efforts to improve cooperation produced some impressive counterterrorism successes, including the capture and prosecution of those involved in the 1993 World Trade Center attack.[65]

Finally, the CIA developed much stronger relationships during this period with foreign intelligence services. According to the Congressional Joint Inquiry into September 11, the move stemmed from the realization among several CIA officials that "traditional U.S. intelligence techniques were of limited value in penetrating and countering" al Qaeda cells.[66]

Although all three of these initiatives were moves in the right direction, they were small steps where large leaps were required. For example, while the bin Laden unit was a brilliant innovation, the station was staffed with relatively junior level people and was considered such a poor assignment that no one from the CIA's Directorate of Operations wanted to run it.[67] As one former clandestine official noted, "it's so smart to set up an Osama bin Laden station, but then it gets stood up with a GS-13 [mid-level] analyst and a few others?! . . . The measure of true commitment is where your A+ people are. We didn't put the right people in that place."[68] Counterterrorism staffing levels, moreover, did not begin to keep pace with the threat. CIA clandestine chief James Pavitt told the 9/11 Commission that he believed staffing levels were "woefully, woefully inadequate to the threat that was out there."[69] The Congressional Joint Inquiry agreed, finding that the bin Laden station and its parent unit, the CIA's Counterterrorist Center, did not receive any substantial infusions of personnel or resources until after 9/11.[70] The Joint Inquiry found that on the morning of September 11, 2001, only five analysts were assigned full-time to al Qaeda.[71]

Similarly, the exchange of officials between the CIA and FBI began to chip away at the intense suspicion and outright hostility between these two agencies that had metastasized over decades. But the road to interagency collaboration was long and difficult. Resistance was so strong that insiders in both agencies referred to the FBI/CIA swaps as the "hostage exchange program." One of the FBI agents tapped to participate in the program turned down the assignment and went to the CIA only after he was ordered to report there. "A detail assignment [to the CIA] was like death," he recalled. "I thought, 'I don't know these people. I don't like these people. I don't trust these people.' "[72] Although the agent would eventually support efforts to improve CIA-FBI cooperation, he and many others were swimming against the currents of prevailing agency culture on both sides. As chapter 5 discusses, distrust between the FBI and CIA was so ingrained that even in the summer of 2001, when intelligence chatter was spiking about an imminent terrorist attack, CIA officials missed four opportunities to share key pieces of information about the plot with their FBI counterparts.

Strengthening liaison relationships with foreign intelligence services was also a good idea, but one that arose from the realization that the CIA's own clandestine Directorate of Operations could not penetrate al Qaeda. Below, I discuss in greater detail why the CIA's clandestine service was in such disarray and why efforts to revamp it did not succeed. The point, however, is that this reform, while valuable, also hinted at serious trouble: establishing closer bonds with foreign intelligence services was a workaround. It mitigated the damage caused by weaknesses in the CIA's own clandestine service, but did not attempt to fix the underlying problem.

SUMMARY

For those determined to revamp and retool the CIA to fight a new enemy, the mid-1990s was a time of great effort and disappointment. By 1996, the contours of the post–Cold War world had come into focus and intelligence reform was in the air. With five different studies calling for varying degrees of change, the Congressional Intelligence Committees took up the charge with a vengeance, pressing for a sweeping overhaul of the U.S. Intelligence Community and dramatic changes to the CIA. They did not get far. In both the House and Senate, intelligence reform bills were swiftly and roundly attacked by the Pentagon and defense oversight committees. With intelligence reform derailed and the president staying on the sidelines, the CIA was on its own. The agency made progress in improving its counterterrorism capabilities, but as intelligence officials soon learned, these efforts were nowhere near enough.

Phase Three: Failed Reforms from Within, 1998–2001

The CIA was jolted into its third adaptation phase on the morning of August 7, 1998, when al Qaeda operatives detonated two truck bombs simultaneously outside U.S. embassies located four hundred miles apart, in Dar es Salaam, Tanzania, and Nairobi, Kenya. The bombings, which revealed sophisticated operations and years of careful planning, killed hundreds, wounded thousands, and delivered a wake-up call to the U.S. Intelligence Community: the time for change was overdue.[73] Between 1998 and 2001, four blue-ribbon panels examined U.S. counterterrorism policy and capabilities.[74] Again, the calls for reforming U.S. intelligence agencies were widespread but focused on the same major issues: information sharing, cross-agency coordination, strategic thinking, and human intelligence collection. This time, however, the most serious reform efforts took place inside the CIA, not Congress.[75] Director of Central Intelligence George Tenet launched a series of initiatives to dramatically enhance Intelligence Community integration, improve strategic analysis in counterterrorism, and rebuild the CIA's clandestine service. All of Tenet's proposed changes encountered strong resistance, leading to limited successes and in many cases outright defeat.

ENHANCING INTEGRATION

Tenet's first prong of attack was to improve integration across the U.S. Intelligence Community. In December 1998, four months after the embassy bombings, he issued a memo declaring, "We must now enter a new phase in our effort against Bin Ladin. . . . We are at war. . . . I want no resources or people spared in this effort, either inside [the] CIA or the Community."[76]

At about the same time, he announced the completion of an ambitious strategic plan for the entire U.S. Intelligence Community: it was the first strategic plan developed since the Cold War's end.[77] The "DCI's Strategic Intent for the United States Intelligence Community" set comprehensive and aggressive goals in five areas: unifying the Community, developing a first-rate work force, creating new sources and methods of intelligence collection, improving information sharing, and revolutionizing resource allocation. It also made clear that technology was the key to success. Acknowledging that traditional intelligence processes "have not kept pace with the new information age," the plan called for adopting a new intelligence business model of "virtual enterprises," computer and communications networks that enable linkages across issues, experts, and agencies in real time.[78] Finally, Tenet tried to break down logistical and cultural walls between intelligence agencies to improve collaboration. He sent directives that required a standard blue security badge be issued to all U.S. intelligence officials so that they could move more freely between agencies located in different facilities and he mandated intelligence officers serve in intelligence agencies outside their own for promotion to senior ranks.

None of these initiatives succeeded. The 9/11 Commission and Congressional Joint Inquiry found that Tenet's declaration of war memo had almost no impact: only a handful of agency heads ever received it, and all of them ignored it.[79] Lietenant General Kenneth Minihan, director of the National Security Agency, said that he received a copy, but thought the memo applied only to the CIA, not his agency. CIA officials, on the other hand, thought the memo was intended for the rest of the Intelligence Community and did not apply to them.[80] These reactions were not at all unusual. As one intelligence official noted, standard practice in the Intelligence Community was to use the "two parent approach: if mom says no, go to dad." When asked to do something by the DCI, agencies would routinely "go out and find some bozo regulation that says why they cannot do it." Conversely, the official noted, "If the secretary of defense asks them, they go out and find some bozo directive from the DCI."[81] The House and Senate Intelligence Committees' Joint Inquiry concluded that Tenet's memo failed to galvanize the Intelligence

Community, leaving it "fragmented [and] without a comprehensive strategy for combating bin Ladin."[82]

Tenet's strategic plan fared even worse. The DCI's top deputies soon learned that they lacked basic information and abilities to begin putting the plan into action. No one, for example, knew how many analysts worked in the United States Intelligence Community or what expertise they had.[83] The same was true for intelligence collection. When Charlie Allen began assessing U.S. collection efforts, he found gaping holes. Among them: no one in the entire U.S. Intelligence Community was looking at Baghdad, Saddam Hussein's power base.[84] Other parts of the plan were fiercely resisted. In 1999, for example, the DCI's office launched a new computer initiative called ICMAP that would have established a tracking system for intelligence collection requests. Before, analysts could ask intelligence collection agencies to gather information on a certain target, but had no way of knowing where their request ranked on the collecting agency's priority list or determining whether it had been done—making it difficult to set priorities or hold agencies accountable. ICMAP promised to fix these problems. But it was opposed by the National Security Agency and other collection agencies, which feared losing turf, power, and control over their own activities.[85] As one intelligence official and ICMAP supporter commented, "Somebody should have been shot for blocking this."[86]

Tenet's security badge and promotion directives also went down to defeat. Although a standard blue security badge was issued to all intelligence officials, the new badges did not actually enable individuals to work more easily across agency lines. Some employees refused to carry the Community blue badges out of loyalty to their home agency.[87] One National Security Agency (NSA) official, for example, superglued the laminate back onto his old NSA green badge and refused to give it up until he was finally barred by security officers in the NSA lobby. When asked why he had done it, he declared, "I work for NSA, not the Community."[88] His was not an isolated or unusual reaction: entire agencies circumvented the directive, most often by issuing their own badges and requiring both passes for admission to their facilities. Even the DCI's own staff had badges that allowed them access to just two of the thirteen U.S. intelligence agencies they were supposed to be overseeing.[89]

Meanwhile, Tenet's directive requiring intelligence officials to work in different intelligence agencies was ignored. As one defense intelligence official explained, "other than going to the other agencies and saying 'please, please, please do this,' Tenet had no authority to do this in the Defense Department. . . . There was no hammer behind it." After the directive first came out, he recalled, "We looked at the candidates [for promotion to senior intelligence service]. Only 3 percent of them had met the rotational qualification for promotion. We had two choices: get a waiver or ignore the directive. We ignored it. What was the downside? Nothing."[90]

IMPROVING STRATEGIC ANALYSIS

Tenet also sought to improve strategic analysis of terrorist threats. This should not be a surprise: the CIA's primary mission had always been to provide integrated strategic analysis and warning for the U.S. Intelligence Community, and by 1998 terrorism clearly ranked among the top threats to U.S. national security.[91] It is important to note that strategic analysis is a particular type of intelligence analysis. While much intelligence analysis is tactical in nature—examining specific questions that often demand fast answers, such as where to target an Air Force missile—strategic analysis works on a longer time frame and takes a broader view. Piecing together bits of information, identifying gaps, and noticing patterns, strategic analysis is designed to provide a better picture of threats and scenarios over the horizon. Done well, strategic analysis focuses intelligence collection efforts and enables policymakers to pinpoint threats and develop policies to address them before crises erupt or disaster strikes. Done poorly, or not at all, strategic analysis leaves policymakers flying blind, caught in the present without a view of the future.[92]

During the Cold War, strategic analysis of the Soviet threat was challenging, but far more straightforward. The enemy had territory on a map, officials in embassies that issued policies and made demands, and a military that paraded its deadliest weapons through Red Square for everyone to see. Soviet planning, moreover, was so bureaucratized that when Nikita Khrushchev secretly tried to deploy nuclear missiles to Cuba in October 1962, the launch sites were built without camouflage, enabling American U2 surveillance planes to spot them. How could this be? Soviet officials on the ground were carefully following construction regulations developed in the Soviet Union, where camouflage had always been unnecessary.[93]

Strategic analysis of threats to U.S. national security became much more complex and difficult after the Soviet Union's collapse. As one intelligence official reflected, "we were dealing with a rapidly changing world. Don't forget, we had been focused almost exclusively on the Soviet Union for a long time. . . . you woke up every morning and it was there. Terrorism represent[ed] something very different than what the Soviet Union was for us."[94] Suddenly, strategic analysis required considering weak states rather than great powers, and understanding the large destructive power of small groups of individuals that moved across borders, were driven by fanaticism, untied to national governments, and hidden from view. Tracking this threat, along with the old and other emerging dangers, was a tall order.

Even so, the CIA's efforts to adjust strategic analysis from the Soviet Union to the rise of terrorism did not maximize prospects for success. Strategic analysis of al Qaeda was supposed to be coordinated across the Intelligence Community and produced by the CIA's Counterterrorist Center. The center, however, was not housed as a stand-alone unit or placed inside the CIA's analytic branch, the Directorate of Intelligence. It was embedded in the Directorate of Operations, which runs clandestine human intelligence operations. This location made all the difference. Because it was viewed as an operations shop, the Counterterrorist Center had difficulty attracting top-flight analysts and focused more on reporting current activities in the field than analysis.[95] Deputy Director of Central Intelligence John McLaughlin admitted that even the Counterterrorist Center's designated analysis group dealt mostly with intelligence collection issues, not strategic analysis.[96] By the end of 2000, CIA Director Tenet had become so concerned about the inadequacy of the Counterterrorist Center's strategic analysis that he appointed a senior manager to address the problem. A few months later, he went further, establishing a new ten-person strategic assessments branch inside the center. Even then, the Counterterrorist Center struggled to fill the slots. The new chief of the strategic assessments branch started work on September 10, 2001, a day before the World Trade Center and Pentagon attacks.[97]

Here, too, Tenet's concerns were well founded. Here, too, his efforts were laudable. And here, too, they floundered. In retrospect, the CIA's strategic analysis about Osama bin Laden and his al Qaeda network before September 11 missed several key issues and identified other important patterns only to overlook them later. Thousands of intelligence reports were written about al Qaeda in the years preceding 9/11.[98] None of them, however, provided a broad picture of critical issues such as bin Laden's strategy, his historical role in terrorist attacks, or the threat that al Qaeda posed to the United States.[99] What's more, the most impressive piece of strategic analysis, distributed in the summer of 1995, attracted little notice over the next six years. The piece was a National Intelligence Estimate (NIE) called "The Foreign Terrorist Threat in the United States."[100] National Intelligence Estimates are not just any intelligence reports; they are considered the gold standard of Community-wide intelligence assessments, produced by the director of central intelligence's own interagency think tank, the National Intelligence Council.[101] In the words of one former intelligence official, "NIEs are supposed to give the best, big picture understanding of the whole Intelligence Community on a vital problem laden with serious uncertainties." [102]

The 1995 National Intelligence Estimate specifically predicted future terrorist attacks against targets in the United States. It warned that such attacks would be carried out by groups of "transient" individuals with "loose affiliations" similar to the group that carried out the 1993 World Trade Center attack. It also warned that potential targets included the White House, the Capitol, economic symbols such as Wall Street, critical infrastructure such as power grids, and civil aviation generally. According to the 9/11 Commission, the 1995 Estimate was "an excellent summary of the emerging danger, based on what was then known."[103]

The 1995 National Intelligence Estimate should have informed and generated subsequent strategic analyses, serving as a touchstone for considering the meaning of new intelligence and making new judgments about the nature and danger of the evolving terrorist threat. It didn't. Over the next two years, U.S. intelligence agencies made important new discoveries about bin Laden and al Qaeda, learning that bin Laden was a mastermind rather than merely a financier of international terrorism and that al Qaeda had been involved in other terrorist attacks against Americans, most notably the 1993 shoot-down of U.S. Army Black Hawk helicopters in Mogadishu, Somalia.[104] None of this information made its way into the 1997 updated National Intelligence Estimate. The 1997 NIE devoted just three sentences out of six pages to bin Laden and did not mention al Qaeda once.[105]

More stunning, 1997 was the last time *any* National Intelligence Estimate focused on foreign terrorism until the September 11, 2001, attacks.[106] Even after the embassy bombings of 1998, after the foiled Millennium attacks of late 1999, after the bombing of the U.S.S. *Cole* in 2000, after Director Tenet warned Congress that there "was not the slightest doubt" bin Laden and his allies were planning more attacks against the United States,[107] and after the FBI placed Osama bin Laden on its Ten Most Wanted list, the U.S. Intelligence Community produced no National Intelligence Estimate that laid out its best strategic judgments about the United States' principal enemy. As one former member of the National Intelligence Council noted, "The lack of an NIE is a strong piece of evidence that Director Tenet and the Intelligence Community failed to take a strategic view of the terrorism threat.[108]

REBUILDING HUMAN INTELLIGENCE

Finally, Tenet focused on rebuilding the CIA's human intelligence capabilities, devoting more time to the issue by orders of magnitude than any other.[109] Tenet and other senior intelligence officials knew that human intelligence was pivotal to unraveling and thwarting terrorist attacks. "The key to the whole game," said one CIA official after 9/11, "is to penetrate the organization and get inside the plot. I understand the targeting doctrine of al Qaeda. The question is, when, why, where, and how is it going to happen?"[110]

After the embassy bombings, Tenet conducted a comprehensive review of clandestine human intelligence capabilities and launched a new operational strategy for going after al Qaeda called "The Plan." The Plan focused on capturing bin Laden and included measures to hire better clandestine officers with counterterrorism skills, recruit more spies inside Afghanistan, close gaps in technical intelligence, and penetrate al Qaeda directly.[111] Notably, however, this new human intelligence strategy included no estimates of the threat that bin Laden's network posed to the United States, no significant participation by the FBI or any other intelligence agencies outside the CIA, no decisions to shift or downgrade other intelligence priorities, and no apparent infusion of resources to execute the strategy.[112] Although The Plan produced increased reporting on al Qaeda in Afghanistan and new options for capturing Osama bin Laden there,[113] none of the options was believed to have more than a 15 percent chance of success.[114] Before 9/11, the CIA never succeeded in getting any human sources inside al Qaeda's leadership.[115] Indeed, the CIA's Directorate of Operations had grown so risk averse that the vast majority of clandestine case officers during the 1990s spent most of their time in Washington rather than recruiting assets overseas.[116] Tenet admitted to the 9/11 Commission that while he believed the CIA had positioned itself "very well" to take down bin Laden's Afghan sanctuary, the CIA "never penetrated the 9/11 plot."[117] Many agreed. James Pavitt, who headed the CIA's clandestine directorate of operations, told the 9/11 Commission, "We simply failed to uncover the necessary intelligence to penetrate Al Qaida at the appropriate level—at the leadership level—to stop the attacks."[118] The Congressional Joint Inquiry issued a more severe assessment: "Prior to September 11," the Inquiry concluded, "the Intelligence Community did not effectively develop and use human sources to penetrate the al-Qa'ida inner circle. This lack of reliable and knowledgeable human sources significantly limited the Community's ability to acquire intelligence that could have been acted upon before the September 11 attacks."[119]

And in 2003, six former top ranking intelligence officials with more than 200 years of collective experience wrote a highly unusual public article in the *Economist* that singled out human intelligence as the most important shortcoming before 9/11. "Despite the best efforts of our law-enforcement and intelligence agencies," they wrote, "the fact remains that secret members of a conspiratorial foreign organization operated clandestinely abroad and in this country for almost a decade before September 11th to plan, lay the groundwork for and successfully carry out a surprise attack on the United States. . . . We simply did not have enough actionable information from spies inside al-Qaeda." They went on to issue a strong call for better and more human intelligence. "Our collective experience makes it absolutely clear that the *only* way to uncover and destroy terrorist activity is to *penetrate the organizations engaged in it*. And the best way to do this is to place spies in their innermost councils [emphasis theirs]."[120]

Summary

The CIA's failure to adapt to the rise of terrorism was not for lack of effort, talent or dedication. At first, the agency labored simply to survive. In the early 1990s, while some policymakers saw new and uncertain dangers, most believed the United States had entered a time of peace and pushed for deep reductions in defense and intelligence spending. In this political context, "change" for the CIA meant cutting costs. The agency fulfilled this mandate—ironically, cutting back at precisely the moment it needed to retool, reinvest, revamp, and rebuild. Adaptation entered a second phase in 1994, when the Ames and National Reconnaissance Office scandals led to a number of critical reviews of U.S. intelligence agencies. The combination of scandal and study triggered a major push inside Congress to pass sweeping intelligence overhaul. Reform legislation, however, was defeated by opposition from the Pentagon and its congressional oversight committees. As a result, for most of the decade the CIA was left marching alone, without the help of any major new statutory or executive authorities. The third adaptation phase began after the 1998 embassy bombings, when Director Tenet tried a new approach: reforming from the inside. Although he labored mightily, Tenet did not get far. He was unable to get the Intelligence Community focused on al Qaeda, implement his strategic plan, institutionalize cross-agency assignments, develop a robust strategic analysis capability in the Counterterrorist Center, capture bin Laden, or penetrate al-Qaeda's senior ranks. Even his own staff did not have security badges allowing them access to most of the agencies in the Intelligence Community. On the eve of September 11, 2001, the director of central intelligence was waging a two-front war, battling al Qaeda outside the corridors of Washington and his own intelligence colleagues on the inside. And he was losing against them both.

Explaining Adaptation Failure in the CIA

Two major conclusions can be drawn from examining the CIA's adaptation efforts. First, the quantitative analysis of intelligence reform recommendations in chapter 2 was on target: the CIA did not adapt to the rising terrorist threat. Second, the adaptation model developed in chapter 3 offers a powerful explanation of this failure. The nature of organizations, rational self-interest, and the fragmented structure of the U.S. federal government proved a deadly combination, blocking reform initiatives from every quarter.

Why Internal Reforms Faltered: The Nature of Organizations

At first glance, one would expect internal CIA reform initiatives to have the greatest prospects for success, for two reasons. First, the director of central intelligence exercised far more control over the CIA than the rest of the U.S. Intelligence Community, with statutory power over the agency's budgets, personnel, and mission, and decades of being viewed as the unchallenged agency leader. Second, internal reforms by definition could be implemented by the CIA unilaterally, without the assistance or cooperation of legislators, presidents, or other executive branch agencies.

Yet even in this best case scenario, counterterrorism initiatives faltered. The reform studies show that most recommended internal reforms never got anywhere: of the twenty-three CIA reform recommendations that could be implemented through unilateral agency initiatives, twenty-one, or 91 percent of the total, generated no action at all. Moreover, as discussed earlier, the reforms that were tried did not get very far: the National Performance Review's personnel reductions, the creation of the bin Laden unit, efforts to revamp the spy service and improve strategic analysis inside the Counterterrorist Center—all of these initiatives were launched inside the CIA but foundered.

The nature of bureaucratic organizations is to blame. All organizations have difficulty changing, and the CIA was almost perfectly designed to resist change from within. While all leaders confront bounded rationality problems—making decisions with some degree of uncertainty and information about the future—CIA officials operated in a world so riddled with uncertainty and imperfect information that even the past was not always clear. As Mark Lowenthal, former assistant director of central intelligence for production, put it, "We are in the mosaics business, but every day, the size, shape, and color of the glass changes."[121]

In addition, the CIA faced rampant structural secrecy problems. Here, too, the difficulty was typical of all organizations but the extent of it was unusual in the CIA. Recall that structural secrecy refers to the internal divisions of labor within organizations that make it hard for one part of the organization to know what other parts of the organization are doing or learning. While most businesses and agencies have trouble learning from within, they are constantly interacting with outsiders—investors, interest groups, reporters, industry analysts, to name a few—who provide information channels, outside criticism, and incentives for the organization to learn about itself, correct weaknesses, and improve performance. The CIA did not have this advantage. It was built and designed to operate in secret, with strict rules governing contact between individuals, even those within the agency, a classification system designed to protect information rather than share it, and a host of other security measures separating the agency from the rest of the outside world. This isolation not only made oversight and learning difficult, it made internal social norms, habits, and cultural values all the more important in daily agency life. Left alone, agency officials grew more attached to the internal bonds that kept them working together.

Time, finally, made everything worse. For any organization, change becomes harder with time, as habits and policies and cultures become ingrained. For the CIA, the demand for change came after forty years—an entire organizational lifetime—of fighting the same enemy.

Together, bounded rationality, structural secrecy, and the liability of time kept the agency from adapting to the rising terrorist threat, even when the director of central intelligence demanded it. Director Tenet's efforts to improve strategic analysis and rebuild the clandestine service provide portraits of these forces at work.

STRATEGIC ANALYSIS

In many ways, Tenet's efforts to improve strategic analysis in the Counterterrorist Center were defeated before they ever began. As noted above, the center began in 1986 as a new unit inside the CIA's clandestine Directorate of Operations. For strategic analysis, this location was akin to operating behind enemy lines: The DO was home to people who ran spies, stole secrets, and conducted clandestine operations, not for egghead analysts who sat behind desks piecing together information about future threats. The DO's traditional focus on intelligence collection and operations, combined with the constant pressure to respond to near-term threats, ensured that the Counterterrorist Center would give short shrift to strategic analysis from day one. That is exactly what happened. Cofer Black, who headed the Counterterrorist Center from 1999 to 2002, testified after 9/11 that during his tenure, investment in tactical intelligence far outstripped resources dedicated to strategic intelligence. "We have under-invested in strategic," he declared, because "tactical is where the lives are saved."[122]

The DO's culture only made matters worse, hindering information sharing between collectors and analysts inside the center from its inception. While all intelligence officials believed in the importance of protecting sources and methods, nowhere was the "need to know" more deeply rooted than inside the DO. Viewing themselves as members an elite group, working in spectacular isolation, upholding the protection of sources and methods as a cardinal virtue, DO officers tended to view analysts with suspicion, even disdain. So deep was the divide between DO officers and analysts that when the Counterterrorist Center was first created, DO personnel assigned there requested additional safes and procedures to keep their information out of the hands of the analysts working alongside them, despite the fact that the center was designed to foster precisely this kind of collaboration between analysts and collectors and everyone held the same level of security clearance.[123] Old attitudes proved hard to change. Fifteen years later, after the September 11, 2001, terrorist attacks, many analysts still complained about the lack of trust between collectors and analysts across the Intelligence Community.[124]

Career incentives further reinforced the status quo, effectively discouraging analysts from producing strategic analysis—particularly in counterterrorism—even when the director of central intelligence requested it. For years, performance evaluations had reviewed CIA analysts based on the number of reports they produced, and valued current intelligence products such as the President's Daily Brief more than longer-term analytic products. This trend only grew worse in the 1990s, as policymakers began demanding more current intelligence in response to the rise of CNN and twenty-four-hour news cycles.[125] For career-minded analysts, the message was clear: stay away from strategic assignments. Indeed, the only thing worse than a strategic assignment was a strategic assignment located outside the CIA's analytic branch—precisely what Director Tenet advocated in 2000 and 2001. Little wonder the DCI found the center's strategic analytic capabilities so weak and struggled with little success to fix them before September 11. In 2001, even with Tenet's insistence that ten new analysts be assigned to the center (which was itself viewed as a major bureaucratic victory),[126] senior analysts managed to avoid it, leaving more junior analysts to fill the ranks. The average experience of counterterrorism analysts was just half that of analysts in the CIA's analytic branch, the Directorate of Intelligence.[127] In a profession where analytic judgment requires time more than anything else to develop, this experience gap had serious consequences. As one intelligence official testified, the Counterterrorist Center simply did not have enough experienced analysts to produce the number of sophisticated, in-depth analyses that were required.[128] Career incentives meant that the unit most in need of experienced analysts to conduct strategic analysis of the nation's most serious threat did not have them.

CLANDESTINE SERVICE

Old structures, habits, policies, and thinking also doomed Tenet's efforts to rebuild the CIA's clandestine service in the late 1990s.

To be sure, infiltrating a terrorist cell is no easy task. As one former senior intelligence official put it, "It's just so hard to do, getting at the people we need to get at. It was different when we were going after foreign governments. Terrorist groups are a totally different target." He continued:

> I'll never forget a video I saw . . . that was an al Qaeda training video. The first pictures were of young Muslim men talking, taking an oath of allegiance, talking about fighting Jihad. The next pictures were the same people lying dead. And this was a recruiting video. And I thought, "how in the world do we put people in there?" Not only are we asking them to do horrible things, but we may be asking them to martyr themselves. That's not to say we shouldn't be trying.[129]

A former CIA operative described the problem more colorfully: "It's hard and dangerous work, and it's done in places where diarrhea is the default setting."[130] Even the House and Senate Intelligence Committees' Joint Inquiry into the September 11 attacks, which spared no criticism of U.S. intelligence agencies, noted that terrorist groups posed far greater challenges than other targets. "The penetration of al-Qa'ida by an Intelligence Community human asset is an exceptionally difficult task," the Committees' final report concluded. "Intelligence Community officials in several agencies told the Joint Inquiry that members of Usama Bin Ladin's inner circle have close bonds established by kinship, wartime experience, and long-term association. Information about major terrorist plots was not widely shared within al-Qa'ida."[131]

While it is true that penetrating bin Laden's inner circle was exceptionally difficult, it is also true that the CIA was in no shape to succeed. The CIA's human intelligence efforts before September 11 were doubly hamstrung—first, by the inherent challenges of penetrating terrorist groups, and second by the agency's own weaknesses.

Years after the Soviet Union's collapse, clandestine human intelligence operations were still frozen in a Cold War model: most undercover operatives continued working under official covers, posing as U.S. government employees in American embassies around the world and attending diplomatic events and parties where they would recruit foreign military officials, party members, and other bureaucrats to spy for the United States. One veteran clandestine operative described the usefulness of the model this way: "The guy in the embassy was appropriate for the last fifty years because the secrets you wanted resided in a defense minister's safe or a prime minister's office. They were in governments."[132] The Cold War's end, however, required radically different approaches. These included much greater use of nonofficial covers (NOCs, pronounced "knocks"): clandestine case officers who worked under affiliations—such as businessmen or members of anti-American organizations—that were unconnected to the U.S. government, traveled quietly into and out of foreign countries, and sought to penetrate small nongovernment groups such as terrorist cells or nuclear weapons traffickers rather than large foreign government agencies.

Despite Director Tenet's efforts to rebuild the clandestine service, these kinds of new approaches never took hold.[133] In the words of one former clandestine officer, many in the DO's leadership felt, "we've been doing this for twenty years." While a few pushed for greater use of NOCs and a more vigorous effort to fundamentally rethink the craft of human intelligence, they became marginalized while the rest of the DO "just kept driving down that set of tracks, working through diplomatic receptions, and areas that we knew there were no terrorists."[134] According to several former DO officials, the number of NOCs from 1990 to 2001 remained flat.[135] As another lamented, "We were resistant to change. We had a comfort zone and we were going to stay right there."[136]

Here, too, resistance to change stemmed from past practice, incentives, culture, and history. For generations, newly hired case officers were taught how to detect car bombs but not how to understand and work effectively in foreign cultures.[137] In fact, instructors often told trainees that cultural distinctions did not matter, that an operation was the same, regardless of where it took place or what it was targeting—an attitude captured by the saying, "an op is an op."[138] Developing deeper country or linguistic expertise throughout an officer's career was not encouraged. DO policy required frequent rotations to different countries and rewarded generalists, not specialists, with promotions and assignments.[139] Robert Baer, one of the CIA's veteran Middle East agents, put it this way: "The DO has an attitude that people are fungible. It's like General Motors. It's a Harvard Business School idea. It's the wrong approach. We need to build expertise, train people and keep them in one area for longer periods of time."[140] When Baer tried to enroll in a master's program in Middle Eastern studies at night, on his own time, the CIA resisted. In the end, the agency approved his studies, but refused to pay for the entire program, insisting on separate approvals for every course instead. "No one in the DO ever goes to graduate school," Baer complained. "We don't want people to have advanced degrees."[141]

Incentives also directed the DO's focus toward immediate needs rather than longer-term collection. One former DO official recalled that in the early 1990s he initiated a review to determine human intelligence needs over the next decade. But when he asked the national security advisor and other members of the NSC staff what human intelligence they needed in the future, he "quickly discovered that almost universally the answer was, 'I don't know, but King Hussein is going to visit tomorrow. Can you tell me what he's going to ask me?' "[142] Policymaker demands kept strategic collection on the back burner. Another former clandestine officer joked that responding to current intelligence demands had become such a way of life, strategic thinking for the head of the DO consisted of "studying the time, date and place for the next meeting."[143]

Finally, DO personnel policies were designed to keep poor performers and those who were either unable or unwilling to adapt to new challenges rather than weeding them out or helping them improve their performance. One former clandestine official described the performance evaluation system with notable frustration:

> Look at the way we discipline people when somebody screws up. We informally refer to it as "putting somebody in the box." Alright. And we put them in the penalty box for one to two years, no promotions, no bonuses, no key assignments. What we don't do is we don't look at that mistake and try to address that mistake and give them extra training or assistance to improve or to repair what was wrong with that person. So we put them in the penalty box. The person that penalized them sooner or later moves on or retires or dies, and so then all is forgotten and forgiven, and the person back there with the same flaws is back in line."[144]

Another former clandestine service officer noted, "You know, normally if you have a marginal performer, not a total failure

but a marginal performer . . . you may even inflate his performance evaluation grades" in order to move him into another
assignment.[145]

In short, as the threat shifted, the DO did not, training officials
in old ways of doing business, using outdated models for recruiting spies, and following old rules of the game that stifled innovation and let mediocrity go unchecked. While terrorism posed extraordinary challenges for any human intelligence service, it
proved impossible for one designed decades earlier for a different enemy. In the end, Tenet's rebuilding efforts failed because
rebuilding was not enough. Transforming the DO required dismantling virtually every aspect of the clandestine service.

Why Executive Branch Reforms Failed: Rational Self-Interest

Executive branch reforms—initiatives that required the assistance of agencies and officials working outside the CIA to succeed—offered a second path toward adaptation. These also
failed, but for a different reason: rational self-interest, which discouraged presidents from undertaking major reform in the first
place and led bureaucrats to block virtually everything the director of central intelligence tried to do.

Presidents were the dogs that did not bark in this story. Rather
than attempting intelligence overhaul, they avoided it. Between
1991 and 2001, Presidents George H. W. Bush, Bill Clinton, and
George W. Bush led no legislative campaigns to reform the U.S.
Intelligence Community and did not engage when Congress
tried to act on its own. Even more telling is the fact that these
three presidents all eschewed using their unilateral powers of
office to mandate intelligence reform from the White House. Together, Presidents Bush, Clinton, and Bush issued a total of 555
executive orders[146] and an estimated 257 national security directives[147] before the September 11 attacks.[148] These kinds of unilateral measures could have dramatically changed the structure,
policies, and culture of the U.S. Intelligence Community to combat terrorism. None of them tried, because restructuring and reforming U.S. intelligence agencies threatened to produce the
worst possible outcome from the president's perspective: high
political costs, low political benefits, and uncertain results. These
presidents, like their predecessors, knew that intelligence reform

would draw fierce opposition from the Defense Department, generate little public interest, and might not succeed. Instead, the post–Cold War presidents opted for lower cost, minor changes, using their unilateral powers to mandate reviews, establish commissions, declare priorities (without enforcing them) and attempt other relatively insignificant modifications.

After the Soviet Union collapsed, for example, President George H. W. Bush, the only president to have served as a former director of central intelligence, refused to order or require any specific changes to U.S. intelligence. Instead, he opted for a lower cost initiative: directing a review of Intelligence Community needs for the future.[149]

President Clinton also treaded carefully. In 1995, he issued two Presidential Decision Directives (PDDs) on intelligence and counterterrorism. The first, PDD-35, tried to set intelligence collection and analysis priorities.[150] But there were so many priorities clustered at the top, the directive ended up dividing them into Tiers 1A and Tier 1B, with the very highest priorities counter-intuitively assigned to Tier Zero.[151] As time passed, Clinton and then Bush officials added new priorities to the list but never removed or downgraded old ones. By 9/11, the National Security Agency had 1,500 formal requirements, and no fewer than 200,000 "Essential Elements of Information" that were desired by policymakers. Intelligence officials told the Congressional Joint Inquiry after the terrorist attacks that the prioritization process was cumbersome, confusing, and so broad as to be meaningless.[152]

Notably, transnational terrorism was relegated to Tier 3, the lowest priority level, behind supporting U.S. military operations (including humanitarian missions) and preventing crises and conflicts with hostile states.[153] As one former senior intelligence official complained, "PDD-35 was a way to deal with mission confusion. It turned out to be stupid, because you have Afghanistan on the 10th of September as a Tier 3 issue. The military hadn't ordered a new map of Afghanistan in 4 years because why would you? It was Tier 3 country. It shouldn't have been a Tier 3 country. Hello?"[154]

The second 1995 presidential directive, PDD-39, declared terrorism a matter of national security and assigned responsibilities to various agencies.[155] Three years later, Clinton tried to move further, issuing two more Presidential Decision Directives which established a new National Coordinator for Counterterrorism and offered a ten-point program for integrating counterterrorism efforts across the U.S. government.[156] Here, too, however, the president never invested the political capital to translate these documents into meaningful change. The Congressional Joint Inquiry concluded that Clinton's counterterrorism directives did not "appear to have much impact."[157] Other than the counterterrorism coordinator himself, Richard Clarke, not a single Joint Inquiry witness pointed to the directives as the guiding policy governing U.S. counterterrorism efforts.[158] And even Clarke wrote that the directives gave him "the appearance of responsibility for counterterrorism, but none of the tools or authority to get the job done."[159]

When George W. Bush came to office in 2001, four different counterterrorism commissions had recently published major reports and issued forty-nine recommendations for changes to U.S intelligence agencies.[160] The new president's response was to order yet another intelligence review.[161]

In sum, these very different presidents behaved in similar ways. Two Republicans and one Democrat, two former governors with almost no foreign policy experience and one of the most experienced foreign policy presidents in American history, all confronted a dysfunctional U.S. intelligence system and chose to leave it alone. Rational self-interest explains why. Although individuals have their own ideas, skills, and policy preferences, institutional incentives and capabilities exert a powerful influence, making some courses of action easier and more costly than others. For presidents, the political calculus was clear: leading intelligence reform from the White House threatened to expend precious political capital, inflame bureaucratic rivalries, deflect attention from other policy issues higher on their agendas, and promised only limited success at best. The political costs of executive branch intelligence reform were too great.

Rational self-interest also explains the failure of executive branch reforms launched by the director of central intelligence. With almost no control over budgets, personnel, or programs in twelve of the thirteen intelligence agencies, the DCI could request but could not demand that other intelligence agencies comply with his directives. They didn't. Tenet's declaration of war against bin Laden was disregarded, his strategic plan thwarted, his directive to require temporary rotations across U.S. intelligence agencies ignored, his order to streamline Community security procedures circumvented. From the perspective of bureaucrats in these other intelligence agencies, opposition was the only choice: the DCI's reform efforts threatened the very power and autonomy they valued most.

Why Legislative Reforms Failed: The Fragmented Federal Government

Legislative reforms provided a third and final path to adaptation. These failed as well, for predicted reasons. Both the 1992 and 1996 intelligence reform bills proposed sweeping reforms of the CIA and the rest of the U.S. Intelligence Community. Not surprisingly, in both instances, the bills generated intense opposition from the Defense Department and its supporters on the Congressional Armed Services Committees. While such opposition was to be expected, the fragmented structure of the U.S. federal government made it lethal. Indeed, reform bill opponents did not have to work very hard to win. Separation of powers, the congressional committee system, the bicameral legislature, congressional committee rules and norms such as majority voting and the filibuster created a system that stacked the deck against change. To succeed, any new bill had to win not one, but a series of majority votes in different subcommittees and committees in both houses of Congress. The political system created multiple veto points in the legislative process, allowing opponents numerous opportunities to either kill or fatally hobble a new bill. In the case of intelligence reform, any reform bill had to get past its most bitter enemies in Congress to survive.

SUMMARY

Adaptation was a losing battle for the Central Intelligence Agency. CIA leaders, outside experts, and legislators all tried to transform the agency during the 1990s to meet the rising terrorist threat, but in the end they did not stand a chance. Internal reforms were up against a powerful foe: the CIA itself, whose structures, habits, cultures, and procedures had grown impervious to change after decades of fighting the Cold War. At the same time, rational self-interest doomed executive branch reforms to make the CIA and the rest of the Intelligence Community work better together, discouraging presidents from even trying and encouraging bureaucrats to ignore, resist, or circumvent reform efforts led by the director of central intelligence. Finally, the fragmented structure of the federal government meant that legislative reforms had to get past the gauntlet, winning majority votes from their most bitter opponents in the Congressional Armed Services Committees. While House and Senate Intelligence Committee members had urged overhaul for years, no serious bill ever managed to make it through. As one Congressional Intelligence Committee staffer lamented, "the intelligence committees just didn't have the juice to get much done."[162]

The result was that as al Qaeda operatives learned how to use low-tech weapons like box cutters and truck bombs, U.S. intelligence budgets continued overfunding high technology and underfunding human intelligence. As bin Laden's suicide Jihadists traveled from caves to condominiums, the CIA's clandestine Directorate of Operations continued operating out of U.S. embassies and working the diplomatic circuit to recruit spies. While bin Laden and his associates spent years devising plans for their terrorist attacks, carefully and patiently working out the details, the CIA became CNN with secrets, responding to the "crisis du jour" more than producing longer-term strategic analysis about dangers looming over the horizon. As a new enemy grew stronger, an old bureaucracy remained stuck.

CHAPTER 5

Signals Found and Lost

THE CIA AND 9/11

> You can say whatever you want. You can say the FBI
> screwed us all, State screwed this all up. But at the end
> of the day, these were nineteen people that, if I remember
> correctly, didn't come from the United States. They came
> from the foreign arena, where we own the turf.
> —Former CIA clandestine officer[1]

ON JANUARY 8, 2000, the CIA suddenly lost track of three suspected al Qaeda operatives traveling from Kuala Lumpur, Malaysia to Bangkok, Thailand. Several days earlier, CIA officials had rushed to establish surveillance operations in Malaysia, believing—correctly—that "something nefarious might be afoot."[2] The operation was deemed so important that regular updates were sent to Director of Central Intelligence George Tenet, National Security Advisor Sandy Berger, and FBI Director Louis Freeh. Nobody, however, was prepared for what happened next. When the meeting disbanded, the trail went cold. The three operatives were tracked as far as a Bangkok-bound commercial flight. Although U.S. officials in both Kuala Lumpur and Washington sent urgent requests to Bangkok for help, by the time their messages arrived the terrorists had disappeared. Intelligence officials now know that two of them, Khalid al-Mihdhar and Nawaf al-Hazmi, flew to the United States a few days later, where they settled in California and prepared for their September 11 suicide hijacking mission. The third, Khallad bin Attash, went on to plan the bombing of the USS *Cole* which killed seventeen American sailors in the fall of 2000.[3]

What went wrong? At first glance, the answer appears to be just about everything. In an era of instant communications, three terrorists sitting on a plane for two hours reached Bangkok faster than the CIA's own urgent messages. No one inside the Central Intelligence Agency seemed to think ahead, about how they would continue tracking these suspects once they left Kuala Lumpur. On January 8, CIA officials knew the full name of one of the men, Khalid al-Mihdhar, and that he held a U.S. visa. Apparently, however, they did not consider the possibility that al-Mihdhar might actually use his visa to travel to the United States. In addition, working level and senior CIA leaders did not even realize all of the information they had, information that could have potentially salvaged the tracking operation. The CIA was the lead agency, but CIA officials never asked other intelligence agencies to check what they knew. A search of the National Security Agency's database would have quickly revealed the full name of the second terrorist, Nawaf al-Hazmi. A search of the State Department's records would have uncovered that he, too, held a U.S. visa, which he presumably intended to use. Management of the operation was so disjointed that the head of the CIA's bin Laden unit believed, and told his bosses, that the suspects were still being monitored in Kuala Lumpur five days after they had already disappeared into the streets of Bangkok.[4] Finally, the tracking effort seems to have vanished as quickly as the terrorists: No one at the CIA considered resuming surveillance of these men for the next year and a half.[5]

Probing more deeply, however, reveals that this Keystone-Cops picture, with seemingly incompetent individuals making one bad decision after another, is misleading. The real picture is worse. The Malaysia tracking failure was just one of eleven known opportunities the CIA had to potentially disrupt the September 11 plot. The agency missed every one of them, for the same reason: longstanding organizational weaknesses in the CIA made it likely, perhaps even unavoidable, that smart people would do dumb things.

In the previous chapter, I explained why, despite the best efforts of intelligence officials and policymakers, the CIA was unable to adapt to the rising terrorist threat after the Cold War ended. This chapter takes a hard look at consequences, at what role failed organizational adaptation played in the September 11 attacks.

I begin by going back to Malaysia, showing how the tracking failure stemmed more from organizational deficiencies than individual errors. Next I provide an overview of ten more specific opportunities the CIA had, and missed, to potentially stop the September 11 attacks. I then revisit these missed opportunities using an organizational lens, tracing the connection between the CIA's nagging organizational problems and its performance failure. Finally, I consider and rebut the strongest criticism of my argument.

THE MALAYSIA TRACKING FAILURE: A SECOND CUT

Viewing the Malaysia tracking failure through an organizational lens reveals a very different picture. This missed opportunity was not the result of individual error or isolated mistakes, but pervasive and longstanding weaknesses in the CIA's structure, culture, and incentives.

Above all, surveillance of the three terrorists faltered because the CIA's internal structure left no single person or office in charge of the case. As the 9/11 Commission concluded, the CIA's field office structure focused on where, not who; it was designed to cover broad territory rather than track specific terrorists.[6] The Kuala Lumpur field office ran surveillance while the terrorists stayed in Malaysia. Bangkok ran the operation once it realized the terrorists had arrived in Thailand. Nobody, however, was responsible for managing the transition between these two offices or picking up the trail once it had been lost. Back in Washington, the Directorate of Operations, which oversaw all clandestine activities; the Counterterrorist Center, which was supposed to integrate counterterrorism intelligence collection, analysis, and operations; and the CIA's Osama bin Laden unit were all watching the operation closely. But they were not overseeing it. This was not a mistake. It was standard practice. As one career clandestine officer put it, the structure was "as close to medieval architecture in management as you could find," with personnel, resources, and power controlled by geographic barons managing the field divisions.[7]

Structural and cultural pathologies also explain why the CIA failed to get vital information about the terrorists from the National Security Agency and State Department even though it was designated the lead agency. Fragmentation across U.S. intelligence agencies meant that CIA officials had ready access only to information in their own databases. Getting the full picture required asking other agencies to join efforts. But this required thinking about the Intelligence Community as a unified team, something that was not natural for CIA officials. Instead, CIA officers approached this case like they had approached every other case for decades: with a deeply ingrained parochial perspective—described by one government official as a "me, my, mine" view of the world—that naturally focused on the agency's own actions and information rather than integrating efforts across the entire Intelligence Community.[8] CIA officials neglected to ask the National Security Agency and State Department what they knew about the Kuala Lumpur terrorists not because they fell down on the job, but because they never considered it to be their job.

Finally, incentives were also at work. After the September 11 attacks, CIA officials told congressional investigators and the 9/11 Commission that they were overwhelmed by the daily press of business and had little time for important but longer-term projects, even ones that sought to track the whereabouts of al Qaeda operatives holding U.S. visas. In the words of the CIA's Counterterrorist Center Director Cofer Black, this operation was one among many and, because of its longer-term nature, was not considered "heavy water."[9] Without strong incentives to reward analysts for peering over the horizon, following cases over time, and developing strategic intelligence, the urgent crowded out the important.

These organizational problems led the agency to fail again. Between January 2000 and September 11, 2001, the CIA had ten other known opportunities to penetrate and possibly thwart the World Trade Center and Pentagon attacks. It missed every one.

MISSED OPPORTUNITIES 2, 3, AND 4: WATCHLISTING

At the same time the CIA lost Khalid al-Mihdhar and Nawaf al-Hazmi in Bangkok, it also failed to place al-Mihdhar on the State Department's watch list denying him entry into the United States or notify the FBI. The CIA missed another watch list opportunity in March 2000, when officials finally identified Nawaf al-Hazmi by his full name and learned that he had already entered the United States. Failure struck again in January 2001, when the CIA learned that a third Kuala Lumpur operative, Khallad, was a key figure in the bombing of the USS *Cole*. This new piece of information was viewed as highly significant, since it directly and definitively linked both al-Mihdhar and al-Hazmi to a significant al Qaeda figure.[10] Khallad, in fact, was later described by one FBI counterterrorism official as "a major league killer."[11] Yet for the third time in a year, nobody at the CIA notified the FBI or State Department to keep al-Hazmi and al-Mihdhar out of the country or find them if they were already here.

Although it is impossible to determine what might have been, intelligence officials now know that in January 2001, al-Mihdhar was temporarily outside the United States; watchlisting him could have resulted in denying him a U.S. visa.[12] It is also possible that this information would have prompted the FBI to locate and watch al-Hazmi, who was still inside the United States. The two terrorists should not have been all that difficult to find: both of them had numerous contacts with an FBI informant while they were living in San Diego,[13] al-Hazmi was listed in the San Diego telephone directory,[14] al-Mihdhar used his real name to obtain a California photo identification card,[15] both used their real names on a rental agreement,[16] and al-Mihdhar's correct address was found by the FBI's information technology center, using nothing but his name and open sources, in just a few hours the night of September 11.[17]

Nawaf al-Hazmi, moreover, was not just any hijacker. He is believed to have been second-in-command of the entire operation.[18] Intelligence officials now know that al-Hazmi made personal contact with individuals from at least three of the four hijacking teams between May and July of 2001, perhaps earlier.[19] Al-Hazmi was a key link between multiple elements of the plot.

These retrospective facts suggest that had the FBI been properly notified at any of the three watchlisting opportunities, there was a very real possibility that the bureau would have chosen to investigate these two men, that one or both would have been found, and that surveillance would have led the FBI to all but one of the hijacking teams weeks, and possibly even months, before the attacks occurred. Indeed, according to the FBI agent who handled the San Diego informant who knew the two hijackers, the CIA's information about al-Mihdhar and al-Hazmi "would have made a huge difference." Testifying before the Congressional Joint Inquiry into September 11, the FBI agent reflected: "We had the predicate for a [deleted] investigation if we had that information. . . . [W]e would immediately go out and canvass the sources and try to find out where these people were. . . . [T]hey were very close—they were nearby—[and] . . . we would have used all available investigative techniques. We would have given them the full court press."[20]

To be sure, the agent's views are speculative and made in the aftermath of tragedy. However, as the Joint Inquiry more soberly concluded, "the informant's contacts with the hijackers, had they been capitalized on, would have given the San Diego FBI field office perhaps the Intelligence Community's best chance to unravel the September 11 plot."[21] Instead, information about al-Hazmi and al-Mihdhar was not passed to FBI officials until August 23, 2001, just nineteen days before the two terrorists hijacked Flight 77 and crashed it into the Pentagon.

Missed Opportunities 5, 6, 7, and 8: Information Sharing

The CIA missed four more operational opportunities when officials failed to share what turned out to be key pieces of information with their counterparts at the FBI.[22] In January 2000, a CIA employee spoke to two FBI employees about the activities of Khalid al-Mihdhar in Malaysia, but did not tell them about al-Mihdhar's U.S. visa.[23] In May 2001, a CIA official detailed to the FBI's International Terrorism Operations Section became concerned about the spike in threat reporting indicating an imminent terrorist attack. Searching through old CIA cables, he learned of al-Mihdhar's U.S. visa, al-Hazmi's travel to the United States, and Khallad's attendance at the Malaysia meeting. The CIA official concluded that, "something bad was definitely up."[24] Yet he never shared any of this information with his colleagues at the FBI or asked them to determine whether any of these terrorists were in the United States.[25]

That same month, another CIA official had the chance to disclose information about the plot to an FBI counterpart but did not. The CIA official, an analyst who was trying to identify someone else in U.S. custody in connection with the *Cole* bombing, showed an FBI Intelligence Operations Specialist a picture of al-Mihdhar but said nothing about the fact that the picture had been taken at a meeting with Khallad, that al-Mihdhar held a U.S. visa, or that he might travel to the United States.[26]

On June 11, the same CIA analyst met with FBI agents from the New York field office who were investigating the *Cole* case. The New York agents were also shown copies of al-Mihdhar's photo. But they were told only his name. One of the New York agents pressed for more information, asking, "Why were you looking at this guy? You couldn't have been following everybody. . . . What was the reason behind this?"[27] He didn't get an answer. The CIA analyst said that the information could not be passed, but might be shared in the days and weeks to come. It wasn't, despite repeated inquiries by the FBI agent.[28]

MISSED OPPORTUNITIES 9, 10, AND 11: ANALYSIS

Finally, the CIA missed three opportunities to piece together new and old information that might have led to discovery of the plot. On June 12, 2001, the CIA disseminated a report to all Intelligence Community agencies reporting that Khalid Sheikh Mohammed (KSM), who was already under indictment for his role in the 1995 Bojinka terrorist plot (which included plans to crash airplanes into the CIA headquarters), was one of bin Laden's most trusted lieutenants and was actively recruiting operatives to travel outside Afghanistan, including to the United States, to plan terrorist-related activities.[29] But because KSM had been indicted, responsibility for his case rested in the Renditions Branch of the CIA's Counterterrorist Center. That office focused on locating him for arrest, not analyzing information about him in the context of other possible terrorist plots. As a result, the report accurately identified KSM's role—he did, in fact, arrange travel of the hijackers to the United States and was the mastermind of the September 11 plot—but the report never connected KSM to other information inside the CIA about Khalid al-Mihdhar's visa or Nawaf al-Hazmi's arrival in the United States.[30]

The most controversial and widely known incident occurred on August 6, 2001, when the CIA delivered a briefing to President Bush entitled, "Bin Ladin Determined to Strike in U.S."[31] The report was part of the President's Daily Brief (PDB), the most highly classified and important current intelligence product in the U.S. government, and was prompted by the president's questions about the possibility of a domestic al Qaeda attack. This was a golden opportunity for the CIA to distill the best intelligence from across the U.S. Intelligence Community and present it directly to the president.

To some, the PDB, which was disclosed in a set of explosive 9/11 Commission hearings televised live in the spring of 2004, appeared to provide a smoking gun, proof that the Bush administration had been warned about al Qaeda's intention to strike inside the United States but failed to take that warning seriously enough. A closer examination of the declassified document, however, suggests something quite different: the August 6th CIA report was a tragically shoddy piece of intelligence analysis that provided unimportant information, false reassurances, wrong information, and failed to include the best intelligence available about al Qaeda operatives in the United States, information that might have made a difference.

For starters, the PDB consisted mostly of historical information about bin Laden's interest in striking the United States, information the president later said he already knew.[32] A word count shows that 82 percent of the document (the entire first page) discussed reporting about al Qaeda and other terrorist activities between 1993 and 1999, while just 18 percent of the document (two paragraphs on the second page) addressed intelligence about current bin Laden activities.[33]

The August 6th PDB also provided false assurances that the FBI was aggressively investigating terrorist threats directed at the United States homeland. Although the memo warned that "Al-Qa'ida members—including some who are US citizens—have resided in or traveled to the US for years, and the group apparently maintains a support structure that could aid attacks," it gave the distinct impression that the FBI had the domestic threat covered. The memo's concluding paragraph noted, "the FBI is conducting approximately 70 full field investigations throughout the US that it considers bin Laden-related."[34] President Bush later told the 9/11 Commission that he remembered thinking it was heartening that seventy investigations were underway.[35] Bush's national security advisor at the time, Condoleezza Rice, also testified that the report suggested the FBI was handling the threat posed by potential domestic sleeper cells. She told the commission, "I . . . understood that . . . the FBI was pursuing these al Qaeda cells. . . . In the August 6th memorandum it says that there were 70 full field investigations underway of these cells. And so there was no recommendation that we do something about this . . . the FBI was pursuing it."[36] But the FBI was not pursuing sleeper cells aggressively. Officials later admitted to the 9/11 Commission that the number of full field investigations had been exaggerated (counting individuals under investigation rather than separate investigations and considering all terrorist financing cases as "bin Ladin-related"). And at the very moment the PDB was being delivered to the president, an FBI memo by a Phoenix special agent recommending more aggressive action to investigate whether bin Laden operatives were enrolling in U.S. flight schools was gathering dust at FBI headquarters.

Two of the three other pieces of current intelligence in the PDB also turned out to be wrong.[37] The memo noted uncorroborated "sensational reporting" from foreign intelligence services that bin Laden wanted to hijack a U.S. aircraft to gain the release of extremists held in the United States; there was no mention of the possibility of using airplanes as missiles. The PDB also reported that FBI information indicated "patterns of suspicious activity" in the United States "consistent with preparations for hijackings or other types of attacks, including recent surveillance of federal buildings in New York." Although this statement sounds ominous in retrospect, the casing of New York targets was a coincidence, not a forewarning: The memo's reference to "surveillance of federal buildings in New York" turned out to be Yemeni tourists taking photographs.[38]

These sins of commission were accompanied by more glaring sins of omission. The PDB never mentioned key pieces of information that various individuals in the Intelligence Community already believed to be important: namely, that Khalid al-Mihdhar and Nawaf al-Hazmi had attended an al Qaeda meeting in Malaysia with a major bin Laden figure, that al-Mihdhar held a

Bin Ladin Determined To Strike in US

Clandestine, foreign government, and media reports indicate Bin Ladin since 1997 has wanted to conduct terrorist attacks in the US. Bin Ladin implied in US television interviews in 1997 and 1998 that his followers would follow the example of World Trade Center bomber Ramzi Yousef and "bring the fighting to America."

> After US missile strikes on his base in Afghanistan in 1998, Bin Ladin told followers he wanted to retaliate in Washington, according to a ███████████ service.

> An Egyptian Islamic Jihad (EIJ) operative told an █████ service at the same time that Bin Ladin was planning to exploit the operative's access to the US to mount a terrorist strike.

The millennium plotting in Canada in 1999 may have been part of Bin Ladin's first serious attempt to implement a terrorist strike in the US. Convicted plotter Ahmed Ressam has told the FBI that he conceived the idea to attack Los Angeles International Airport himself, but that Bin Ladin lieutenant Abu Zubaydah encouraged him and helped facilitate the operation. Ressam also said that in 1998 Abu Zubaydah was planning his own US attack.

> Ressam says Bin Ladin was aware of the Los Angeles operation.

Although Bin Ladin has not succeeded, his attacks against the US Embassies in Kenya and Tanzania in 1998 demonstrate that he prepares operations years in advance and is not deterred by setbacks. Bin Ladin associates surveilled our Embassies in Nairobi and Dar es Salaam as early as 1993, and some members of the Nairobi cell planning the bombings were arrested and deported in 1997.

Al-Qa'ida members—including some who are US citizens—have resided in or traveled to the US for years, and the group apparently maintains a support structure that could aid attacks. Two al-Qa'ida members found guilty in the conspiracy to bomb our Embassies in East Africa were US citizens, and a senior EIJ member lived in California in the mid-1990s.

> A clandestine source said in 1998 that a Bin Ladin cell in New York was recruiting Muslim-American youth for attacks.

We have not been able to corroborate some of the more sensational threat reporting, such as that from a ███████████ service in 1998 saying that Bin Ladin wanted to hijack a US aircraft to gain the release of "Blind Shaykh" 'Umar 'Abd al-Rahman and other US-held extremists.

continued

For the President Only
6 August 2001

Figure 5.1a. President's Daily Brief, August 6, 2001.

— Nevertheless, FBI information since that time indicates patterns of suspicious activity in this country consistent with preparations for hijackings or other types of attacks, including recent surveillance of federal buildings in New York.

The FBI is conducting approximately 70 full field investigations throughout the US that it considers Bin Ladin-related. CIA and the FBI are investigating a call to our Embassy in the UAE in May saying that a group of Bin Ladin supporters was in the US planning attacks with explosives.

For the President Only
6 August 2001

Figure 5.1b. President's Daily Brief, August 6, 2001.

U.S. visa, and that al-Hazmi had already traveled to the United States; that KSM, one of bin Laden's most trusted operatives, was recruiting terrorists to travel to and plan terrorist activities in the United States; that dramatic spikes in intelligence chatter suggested an imminent catastrophic terrorist attack against American targets somewhere in the world; and that a star FBI agent believed that bin Laden might be sending operatives to the United States for flight training.

The last missed opportunity occurred in late August, when Director of Central Intelligence George Tenet and his deputy, John McLaughlin, were both informed that the FBI had arrested a man named Zacarias Moussaoui, and that the CIA and FBI were working the case.[39] Moussaoui, an Islamic extremist who had aroused suspicion at a Minneapolis flight school, pleaded guilty to six counts of conspiracy in the September 11 attacks and became the only person convicted in the United States in connection with the plot. Back in August 2001, however, no one connected Moussaoui to other information about al-Mihdhar's visa, al-Hazmi's travels, their connections to bin Laden, reports about KSM, or the alarming levels of threat reporting. Director Tenet told the 9/11 Commission that by late July "the system was blinking red" and that it could not "get any worse," but the system was unable to make sense of the pieces of information it had.[40]

The Organizational Roots of Failure

The CIA's inability to capitalize on all of these opportunities stemmed from the same organizational causes. First, structural fragmentation raised exceptionally high barriers for any activity requiring collaboration across agency lines, and counterterrorism efforts—placing suspected al Qaeda operatives on watch lists, sharing information between the CIA and FBI, and drafting intelligence assessments for the president—required precisely this kind of collaboration. In a system hardwired to keep agencies apart, talented and dedicated officials could only do so much to make them work together. Even in 2001, despite Director Tenet's strategic plan calling for greater unity of effort across agencies, the Intelligence Community lacked basic managerial tools such as a Community-wide financial accounting system and a computer architecture that could integrate counterterrorism data across all the different agencies.[41] Lines between the CIA and FBI were so hardened that temporary assignments between the two agencies were known as the hostage exchange program, and standard operating procedures excluded the attorney general from receiving CIA reports in the President's Daily Brief.[42]

Structural fragmentation also made it likely that trails would go cold, information would not be shared, and dots would not get connected because everyone assumed that the responsibility for specific tasks rested, at least in part, someplace else: Washington officials looked to the field to find the whereabouts of al-Mihdhar, al-Hazmi, and Khallad; lower-level CIA employees believed authority for sharing information resided with their superiors when it did not; the CIA's Renditions Unit focused only on finding KSM and assumed others in the CIA would analyze any intelligence leads his case produced. Even the director of central intelligence said he took no action after receiving his briefing about the FBI's arrest of Zacarias Moussaoui in Minneapolis—a briefing titled, "Islamic Extremist Learns to Fly"—because he viewed it as an FBI case.[43] Indeed, Director Tenet called the structural divide between the CIA and FBI the most serious weakness in U.S. counterterrorism capabilities before September 11, telling the 9/11 Commission, "most profoundly, we lacked a government-wide capability to integrate foreign and domestic knowledge, data, operations, and analysis. Warning is not good enough without the structure to put it into action."[44] The commission agreed, finding that "the terrorists exploited deep institutional failings within our government."[45]

Organizational culture also had debilitating effects on the CIA's counterterrorism efforts. Different CIA officials on more than one occasion neglected to watchlist two of the September 11 hijackers, share information, and distill vital pieces of intelligence scattered throughout the Community in large part because they were steeped in an organizational culture that regarded these activities as unnatural acts: embracing new tasks, thinking beyond the agency, and sharing secrets all ran against the grain of everything CIA officers had known, believed, and cherished for years. The CIA was much more than a job; it was a brotherhood, filled with lifelong members that shared a commitment to country, a willingness to sacrifice, and the knowledge that nearly everything they did would have to stay secret. In this kind of insulated environment, Cold War habits (which never gave high priority to placing suspected terrorists on watch lists), parochial agency perspectives, and cherished values about the vital importance of protecting information rather than sharing it had a powerful grip.

Finally, career incentives exacerbated structural and cultural deficiencies. Clinton administration Attorney General Janet Reno made no bones about the fact that employees were not rewarded for interagency work. "At the FBI in particular, agents are not trained to share information with other agencies," Reno told the 9/11 Commission. "Nor are they evaluated and rewarded based on their ability to generate and share information that other agencies might find useful. . . . This must change."[46] DCI George Tenet had tried years earlier to change the incentive structure to foster greater cross-agency collaboration, requiring rotational assignments to other intelligence agencies for promotion. The program did not succeed because agencies did not want to send their best people away and because rising stars knew that leaving their home agency meant getting off the fast track to career success. As one senior intelligence official noted, "Managers are only in the job three years. They want their good people to stay. They can't send them off for one or two years . . . [because] they are very concerned about what happens on their watch."[47] Agencies were still struggling with this issue years after September 11. As another senior intelligence official noted in 2004, "We need to create the incentive structure to evaluate people's performance in collaboration and teamwork. The leadership structures need to make clear that it's not just expected, it's demanded. We are not there yet."[48]

In addition to discouraging desired behavior, career incentives allowed undesired behavior to go unpunished, particularly when it came to sharing information. As one senior intelligence official noted, "No one's career is ever ruined by being too restrictive about classified information."[49]

Incentives impeded analysis as well. One reason why CIA officials did such a poor job synthesizing counterterrorism information before September 11 is that they operated in a system that prized output and immediacy more than quality and importance. Individual incentives had the collective effect of creating system-wide knowledge gaps about key counterterrorism issues. Between 1998 and 2001, the CIA produced hundreds of analyses about Osama bin Laden and al Qaeda in the President's Daily Brief and other reports,[50] with forty different PDB reports in 2001 alone.[51] Not one of them provided a broad overview of al Qaeda's involvement in past terrorist activities, a comprehensive view of al Qaeda's strategy, or its relationships with other governments. And none assessed the nature or scale of the threat that Osama bin Laden's terrorist network posed to the United States.[52] CIA assessments pointed out the trees but never provided a picture of the forest.

In sum, the Cold War's end left the CIA with a structure splintered into disparate units and no fusion between them; with an organizational culture that viewed intelligence from a parochial perspective, resisted new tasks, and valued keeping secrets above all else; and with career incentives that discouraged interagency collaboration and analysis of big picture issues. These deficiencies struck at the core of how CIA officials perceived and performed their jobs, making it likely that terrorist trails would get lost and information would fall between the cracks.

RED FLAGS IN A SEA OF RED FLAGS?

Critics will argue that this account of missed opportunities is unfair: It has often been said that U.S. intelligence agencies must be right 100 percent of the time, while terrorists need to succeed only once. Many have also suggested, quite correctly, that sifting through massive volumes of intelligence for clues to a surprise attack is an inherently daunting challenge. Roberta Wohlstetter's classic study of the Japanese attack at Pearl Harbor found that in 1941, various U.S. intelligence agencies had pieces of information about the impending attack, but nobody could distinguish these warnings from all of the background noise.[53] As Bruce Berkowitz writes, "this problem of signal-to-noise ratio is so fundamental in the intelligence business that today, if one refers to the 'Roberta Wohlstetter problem,' almost everyone knows exactly what you are talking about."[54] Sixty years later, these challenges may be even worse. When Wohlstetter wrote her book in 1962,

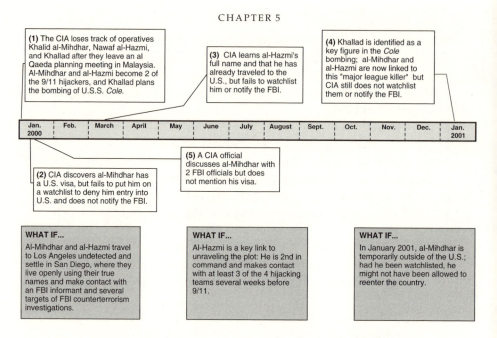

(1) The CIA loses track of operatives Khalid al-Mihdhar, Nawaf al-Hazmi, and Khallad after they leave an al Qaeda planning meeting in Malaysia. Al-Mihdhar and al-Hazmi become 2 of the 9/11 hijackers, and Khallad plans the bombing of U.S.S. *Cole.*

(3) CIA learns al-Hazmi's full name and that he has already traveled to the U.S., but fails to watchlist him or notify the FBI.

(4) Khallad is identified as a key figure in the *Cole* bombing; al-Mihdhar and al-Hazmi are now linked to this "major league killer" but CIA still does not watchlist them or notify the FBI.

| Jan. 2000 | Feb. | March | April | May | June | July | August | Sept. | Oct. | Nov. | Dec. | Jan. 2001 |

(5) A CIA official discusses al-Mihdhar with 2 FBI officials but does not mention his visa.

(2) CIA discovers al-Mihdhar has a U.S. visa, but fails to put him on a watchlist to deny him entry into U.S. and does not notify the FBI.

WHAT IF...
Al-Mihdhar and al-Hazmi travel to Los Angeles undetected and settle in San Diego, where they live openly using their true names and make contact with an FBI informant and several targets of FBI counterterrorism investigations.

WHAT IF...
Al-Hazmi is a key link to unraveling the plot: He is 2nd in command and makes contact with at least 3 of the 4 hijacking teams several weeks before 9/11.

WHAT IF...
In January 2001, al-Mihdhar is temporarily outside of the U.S.; had he been watchlisted, he might not have been allowed to reenter the country.

Figure 5.2a. Timeline of the CIA's 11 Missed Opportunities.

there were 5,000 computers in the world, no fax machines or cellular phones. Today the National Security Agency, which collects signals intelligence, must contend with 180 million computers, fourteen million fax machines and forty million cell phones.[55] The agency's information intake is astounding: it operates a dozen or more listening posts around the world, each one of which intercepts two million faxes, e-mails, telephone calls and other signals every *hour.*[56] That's about 200 million pieces of intelligence in a regular workday; little wonder less than 1 percent of it is ever decoded, translated, or processed.[57] The FBI's former counterterrorism chief described the challenges of preventing the September 11 attacks in this way:

> There were a lot of red flags prior to 9/11. And once 9/11 occurred it's real easy to go back and pick out the red flag in the ocean of red flags and say "You should have done this" or "You should have seen this." And the threat to aviation is certainly one of the areas that we received threat reporting on. It was not the only area. We had threats to malls, threats to power plants, threats to assassinations. Across the board we have threats coming in every day. And if something happened today concerning a small boat at-

116

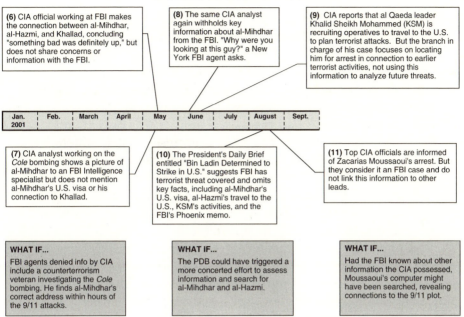

(6) CIA official working at FBI makes the connection between al-Mihdhar, al-Hazmi, and Khallad, concluding "something bad was definitely up," but does not share concerns or information with the FBI.

(8) The same CIA analyst again withholds key information about al-Mihdhar from the FBI. "Why were you looking at this guy?" a New York FBI agent asks.

(9) CIA reports that al Qaeda leader Khalid Sheikh Mohammed (KSM) is recruiting operatives to travel to the U.S. to plan terrorist attacks. But the branch in charge of his case focuses on locating him for arrest in connection to earlier terrorist activities, not using this information to analyze future threats.

| Jan. 2001 | Feb. | March | April | May | June | July | August | Sept. |

(7) CIA analyst working on the *Cole* bombing shows a picture of al-Mihdhar to an FBI Intelligence specialist but does not mention al-Mihdhar's U.S. visa or his connection to Khallad.

(10) The President's Daily Brief entitled "Bin Ladin Determined to Strike in U.S." suggests FBI has terrorist threat covered and omits key facts, including al-Mihdhar's U.S. visa, al-Hazmi's travel to the U.S., KSM's activities, and the FBI's Phoenix memo.

(11) Top CIA officials are informed of Zacarias Moussaoui's arrest. But they consider it an FBI case and do not link this information to other leads.

WHAT IF...
FBI agents denied info by CIA include a counterterrorism veteran investigating the *Cole* bombing. He finds al-Mihdhar's correct address within hours of the 9/11 attacks.

WHAT IF...
The PDB could have triggered a more concerted effort to assess information and search for al-Mihdhar and al-Hazmi.

WHAT IF...
Had the FBI known about other information the CIA possessed, Moussaoui's computer might have been searched, revealing connections to the 9/11 plot.

Figure 5.2b. Timeline of the CIA's 11 Missed Opportunties.

tacking somewhere in one of our harbors in the U.S., we'd probably have information about that. So it's a mass of information and it's a sea of threats, and it's like working against a maze. If you know where the end point of a maze is, it's certainly easier to work your way back to the starting point than trying to go through the maze and sort out all the red flags."[58]

These criticisms are understandable, but ultimately unconvincing, for three reasons. First, every one of the eleven missed opportunities involved information that CIA and other officials had already distinguished from the background noise. Remember that back in January of 2000, CIA leaders were so convinced about the potential significance of the al Qaeda meeting in Malaysia, they not only set up surveillance of it, but provided regular updates to the FBI director, the head of the CIA, and the national security advisor. CIA officials knew this particular al Qaeda meeting was important. They treated it as important. They were primed by reports of potential terrorist attacks surrounding the Millennium. They were tipped off to the meeting by sources considered to be the very best on al Qaeda.[59] They

117

believed "something nefarious" was afoot. And nothing they learned suggested otherwise. Nobody and nothing ever indicated that these suspected terrorists were wrongly targeted, that the meeting was for innocent purposes, that something nefarious was not in fact afoot. A year and half before 9/11, Khalid al-Mihdhar, Nawaf al-Hazmi, and Khallad were singled out. The Wohlstetter problem had been overcome. It was only then that the system broke down. The 9/11 Commission staff statement investigating the Malaysian tracking and watchlisting failures concluded, "We believe every available resource should have been devoted to learning who these people were, and trying to spot and track them."[60] This never happened. The signal was not missed. It was found and then lost.

Second, CIA officials were not searching for red flags in an endless sea of possible threats. They were focused on terrorism and al Qaeda. In the spring and summer of 2001, the U.S. intelligence system was, in Director Tenet's words, "blinking red" with an unprecedented crescendo of reports suggesting an imminent and catastrophic terrorist attack against American targets somewhere in the world. In June, and again in July, intelligence agencies warned senior U.S. government officials that attacks were expected to "cause major casualties" and would "occur with little or no warning."[61] Many intelligence officials told the 9/11 Commission that they realized something terrible was in the offing and were working desperately to stop it.[62] American embassies were warned of the possibility of attack. Military exercises were cancelled and alert levels raised. All fifty-six FBI field offices in the United States were called and told to get their evidence teams ready to investigate attacks at a moment's notice. The president was briefed repeatedly about al Qaeda's intention to strike American targets.[63] To be sure, most of the threat reporting pointed overseas. The September 11 attacks, however, were not bolts from the blue. U.S. intelligence officials and senior policymakers knew an attack was coming and that al Qaeda was behind it. This information alone narrowed the scope of inquiry considerably. The intelligence challenge was still formidable, but it was not impossible. CIA officials still had to find the red flags, but with one major advantage: they had a pretty good idea of what they were looking for.

Yet the CIA failed to use this advantage to focus its own intelligence collection and analysis efforts in a systematic way. Nor did the agency ever develop a comprehensive collection and analysis plan for the rest of the Intelligence Community. What al Qaeda information did U.S. intelligence agencies already possess? What questions still needed to be answered, and in what priority? What kinds of intelligence could fill in the gaps? Which agencies and people were best suited for the job, and how could they work together most productively? These questions were never asked or answered.[64] Instead, the nation's best intelligence professionals were cast adrift, left to piece together what they knew based on what they could get. Tellingly, even the eventual watchlisting of al-Mihdhar and al-Hazmi nineteen days before the attacks was not part of any formal assignment, but came from two FBI analysts and a CIA analyst who reviewed the information on their own.

Third, although it is true that no organizational arrangement guarantees 100 percent success, in this case the CIA's organizational weaknesses led to 100 percent failure. The agency did not miss some of the eleven opportunities it had to potentially disrupt the September 11 attacks. It missed them all. A track record that poor suggests something more fundamental is broken.

CHAPTER 6

Real Men Don't Type

ADAPTATION FAILURE IN THE FBI

The facts speak for themselves. It is indisputable
that the FBI did not adapt.
—Former senior FBI official[1]

ADAPTING TO THE RISE of terrorism after the Cold War proved
an even more daunting task for the FBI than the CIA. Although
the Central Intelligence Agency had to face a new terrorist
enemy during the 1990s, its core mission—collecting and analyzing intelligence—remained unchanged. The Federal Bureau of
Investigation was not so lucky. Preventing terrorists from killing
Americans was nothing like arresting bank robbers or any other
aspect of the bureau's eighty-year-old crime fighting mission. In
counterterrorism, success hinged on moving fast, looking ahead,
and connecting information across cases. Law enforcement, by
contrast, required working slowly and meticulously to avoid
tainting evidence rather than quickly to forestall catastrophe;
looking backward to solve past crimes rather than forward to
stop future attacks; working one case at a time rather than
tracking leads between them; and guarding, not sharing, information so that it could be admitted in court to win a conviction.
For the CIA, adapting to terrorism meant doing the job differently. For the FBI, it meant doing a different job entirely.

Like the CIA, the FBI did not succeed. Indeed, the two agencies' failed counterterrorism efforts bear strong similarities. In
both cases, initial responses to the changing threat environment
were muddled, with the CIA struggling to define itself and the
FBI fighting to defend itself in the aftermath of the Waco and
Ruby Ridge disasters. In both cases, external reforms amounted
to little. Congressional efforts to reform the CIA failed twice, in
1992 and 1996. Congress made even less progress with the FBI.

Although legislators succeeded in expanding the bureau's legal jurisdiction over terrorism cases and increased FBI budgets, they never paid serious attention to the FBI's counterterrorism capabilities or its floundering internal reform efforts. For both agencies, presidents avoided making major changes, preferring instead to address counterterrorism weaknesses through executive directives that proved ineffectual. Internal reforms fared no better. In the late 1990s, just as Director of Central Intelligence George Tenet attempted to change the CIA from the inside, senior FBI officials desperately tried to fix the FBI's longstanding counterterrorism deficiencies from within. They, too, did not succeed.

Below, I begin by tracing the FBI's organizational deficiencies. Next I provide a more detailed view of the bureau's counterterrorism efforts between 1991 and 2001. Finally, I show how the nature of organizations, rational self-interest, and the fragmented structure of the federal government blocked success.

THE FBI'S ORGANIZATIONAL DEFICIENCIES

Like the Central Intelligence Agency, the FBI was hobbled by weaknesses in organizational structure, culture, and incentives. These are summarized in figure 6.1 and discussed in greater detail below.

Structure: Leaving Gaps, Building Fiefdoms

The FBI faced structural problems on two fronts. Externally, the bureau was caught in an Intelligence Community that artificially divided intelligence responsibilities by geography, leaving huge gaps in coverage. The CIA and other agencies were responsible for tracking terrorists abroad, while the FBI was supposed to watch them at home. Nobody, however, was clearly responsible for monitoring the communications or movements of suspected terrorists *between* the United States and foreign countries. The result was that terrorists could operate seamlessly across borders but the U.S. Intelligence Community could not.

The bureau's traditional law enforcement mission exacerbated these gaps. The Federal Bureau of Investigation was established

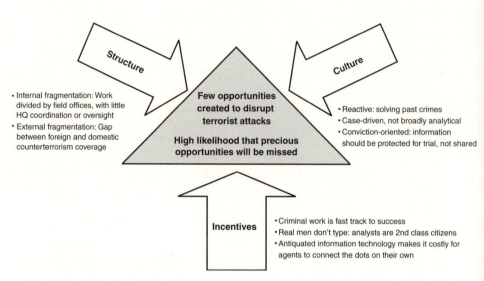

Figure 6.1. The FBI and 9/11: The Organizational Roots of Failure.

by U.S. Attorney General Charles Bonaparte in 1908, nearly forty years before the CIA, to investigate possible violations of U.S. federal laws on U.S. soil.[2] The bureau eventually assumed responsibility for rooting out foreign spies and terrorists operating inside the United States and briefly collected intelligence in Latin America during World War II. Yet FBI officials never considered intelligence their core business, and other officials never considered the FBI a major part of the Intelligence Community.[3] Spies stole secrets, operated abroad, and worked in the shadows of the law; Hoover's special agents, by contrast, were supposed to nab criminals at home and operate in the light of day, granting suspects all of the liberties and procedural protections guaranteed by the U.S. Constitution. The FBI was considered so peripheral to intelligence that before 9/11, the attorney general did not receive the President's Daily Brief, the most important Community-wide current intelligence report.[4]

At the same time, the bureau's internal structure was highly decentralized, with power concentrated in fifty-six local field offices, each run by a special agent-in-charge, or SAC.[5] Field offices existed from the bureau's inception.[6] But it was legendary Director J. Edgar Hoover who expanded and institutionalized the field office system during his forty-seven-year reign. Between

1924 and his death in 1972, Hoover initiated the practice of evaluating field office performance based on quantifiable statistics such as the number of arrests and convictions produced. He standardized forms and processes across the different field offices. And the FBI Director held SACs directly accountable for the work and mistakes of their subordinates.[7] By the 1990s, field office primacy had become so ingrained that some joked the FBI consisted of "fifty-six field offices with a headquarters attached."[8] It is fair to say that when the Cold War ended, the FBI was less a single agency than a system of fifty-six affiliated agencies, each of which set its own priorities, assigned its own personnel, ran its own cases, followed its own orders, and guarded its own information.[9] As former Attorney General Richard Thornburgh put it, the FBI's traditional system was one of "decentralized management of localized cases."[10]

Such a structure was well suited for prosecuting individual criminal cases and responding to local law enforcement priorities throughout the Cold War. But it was poorly designed for managing a coordinated national counterterrorism program. After September 11, the FBI admitted that its traditional field office structure "had a number of failings." Among them, information tended to become "stove-piped" in individual offices rather than pooled or assessed in a coordinated fashion; offices could (and did) pursue their own cases and ignore national priorities such as counterterrorism; and the system left even senior FBI officials in the dark, unaware of what their own agents knew or did and unable to coordinate FBI activities with other U.S. government agencies.[11]

Law Enforcement Culture

Grafted onto these structural weaknesses was a law enforcement culture that had taken root during eight decades spent pursuing the same mission. Everything in the bureau, from the photographs of award-winning agents placed outside the director's office to new agent training programs, reinforced the idea that agents were supposed to be reactive, case-driven, and conviction-oriented, working cases one by one and protecting information for use in trial.

Here, too, J. Edgar Hoover left an indelible imprint. From dress codes to new agent training to the plaque he placed in every field office titled, "Loyalty,"[12] Hoover spent four decades setting and enforcing rigid standards about what it meant to be an FBI agent. Protecting the bureau from embarrassment was foremost on Hoover's list of virtues. As Robert Lamphere, who was an FBI agent in 1941, described it, "Our self-esteem became interconnected with the FBI's image, and we took our strength from our membership in the organization."[13] While this attitude cultivated a sense of institutional loyalty and professionalism, it also bred an intense fear of failure, an unwillingness to admit or examine mistakes, and a refusal to reflect on how to improve performance. As one former FBI official observed:

> I think that Hoover built what was probably given the times an extraordinarily modern, effective and admirable law enforcement agency. And he did it by being a terribly hard master, by getting involved in details at every level ... involved in the dress code, giving people extraordinary retirement benefits. . . . But there was always the constant threat of outer darkness. If you screwed up and embarrassed the bureau, you'd get cast off into outer darkness. . . . I personally believe while these guys will still go through a locked door with a gun behind it, sitting time after time at a meeting [during the 1990s], when someone senior in the FBI said, "the sky is yellow" and everyone else knew it was blue, they didn't say anything. And that's why.[14]

Former FBI Director Louis Freeh reveals just how much Hoover's culture of institutional self-protection persisted in his 2005 memoir, *My FBI*. Freeh, who began his career as an FBI street agent investigating organized crime in the 1970s and ran the bureau from 1993 until the summer of 2001, declares his greatest lifetime achievement on page viii: "Never once did I say or do anything that embarrassed or caused harm to the FBI or the country."[15] This is a stunning statement in light of the September 11 terrorist attacks, the wealth of evidence uncovered by both the Congressional Intelligence Committees and the 9/11 Commission about the FBI's shortcomings in counterterrorism, and the widespread calls for reform. Out of 318 pages, in fact, Freeh devotes just twenty-five to September 11, most of which blame Congress for insufficiently funding the FBI (despite the fact that the FBI received *more* money for counterterrorism than the president requested five out of seven fiscal years between 1995 and 2001)[16] and the Clinton administration for not taking a more aggressive posture against terrorism. Only a single page ponders whether the bureau itself could have performed better.[17] Freeh's answer is no.

In addition to instilling institutional loyalty, Hoover worked assiduously to develop a culture and image of FBI agents as men of action, both inside and outside the bureau. Hoover became a public relations machine, offering cooperation only with those producers and reporters who portrayed the FBI in a positive light.[18] By the 1930s, Hoover's G-men appeared on everything from bubble gum cards to the big screen.[19] In 1935 alone, sixty-five movies featured the FBI. All of them glorified FBI agents as intrepid heroes, guns in hand, who worked the streets to solve crimes and always got their man.[20] This image took strong hold inside the FBI as well. For an ambitious FBI agent, the goal was to work a case, not sit behind a desk. One unintentional consequence of this action culture was an aversion to technology and analysis—an aversion that would prove disastrous during the 1990s. After the September 11 attacks, one veteran agent described the prevailing old-school FBI attitude as, "real men don't type. The only thing a real agent needs is a notebook, a pen and gun, and with those three things you can conquer the world."[21]

For years, this law enforcement orientation served the bureau well. The problem came when the Cold War ended and counterterrorism required a radically different approach. Suddenly, agents who had devoted careers to investigating past tragedies were supposed to prevent them. Officials were expected to work across cases rather than within them. An organization geared to guarding information was now supposed to share it. And the most highly prized result was no longer a conviction, but a non-result: the absence of terrorist attack. The bureau's new counterterrorism mission required radical shifts in how everyone from street agents to senior officials viewed their jobs. It was all too much, too fast. When the terrorist threat emerged, the law enforcement culture that had been one of the FBI's greatest strengths became one of its greatest liabilities.

Misplaced Incentives

Organizational incentives reinforced these cultural pathologies, encouraging agents to focus on traditional criminal work instead of counterterrorism and spend their time solving individual cases rather than analyzing broad trends. As one blue-ribbon commission noted in 2005, "Law enforcement work has long been the surest route to professional advancement within the Bureau."[22] It did not take much for new FBI agents to realize that criminal cases offered the fast track to success. The bureau's new agent training course devoted just twenty-eight out of 680 hours to counterintelligence and counterterrorism.[23] Resources overwhelmingly supported criminal work at the expense of counterterrorism. And plum assignments such as managing FBI field offices far more often went to agents from the Criminal Division than anywhere else.[24] As one former FBI agent put it, "Counterintelligence and counterterrorism was a dumping area for problem children in the late 1980s and early 1990s."[25]

Incentives also discouraged analysis. Because success was determined primarily by criminal case statistics, analysts were considered second-class citizens, nonessential employees who could be transferred away from strategic analysis to do just about anything that supported case work, including answering phones and emptying the trash.[26] Before September 11, FBI personnel policies expressly prohibited analysts from being promoted to senior positions.[27] The bureau had no dedicated career path for analysts.[28] Nor did it have any "professional reports officers," positions which were considered vital in intelligence, to assess and disseminate information from the FBI to other agencies.[29] As an old FBI joke put it, there were only two kinds of people in the bureau: agents and furniture.

At the same time, the bureau's computer inadequacies made it extremely costly for agents to conduct their own analysis. As the 9/11 Commission concluded in a staff statement, "The FBI did not have an effective system for storing, searching, or retrieving information of intelligence value contained in its investigative files."[30] With billions of records kept in paper files,[31] computers so old that it took twelve commands to store a single document,[32] different databases that could not perform integrated searches,[33] and e-mail so unreliable that messages often went unread,[34] even agents interested in connecting the dots between cases could not make headway easily.

In sum, when the Cold War ended in 1991, the FBI was a fully developed, eighty-three-year-old organization with a well defined and stable law enforcement mission codified by law, a highly decentralized field office structure, and a powerful organizational culture that prized loyalty and action above analysis and technology.

ADAPTATION AFTER THE COLD WAR

FBI counterterrorism efforts can be roughly divided between the early 1990s and the late 1990s. During the first half of the decade, America's principal law enforcement agency continued to do what it had always done: catch criminals. Although the Cold War's end changed everything overnight for the CIA, it did not create such a sudden and dramatic shift in the FBI's external environment. Instead, the bureau made only halting steps toward change, gradually adding terrorism to the bottom of a long list of crimes in its jurisdiction.

In 1995, however, a trifecta of terrorist developments—the capture of the architect of the 1993 World Trade Center bombing, a chemical terror attack on the Tokyo subway, and the bombing of the U.S. federal building in Oklahoma City—triggered a more concerted focus on terrorism inside the United States. By 1998, a handful of senior FBI officials were desperately trying to transform the bureau into a twenty-first-century counterterrorism agency, with the technological capabilities, analytic capacity, and proactive mentality to thwart attacks before they occurred. Racing against time, they made slow and painful progress, generating more resistance than results.

The Early 1990s: Halting Steps and Short-Lived Victories

Initially, the Cold War's end did not change much for the FBI. Instead, the bureau continued to concentrate its efforts on fighting crime. Although the FBI had assumed responsibility for investigating terrorism cases and catching foreign spies for years, these activities had always ranked low on its priority list compared to criminal activities such as violent crime, organized crime, and drug trafficking. In the words of FBI special agent Kenneth Williams, author of the famous Phoenix memo (which warned in July 2001 that al Qaeda terrorists might be enrolling in U.S. flight schools), counterterrorism and counterintelligence were considered the "bastard step children" of the FBI because they did not generate the arrest and conviction statistics that criminal programs did.[35] When the Soviet Union collapsed in 1991, fewer than fifty people were working in the FBI's counterterrorism section, the unit that oversaw all terrorism and intelligence matters.[36] Indeed, some evidence suggests the bureau saw the Soviet Union's collapse as an opportunity to devote even less attention to national security issues. In January 1992, three hundred special agents in the field were reassigned from counterintelligence duties to violent crime investigations.[37] The FBI's own history proudly notes that the Cold War's end provided "an unprecedented opportunity to intensify efforts in burgeoning domestic crime problems" while its national security programs in counterintelligence and counterterrorism were being rethought and retooled.[38]

After the February 1993, terrorist bombing of the World Trade Center, the FBI took some steps to improve its counterterrorism capabilities and scored some operational successes. In 1994, the bureau established a Radical Fundamentalist Unit in headquarters to handle counterintelligence, coordinate intelligence operations outside of the United States, and oversee criminal investigations of radical fundamentalist terrorists.[39] The same year, Congress passed laws making material support to terrorism a federal crime for the first time[40] and enhancing the bureau's ability to conduct surveillance of digital communications and stored data.[41] FBI agents also succeeded in identifying the perpetrators of the World Trade Center bombing (capturing some immediately and all of them eventually) and in disrupting a major plot to blow up other New York City landmarks, including the United Nations and the Lincoln and Holland Tunnels.

These developments, however, were short-lived victories. The 1993 World Trade Center bombing raised the FBI's level of concern about terrorism inside the United States, but the attack did not cause the bureau to adjust its priorities, shift resources, or transform its capabilities to combat terrorism more effectively. In April 1994, a year after the World Trade Center attack, newly appointed FBI Director Louis Freeh made clear that his top priority would continue to be crime, not terrorism. "It's time to stop fooling around," he told a Senate Appropriations Subcommittee during its annual budget hearing of the FBI. "Crime in the United States is a disaster . . . of the first magnitude."[42] One year later, in March of 1995, Freeh reiterated his dedication to the FBI's traditional mission, assuring members of the House Appropriations Committee that thanks to their budget increases, 246 newly minted FBI agents would soon be assigned to investigate "such FBI priorities as violent crimes, drugs, and organized crime." He did not mention terrorism.[43] Even counterterrorism funds did not end up supporting counterterrorism activities. An independent review of the FBI chaired by former Attorney General Richard Thornburgh found that after the 1993 World Trade Center attack, FBI field offices diverted counterterrorism resources to violent crime, drug trafficking, and other traditional priorities.[44]

Instead, the FBI spent the early 1990s looking backward, not forward, defending itself and rebuilding its reputation after a string of scandals. These included the 1992 standoff in Ruby Ridge, Idaho, when FBI agents pursuing Randall Weaver in connection with weapons charges accidentally shot and killed Weaver's wife; the disastrous 1993 siege of the Branch Davidian cult compound in Waco, Texas, which ended when an FBI assault to seize a cache of weapons prompted cult members to set fire to the compound, killing eighty people; and the sacking of FBI Director William Sessions over concerns about ethics violations. The Ruby Ridge and Waco standoffs, in particular, captured headlines, ignited a political firestorm in Washington, and called into question the FBI's basic competence as a law enforcement agency.[45] By 1995, after congressional hearings investigated the two incidents, public confidence in the FBI had plummeted. An April 1995 Gallup poll reported that 39 percent of Americans feared the federal government posed an immediate threat to their civil liberties, and an August 1995 Pew poll found that only 16 percent of Americans held a very favorable impression of the bureau.[46]

The Late 1990s: Waking Up

The FBI's wake-up call began with three terrorist incidents in 1995. In January, an accidental explosion in Manila led the Philippine National Police to the bomb-making lab of Ramzi Yousef, the mastermind of the 1993 World Trade Center attack. Inside they found evidence of a new terrorist plot to blow up twelve American airplanes in Asia, assassinate the pope, bomb U.S. and Israeli embassies in Manila, and crash an airplane into CIA headquarters. Filipino police quickly arrested an accomplice, Abdul Hakim Murad, and the FBI nabbed Yousef in Pakistan a few weeks later. In March, a Japanese apocalyptic religious cult named Aum Shinrikyo released sarin nerve gas in a Tokyo subway, killing twelve people and injuring five thousand. It was the first-ever terrorist attack with a weapon of mass destruction. One month later, Timothy McVeigh detonated a truck bomb outside the Alfred P. Murrah Federal Building in Oklahoma City, killing 168 Americans in what was then the worst terrorist act in U.S. history. Coming in such rapid succession, these three incidents raised a new and frightening prospect: small groups of fanatics—both homegrown and foreign—could inflict catastrophic damage without warning, by combining terrorist tactics with weapons of mass destruction.

The FBI responded by creating a headquarters Counterterrorism Center and a special unit focused exclusively on Osama bin Laden, launching the first exchange of senior FBI and CIA counterterrorism officials, and expanding the bureau's legal attaché offices overseas to forge closer relationships with foreign law enforcement officials.[47] Between 1996 and 2001, the number of foreign FBI offices nearly doubled, from twenty-three to forty-four. New offices were located in places such as Cairo, Islamabad, Tel Aviv, and Riyadh—as Director Freeh put it, "places that matter in the fight against terrorism."[48]

REFORM TURNS RADICAL: THE 1998 STRATEGIC PLAN

To some, it quickly became apparent that even these measures were inadequate. In 1997 Robert "Bear" Bryant, the FBI's second highest official, spearheaded a radical new strategic planning effort that focused on upgrading the bureau's counterterrorism capabilities. Where previous strategic planning efforts had focused on incremental adjustments—in the words of one former official, "restating the work we did [and] adding a five percent improvement factor"—Bryant's strategic planning sought dramatic changes in the FBI's core mission and culture. "Before, it was 'here's how we can do a few things better,'" said the official. "This time, it was 'we cannot continue the way we are.' "[49] For the next year, Bryant and his team met with every FBI investigative program, many of the field office SACs and the FBI's top brass to, in the words of one planner, "soften the underbelly of the organization."[50]

Bryant's plan was released in May of 1998 and called for changes that were nothing short of revolutionary. First, the plan reversed the FBI's traditional strategic priorities, placing terrorism, espionage, and other national security threats—issues that posed the greatest danger to the largest number of people for which the bureau held exclusive jurisdiction—at the top of the priority list for the first time in FBI history. Meanwhile, crimes against individuals and property, which fell under the jurisdiction of many other law enforcement agencies but had been the FBI's bread and butter work for decades, consuming most of the bureau's resources, were downgraded to the bottom of the priority list.[51] "When you looked at the strategic plan," said one former FBI agent, "and considered where we put our resources, we were 180 degrees from where we needed to be."[52]

Second, the plan mandated dramatic improvements in the FBI's intelligence collection and analysis capabilities. Notably, the strategic plan argued that intelligence was not simply a counterterrorism tool, but a vital element of twenty-first-century law enforcement more generally. "Crime is increasingly more sophisticated, creating demands on the FBI to develop strategies to prevent rather than merely respond to new and emerging crime," the report noted. "This will require an intelligence capability far different than that which has supported the FBI's efforts over the past several decades."[53] The report declared that existing FBI capabilities were "inadequate to the task of the future,"[54] with declining numbers of human sources, unqualified and poorly trained analysts, no ability to produce longer-term strategic intelligence analyses, poor cooperation between FBI programs as well as with other intelligence agencies, an electronic information system incapable of transmitting or inte-

grating information within the FBI, and an organizational culture that did not understand how to use intelligence or appreci-
ate its importance.[55] One former government official described
the situation in less diplomatic terms: "Any blind monkey coming off the street could have told you there wasn't anybody in
the FBI doing intelligence analysis."[56]

Third, the strategic plan emphasized the urgent need to upgrade the bureau's obsolete information technology systems.
The report found that existing technologies and computer capabilities were so outdated, agents were still keeping much of their
information in paper files, often could not access information
outside their own offices, and could not send e-mail even within
the FBI.[57] The report was clear: "The investigative challenges facing the FBI in the 21st century will require major enhancements
to existing IT capabilities."[58]

Fourth, and finally, the strategic plan called for a wholesale
cultural shift in the FBI from its reactive law enforcement past
to a more proactive, intelligence-oriented future. The report
stated on page two, "a large part of the FBI mission is inherently
reactive, and rightly so. . . . The FBI's unparalleled record of
solving major cases plays a significant role in the FBI's self
image. When the FBI can apprehend a terrorist, return a child
safely to its family . . . each member of the FBI workforce believes that he or she has done his/her job."[59] However, the strategic plan took pains to lay out that times had changed with the
Cold War's end and the dawning of an information revolution.
"Unprecedented, and in some cases wholly unforeseen, changes
in the world over the past five years have dramatically altered
the world of international crime," the report observed. New
threats required a new kind of law enforcement agency that
could prevent as well as respond. As the report concluded,
"Meeting the strategic goals requires that the FBI supplement
its reactive capability with bold and innovative proactive efforts
designed to deter and prevent—to the maximum extent feasible—criminal activities that threaten vital American interests."[60]

STRUCTURAL REORGANIZATION AND MAXCAP 05

Two significant reform initiatives quickly followed. First, in November 1999, the FBI underwent a major reorganization. For the
first time, counterterrorism activities would be handled in a sep-

arate, stand-alone Counterterrorism Division rather than as a component of another division.[61] In addition, intelligence activities, which had previously been "owned" by the various operational divisions, were consolidated into a single Investigative Services Division. The move was intended to raise the stature of analysts, house them all in one place, and encourage sharing across different operational programs (such as white-collar crime and counterterrorism).[62] As FBI Director Louis Freeh later told the 9/11 Commission, "Nobody in the Executive or the Congress suggested we do this. We did it because we were focused on enhancing this critical program. This major reorganization of FBIHQ [headquarters] and CT [counterterrorism] assets in our 56 Field Offices represented a major commitment to preventing terrorism and enhancing our intelligence bases."[63]

Second, in 2000, the Counterterrorism Division's new chief, Dale Watson, launched an ambitious program to enhance the FBI's counterterrorism capacity where it counted most: in the field. Called MAXCAP 05, Watson's program sought to achieve what he called "maximum feasible capacity" in counterterrorism across the FBI's fifty-six field offices by 2005.[64] The plan established baseline capabilities at every field office, identified gaps, set targets for improvement, and held individual field office SACs accountable for the results in their own performance evaluations. Moreover, each field office's progress was measured according to a color system: green for good, yellow for improving, and red for inadequate. Or in the words of one former FBI official, "red being we don't know shit, yellow being we're getting better, green being we're okay, we understand the terrorist presence and stand a chance."[65] Watson retained final say over each office's rating and presented a report to the FBI director days before 9/11 that included a map of the United States with the color grades of all of the field offices on it, along with supporting documents.[66]

In short, Bryant's strategic plan, the organizational restructuring, and Watson's MAXCAP 05 plan signaled a new and dedicated internal effort to revolutionize the Federal Bureau of Investigation. The strategic plan laid bare the bureau's critical weaknesses, identified terrorism as the FBI's most important priority, and articulated a comprehensive strategic vision to combat it. As the 9/11 Commission later concluded, "If successfully implemented, this would have been a major step toward addressing terrorism systematically, rather than as individual unrelated cases."[67] Reorganizing counterterrorism and intelligence was intended to strengthen the bureau's focus on terrorism and its analytic capacity across a broad range of program areas. MAXCAP 05 sought to turn the strategic plan into reality by developing a concrete program for improving counterterrorism capabilities in the field. Between 1997 and 2001, Bryant, Watson and other FBI officials worked feverishly to reform the FBI. "The issue was not a lack of commitment," said one former FBI official. "The staff that went to Counterterrorism Division . . . intensity was their middle name."[68]

FAILING ON ALL FRONTS

It was not enough. By September 11, 2001, every reform initiative had failed. The 1998 strategic plan made terrorism a top FBI priority in theory, but never in practice. Between 1998 and 9/11, counterterrorism spending remained flat,[69] 76 percent of all field agents continued to work on criminal investigations unrelated to terrorism,[70] the number of special agents working international terrorism cases actually declined,[71] and field agents were often diverted from counterterrorism and intelligence work to cover major criminal cases.[72] The 9/11 Commission found that only 1,300 of the FBI's 21,000 employees, or 6 percent of the bureau's total work force, were field agents working on terrorism in 2001.[73] On September 11, in fact, more FBI agents—hundreds more—were investigating white-collar criminals than suspected terrorists.[74]

Moreover, counterterrorism continued to attract low levels of attention as well as resources. Former White House counterterrorism czar Richard Clarke told congressional investigators that with the exception of the New York field office, which had been the primary office investigating terrorist incidents for years, the FBI's field offices around the United States were "clueless" about counterterrorism and al Qaeda before September 11.[75] Clarke personally visited several field offices during 2000, asking each one what they were doing about al Qaeda. The responses he received were alarming. "I got sort of blank looks of 'what is al-Qa'ida?'" he recalled.[76] The 9/11 Commission found the same problem at work in the summer of 2001, concluding that there was "little evidence" that any field office outside of New York understood or appreciated the terrorist threat, despite dramatic spikes in intelligence chatter warning of an imminent terrorist attack and despite direct telephone calls from Acting FBI Director Thomas Pickard to every field office in July explicitly discussing the heightened terrorist threat level.[77]

The strategic plan's mandate for improving intelligence collection and analysis also produced no meaningful change. The 9/11 Commission curtly concluded that the FBI's collection of "useful intelligence from human sources" was "limited," with a roster of mediocre sources, no system for validating the credibility of human source reporting, and poorly developed mechanisms for sharing intelligence either within the FBI or with other intelligence agencies.[78] In addition, electronic surveillance of terrorist communications continued to be artificially divided between the National Security Agency, which monitored communications abroad, and the FBI's domestic surveillance of terrorists inside the United States. As the Congressional Joint Inquiry concluded, this divide left no agency responsible for collecting information transmitted between U.S.-based and foreign terrorist cells or considering how a terrorist group might target the United States itself.[79]

Intelligence analysis also continued to languish. The bureau tried several times to hire more and better analysts during the 1990s. However, because analytic work, especially longer-term strategic analysis, was not considered essential for solving cases, analysts were frequently given menial support duties that included photocopying, emptying the trash, and answering phones.[80] Many high quality analysts quickly left, leaving an understaffed and unqualified work force. In 2001, the FBI had a grand total of eleven al Qaeda analysts,[81] only one of whom was assigned to produce longer-term strategic assessments of the terrorist network.[82] In fact, the bureau's only strategic assessment of the terrorist threat to the United States, a draft report submitted in September 2001, was considered too shoddy to be of any use. Among its glaring omissions, the report never addressed the likelihood of terrorist attack, never assessed the capabilities of different terrorist groups, never identified critical intelligence requirements, and made no recommendations to FBI management about how to develop a counterterrorism strategy or prioritize resources.[83] Richard Clarke concluded: "The FBI did not provide analysis. The FBI, as far as I could tell, didn't have an analytical shop. They never provided analysis to us, even when we asked for it, and I don't think that throughout the ten-year period we really had an analytical capability of what was going on in this country."[84]

The bureau continued to be plagued by glaring analytic deficiencies years after 9/11. In 2002, an internal FBI study found that two-thirds of the bureau's analysts were unqualified to do their jobs[85] and a report issued by the Justice Department Inspector General's Office concluded that the FBI "lacked a professional corps of intelligence analysts with a defined career path, standards for training . . . or a system for effectively deploying or utilizing analysts to assess priority threats."[86] In 2004, an FBI field office report found that analysts were still being assigned clerical and secretarial duties.[87] In March 2005, a blue-ribbon presidential commission chaired by Judge Laurence Silberman and former Senator Charles Robb (D-VA) harshly criticized the FBI's progress, noting that the bureau was producing few strategic analyses and was "still far from having the strong analytic capability that is required."[88] In December 2005, the 9/11 Commission's Public Discourse Project issued its first report card on intelligence reform. In it, Commission Chairman Thomas Kean and Vice Chairman Lee Hamilton highlighted concerns about ongoing "deficiencies in the FBI's analytic capabilities."[89] As one former government official bluntly put it, "there is still no such thing as a law enforcement intelligence product. There's no methodology. It's, 'Why don't you read these files and tell me what you see?'"[90]

A TRAIN WRECK IN SLOW MOTION

Efforts to modernize the Bureau's obsolete information technology (IT) systems can only be described as feckless. Between 1997 and 1999, legislators were so concerned that the FBI was incapable of implementing a successful IT modernization program, they refused to fund the bureau's proposed $430 million Information Sharing Initiative.[91] Their concerns were justified. As former Attorney General Janet Reno later explained, "Unfortunately, the FBI had faced extensive delays and cost overruns in the deployment of its previous major technology programs, so it faced major challenges convincing the Congress to provide significant new funding for this initiative."[92] The FBI's main information system at the time, the Automated Case Support system (ACS), had cost $67 million and was obsolete from its inception.[93] Launched in 1995 with 1980s technology, the system used function keys instead of "point and click" mouse technology or icons, could not store graphics or picture files, required twelve separate commands to store a single document, and proved so unreliable that many agents continued storing case information in paper files and transmitted electronic data using forty-two different and unconnected information systems to circumvent ACS problems.[94] Chief among them was the ACS system's inability to perform data searches using more than one word. In the fall of 2001, for example, an agent interested in flight schools could search for the word "flight" or the word "schools" in some FBI case files but not for "flight schools." By contrast, the CIA had been able to search for full phrases on its computers since 1985.[95] As Acting FBI Director Thomas Pickard put it, "The FBI computer system was the joke of Washington, D.C. The FBI knew it, DOJ [the Department of Justice] knew it, and Congress knew it."[96]

Yet FBI Director Freeh, who ordered his own computer removed from his office because he never used it, was slow to act.[97] In the spring of 2000, two years after the strategic plan was released, Attorney General Janet Reno was so concerned that "the FBI didn't know what it had," she sent three separate memos to the FBI director demanding urgent action.[98] On February 29, 2000, Reno asked the FBI to "develop and implement a system to ensure the linkage and sharing of intelligence evidence and other information" among all parts of the FBI, and to have the system in place by October 1, 2000.[99] On March 8, 2000, Reno issued a second memo that noted, "the bottom line is that we must develop a capacity within the Federal Bureau of Investigation in all fields to identify relevant information and share it internally, and then share it securely with other agencies."[100] And in May she wrote that it was imperative that the bureau "immediately develop the capacity to fully assimilate and utilize intelligence information currently collected and contained in FBI files, and use that knowledge to work proactively to identify and protect against emerging national security threats."[101] As Reno later explained, she believed that enhancing existing computer systems would be "helpful," but it was also important "for people to begin to look at manually what they could do and to find out what they had and what they didn't have."[102] Finally, in June 2000, Freeh appointed the bureau's first professional chief information officer, an IBM veteran named Bob Dies, and in the fall of 2000 convinced Congress to fund a new, $500 million information technology modernization program named Trilogy.

It was too little, too late. At the time of the September 11, 2001, attacks, half of all of the FBI's records—six billion pages—were still being stored in paper form.[103] The FBI's technology systems were several generations behind industry standards.[104] Most of the bureau's desktop computers were so old that they could not use standard software or connect to the Internet.[105] Agents had to write interview notes by hand, retype them into their computers, and store other case-related documents and photographs in manila envelopes.[106] E-mail was so slow and unreliable that agents often resorted to faxing important documents instead.[107] Management of information technology programs and investments continued to be splintered across several operational divisions, with no consolidated control or high-level attention.[108] In short, as al Qaeda was mastering twenty-first-century terrorist warfare, the FBI was struggling to bring its technology systems out of the Dark Ages. Without modern computer networks to collect, integrate, and share information, individual agents were left groping in the dark, searching for clues and piecing together what information they could unearth through personal contacts and gut instinct. As one former FBI official reflected with frustration, "If you really understood what domestic intelligence was, *nothing* would have stood in the way of getting the computer piece right. It's the heart of intelligence."[109]

After September 11, the Trilogy information modernization program proved to be precisely the disaster that Congress had feared all along. Robert Mueller, who became FBI director just one week before 9/11, quickly announced that Trilogy was one of his top reform priorities.[110] Nearly four years later, however, he was forced to declare failure. In February 2005, Mueller announced that Trilogy's cornerstone electronic case filing system, which had already run behind schedule and over budget, cost $170 million, and burned through five different chief information officers and ten project managers, was being scrapped because it did not work.[111] "It's unbelievable," fumed Senator Patrick Leahy (D-VT). "It's been a kind of train wreck in slow motion. . . . Back in 2000, when we began discussions about Trilogy as a way to bring the FBI's antiquated system into the 21st century, we were warned of dire consequences to our security and our safety if the improvements weren't imminent, if we didn't get the money so we could be done right away. Well, we responded . . . But time and again, it has fallen victim to escalating costs and implementation concerns, mismanagement and so on. . . . The $170 million seems to have evaporated."[112]

LOSING THE CULTURE WAR

The final element of the 1998 strategic plan sought to transform the bureau's culture, reshaping the organization from a reactive, conviction-oriented law enforcement agency to a proactive, domestic intelligence organization. This was a monumental shift for an organization where street agents reigned supreme and analysts were considered glorified secretaries; where the weapon of choice was a gun, not a computer; where individual cases, not broad threats, ruled the day; where the job began at a crime scene and ended in court; and where careers were made or broken by arrest, prosecution, and conviction statistics rather than the absence of catastrophic attack.

Above all, transforming the FBI's culture required two profound changes in the way rank and file agents did their jobs: sharing information rather than protecting it for possible use in trial, and preventing rather than responding to disaster. The bureau failed at both. Information sharing problems remained rampant. Inside the FBI, information continued to be "owned" by individual case agents and rarely shared, even with agents in the same squad.[113] Even criminal and terrorism agents investigating the same suspects refused to share information: concern about compromising a conviction ran so deep that most FBI agents believed—wrongly—that they were prohibited by law from passing nearly all information between investigations of criminal wrongdoing and investigations designed to gather intelligence about potential terrorist activity.[114] The result was that nobody inside the FBI knew what anybody else inside the FBI was doing. During the summer of 2001, for example, three different FBI field offices uncovered tantalizing clues about potential terrorist activity inside the United States: an agent in the Phoenix office wrote a memo warning that Osama bin Laden might be sending terrorists to train in U.S. flight schools and urged the bureau to investigate the matter; Minneapolis field agents became concerned that a radical fundamentalist named Zacarias Moussaoui might be connected to a larger terrorist hijacking plot and arrested him; and the New York field office began a manhunt for suspected terrorists Khalid al-Mihdhar and Nawaf al-Hazmi, who were believed to be living in the United States and who would later crash American Airlines Flight 77 into the Pentagon. Yet none of the agents working these leads were aware of the other developments.[115] Almost none of the FBI's field offices had any inkling of any of these investigations.[116] And the FBI's top cop, Acting Director Tom Pickard, was completely in the dark, learning about the Phoenix memo, Moussaoui's arrest, and the search for al-Hazmi and al-Mihdhar only after the September 11 terrorist attacks.[117]

Information sharing between the FBI and other government agencies was even worse.[118] The Congressional Joint Inquiry found that before 9/11, FBI agents did not routinely disseminate information acquired in the course of terrorism investigations with the rest of the U.S. Intelligence Community.[119] Nor did the bureau share information with the president's top foreign policy advisors. In the words of one former National Security Council official, the FBI was an informational "black hole," repeatedly withholding information from senior White House officials on the grounds that sharing relevant counterterrorism information could compromise pending investigations.[120] So pervasive was the case-oriented law enforcement mentality, when FBI headquarters received the Phoenix memo in the summer of 2001, an analyst there forwarded the document to the Portland FBI field office because he thought it could help with a criminal investigation there, but never passed it on to the Central Intelligence Agency.[121] No one else in the FBI did either, despite the memo's explicit request that FBI headquarters "discuss this matter with other elements of the U.S. Intelligence Community and task the community for any information that supports Phoenix's suspicions."[122] Focused on solving cases rather than collecting information, FBI officials were unable to see the intelligence value of a memo that reported suspicious flight school training of foreign Islamist extremists inside the United States.

Moving the bureau from a reactive to proactive orientation proved equally difficult and unsuccessful because it required a fundamental shift in how FBI agents viewed their jobs. For decades, FBI agents had been helping local communities solve crimes. They were recruited, trained, and rewarded for scoring victories, catching bad guys, serving justice, and closing cases. Proactive counterterrorism work, by contrast, required agents to work national issues, not local ones, and dedicate resources and concentrate attention to things that might never happen rather than addressing pressing problems that already existed. "Put yourself in the position of the SAC told to think about the terrorism problem," one former official explained. "You've got to figure out who might be putting together a camp of terrorism. Meanwhile there are bank robberies going on. It's an unnatural act."[123] Resistance to such changes was swift and strong. Here's how one former FBI official described the SACs' reaction to the plan at a special national meeting with Director Freeh and other senior headquarters officials: "Louis rolls out how we have to be more proactive and not reactive . . . [and] the SACs, the senior cardinals of the church, say . . . 'Let me get this right. I'm going to be evaluated in Cleveland on white-collar crime that doesn't take place?' There was absolutely no comprehension."[124]

Even the FBI's top leaders seemed unable to make the leap from reaction to prevention. On July 19, 2001, FBI Acting Director Tom Pickard held a conference call with all of the FBI field office SACs during which he warned of the heightened threat of terrorist attack. His recommendation, however, was all reaction: Pickard urged field offices to have their evidence response teams ready to investigate an attack at a moment's notice.[125]

In sum, Bryant's 1998 strategic plan was long on vision but short on execution. Before September 11, 2001, not a single element of the plan had been successfully implemented. As the Justice Department Inspector General later concluded, the 1998 strategic plan "identified numerous vulnerabilities and weaknesses in the FBI's capabilities to deal with the general terrorist threat, but before September 11 this identification did not result in the fundamental changes in the FBI necessary to correct the deficiencies."[126]

LAST GASPS

The bureau's efforts to reorganize headquarters and revamp counterterrorism capabilities in the field proved equally unsuccessful. The creation of a Counterterrorism Division did not, in fact, lead to a significant shift of resources either at headquarters or in the field.[127] Intelligence reorganization fared even worse. Although the new Investigative Services Division was intended to streamline and improve intelligence collection and analysis, it came under immediate attack from operational managers in the Criminal, Intelligence, and Counterterrrorism Divisions who wanted to retain control over their own intelligence assets. The division proved so ineffective that it was dismantled soon after 9/11.[128]

Finally, there was Dale Watson's MAXCAP 05 counterterrorism program. In September 2001, as nineteen al Qaeda hijackers were making final preparations for their attack, Watson delivered a frightening progress report to the FBI's new director, Robert Mueller. In it was a MAXCAP 05 map of the United States that was completely covered in red. After a year of feverish work rolling out his counterterrorism improvement program, Watson concluded that every single one of the FBI's fifty-six field offices was still failing.[129] His counterterrorism report was considered so embarrassing to the bureau, it was highly classified and only a handful of copies were ever produced.[130] Watson told the 9/11 Commission that implementing MAXCAP 05 was the hardest thing he had ever done in his life.[131] As one former FBI counterterrorism official put it, "There were a few of us swimming upstream, and there were lots of people throwing rocks at us from the side."[132]

MISSING IN ACTION: THE PRESIDENT AND CONGRESS

Between 1995 and 2001, nearly all of the reform action was taking place inside the FBI, not the White House or Congress. President Clinton's efforts to transform the FBI during this period consisted of three measures: a disappointing legislative initiative after the Oklahoma City bombing in 1995 to expand the bureau's counterterrorism authorities; a 1995 presidential directive assigning terrorism responsibilities to various agencies; and a package of 1998 directives which sought to improve the counterterrorism interagency process by establishing a counterterrorism czar in the White House.[133] None of these initiatives amounted to much. The president's final antiterrorism bill, the Antiterrorism and Effective Death Penalty Act of 1996, was attacked by an unusual coalition of interest groups and lawmakers from both the left and right, all of whom feared granting more authority to the nation's most powerful law enforcement agency in light of the Ruby Ridge and Waco debacles. The final bill was so gutted of substantive provisions, Representative John Conyers (D-MI) described it as "a low-grade crime bill—cats and dogs from the Judiciary Committee . . . that have nothing to do with fighting terrorism."[134] At the bill's signing ceremony, President Clinton took the unusual step of criticizing the law he was enacting. Complaining that the bill "should have been stronger," the president listed the omission of provisions that his administration had sought. These included changes that would have enabled the FBI to follow terrorists across different telephones with a single court-ordered wiretap and would have granted FBI agents the same access to hotel, telephone, and other records of suspected terrorists that used-car dealers already had.[135]

The Presidential Decision Directives, moreover, did not succeed in forging an integrated government-wide counterterrorism strategy and did not begin to address any of the fundamental shortcomings identified by the FBI's own strategic plan or MAXCAP 05. Although Clinton's 1995 Presidential Decision Directive 39 listed preventing terrorist attack as one of its four cornerstone programs, the directive did not appear to envision a major FBI role in intelligence collection, analysis, or terrorism prevention.[136] Instead, the bureau was granted marching orders to continue what it had already been doing: investigating terrorist incidents after they occurred.[137] The Congressional Joint Inquiry found that the 1998 counterterrorism directives also had little impact.[138] Finally, relations between the FBI and the Clinton White House appear to have grown both distant and hostile by the end of 2000.[139] Director Freeh writes that between November 1997 and the bombing of the USS *Cole* in October 2000, high noon for the bureau's internal counterterrorism reform initiatives, he did not speak with the president once.[140]

The Bush administration remained just as disengaged. In 2001, the newly elected president retained but demoted Clinton's national counterterrorism czar, Richard Clarke, and launched an al Qaeda strategy review that focused on foreign policy, not domestic counterterrorism capabilities.[141] Although Bush ordered a vice presidential task force to examine domestic preparedness in May, his attorney general at the same time downgraded terrorism in the Justice Department's budget process.[142] FBI counterterrorism chief Dale Watson recalled that when he heard that gun crimes, narcotics trafficking, and civil rights had eclipsed terrorism on the Justice Department's budget priority list, he nearly fell out of his chair.[143]

In short, the disconnect between internal FBI reform efforts and presidential inaction is striking: while top officials inside the FBI were racing against time to transform the bureau, presidents were not.

Congress, meanwhile, neglected its oversight of the FBI. None of the major committees overseeing the FBI—the House and Senate Judiciary, Intelligence, and Appropriations Committees—took seriously the task of questioning the FBI's counterterrorism capabilities, assessing the bureau's progress in adapting to the terrorist threat, pressing for change inside the FBI, or passing new legislation. Between the start of the FBI's strategic planning process in 1997 and September 11, 2001, subcommittees of the House and Senate Appropriations Committees held a total of ten annual budget hearings in which legislators discussed FBI priorities and problems. Terrorism was almost never mentioned. Together, the House and Senate transcripts totaled approximately 139,000 words, only 118 of which were "terrorism" or "counterterrorism." To put these numbers into perspective, if one were to convert the hearing transcripts into a paperback book, it would be 385 pages long, with the words "terrorism" and "counterterrorism" filling less than a single page.[144] In March 1999, just seven months after the al Qaeda attacks on U.S. embassies in Africa, the Senate Appropriations Subcommittee spent more time discussing the bureau's plans to purchase a private plane than its counterterrorism efforts.[145]

Meanwhile, the Judiciary Committees, which had primary oversight for all Justice Department agencies, spent the 1990s responding to headlines and investigating a never-ending list of scandals rather than improving the FBI's counterterrorism capabilities.[146] These included the Ruby Ridge and Waco standoffs, the 1996 bungled investigation of the Atlanta Olympic bombings, the botched Wen Ho Lee counterintelligence investigation of 1999, the 2001 discovery that veteran FBI agent Robert Hanssen had been spying for the Russians, and the postponement of Timothy McVeigh's execution in the Oklahoma City bombing case in May 2001 after officials learned the FBI had inadvertently failed to turn over more than 4,400 pages of documents to McVeigh's defense attorneys. Between 1992 and 2001, the House and Senate Judiciary Committees held eighty-seven hearings where FBI officials were called to testify. Only fifteen of them focused on terrorism.[147] Indeed, the Judiciary Committees' efforts to help the FBI adapt to terrorism between 1995 and 2001 consisted of just two measures, both of them ineffective: blocking, and then funding, the ill-fated Trilogy information technology modernization program and passing the Antiterrorism and Effective Death Penalty Act in 1996,[148] a bill that was so watered down, it became known as the "better-than-nothing antiterrorism bill."[149]

As the terrorist threat grew and internal FBI reform efforts intensified, lawmakers paid even less attention to the bureau's counterterrorism problems. Six weeks before the September 11 attacks, the Senate Judiciary Committee held confirmation hearings for FBI Director nominee Robert Mueller. The substance of the hearings is revealing. For two days, fourteen senators peppered Mueller with ninety-four questions on topics ranging from bank fraud to racial profiling. Only three questions—all from a single senator, John Edwards (D-NC)—asked how the future FBI director planned to address terrorism. What's more, several members of the committee demonstrated a stunning lack of awareness of the FBI's counterterrorism mission, its declared priorities, or its ongoing problems. Senator Charles Schumer (D-NY) said he believed the FBI was doing "an excellent job as they always did" in terrorism investigations and asked whether the counterterrorism function had hurt other missions inside the bureau.[150] Senator Dianne Feinstein (D-CA) declared that the FBI director is "a job that I believe demands someone who can remain focused on the core mission of the bureau—solving crimes and catching criminals."[151] And Senator Jeff Sessions (R-AL) advocated rewarding agents for pursuing local law enforcement priorities rather than national ones such as terrorism.[152] On the eve of 9/11, three years after the launch of the strategic plan, and one year after MAXCAP 05 got underway, the committee charged with vetting the new FBI director, protecting the national interest, and ensuring the FBI's effectiveness spent more time demanding to know what the bureau was doing about parental kidnapping, digital piracy, and the number of agents in Wisconsin than the FBI's counterterrorism reform initiatives.[153]

The House and Senate Intelligence Committees did not fill the gap. Together, the committees held scores of open and closed hearings about other issues between 1998 and 2001, but only ten on counterterrorism.[154] The FBI does not appear to have been a major focus of any of them. One intelligence lawmaker bluntly admitted that the committees never saw the FBI's 1998 strategic plan, noting, "If Louis Freeh had some cosmic plan to reform the FBI, he never unveiled it to anyone I knew."[155] An Intelligence Committee staffer concurred. "The committees' forays into the FBI were episodic at best," the staffer said. "Enormous amounts of attention went into counterintelligence . . . but there was no systematic strategic look at what the FBI was doing in counterterrorism."[156] The 9/11 Commission called the Intelligence Committees' oversight "not impressive,"[157] and concluded that Congress as a whole did not do its job. "Congress gave little guidance to executive branch agencies," the commission noted, "did not reform them in any significant way, and did not systematically perform oversight to identify, address, and attempt to resolve the many problems in national security and domestic agencies that became apparent in the aftermath of 9/11."[158]

EXPLAINING ADAPTATION FAILURE IN THE FBI

The FBI's counterterrorism efforts tell a tragic tale of an agency that recognized a new threat, understood the imperative for organizational change, and tried but failed to adapt. As in the CIA's case, adaptation failure stemmed not from individual failures but systemic ones. Here, too, three enduring realities—the nature of organizations, rational self-interest, and the fragmented structure of the American federal government—explain why internal reforms did not succeed and why external reforms were never tried.

Reforming From Within

In many ways, the FBI was better equipped to undertake internal reform than the CIA. The director of central intelligence was supposed to manage thirteen different intelligence agencies, twelve of which were largely outside his statutory control. The FBI director, by contrast, had only one agency to run, and he came armed with a statutory ten-year term and strong legal authorities to get the job done. While the CIA operated mostly in the shadows, collecting and analyzing intelligence in secret, the FBI operated mostly in the open, requesting warrants, tailing suspects, and investigating cases according to extensive rules and procedures designed to protect civil liberties and maintain the public trust. For the CIA, managing the field meant overseeing clandestine agents in remote reaches of the world, places like Kandahar and Kuala Lumpur. For the FBI, it meant calling Kansas City.

Yet the FBI still found itself fighting a losing battle. Factors inherent in the nature of organizations—bounded rationality, structural secrecy, and the liability of time—explain why. Consider first bounded rationality, or the natural limits that often prevent even the best leaders from making optimal, adaptive decisions. Like the CIA, the FBI faced unavoidable and profound uncertainties about the changing nature of the world in the early 1990s. The CIA initially responded by instituting a mindless cost-cutting program. The FBI responded by clinging to its old crime-fighting mission. The agencies' responses were different, but their cause was the same: the Cold War had ended, but in the early 1990s no one had the information or capacity to know what might take its place.

Structural secrecy, the tendency of all organizations to divide work in ways that impede organizational learning, also played a large role. Like the CIA, the FBI was a tightly knit, highly decentralized organization. The bureau's fifty-six field offices were separate fiefdoms, run by SACs who called their own shots and all too often answered to no one. This structural fragmentation impeded adaptation in two major ways. First, it kept the bureau from knowing what it knew. Because individual field offices controlled their own cases, learning across offices was difficult, costly, and rarely done. This was particularly true in counterterrorism, where responsibility for bin Laden-related cases resided almost exclusively in the New York field office[159] and where very few field office heads in the rest of the United States had any counterterrorism experience.[160] As Dale Watson found, the field office structure made even straightforward tasks such as identifying baseline counterterrorism capabilities across the bureau excruciatingly difficult.

Second, the FBI's decentralized field office system fueled resistance to change. Recognizing the need for reform in a headquarters strategic planning document was one thing. Convincing fifty-six largely autonomous units to implement reform in the field was another. When Deputy Director Bear Bryant rolled out the bureau's new set of priorities, field offices ignored him. When a headquarters directive told field offices to send communications electronically rather than by hard copy, almost nobody complied.[161] Even after Director Freeh blessed Watson's MAX-CAP 05 counterterrorism program, many field offices continued to resist. The FBI's own review after 9/11 concluded that the field office structure "allowed . . . field offices to assign varying priorities and resource levels to terrorist groups and threats . . . impeded oversight by FBI leadership, and it complicated coordination with other federal agencies and entities involved in the war against terror."[162] Field office power was so strong that one year after September 11, the FBI's second in command, Bruce Gebhardt, complained in a memo that he was "amazed and astounded and at a loss to understand" why some offices were still failing to follow Director Mueller's clear orders to make counterterrorism their top priority.[163]

Finally, the passage of time made adaptation all the more difficult. The FBI had been chasing criminals for eighty-three years before the Soviet Union collapsed, and had been under the reigns of legendary Director J. Edgar Hoover for forty-seven of them, longer than the CIA had been in existence. By 1991, the bureau's law enforcement mission, procedures, career incentives, and culture had set like stone. From training to promotions to awards, FBI agents got the message that the traditional path of making arrests and working cases, not stopping attacks and analyzing intelligence, was the road to success. Throughout the 1990s, new agents continued to receive more time for vacation than counterterrorism training.[164] Career incentives still rewarded agents for arrests, indictments, and convictions, all of which were more likely products of traditional criminal investigations than lengthy terrorism investigations. Internal rules had for years prohibited analysts from being promoted to senior ranks.[165] And the bureau continued to give its most important rewards and recognition overwhelmingly to agents who were steeped in the bureau's old ways. Between 1992 and 2001, nearly a hundred FBI officials were honored with the federal government's highest Civil Service honor, a Presidential Rank Award.[166] These annual awards were no small matter, carrying prestige and a cash bonus equivalent to between 20 and 35 percent of the winner's annual salary. According to Carol Bonosaro, president of the Senior Executives Association, the awards were treated with exceptional fanfare at the FBI compared to other agencies. Winners had their photographs displayed outside the director's office for the following year and were honored at a special ceremony and reception hosted by the FBI director and the attorney general and attended by their families.[167] In short, the awards provide a useful gauge of FBI culture, of what it meant to be a star FBI agent, what kinds of work the bureau valued, and the extent to which these ideas changed over time.

Analysis of the awards reveals that old attitudes proved extraordinarily difficult to change. As table 6.1 shows, 59 percent of award recipients from 1992 to 2001 were recognized for outstanding criminal work, the FBI's traditional mission. Only 14 out of 92 award winners, or 15 percent of the total, were honored for work in counterterrorism and counterintelligence.

In addition, counterterrorism work continued to get little recognition even after 1997, when the FBI began highlighting its importance and launched major reform initiatives. As figure 6.2 shows, between 1997 and 2001, 55 percent of all presidential rank awards still recognized criminal work, while only 18 percent went to officials for counterintelligence and counterterrorism. Moreover, closer examination finds that awards for preventive work in counterintelligence and counterterrorism actually declined over time. Between 1992 and 1996, four of the five

TABLE 6.1

Criminal Focus of FBI Presidential Rank Award Winners, 1992–2001

Year	Criminal Awards	Counterterrorism, Counterintelligence Awards	Other	Total
1992	4	1	4	9
1993	8	1	2	11
1994	3	1	1	5
1995	5	1	1	7
1996	7	1	3	11
1997	7	0	4	11
1998	5	2	2	9
1999	4	3	4	11
2000	3	3	2	8
2001	8	1	1	10
Total	54	14	24	92
% of Total	59%	15%	26%	100%

Source: Textual analysis of Presidential Rank Award citations in annual FBI awards programs, 1992–2001.

counterintelligence and counterterrorism officials receiving Presidential Rank Awards were recognized for their outstanding preventive work. By contrast, only two of the nine counterintelligence and counterterrorism winners during the 1997–2001 period were honored solely for exceptional proactive efforts. The rest were recognized for conducting after-the-fact investigations and other more traditional activities. In short, while FBI reformers were urging new approaches, the bureau's highest honors were still showcasing old ways.[168]

Taken together, bounded rationality, structural secrecy, and the liability of time created powerful barriers to internal change. All organizations have a hard time adapting under the best of circumstances, and the FBI's circumstances were far from the best. In the early 1990s, FBI leaders faced an external environment that was radically different from the past but was harder to see and understand. By the late 1990s, when they finally recognized the threat and the urgent need to adapt, they could not. Switching priorities from crime to terrorism, getting cops to act like analysts, rewarding agents based on nonevents rather than

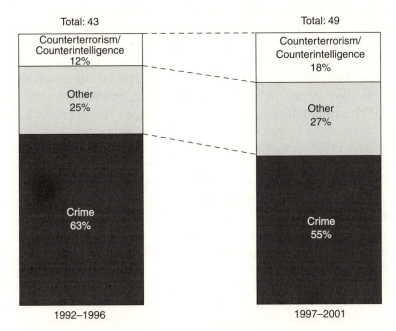

Figure 6.2. Comparison of FBI Presidential Rank Awards,
Early versus Late 1990s.
Source: Textual analysis of Presidential Rank
Award citations in annual FBI award programs, 1992–2001.

tangible statistics—all of these things hinged on the simultaneous cooperation of fifty-six autonomous field offices and meant undoing an organizational culture that had been carefully cultivated for nearly a hundred years.

Understanding the Absence of Action: Rational Self-Interest

Executive branch reform offered a second route to adaptation. Here, too, the FBI's story bears a strong resemblance to the CIA's. In both cases, presidents avoided reform and other executive branch officials undermined it. And in both cases, rational self-interest explains why.

Consider presidents first. In chapter 4, I showed how all three post–Cold War presidents, George H. W. Bush, Bill Clinton, and George W. Bush, were aware of the need for radical change in

151

the U.S. Intelligence Community but chose to make only minor changes through direct, unilateral executive actions. Their political agendas, personal beliefs, and individual leadership styles could not have been more different, but their cost-benefit calculations were driven by the same imperatives of office: all three presidents wanted to improve intelligence, but none wanted to incur the political costs of a major Pentagon fight or take valuable time away from other issues on their agendas.

In the FBI's case, three factors made reform costly from the president's perspective. The first was the bureau's public role. Reforming the FBI meant telling Americans that Hoover's G-men would be spending less time catching drug traffickers and violent criminals in their neighborhoods in order to find potential terrorist cells somewhere else that might never do anything. As one former FBI agent put it, "the FBI is a public institution. It can't stand with its hands in its pockets while gang murders are terrorizing the population of the community they serve. There is tremendous pressure to put every shoulder to the wheel to serve the community."[169]

The second factor was the politics of scandal. The 1990s were not good years for the Federal Bureau of Investigation, with Waco and Ruby Ridge followed by a seemingly endless parade of problems. Public trust in the FBI had eroded so much that even after the Oklahoma City bombing of 1995, President Clinton was unable to gain passage of his desired counterterrorism reforms. No one, it seems—not leftist members of the American Civil Liberties Union or right-wing members of the National Rifle Association—wanted to expand the powers of the agency that had made Waco a household name. After his failed 1996 effort, Clinton never tried again, for good reason. From the president's vantage point, FBI reform meant getting back to basics on the criminal side of the house—arresting people without killing them, reading suspects their rights before interrogating them, and providing documents to attorneys before a defendant ended up on death row. In the scandal-ridden climate of the 1990s, the political costs of improving the FBI's counterterrorism program were exceptionally high.

Third, and finally, reform meant taking on the FBI. The bureau was bound to oppose any presidential reform efforts that meant reversing traditional priorities, overhauling procedures, or transforming its age-old culture, and presidents knew it. In short, major executive overhaul risked public outrage, congressional opposition, and FBI resistance. Little wonder, given these three considerations, that Presidents Clinton and George W. Bush settled instead for broad interagency coordination directives and bottom-up reviews.

Rational self-interest also led Attorneys General Janet Reno and John Ashcroft to undermine reform. Like every other attorney general, these two officials were responsible for running the entire Department of Justice. And that meant focusing first and foremost on prosecutions, not prevention. In 1995, for example, Reno announced new guidelines to regulate the passing of information between criminal and intelligence investigations inside the FBI. Although the effects of these guidelines have been fiercely debated, their origins have not: they stemmed from fears that information gathered in the FBI's intelligence investigation of Russian spy Aldrich Ames was improperly shared with the bureau's own criminal investigators and that this transmittal could have jeopardized a conviction had the case gone to trial.[170] Concerned that important counterintelligence court cases might be lost in the future, Reno had Deputy Attorney General Jamie Gorelick issue guidelines that, in Gorelick's own words, "[went] beyond what is legally required."[171] The point is not whether these particular guidelines impeded information sharing—indeed, there is much evidence suggesting that culture, more than rules, stymied information sharing within the FBI and between the FBI and CIA. The point is that this attorney general, like every attorney general, faced competing interests when it came to intelligence and criminal investigations, and had powerful incentives to put criminal cases first.[172]

Although George W. Bush's attorney general, John Ashcroft, criticized Reno and Gorelick for issuing the guidelines after September 11,[173] Ashcroft faced the same incentives and reacted in much the same manner before the attacks occurred. As noted above, in the spring of 2001, Ashcroft deliberately downgraded terrorism in the Justice Department's budget request, declaring that traditional crimes such as drug trafficking would be higher priorities for the coming year.

In sum, rational self interest provides a compelling explanation for why two different administrations reacted to the terrorist threat in much the same way.

The Fragmented Federal Government

Legislation offered a third route to adaptation that was never
taken. In the CIA's case, rational self interest and the fragmented
structure of government ensured that intelligence reform would
be defeated by Pentagon supporters in the Armed Services Committees. In the FBI's case, these same forces guaranteed that FBI
reform would never be seriously considered at all. During the
1990s, responsibility for terrorism was splintered across at least
nineteen different congressional committees, with oversight of
the FBI divided among at least six: Appropriations, Intelligence,
and Judiciary Committees in both the House and Senate.

It was no secret that this fragmented oversight system desperately needed fixing. Restructuring the Congress was recommended in seven of the twelve intelligence and terrorism studies
between 1991 and 2001.[174] Yet Congress never acted. In fact, Congress was the only government entity that failed to implement a
single recommendation for reform during the decade—a record
worse than either the CIA's or the FBI's. As one former White
House official reflected, Congress's own organizational problems
erected serious barriers to change. "Every time a member of Congress stands up they say we have to reform intelligence, we have
to reform the State Department, it is time we integrate our economic policies, et cetera . . . you have to start with the committee
structure and nobody has ever been able to crack that."[175]

Because of this fragmented congressional committee system,
everyone seemed to think that overseeing the FBI's counterterrorism program was somebody else's job. One Intelligence Committee staffer noted, "the implicit deal was that the intelligence committees would deal with intelligence and judiciary would handle
the rest."[176] But Judiciary Committee members believed FBI intelligence issues fell under the Intelligence Committees' bailiwick.
The result was that before 9/11, oversight of the FBI's counterterrorism program was overlooked by both sets of committees.

Electoral incentives, moreover, impelled legislators to focus on
local concerns and headline scandals rather than the develop-

ment of long-term capabilities inside the FBI. As Phoenix Special Agent Kenneth Williams was writing his warning memo about bin Laden operatives at U.S. flight schools, members of the Senate Judiciary Committee were drafting questions for FBI director designate Robert Mueller about Ruby Ridge, Waco, and whether bank fraud and digital piracy could be made higher priorities.[177]

SUMMARY

The nature of organizations, rational self-interest, and the fragmented structure of the federal government made adaptation all but impossible for the FBI. Although "the light went on" for some inside the bureau, individual reformers, however prescient and powerful, were no match for an old, hidebound, proud, and decentralized law enforcement agency. Nor did they get much help. Rational self-interest kept presidents on the sidelines and encouraged Justice Department leaders to put criminal cases ahead of terrorism prevention. Congress, meanwhile, was too fragmented and too focused on investigating the scandal *du jour* to produce meaningful oversight or legislative reform.

CHAPTER 7

Evidence Teams at the Ready

THE FBI AND 9/11

> Someday someone will die . . . and . . . the public will not
> understand why we were not more effective and throw-
> ing every resource we had.
> —E-mail from New York FBI agent to FBI headquarters,
> August 29, 2001[1]

ON THE NIGHT OF September 11, 2001, as the World Trade Center lay smoldering nearby, an anguished New York FBI agent tested a hunch.[2] He submitted the name of hijacker Khalid al-Mihdhar to the bureau's information technology center to see what a search of public records would uncover. Within hours, the agent received al-Mihdhar's correct address in San Diego.[3]

Although the FBI had just nineteen days to find al-Mihdhar and his colleague, Nawaf al-Hazmi, before they hijacked Flight 77, time was not the FBI's greatest impediment. The FBI was. It turns out that al-Mihdhar and al-Hazmi were hiding in plain sight, using their real names on rental agreements, travel documents, bank accounts, credit cards, auto insurance, and telephone listings.[4] The two terrorists also were operating right under the FBI's nose, living with an FBI informant[5] and making contact with several targets of past and ongoing FBI counterterrorism investigations in San Diego over a period of several months.[6] None of this information was known before 9/11 because the FBI was not searching for it. No FBI official ever asked the San Diego field office, or the bureau's fifty-five other field offices, to query informants or check records for connections to the two operatives. Nobody asked the FBI's own white-collar crime unit or the treasury department's financial crimes enforcement network to search their databases for credit card and bank information, steps that helped quickly identify nearly all of the nineteen hijackers soon after the attacks.[7] And nobody in the bureau notified the Federal Aviation Administration (FAA) to include al-Mihdhar and al-Hazmi in the FAA's August 2001 security directives, which warned that terrorists might be traveling on commercial airlines and directed that anyone listed in the advisory be subjected to detailed searches of their persons, carry-on bags, and checked luggage before boarding.[8] Instead, the manhunt for the two terrorists was assigned to a single FBI office, New York. It was designated a low priority intelligence investigation rather than a high priority criminal investigation. It was labeled "routine,"[9] the lowest level of precedence.[10] And it was given to a junior agent who had never led an intelligence investigation before.[11] When al-Mihdhar and al-Hazmi boarded the airplane on the morning of September 11, the FBI was nowhere close to finding them.[12]

Al-Mihdhar and al-Hazmi began their journey by evading CIA surveillance abroad and ended it by escaping FBI detection at home. The two terrorists needed no secret identities or high tech gadgets to succeed. They needed only for the CIA and FBI to conduct business as usual. The adaptation failure of both agencies during the 1990s left the United States vulnerable to catastrophic terrorist attack.

In chapter 5, I traced the connection between the CIA's failure to adapt and its failure to perform, showing how debilitating organizational weaknesses prevented the agency from capitalizing on eleven different opportunities to penetrate and potentially disrupt the 9/11 plot. In this chapter, I conduct the same exercise for the FBI. The details are different but the story is all too familiar: organizational weaknesses sowed the seeds of failure. In the weeks before 9/11, FBI agents had twelve opportunities to penetrate and possibly stop al Qaeda's operation. Like the CIA, they missed them all. Structural weaknesses, cultural pathologies, and counterproductive incentives—all of the organizational problems that had eluded reform throughout the 1990s—explain why.

THE MANHUNT REVISITED

Organizational weaknesses go a long way toward explaining why the FBI conducted such a half-hearted effort to find al-Mihdhar and al-Hazmi nineteen days before September 11. From the outset, the bureau's decentralized structure ensured that what should have been a nationwide effort was instead the focus of a handful of people in a single FBI office. This particular case was not bungled. It was handled like every other: assigned to a lead FBI field office for investigation with little central oversight or coordination from headquarters.[13]

Culture also played an important role. It turns out that the FBI analyst who requested the manhunt actually believed the matter had some urgency. She was so worried about finding al-Mihdhar, in fact, that she called an agent in New York's bin Laden squad to alert him even before finishing her formal request. This was something she had never done before.[14] A few days later, she sent him an e-mail urging, "I . . . want to get this going as soon as possible."[15] In addition, when another counterterrorism agent pressed to have the manhunt opened as a full-scale, high priority criminal investigation, she explicitly considered the matter and sought legal advice. Yet she ultimately assigned the manhunt the lowest possible priority: a "routine" intelligence case. Why?

The answer lies in pervasive attitudes and beliefs, not individual errors. Like nearly all FBI officials, the analyst believed that criminal investigations—which are designed to solve past crimes—took precedence over intelligence investigations designed to gather information about possible future attacks. After September 11, the analyst told Justice Department officials that although she considered finding al-Mihdhar to be important, this investigation was "no bigger" than any other intelligence investigation at the time.[16] Good instincts led the analyst to take unusual steps to expedite the search, but old attitudes prevailed: when pressed to prioritize the manhunt relative to the bureau's traditional law enforcement work, she put down "routine."

Culture also explains why the analyst mistakenly designated the manhunt an intelligence investigation. Here the question involved "the wall," a set of laws and internal guidelines that regulated information sharing between two types of counterterrorism cases: criminal investigations seeking prosecution for specific past attacks and intelligence investigations seeking information about potential future attacks. In reality, the legal barriers to passing information across this divide were low. However, over time, the bureau's penchant for protecting information for trial had twisted reality, fostering the widespread belief that criminal and intelligence cases had to remain separate. In August 2001, the FBI analyst, her supervisor, and an FBI legal expert all believed that they were not allowed to authorize a full-scale criminal investigation to find the terrorists because the original tip about al-Mihdhar had come through intelligence channels.[17] They were wrong.[18] And they were not alone. Attorney General Janet Reno told the 9/11 Commission that information sharing problems throughout her tenure were rampant, severe, and stemmed from "agency culture and lack of understanding."[19]

Incentives, finally, made everything worse. Although the New York field office had unparalleled experience in terrorism cases, even there most resources went to investigating past attacks, not thwarting future plots. From October 2000 to June 2001, all but one of the agents in the office's Osama bin Laden squad were designated criminal agents who sought to prosecute terrorists for crimes that had already occurred.[20] This left just one person in the FBI's leading counterterrorism office to investigate information about all future al Qaeda plots. It was not considered an attractive assignment. The agent described himself as the squad's "leper," and was overwhelmed with work.[21] By August 29, 2001, when New York officially opened its investigation of al-Mihdhar and al-Hazmi, a second intelligence agent had joined the squad. He had just finished his rookie year in the bureau, had spent less than eight weeks on the bin Laden squad, and had never led an intelligence investigation before.[22] This junior agent was tapped for the manhunt because of his inexperience, not despite it. In an organization where convictions made careers, finding and interviewing two potential terrorists went to one of the office's least experienced investigators because it was one of the least desirable jobs.

In short, the bureau's structure, culture, and incentive system made it unlikely that al-Mihdhar or al-Hazmi would be found. The decentralized field office structure guaranteed that the alarm would be sounded in only one place. The FBI's law enforcement culture ensured that the alarm would be muffled by criminal cases and priorities. And incentives promised that those with the least experience and expertise would be answering the call. Although an all-out effort might not have succeeded in nineteen days, the bureau's half-hearted approach was destined to fail.

These same organizational problems prevented the FBI from capitalizing on eleven other opportunities between July and September 2001.

MISSED OPPORTUNITIES 2 AND 3: THE PHOENIX MEMO

In May 2001, a veteran FBI agent named Kenneth Williams began reading old files to get up to speed for his new counterterrorism assignment in Phoenix. He became increasingly alarmed by what he found: a large number of Islamist extremists enrolling in Arizona flight schools. Williams himself had interviewed one of them a year earlier, in April 2000. The subject had a poster of Osama bin Laden in his apartment and said he considered the United States government to be a legitimate target of Islam.[23] By the summer of 2001, Special Agent Williams realized that his subject was not an isolated case. On July 10, Williams sent a memo to six officials at FBI headquarters[24] and two agents on different international terrorism squads in the FBI's New York field office[25] warning that he believed "a coordinated effort by Usama bin Laden (UBL)" was underway "to send students to the United States to attend civil aviation universities and colleges."[26] The memo discussed ten individuals who were the subject of FBI investigations.[27] It also recommended that the bureau begin compiling lists of civil aviation colleges in the United States, establish relationships with those schools, consider seeking authority to obtain visa information about foreign flight school students, and most importantly, discuss the issue with other intelligence agencies so that they could gather additional information.[28]

The Phoenix memo produced two missed opportunities. The first was the chance to alert and engage a broader circle of FBI and intelligence officials about the terrorist threat two months before the attacks. Although the memo contained no direct warning of the September 11 plot, it was a timely and outstanding piece of strategic analysis that reached across cases, noticed a disturbing pattern with potentially serious implications for U.S.

national security, and recommended specific next steps to involve additional FBI field offices and other U.S. intelligence agencies. As FBI Director Robert Mueller later reflected, "You are not going to have a better intelligence product than the Phoenix memo."[29] But before 9/11, almost no one knew or did anything about it. The Congressional Joint Inquiry found that Williams's memo "generated little or no interest" at either FBI headquarters or the New York office.[30] It was sent to just one FBI field office, Portland, because one of the ten suspects had a connection to a local case.[31] It was never forwarded to any managers at FBI headquarters, the CIA, or any other intelligence agency.[32] As Director Mueller admitted, "the Phoenix memo should have been disseminated to all field offices and to our sister agencies, and it should have triggered a broader analytic approach."[33]

Second, the primary person named in the Phoenix memo turned out to be an associate of hijacker Hani Hanjour, but he was never investigated before September 11. FBI officials now believe that the two men trained in the same Arizona flight school beginning as early as 1997, continued meeting there at least until 2000, and may have reconnected in June 2001 as part of the September 11 operation.[34] But for bureaucratic reasons discussed below, this connection to the plot was never pursued before the attacks. The suspect was singled out in the Phoenix memo and then lost.

Missed Opportunities 4 and 5: Zacarias Moussaoui

One month later, the FBI missed perhaps its best chance to derail the September 11 attacks when Minneapolis field agents arrested a French citizen of Moroccan descent named Zacarias Moussaoui. Moussaoui has since admitted to being a member of al Qaeda, in April 2005 pleaded guilty to six counts of conspiracy to commit terrorism in the 9/11 plot, and in 2006 was sentenced to life in prison, becoming the only person convicted in the United States in connection with the attacks.[35]

The lucky break came on Wednesday, August 15, 2001, when an employee of the Pan American International Flight School called the local Minneapolis FBI field office about a suspicious foreign student who had paid more than $6,000 in cash for training on a Boeing 747 flight simulator but lacked all of the usual qualifications—including a pilot's license—and seemed unusually interested in the operation of the plane's doors, take-offs and landings.[36] Minneapolis field agents immediately opened an intelligence investigation, interviewed Moussaoui, and concluded that he, along with "others yet unknown" were probably plotting to seize control of an aircraft.[37] They were right. But they then made two crucial errors. First, instead of initiating surveillance of Moussaoui, agents quickly arrested him, losing a potentially valuable opportunity to uncover intelligence about the plot. As September 11 neared and the hijacking teams converged for their flights, Moussaoui was sitting in a Minnesota jail.

Second, Minneapolis field agents spent the next four weeks on a wild goose chase trying to get a warrant under the Foreign Intelligence Surveillance Act (FISA) to search Moussaoui's belongings.[38] They failed because they were operating in near total isolation and because FBI officials in both Minneapolis and headquarters misunderstood the legal requirements for investigating a suspected terrorist who had not yet committed a crime.

Whether different actions could have resulted in different outcomes will never be known. However, this much is clear: when officials searched Moussaoui's belongings after September 11, they found substantial evidence connecting him to Ramzi Binalshibh, one of the core planners of the September 11 plot;[39] nobody on the Moussaoui case knew about the Phoenix memo which could have expedited the warrant and raised questions about a broader al Qaeda operation;[40] and one other FBI field office had a terrorist in custody who could have quickly identified Moussaoui as an al Qaeda member before September 11, but he was never asked.[41]

MISSED OPPORTUNITIES 6, 7, 8, 9, 10, 11, AND 12: PULSING THE SYSTEM AND PUTTING PIECES TOGETHER

Finally, the FBI missed at least seven opportunities throughout the summer of 2001 to pulse the system and put the pieces together. In each case, the threat of a domestic terrorist attack caught the attention of someone somewhere in the FBI, but failed to trigger a broader effort to collect information, share information, or take stock of what the FBI already knew.

The first opportunity arose on July 2, when the FBI's Counterterrorism Division warned other federal agencies, as well as state and local law enforcement agencies, that terrorist attacks in the United States could not be discounted and recommended that personnel "exercise extreme vigilance" and "report specific activities" to the FBI.[42] Apparently, however, no plans were made inside the FBI to do anything with that information. Three days later, on July 5, FBI officials attended a special White House briefing for domestic security agencies about terrorist threat reporting, but took no follow-up steps to query field offices, meet with informants, or check case files to assess what agents across the bureau might know.[43] A third chance came on July 10, when Phoenix Special Agent Kenneth Williams sent his now famous memo to headquarters and the New York office warning that bin Laden might be sending al Qaeda operatives for U.S. flight training. Although Williams asked FBI officials to share his ideas with other U.S. intelligence agencies and take further steps to uncover links between al Qaeda and U.S. flight schools, the memo produced no action. Next, on a July 19 conference call with all fifty-six FBI field office heads, FBI Acting Director Thomas Pickard discussed the heightened terrorist threat level, but instead of asking for information or analysis about potential plots, he asked all field offices to have their evidence teams ready to deploy after an attack.[44] Pickard telephoned field office heads again between July 9 and 31 to discuss their performance evaluations.[45] Once more, he discussed the need to focus on terrorism. Again, however, he directed no proactive investigatory or analytic efforts. The vast majority of field office personnel said they did not perceive any sense of urgency.[46] Next, on August 15, news of the arrest of Zacarias Moussaoui was deemed important enough to reach the director of central intelligence, but was never disseminated to FBI field offices or relayed to senior officials in the FBI's own Counterterrorism Division.[47] Finally, on August 23, when headquarters officials learned that suspected al Qaeda operatives Khalid al-Mihdhar and Nawaf al-Hazmi had probably entered the United States, no steps were taken to determine whether the two might be connected to a broader network or plot.

At each of these junctures, various officials inside the FBI had pieces of information that could have prompted a more concerted investigation but did not. Field offices were not directed

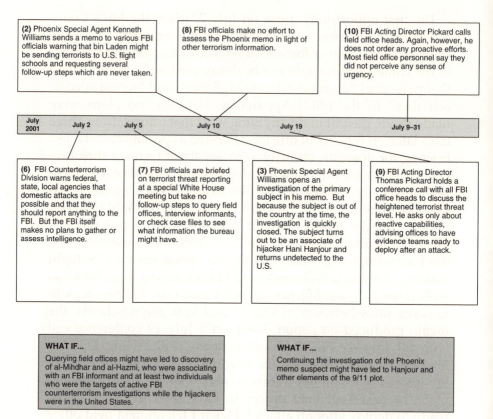

(2) Phoenix Special Agent Kenneth Williams sends a memo to various FBI officials warning that bin Laden might be sending terrorists to U.S. flight schools and requesting several follow-up steps which are never taken.

(8) FBI officials make no effort to assess the Phoenix memo in light of other terrorism information.

(10) FBI Acting Director Pickard calls field office heads. Again, however, he does not order any proactive efforts. Most field office personnel say they did not perceive any sense of urgency.

| July 2001 | July 2 | July 5 | July 10 | July 19 | July 9–31 |

(6) FBI Counterterrorism Division warns federal, state, local agencies that domestic attacks are possible and that they should report anything to the FBI. But the FBI itself makes no plans to gather or assess intelligence.

(7) FBI officials are briefed on terrorist threat reporting at a special White House meeting but take no follow-up steps to query field offices, interview informants, or check case files to see what information the bureau might have.

(3) Phoenix Special Agent Williams opens an investigation of the primary subject in his memo. But because the subject is out of the country at the time, the investigation is quickly closed. The subject turns out to be an associate of hijacker Hani Hanjour and returns undetected to the U.S.

(9) FBI Acting Director Thomas Pickard holds a conference call with all FBI office heads to discuss the heightened terrorist threat level. He asks only about reactive capabilities, advising offices to have evidence teams ready to deploy after an attack.

WHAT IF...
Querying field offices might have led to discovery of al-Mihdhar and al-Hazmi, who were associating with an FBI informant and at least two individuals who were the targets of active FBI counterterrorism investigations while the hijackers were in the United States.

WHAT IF...
Continuing the investigation of the Phoenix memo suspect might have led to Hanjour and other elements of the 9/11 plot.

Figure 7.1a. Timeline of the FBI's 12 Missed Opportunities.

to review files or contact informants for possible clues to a terrorist plot. Analysts were not tasked to assess what the FBI knew. Terrorists in custody were not canvassed. Surveillance was not initiated. Resources were not marshaled. Personnel were not alerted. The result was that threads went unnoticed and unconnected. To be sure, the threads were not ubiquitous or easy to follow. However, the Congressional Joint Inquiry concluded that the 9/11 hijackers had numerous links to a broader al Qaeda support network inside the United States that had already attracted the FBI's attention. Specifically, five of the hijackers—Khalid al-Mihdhar, Nawaf al-Hazmi, Hani Hanjour, Mohamed Atta, and Marwan al-Shehhi—may have had links to as many as fourteen extremists known to the FBI. Four of the fourteen were the targets of active FBI counterterrorism investigations while the hijackers were in the United States.[48] To give just

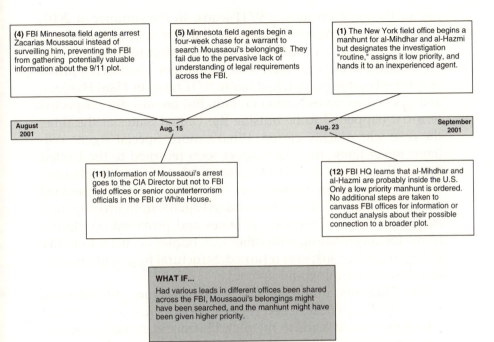

Figure 7.1b. Timeline of the FBI's 12 Missed Opportunities.

a few examples: One previous target of an FBI counterterrorism investigation housed al-Mihdhar and al-Hazmi, cosigned their lease, and held a welcome party for them in San Diego;[49] another extremist who was the subject of an active FBI investigation hired al-Hazmi to work for him;[50] a third, a local imam named Anwar Aulaqi[51] who was the target of an FBI counterterrorism inquiry at the time, became al-Hazmi and al-Mihdhar's spiritual advisor in San Diego, and reconnected with al-Hazmi in Virginia in the spring of 2001.[52] These and other links, however, were never uncovered before September 11 because the FBI never mobilized a coordinated effort to find them.

THE ORGANIZATIONAL ROOTS OF FAILURE

Organizational deficiencies prevented the FBI from capitalizing on all of these opportunities. First, structural fragmentation created an invisible barrier between terrorist investigations at home and abroad that kept one of the FBI's best agents from following one of the most promising 9/11 leads. In the summer of 2001, Phoenix Special Agent Kenneth Williams was onto something. He had detected a coordinated terrorist effort to train pilots in the United States, sent word to headquarters, identified a prime suspect who, it turns out, had ties to 9/11 hijacker Hani Hanjour, and opened an investigation on him. But because the suspected terrorist happened to be outside the United States at the time, the case was quickly closed. What's more, Special Agent Williams never knew that the suspect soon returned to the United States. The reason: once FBI targets traveled outside the country, they were considered somebody else's responsibility. Standard FBI operating procedures discouraged agents from investigating suspects outside of the United States and provided no mechanisms for coordinating with other U.S. border agencies to notify FBI agents when suspects returned. Structural fragmentation ensured that the trail would go cold.[53]

The FBI's decentralized field office structure proved even more crippling. Within a seven-week period, three different field offices uncovered leads to the plot. Phoenix identified a connection between bin Laden and flight schools, Minneapolis arrested a suspicious Jihadist who wanted to fly 747s, and New York began searching for two suspected al Qaeda operatives. Because of the autonomous field office structure, however, none of the agents working these cases knew about the others,[54] and most of the FBI's fifty-three other field offices didn't either.[55] As a result, tantalizing clues surfaced, only to disappear again. Moussaoui's belongings went unsearched when a terrorist in custody could have identified him from al Qaeda's Afghan training camps. A New York agent began searching for al-Mihdhar and al-Hazmi in New York Marriott Hotels[56] completely unaware that the San Diego field office had an informant and several other subjects of past and open counterterrorism investigations who knew both operatives.

These and other dots were never connected because the FBI's organization was designed to keep them apart. FBI field offices were built and expected to work independently, not together. They were designed to pursue individual cases in discrete jurisdictions, not broad plots that spanned the country. And they were given broad latitude to operate, with little direction or oversight from headquarters. This decentralized structure was optimally suited for the FBI's old mission, giving agents great independence to solve criminal cases one by one. For counterterrorism, however, it was a setup for disaster.

The FBI's law enforcement culture also proved debilitating. In all of the missed opportunities described above, FBI officials from top to bottom made the same kinds of mistakes for the same reasons. They pursued specific cases without considering broad trends, favored reaction over prevention, and sought to protect information for trial rather than share it. Officials in headquarters and New York dismissed the Phoenix's memo's strategic analysis because it offered little help with current investigations. Director Pickard urged field offices to be ready to respond to an attack, but never said anything about taking steps to prevent one. A Minneapolis field agent arrested Zacarias Moussaoui because all of his Criminal Division experience told him that arresting a suspect would stop the illegal activity—in his words, it would "freeze the situation."[57] It seems the agent never seriously considered the possibility that Moussaoui was more valuable under surveillance than in jail or that arresting him would freeze the FBI more than the enemy. Finally, officials throughout the bureau misunderstood and misapplied information sharing rules—delaying the Moussaoui warrant and depriving the manhunt of critical resources—because they were steeped in a culture that erred on the side of protecting information so that it could be used in court. The FBI missed all of these clues to 9/11 because most officials were viewing events during the summer of 2001 as they always had: through law enforcement lenses.

Incentives reinforced the worst aspects of FBI culture, encouraging officials to put traditional criminal cases before counterterrorism and operational priorities ahead of strategic analysis. For agents interested in rising up the ranks, the key to success was closing criminal cases, not pondering possible terrorist attacks. As a result, the best agents usually avoided counterterrorism and the best counterterrorism agents usually avoided doing strategic analysis. As Special Agent Williams told Congress, he realized his Phoenix memo would likely go to "the bottom of the pile," because it dealt with the lowest of the bureau's priorities: longer-term analysis in counterterrorism.[58]

Had the memo gone to the top of the pile, moreover, there were few analysts capable of doing much with it. By the summer of 2001, years of personnel policies that relegated analysts to support staff and prevented them from being promoted to senior ranks had taken their toll. In the words of one FBI analyst, the bureau's strategic analysis unit was "on its last legs,"[59] with poor quality products and just one person assigned to handle everything related to al Qaeda.[60] Other pieces of information were not put together in the summer of 2001 for the same reason: thanks to career incentives, there were very few people who could do the job, and even fewer who could do it well.[61] As FBI Assistant Director for Counterterrorism Dale Watson later told Congress, he found not one instance where FBI analysts produced "an actual product that helped out."[62]

At the same time, incentives discouraged field agents from connecting the dots on their own because the bureau's obsolete information technology systems made any search for information exceedingly difficult, time consuming, and ineffective. When Special Agent Williams wrote his Phoenix memo, for example, he was unaware that the FBI had issued several earlier reports expressing similar concerns about terrorists studying at U.S. flight schools because the FBI had no central, user-friendly database to search for relevant cases or reports.[63] Indeed, many agents found FBI computer systems so unreliable that they stopped using them altogether.[64] These technology problems made a bad situation worse. Case agents were already inclined by culture and career advancement to eschew broader analysis and concentrate on individual cases. The bureau's antiquated technology meant that undertaking cross-case analysis would require a superhuman effort.

Summary

The bureau had twelve known chances to follow leads that hinted at impending disaster. In each case, FBI officials missed the lucky break. Organizational factors explain why. Splintered into separate field offices, rewarded for other priorities and blinded by law enforcement culture, the FBI could not make the most of what it had. The FBI's nagging organizational weaknesses gave the 9/11 hijackers the upper hand.

The More Things Change . . .

What's needed for the fix is known. But is it accepted?
Not generally. And is it well on the way to getting implemented? Not at all. Can we say we're really on the way
to remedying the problems that got us into the deep shit
we're in? The answer is no. But we have to. There is no
other way.

—Former senior intelligence official[1]

Hᴜᴛᴏʀʏ ꜱᴜɢɢᴇꜱᴛꜱ that transformative change rarely occurs
during ordinary times. Instead, dramatic departures from the
past often require a large external shock—a tragedy, catastrophic
failure, scandal, or focusing event that challenges conventional
wisdom and exposes the dangers of the status quo. Examples
abound. The Civil War led to ratification of the Thirteenth, Four-
teenth, and Fifteenth Amendments of the U.S. Constitution. The
Great Depression produced Roosevelt's New Deal. World War
II gave rise to the CIA, the United Nations, and the Marshall
Plan. The Cuban missile crisis of 1962 ushered in an era of dé-
tente between the United States and the Soviet Union. By this
reasoning, the adaptation failure of U.S. intelligence agencies before 9/11 may not be surprising. But adaptation failure after
9/11 is. If ever we would expect to find a catalyst for major
change, the worst terrorist attack in U.S. history should be it. As
one senior government official remarked, "You can talk about
how we missed watchlisting two guys, that information sharing
wasn't what it should have been, that there were cultural differences between the FBI and CIA. But find me a time when the
world went to war without a galvanizing event."[2]

Yet nearly six years after 9/11, the Intelligence Community's
most serious deficiencies remain. In this chapter, I examine the
missed opportunities to overhaul the U.S. Intelligence Community since the attacks, the current state of intelligence capabili-

ties, and prospects for the future. Such assessments are always incomplete. Only a rearview mirror in a distant future will reveal how many plots al Qaeda hatched, how many were stopped, and what U.S. capabilities, policies, and actions made a difference. And that's to say nothing of what new enemies may emerge. As one former intelligence official ruefully noted, "By the time we master the al Qaeda problem, will al Qaeda be the problem?"[3] International politics is rife with uncertainty.

Nevertheless, two things are already clear: 9/11 was not enough to jolt U.S. intelligence agencies out of their Cold War past, and future adaptation—to terrorism or any other threat—is unlikely. The nature of organizations, rational self-interest, and the fragmented federal government make intelligence agencies exceptionally impervious to reform, even after catastrophic failure. Adaptation is not impossible, but it is close.

Adaptation Failure since 9/11

There have been two rounds of opportunities to transform U.S. intelligence agencies since 9/11. The first lasted a little more than a year. Between the attacks and December 2002, Congress and the president passed the USA PATRIOT Act, created the Department of Homeland Security, and the Congressional Intelligence Committees launched their Joint Inquiry of 9/11. What policymakers did not do was tackle intelligence overhaul. In the nation's darkest hour, when prospects for intelligence reform were brightest, elected officials chose to place their energies elsewhere. As we shall see, this was no accident; incentives and institutional fragmentation created strong pressures for President Bush and congressional leaders to avoid rather than confront the Intelligence Community's worst problems.

Round two began in July 2004, when the convergence of an extraordinary set of circumstances thrust intelligence reform back onto the political agenda. Again, a sudden turn of events raised the possibility of dramatic change. And again, it was not enough. Although Congress attempted to pass a major restructuring of the Intelligence Community, the 2004 reform bill was obstructed by the same forces that had thwarted reform for decades: bureaucratic resistance, tepid presidential support, and opposition from key congressional committee chairmen who stood to lose and had the power to resist. The Intelligence Reform and Terrorism Prevention Act of 2004 started with high hopes but ended up producing only modest changes.

ROUND ONE: AVOIDING REFORM, 2001 TO 2002

On the evening of September 11, 2001, with smoke still billowing from the Pentagon, congressional leaders gathered on the Capitol steps. Standing shoulder to shoulder, Democrats and Republicans expressed a newfound bipartisanship and a determination to fight terrorism. They then burst into a spontaneous chorus of "God Bless America." Several days later, the *New York Times* wrote that Washington was experiencing a "disaster-driven level of bipartisan civility not seen here in decades."[4] The moment seemed ripe for a major transformation of U.S. intelligence agencies.

Nobody seized the opportunity. Inside Congress, the House and Senate Intelligence Committees decided to investigate the terrorist attacks before considering reform legislation.[5] After twelve expert reports and hundreds of recommendations urging extensive intelligence reforms during the previous ten years, Congress's intelligence watchdog committees announced that they needed to study the issues more. Meanwhile, the White House spent the first forty-five days after 9/11 pressing for the USA PATRIOT Act, which granted the FBI and other law enforcement agencies a number of authorities that had been proposed and scuttled in previous years.[6] In the aftermath of tragedy, both the White House and Congress settled for a quick fix. "The administration wanted to look like they were doing something . . . but there was no effort to connect the contributing factors of 9/11 and what the PATRIOT Act would solve,"[7] noted one congressional staffer. Others agreed. "Everyone wants to do something," said one former FBI official. "It's human dynamics. Logic and common sense are not a part of the formula."[8] Six weeks after 9/11, the new law sailed through Congress with astonishing speed and little debate. Only a single senator, Russ Feingold (D-WI), voted against it.[9] As the FBI official noted, "If you're a member of Congress, following a tragedy like 9/11, are you going to vote against the *PATRIOT Act*?"[10] (emphasis his).

In the following year, the president and Congress missed three more chances to reform the U.S. Intelligence Community. The first came in November 2001, when General Brent Scowcroft delivered a classified report to the White House urging radical overhaul.[11] Scowcroft was no ordinary messenger. He had served as national security advisor to two presidents (Gerald Ford and George H. W. Bush), was considered one of the best informed and most well respected foreign policy officials in Washington, and had recently been appointed chairman of the President's Foreign Intelligence Advisory Board. Scowcroft's report, moreover, had been requested by President Bush himself in May 2001, four months before September 11, as an independent, comprehensive review of U.S. intelligence capabilities.[12] Now, eight weeks after the attacks, Scowcroft turned in his recommendations. They were bold. He urged stripping the three largest defense intelligence agencies from the Pentagon—the National Reconnaissance Office, which builds and runs spy satellites; the National Security Agency, which intercepts signals communications; and the National Imagery and Mapping Agency, which handles imagery and mapping[13]—and placing them directly under the control of the director of cental intelligence.[14] The idea was to give the director of central intelligence real power "to direct" the entire Intelligence Community, "not plead and cajole," said one former official familiar with the report.[15]

Pentagon reaction was swift and lethal: Secretary of Defense Donald Rumsfeld hated the idea.[16] As one former intelligence official paraphrased, "Rumsfeld says 'No fucking way.' He tells Scowcroft to put it into the wastepaper basket."[17] The proposal quickly died.

The next opportunity came in June 2002, when President Bush proposed the creation of a Department of Homeland Security. The move signaled a major policy reversal for the president, who had initially preferred integrating homeland security efforts in a small White House office rather than creating a massive new cabinet department. But with pressure mounting on Capitol Hill to do more, with congressional midterm elections just months away, and with Senator Joe Lieberman's democratic homeland security department bill gaining momentum in Congress, the president had to act fast. On June 6, he abruptly announced a proposal to merge twenty-two different agencies, including the Coast Guard, Customs Service, Immigration and Naturalization Service, Federal Emergency Management Agency (FEMA) and the recently created Transportation Security Administration, into a new homeland security department. "Employees of this new agency," the president announced in a nationally televised address, "will come to work every morning knowing their most important job is to protect their fellow citizens."[18] It would be the largest government reorganization since the 1940s.

Once more, intelligence reform was not a major part of the plan. The overriding purpose of the Homeland Security Department was identifying and protecting critical U.S. targets from terrorist attack, improving emergency response to disasters, and integrating border patrol functions, not revamping the U.S. intelligence system. Although the president's proposal included an intelligence division within the new department, its role was limited and its capabilities weak. The Homeland Security Department's Information Analysis and Infrastructure Protection (IAIP) division was an analysis shop only, charged with analyzing foreign and domestic terrorism threat reporting and assessing U.S. vulnerabilities. It had no power to collect intelligence. It had no tasking authority over other agencies. And it had no ability to knock bureaucratic heads together. Rather than integrating the CIA, FBI, and other intelligence agencies, IAIP was beholden to them for information.[19] Moreover, it was housed outside the DCI's control and inside a behemoth new department whose consolidation was expected to take years.[20] With twenty-two human resource service centers,[21] more than eighty different financial management applications,[22] and 170,000 employees whose jobs ranged from inspecting plants to distributing hurricane relief supplies, the Department of Homeland Security was not likely to produce crack intelligence analysis any time soon. Many feared, in the words of one counterterrorism official, that DHS "[wouldn't] know its ass from its elbow."[23]

Even without intelligence reform in the mix, the homeland security bill proved contentious. By the summer of 2002, business as usual was already returning to Washington. Agencies targeted for absorption in the new department, as well as the congressional committees that oversaw them, began slicing and dicing the president's proposal to protect their own pieces. Secretary of Health and Human Services Tommy G. Thompson launched a campaign behind the scenes to keep units rather than cede them to DHS. "Make sure this doesn't happen!" he told one of his deputies.[24] In Congress, turf trumped party loyalty; Republican-led committees in the House picked apart virtually every aspect of the president's bill. The Judiciary Committee voted against moving the Secret Service to the new department, and also voted to split the Immigration and Naturalization Service in half, moving only part of it to DHS. The Transportation and Infrastructure Committee voted to keep FEMA and the Coast Guard out entirely. The Ways and Means Committee agreed to let the Customs Service move only if the Treasury Department retained management authority over it. In addition, a bitter partisan feud erupted, with Democrats pressing to extend federal employment protections to homeland security workers and Republicans blasting them during an election season for being soft on national security. In the end, it took extensive lobbying (including an unprecedented joint visit to Congress by the administration's top four cabinet officers, Secretary of State Colin Powell, Defense Secretary Donald Rumsfeld, Attorney General John Ashcroft, and Treasury Secretary Paul O'Neill), some bitter wrangling, and the help of the Republican leadership in Congress—which established a special nine-member panel to write the House bill and stacked it with administration supporters who overruled committee votes—to secure passage of the Homeland Security Act of 2002.[25]

No sooner had the ink dried then the president circumvented DHS's new intelligence directorate. On January 28, 2003, just days after swearing in Tom Ridge as the first Secretary of Homeland Security, Bush announced the creation of a new Terrorist Threat Integration Center (TTIC) in his State of the Union address. TTIC ("T-TIC") would report directly to the director of central intelligence and would be responsible for terrorism threat analysis, the same functions that had been assigned to the Homeland Security Department's Information Analysis and Infrastructure Protection Directorate. Ridge was stunned. His deputies were furious. "It was as if the White House created us and then set out to marginalize us," one later recalled.[26] Confusion was rampant. Senators Susan Collins (R-ME) and Joseph Lieberman (D-CT), the chair and ranking members of the Senate Homeland Security and Governmental Affairs Committee, quickly held hearings[27] where they demanded "critically important information about the structure of the Terrorist Threat Integration Center, and how it and other key agencies would share responsibility for the collection, analysis, and dissemination of terrorism-related intelligence."[28] Nearly a year later, little had been settled. "The very fact of TTIC's creation," noted a Markle Foundation expert task force in December 2003, "has caused confusion within the federal government and among state and local governments about the respective roles of TTIC and the DHS."[29]

In short, fourteen months after September 11, the president and Congress passed a major homeland security bill which failed to remedy any of the organizational shortcomings in U.S. intelligence that had left the United States so vulnerable to terrorist attack. The Homeland Security Act of 2002 did not integrate the Intelligence Community, improve human intelligence, change agency incentives and cultures to enhance information sharing, reform the FBI, or match intelligence resources against priorities. What's more, before any ribbons were cut, DHS's intelligence directorate was stripped of its primary function. The Homeland Security Department's Information Analysis and Infrastructure Protection directorate was weak by design and undermined before it ever began.

The fourth and final opportunity for intelligence reform occurred in December 2002, when the Congressional Joint Inquiry issued its final report about the September 11 attacks. The report's nineteen recommendations included establishing a powerful new director of national intelligence, revamping the intelligence priority process, and considering whether a new domestic intelligence agency should replace the FBI. But by then, the momentum for reform was gone. As former Bush Deputy Homeland Security Advisor Richard Falkenrath observed, the report's recommendations "were ignored."[30] Intelligence reform went nowhere for the next year and a half.

The Limits of Catastrophe

In each of these four episodes, crisis was not enough. During the first year after 9/11, lawmakers went 0 for 4 on intelligence reform. These failures were not for lack of information or urgency.

Days after the attacks, as the president and Congress rushed to draft the USA PATRIOT Act, reports were already surfacing about more far-reaching problems in the Federal Bureau of Investigation.[31] In November, at the very moment Defense Secretary Donald Rumsfeld was trashing Scowcroft's sweeping intelligence reform plan behind closed doors, even the *New York Times* editorial page was calling for "radical change."[32] And throughout the fall of 2002, as Bush administration officials lobbied for a new Department of Homeland Security, the House and Senate Intelligence Committees' Joint Inquiry released staggering details about the Intelligence Community's failures leading up to the 9/11 attacks.[33] "[T]he Community made mistakes prior to September 11 and the problems that led to those mistakes need to be addressed and to be fixed," declared Joint Inquiry Staff Director Eleanor Hill.[34] But problems weren't fixed. Intelligence deficiencies were everywhere in the headlines but nowhere on the political agenda.

This was more than a case of bad luck or timing. A track record that poor with tragedy so recent and reforms so urgently needed suggests something more systematic at work. Closer examination reveals that the same enduring realities that prevented adaptation before 9/11 stymied adaptation afterward.

In the weeks following the attacks, elected officials faced strong pressure to do something. But they responded to this pressure in ways that maximized electoral returns and minimized political costs. For the House and Senate Intelligence Committees, this meant investigating what went wrong rather than pushing massive legislative overhaul. Studying the problem had the advantage of demonstrating fast action and resolve without triggering opposition and almost certain defeat by the Congressional Armed Services Committees. As one congressional intelligence staffer bitterly complained in the spring of 2002, "we suck at getting things done. . . . We're a subcommittee of armed services. They swallow our bills."[35]

The same logic explains why 9/11 prompted the president and Congress to pass the PATRIOT Act instead of instituting more sweeping changes to the FBI and the rest of the Intelligence Community. Throwing together old proposals to enhance the FBI's legal authorities was far easier than mandating new and far-reaching changes inside the bureau. Increasing investigatory powers was an FBI crowd pleaser. Demanding that agents do their jobs in fundamentally different ways was quite another matter. The PATRIOT Act made improvements and headlines without making tough choices or raising the hackles of the FBI. From the perspective of executive branch officials and members of Congress, the new law was an ideal response to 9/11. From a national security perspective, it was a squandered opportunity to do more.

Rational self-interest and structural fragmentation also led the president to dismiss reform recommendations from the very intelligence study he had requested. When General Scowcroft submitted his intelligence restructuring plan in November 2001, Secretary of Defense Rumsfeld vehemently opposed it and the president quickly scrapped it. This should not be surprising. Turf-conscious Defense Department officials had been rejecting the same types of reforms for years, and for years presidents had capitulated to their demands, concluding that intelligence reform was not worth the fight. The post-9/11 period was no different. If anything, the costs of intelligence reform may have been even higher: With the onset of military operations in Afghanistan, the president could ill-afford to pick a fight with the Pentagon and its supporters on Capitol Hill.

It should also come as no surprise that when pressure finally forced the president to reorganize the government, he took the path of least resistance. For months, Bush had opposed the creation of a new homeland security department, changing his mind only when it appeared that a democratic bill might pass Congress without his support. Including intelligence reform would have made a difficult government reorganization bill impossible. As it was, the president had to fight hard to win.

Instead, like so many presidents before him, Bush settled for a lower cost approach to intelligence reform: using his unilateral powers of office to mitigate a handful of problems where the odds of success were high and the opposition weak. From September 2001 to August 2004, the president studiously avoided getting embroiled with the Defense Department, opting instead to direct more minor changes through executive orders and announcements. The most significant of these were an executive order tasking the U.S. attorney general with improving coordination of terrorist tracking efforts—an initiative that was still floundering four years later—and the establishment of TTIC.[36] From the president's vantage point, such changes were far more attractive than the alternatives. The Terrorist Threat Integration Center, for example, could be stood up overnight with staff from existing agencies. It could report directly to the director of central intelligence rather than another cabinet official. It required no approval from congressional committees or their powerful chairmen. It posed no serious threat to the Pentagon. And it usurped the power of the one department incapable of fighting back—the Department of Homeland Security, which had not yet opened for business. Like his predecessors, President Bush calculated the costs and benefits of his alternatives. He chose intelligence solutions that were easy and quick instead of difficult and permanent. Catastrophic failure was not enough to alter incentives and institutional realities.

ROUND TWO: THE REFORM THAT WASN'T, 2004

Intelligence reform appeared all but dead until July 2004, when three factors suddenly converged: Director of Central Intelligence George Tenet resigned; the Senate Intelligence Committee issued a scathing report criticizing prewar intelligence assessments of Iraq's weapons of mass destruction;[37] and the 9/11 Commission released its final report.

Together, these three events temporarily suspended the enduring realities that normally impede legislative reform. While bureaucrats ordinarily fiercely oppose such changes, Tenet's resignation removed the Intelligence Community's staunchest and most public defender. During the summer and fall of 2004, as the 9/11 Commission and 9/11 families' groups took aim at U.S. intelligence agencies, there was no public face to defend them. At the same time, the Senate Intelligence Committee's Iraq report momentarily shifted the electoral incentives for members of Congress. During ordinary times, most legislators have little reason to champion intelligence reform, while lawmakers serving on the Armed Services Committees have every reason to block it. But the Senate report was released in the middle of a national election campaign with a tight presidential race, and it linked intelligence failures to an issue that was then gripping the nation: whether legislators had voted to authorize the war in Iraq based on flawed intelligence.[38] Questions about intelligence failures and the Iraq War dogged congressional candidates on the campaign trail everywhere from New York to Nebraska. Intelligence reform was no longer about abstract organizational charts, but about how to avoid making mistakes that were costing American soldiers their lives.

Finally, the 9/11 Commission and the 9/11 families' organizations served as powerful interest groups, lobbying lawmakers and using public media to press their reform agenda. Between July 22, when the commission released its final report, and December 10, 2004, two days after Congress passed the Intelligence Reform and Terrorism Prevention Act, the commission and the families received more national television news coverage than the war in Iraq.[39] These were the first intelligence reform interest groups in U.S. history, and they were powerful forces for change. In interviews, several officials involved in post-9/11 intelligence reform efforts said that the families and the commission were crucial. "It was the kind of ultimate pressure," said one.[40]

Even with all of these advantages, however, the intelligence reform bill was nearly derailed and ultimately diluted by the same forces that had defeated similar efforts for years: vigorous opposition from the Defense Department and prodefense lawmakers on the Congressional Armed Services Committees, and tepid support by the president. Rational incentives and structural fragmentation once again led to disappointment. The 2004 Intelligence Reform and Terrorism Prevention Act produced only modest changes.

The Pentagon: "Trashing Everything."

In the fall of 2004, just like the 1992 and 1996 reform episodes, Defense Department officials savaged legislative proposals to create a powerful new director of national intelligence and streamline the Intelligence Community—two of the principal recommendations of the 9/11 Commission—because these changes threatened to undermine Pentagon control over defense intelligence agencies and the lion's share of the intelligence budget. According to Republican Representative Christopher Shays (R-CT), Secretary of Defense Donald Rumsfeld "just trashed everything about the national intelligence director," in private meetings on Capitol Hill.[41] Other lawmakers from both parties issued similar assessments. One Democrat described Rumsfeld as someone who "was not at all enthusiastic about intelligence reform."[42] Another Republican angrily noted, "the Pentagon for months was working behind the scenes to derail the bill."[43]

The Pentagon's public campaign was equally damaging. Representative Jane Harman (D-CA), the ranking Democrat of the House Intelligence Committee and one of the chief architects of the 2004 reform bill, later remarked, "No one missed the big fights when we were doing the intel reform law with the Pentagon. If any of you missed it, I'm not sure what planet you were on."[44] One key salvo came on October 21, when General Richard Myers, chairman of the Joint Chiefs of Staff, delivered a bombshell letter to House Armed Services Committee Chairman Duncan Hunter (R-CA). In the letter, Myers opposed giving the proposed director of national intelligence strong budgetary authorities over intelligence agencies housed in the Pentagon, arguing that only a Pentagon-controlled budget would ensure sufficient "support to the warfighters."[45] It was a move taken right out of the Defense Department's intelligence reform opposition playbook. In 1992 and 1996, when intelligence reform bills started gathering momentum in Congress, senior defense officials used similar arguments in similar letters sent to Congressional Armed Services Committee chairmen. Both times, the letters helped deliver death blows to the bills.[46]

Although supporting the warfighter proved to be an effective public relations argument, it was a red herring: in reality, nothing in the proposed reforms threatened to disrupt the military chain of command. The real threat was to Pentagon dominance over intelligence collection agencies, a dominance that had over time gutted the Intelligence Community's ability to produce strategic intelligence that anticipated threats and sought to keep warfighters off the battlefield in the first place. Senator Pat Roberts (R-KS), chairman of the Senate Intelligence Committee, drove the point home on national television. Appearing on the November 21, 2004 edition of *Fox News Sunday*, Roberts declared, "I want to point something out. You know, I'm a former Marine. There are no ex-Marines. I am a former Marine, all right? I serve on the Armed Services Committee." His voice grew louder and his tone more angry as he continued: "No bill that I have seen . . . had anything to do with doing any harm to tactical intelligence in regards to that warfighter in the field. . . . There is no reason, if we do intelligence reform, that these agencies we are talking about, these so-called combat support agencies, will not continue to support the warfighter. Nobody is against that."[47]

Despite such rebuttals, intelligence reform still made little headway. As in earlier efforts, Pentagon opposition in 2004 had powerful allies on the House and Senate Armed Services Committees and other prodefense lawmakers who feared diminishing their own jurisdictions if intelligence reform succeeded. Opposition from House Armed Services Committee Chairman Duncan Hunter (R-CA) and House Judiciary Chairman James Sensenbrenner (R-WI) grew so strong that on November 20, House Speaker Dennis Hastert (R-IL) pulled the intelligence reform bill from floor consideration. Senator Susan Collins (R-ME), one of the champions of intelligence reform, called November 20 "the weakest moment" in the 2004 reform battle.[48]

The President: "Get This Thing off our Backs."

The 2004 intelligence reform bill also drew lukewarm public support from the president. "The president was not engaged," declared one democratic lawmaker. "For a long time the White House was in denial about the failure."[49] In press reports and interviews, officials and staffers in both parties agreed.[50] As one former Republican official put it, "The president . . . did absolutely nothing to stop Defense Department lobbying and did not engage after that time. . . . It was less the White House feeling the compulsion to do something. It was, 'Get this thing off our backs.' "[51] Here, too, rational self-interest was to blame. President George W. Bush, like all presidents since Harry Truman, knew that successful intelligence reform required battling, and defeating, his own Department of Defense. Former Senator Gary Hart (D-CO) described the persistence of presidential reluctance this way:

> Imagine the president sitting in the room with a secretary of defense, Harry. The director of central intelligence says, "Mr. President, I cannot do my job unless I have authority over the entire range of intelligence." That's going to require Secretary of Defense

Harry down the table there to give up his intelligence agencies. I'm asking you to introduce legislation to get this to happen." Harry down the table is going to say, "Mr. President, if you do that, you'll destroy the Pentagon." That's just the kind of conversation that goes on.[52]

Congress ultimately passed the Intelligence Reform and Terrorism Prevention Act in December 2004, which created a new director of national intelligence and National Counterterrorism Center, among other changes. However, Pentagon opposition forced lawmakers to weaken substantially the new intelligence chief's legal authorities over two vital levers: control over budgets and personnel across the Intelligence Community. As one former official put it, "the language is fuzzy on both. . . . You're right back to cajoling, wheedling, trying to get cooperation."[53]

A LACK OF PROGRESS REPORT

Six years after the World Trade Center and Pentagon attacks, the U.S. Intelligence Community's worst problems endure. Although legislative, executive, and internal agency initiatives have made many changes to U.S. intelligence agencies, most have created halting progress. Some have made matters worse. None could be declared successes yet. In March 2005, three and a half years after 9/11, the Commission on the Intelligence Capabilities of the United States regarding Weapons of Mass Destruction (the Silberman-Robb Commission) released a report about another intelligence failure: analysis of Iraqi weapons of mass destruction in the run-up to the 2003 Iraq War. The commission found that the Intelligence Community was "dead wrong in almost all of its pre-war judgments."[54] The commission also found the causes of failure to be systemic. Despite the "laudable steps" taken to improve U.S. intelligence agencies, the commission noted that, "we believe that many within those agencies do not accept the conclusion that . . . the Community needs fundamental change if it is to confront the threats of the 21st century." The commission pointedly noted that time and time again, others had targeted the "same fundamental failings," without success. "The Intelligence Community is a closed

THE MORE THINGS CHANGE . . .

world," the commission noted, "and many insiders admitted to us that *it has an almost perfect record of resisting external recommendations*" (emphasis theirs).[55]

Who's in Charge?

The 9/11 Commission found that before September 11, "the intelligence community's confederated structure left open the question of who really was in charge of the entire U.S. intelligence effort."[56] This is still the case today, despite the creation of the director of national intelligence with the passage of the Intelligence Reform and Terrorism Prevention Act of 2004. Indeed, instead of enhancing coordination and centralization, the 2004 legislation has triggered a scramble for turf that has left the secretary of defense with greater power, the director of national intelligence with little, and the Intelligence Community even more disjointed. Many intelligence experts and officials believe that John Negroponte, who became the first director of national intelligence in April 2005, succeeded only in adding yet another bureaucratic layer to an already fragmented system.[57] When Negroponte abruptly announced his resignation in January 2007, his staff had already ballooned to 1,500 people, prompting outcries from members of Congress. "I don't see the leadership," noted Senator Dianne Feinstein (D-CA) in a Senate Intelligence Committee hearing. "What I see . . . is the growth of a bureaucracy over there. And . . . it concerns me very much."[58]

Since 9/11, Pentagon dominance has grown rather than diminished. Details of Defense Department intelligence programs are classified, but public reports suggest an ever-widening expansion of units and activities that often duplicate existing capabilities in other agencies and are not well overseen by either the DNI or Congress. In 2002, the Defense Department quietly and successfully lobbied Congress to pass legislation consolidating Pentagon intelligence activities under a new position, undersecretary of defense for intelligence. In the words of former senior intelligence official John Gannon, the move added "more heft to what already was the IC's thousand pound gorilla."[59] The undersecretary of defense, Stephen Cambone, who served until 2007, dramatically increased the number of clandestine teams conducting secret counterterrorism operations and collecting in-

formation abroad—activities that had traditionally been performed by the CIA.[60] He also expanded Pentagon intelligence activities at home, transforming a small unit called the
Counterintelligence Field Activity (CIFA)—which was created in
2002 to protect U.S. military installations from terrorist attack—
into a sprawling agency with a 1,000-member staff, nine director-
ates, and wide-ranging responsibilities that include conducting
terrorism investigations of Americans inside the United States.[61]
By 2005, CIFA had the authority to give orders to approximately
4,000 Army, Air Force, and Navy investigators in the United
States, in addition to its own staff, making its counterterrorism
investigatory ranks equal to the FBI's.[62] One former senior defense intelligence official described CIFA's evolution this way:
"They started with force protection from terrorists, but when you
go down that road, you soon are into everything . . . where terrorists get their money, who they see, who they deal with."[63]

None of these activities came at the behest of Director Negroponte. Instead, from 2005 to 2007, the nation's first director
of national intelligence labored unsuccessfully to exercise the
powers he had on paper. For example, although the intelligence
reform act gave the DNI power to transfer personnel across different agencies—a measure deemed critical for integrating the
Community—within months of the new law, Secretary Rumsfeld
issued a Defense Department directive that required Pentagon
"concurrence" for any personnel transfers affecting defense intelligence agencies.[64] In October 2006, Representative Jane Harman (D-CA) blasted Secretary of Defense Rumsfeld, calling him
"the best bureaucratic infighter in the history of America," and
complained that "finding a way to outsmart" Rumsfeld on intelligence reform was "a high art" that had "not been mastered."[65]

Other agencies have resisted central management from the director of national intelligence as well. Between 2005 and 2006, a
bureaucratic food fight erupted over the division of staffing and
responsibilities between the CIA's Counterterrorist Center and
the DNI's new National Counterterrorism Center. According to
one DNI official, during the summer of 2005, even when DNI
staffers requested additional parking at CIA headquarters, the
CIA turned them down. "Nothing's changed," complained the
official. "CIA still thinks they're in charge. They don't get that
we *own* those parking spaces."[66]

In interviews, intelligence officials from a variety of agencies expressed grave concerns about the DNI's ability to forge the Intelligence Community into a coherent whole.[67] "The DNI," one noted, "is turning out to be nothing more than another layer on top of sixteen organizations."[68] Another issued an even more negative assessment. "The American public has been sold a bill of goods," he said. "When the next attack happens, an awful lot of people will say, 'How could this happen? We created a DNI.' "[69] Even the DNI's creators share these concerns. In February 2006, Senator Susan Collins (R-ME), one of the chief architects of the 2004 intelligence reform bill, noted, "Director Negroponte has battles to fight within the bureaucracy, and particularly with the Department of Defense. DOD is refusing to recognize that the director of national intelligence is in charge of the intelligence community."[70] In April 2006, the House Intelligence Committee warned that the DNI was heading down the path toward becoming "another layer of large, unintended and unnecessary bureaucracy."[71] Committee Chairman Peter Hoekstra (R-MI) described the report as a "shot across the bow."[72] Ranking member Jane Harman (D-CA), another key player in the creation of the DNI, was even more critical. "The concept behind intelligence reform," she said on national television, "was to create a unified command structure . . . not a bureaucracy. We've said that Mr. Negroponte should stop calling himself ambassador. He's a director. In order to change cultures, you have to lead. You have to make some people mad at you. You have to send new signals."[73]

Instead of sending new signals, however, Negroponte resigned nine months later, leaving the top two DNI posts vacant at the same time. His departure led many to worry that turnover would further bog down the slow pace of reform. "I am deeply troubled by the timing of this announcement and the void of leadership at the top of our Intelligence Community," said Senate Intelligence Committee Chairman Jay Rockefeller (D-WV). "The leadership of the Intelligence Community is too important."[74] By March 2007, the Intelligence Community was in the full throes of leadership transition, with a new secretary of defense, a new undersecretary of defense for intelligence, a new director of national intelligence, a vacant deputy DNI slot, and a CIA leadership team that had been in place less than a year.

Information Sharing and Analysis

Information sharing and analysis, two critical shortcomings raised in the wake of 9/11, have not improved much and in some cases have gotten worse. In 2003, President Bush established the Terrorist Threat Integration Center to provide a hub for analyzing terrorism-related intelligence across the Community. TTIC confused the lines of authority at first, until the 2004 intelligence reform bill expanded the agency's mission and renamed it the National Counterterrorism Center (NCTC). Today, NCTC is widely considered to be one of most successful improvements in U.S. intelligence. Different agency officials now sit in the same room and draft collective analytic reports about terrorism. The Center also has developed a classified counterterrorism Web site, NCTC Online, which provides synthesized terrorism intelligence to policymakers, analysts, and a number of other consumers across the U.S. government.[75]

All that sounds good. Now consider this: Because NCTC's analysts have varying levels of security clearances and come from different agencies, they still see different pieces of information.[76] Most U.S. intelligence agencies have no experience conducting all-source analysis, so the personnel they assign to NCTC are learning on the job. As one senior government official put it, "Eleven organizations sent people to NCTC. Only two of them sent people who knew what they were doing."[77] Officials still resist sharing information with colleagues assigned from other agencies even when the rules allow it.[78] Fusing intelligence is done by humans, not computers; information is stored on nearly thirty separate, incompatible information networks. To access them all, NCTC analysts must use more than a half dozen different computers stacked underneath their desks. "It's a little scary," noted Senator Mike DeWine (R-OH) in a May 2006 Senate Intelligence Committee hearing. "[I]t's like we have duct-taped our systems together. Surely we can do better than this."[79]

This is the shining example. Information sharing in other parts of the Intelligence Community is far more problematic. In 2005 the Silberman-Robb Commission wrote that, "No shortcoming of the Intelligence Community has received more attention since the September 11 attacks than the failure to share information." Yet, despite "literally dozens" of Intelligence Community information sharing initiatives, including executive guidelines and statutory requirements, the commission found that only "minor advances" had been made.[80] The commission urged that the new director of national intelligence make improving the Community's information management system a top priority.[81]

The president quickly responded, appointing a career intelligence official named John Russack to develop a Community-wide information sharing system in June 2005. But Russack was initially given only a two-person staff to do the job.[82] He left seven months later. In December 2005, the 9/11 Commission's Public Discourse Project issued a report card assessing implementation of its recommendations. Information sharing efforts received a D.[83] In July 2006, another expert task force, this time from the Markle Foundation, concluded that improvements had been made, but found "turf wars and unclear lines of authority," officials who "still cling" to old ways of doing business, and a diminishing sense of commitment and determination to improve information sharing.[84] "[A]lmost five years since the terrorist attacks of September 11," the report concluded, "systematic, trusted information sharing remains more of an aspiration than a reality."[85] In January 2007, the Intelligence Community's chief information officer, Major General Dale Meyerrose, offered a similarly discouraging progress report. "The policy that's in place took three years to write, four years to coordinate, and we've not touched it in five," he told the Senate Intelligence Committee. Although Meyerrose noted that his office had been working hard to improve information sharing for over a year and that he expected to produce a series of proposals soon, he underscored that "most of the sharing issues we face are cultural and process rather than technology."[86]

Strategic analysis has not fared any better. In March 2005, the Silberman-Robb Commission found that the pressure to respond to current events was still driving out big picture thinking. "The Intelligence Community we have today is buried beneath an avalanche of demands for 'current intelligence,'" the commission noted.[87] While it found the "pressing need" to meet the tactical demands of military and other requirements necessary, the commission made clear that inattention to strategic analysis posed grave long-term consequences.[88] "Across the board," the commission wrote, "the Intelligence Community knows disturbingly little about the nuclear programs of many of the world's most dangerous actors. In some cases, it knows less now than it did five or ten years ago."[89]

A year later, strategic intelligence again topped the list of unresolved problems. At his May 2006 confirmation hearings to become CIA director, General Michael Hayden singled out rebuilding strategic intelligence as one of the agency's greatest challenges and his top priorities. "We must set aside talent and energy to look at the long view and not just be chasing our version of the current news cycle," Hayden declared, or else the United States would "be endlessly surprised." Hayden bluntly told the committee that doing so would not be easy because of the natural pressures to put current demands ahead of long-term needs. "I actually think it might be worse now than it has been historically," he said, noting that the twenty-four-hour news cycle as well as the operations tempo in Afghanistan, Iraq, and the war on terror have "suck[ed] energy into doing something into the here and now."[90] Outside the hearings, other intelligence officials echoed the theme. John McLaughlin, who served as the CIA's deputy director and then acting director, complained in May 2006 that the demand for instant information had made CIA analysts "the Wikipedia of Washington."[91] Carl W. Ford, Jr., a veteran intelligence official who served in both the CIA and State Department, was even more critical: "We haven't done strategic analysis for so long that most of our analysts don't know how to do it anymore," he told a reporter. Without "fundamental changes" in analysis, Ford noted, "we will continue to turn out the $40 billion pile of fluff we have become famous for."[92]

Human Intelligence

The CIA's human intelligence capabilities have also made little progress since September 11. The reason: to date, the agency's approach to improving human intelligence has focused primarily on increasing the number of spies rather than improving quality or dramatically increasing nontraditional recruitment models to penetrate terrorist groups. In November 2004, the president issued a memorandum that directed the CIA to expand its spy ranks by 50 percent.[93] The agency responded, tripling the number of trained clandestine case officers from 2001 to 2006.[94] But to many intelligence veterans, this was precisely the wrong approach: success requires fewer and better spies operating differently, not more of the same.[95] "The conditions of looking for human intelligence are so different from the Cold War that just more money and more people doesn't guarantee you anything," said former CIA bin Ladin Unit Chief Michael Scheuer.[96] In interviews, several other clandestine case officers agreed. Here's how one CIA veteran described the problem:

> The core element to our business is access. In the Cold War, we wanted to recruit against bureaucracies, and so we were on the diplomatic circuit, we were out there, and that gave us access. We need access, somehow, we need to figure out how do you get access to people that are not on the diplomatic circuit. That's the enemy, that's where they are, that's their battlefield, that's their environment. We need to be in that environment. And we're not going to get there if we sit in the green zone in Baghdad. . . . The whole terrain has shifted, and we still, we haven't shifted with it, except to say, "we want to get back to basics."[97]

"If we were really serious about this," said another, "we would have said the NOC (nonofficial cover) is our primary model of how case officers are deployed. And the exception will be somebody sitting inside an embassy, writing telegrams. But we have never, ever even come close to that position. We have never even contemplated that."[98] John MacGaffin, a thirty-one-year veteran of the CIA's clandestine service, put it more bluntly: "Fifty percent more gets you to 'Stupid.' You'll get 50 percent more of what you've got now."[99]

The FBI

The FBI has attempted the most ambitious changes, with perhaps the most disappointing results. Since 2001, the bureau has made counterterrorism its top priority; hired roughly 1,000 new special agents;[100] doubled its analyst corps;[101] created Field Intelligence Groups to integrate law enforcement and intelligence operations in the field offices; begun training some special agents alongside CIA clandestine case officers to enhance the bureau's human intelligence capabilities;[102] consolidated intelligence, counterterrorism, and counterintelligence functions into a single National Security Branch run by a senior FBI official; and undertaken a massive technology modernization campaign.[103] Interviews with several FBI officials in 2006 and 2007 emphasized the same theme: the FBI is trying to transform itself. As one special agent put it, "We get it. We get it. We really do."[104]

Nevertheless, old law enforcement priorities and attitudes have been slow to change.[105] In 2005, forty-seven of the fifty-six field office heads still came from the Criminal Division.[106] Until 2007, newly hired special agents still received more time for vacation than counterterrorism training.[107] And analysts were still being given secretarial tasks. A 2005 Justice Department survey of more than 800 FBI analysts (two-thirds of the total employed by the FBI at the time)[108] found that on average, analysts were spending only half their time actually doing analysis.[109] Other duties commonly included answering phones, escorting visitors, and collecting the trash.[110] In personal interviews, one FBI analyst who had previous experience as a translator and analyst in another intelligence agency recalled having to spend a week watching repair workers so that FBI office security would not be compromised. One said he was required to work nights and weekends operating the switchboard and escorting the cleaning crew. Another told Justice Department officials that, "A lot of my job doesn't require a college education."[111] Twenty-seven percent of analysts surveyed said that the FBI's special agents—who dominate the bureau—"rarely" or "never" understood what capabilities they had or what functions they were supposed to be performing.[112] Field interviews by the Congressional Research Service and others confirmed the persistence of the old cops-and-robbers culture. As one special agent-in-charge put it, the special agents, not analysts, "will always be the center of the universe."[113]

Changing this law enforcement culture has proven particularly vexing.[114] In May 2006, one FBI official was caught short when asked by a reporter whether FBI agents really wanted to work in the bureau's new National Security Branch, which is the heart of the FBI's counterterrorism, counterintelligence, and intelligence activities. "Not really," the official admitted. "[Agents] say to me, 'Hey, I joined up to arrest people.' "[115] Another FBI official put it this way. "We are working for a better corporate sense of how we employ our resources. We are trying to turn ourselves into an organization that is intelligence driven which has historically been operations driven . . . [but] it's a huge evolutionary process. . . . It's like shifting the direction of an aircraft carrier in mid-stream. . . . Every day it's a battle."[116] Even FBI Director Robert Mueller admitted that one of the bureau's most important continuing challenges is ensuring that "the persons who do not wear the badge and the gun have the equal respect" of others in the FBI. "We're developing that," Mueller noted in January 2007, but added, "We're not where we need to be."[117] In March 2007, the bureau's own Web site still classified FBI employees as either special agents or "professional support staff"—a term that lumped analysts together with secretaries, auto mechanics, janitors, and all other bureau employees.[118]

According to FBI officials, 2006 marked the beginning of a radical transformation in how FBI field offices used intelligence analysis.[119] Dubbed "domain awareness," the new initiative no longer held field office heads responsible for pursuing specific cases. Instead, the special agents-in-charge [SACs] of all fifty-six U.S. field offices were evaluated based on how well they understood the threats to their geographic jurisdictions, how well they identified information gaps surrounding key issues, and how well they devised programs to fill them. "This has been really over the last year a very dramatic shift in how we're approaching problems," noted FBI intelligence directorate chief Wayne Murphy in 2007. He added:

> If a year ago, I asked an SAC to define for me how they understood a particular problem, the way they defined their understanding was framed in terms of how many cases they had. What we've worked to do, and I think successfully, is to create a methodological approach to say you can't say you understand a problem if you define it by what you already know about it. You understand a problem if you have indices to understand it, you've investigated whether it's just smoke or whether there's really a fire there, and you've taken steps to close those knowledge gaps.[120]

As the above description suggests, the domain awareness initiative requires a better understanding of and respect for intelligence analysis. Importantly, however, FBI analysts remain only notional partners in this effort; bureau rules still mandate that senior positions in the field, including the top spot in every U.S. field office, be staffed by FBI special agents—or in the words of one bureau official, the people who "carry guns and risk their lives."[121] These rules mean that analysts must still do battle from below, convincing their special agent superiors that chasing information has as much value as chasing suspects. As one analyst put it, despite progress in domain awareness, "outreach to our own agency" remains an ongoing frustration.[122] John Gannon, a respected senior intelligence official who spent twenty-four years working with the FBI in various positions—including the CIA's analytic branch chief, chairman of the National Intelligence Council, and staff director of the House Homeland Security Committee—offered a more pessimistic assessment. "If you go to the Defense Intelligence [Agency or] if you're CIA," he told the Senate Intelligence Committee in January 2007, "you have analytic structures where any analyst who is working in those organizations can look right up the chain of command to the director, and it is all analytic managers who are reviewing the process and applying rigor to what is done. And ultimately, that analytic system can challenge the agent culture." But, he quickly added, "I don't think that can ever happen out of the FBI system as it is."[123]

Efforts to improve the bureau's antiquated technology systems have been even more feckless. In February 2005, Director Mueller announced he was scrapping the bureau's Trilogy technology modernization program—at the cost of nearly $200 million—because it did not work.[124] A new system, named Sentinel, is now underway. It is expected to cost an additional $425 million and will not be fully operational until 2009. In May 2006, four and a half years after 9/11, the Justice Department's Inspector General testified that, "the FBI still does not have a modern, effective case management records system."[125] Director Mueller himself called the technology modernization program his "greatest frustration." Reflecting on the bureau's continued technology weaknesses in early 2007, he noted:

> I would love to be able to go out and get a contractor and say, "okay, come in and fix it." Part of the problem is that you have to change your business practices, as well. We've probably had the same business practices in place for ninety-eight years of our exis-

tence. And one of the things you do *not* want to do is just tell the technologists to go ahead and change it without changing your business practices. We're in that process. If there's one area of impatience that I have, it's that area [emphasis his].[126]

These and other developments have led to a series of increasingly dire prognoses. In March 2005, the Silberman-Robb Commission noted with concern that the FBI's transformation into an intelligence organization "is still in doubt."[127] In December 2005, the 9/11 Commission issued more alarming warnings. "Reforms are at risk from inertia and complacency," the commission declared in its report card. "[T]hey must be accelerated or they will fail."[128] And in May 2006, John Gannon issued this stark assessment to the Senate Judiciary Committee:

> The salient fact is that, approaching five years after 9/11, we still do not have a domestic intelligence service that can collect effectively against the terrorist threat to the homeland or provide authoritative analysis of that threat. It is not enough to say that these things take time. It could not be clearer from the Intelligence Community's experience over the past 25 years that it is extraordinarily difficult to blend the families of intelligence and law enforcement, and that the Bureau's organizational bias toward the latter for deep-seated historic reasons—is powerful and persistent.[129]

Although Gannon had argued for some time that the FBI was the right agency to develop a domestic intelligence capability after 9/11, by the spring of 2006 he had given up. "[W]atching the FBI struggle with its new national intelligence mandate and recalling earlier interagency 'culture wars' in my career," Gannon declared, "I have changed my mind. I now doubt that the FBI, on its present course, can get there from here."[130]

Making Headlines More Than Progress

Instead, it is fair to say that U.S. intelligence agencies since 9/11 have made more headlines than progress. The CIA has been an agency in turmoil. In September 2004, former House Intelligence Committee Chairman Porter Goss succeeded George Tenet as CIA Director.[131] His twenty-month tenure was steeped in controversy. Several senior agency officials quit in protest over Goss's weak management and fierce personality clashes with Goss's management team, who were viewed as overly partisan. Then, in May 2006, Goss announced his surprise resignation amidst revelations that one of his closest aides, Kyle "Dusty" Foggo, was under investigation in a corruption probe linked to former Congressman Randy "Duke" Cunningham (R-CA). It was a scandal made for the movies, with press reports that Foggo had attended poker parties with prostitutes in—of all places—the Watergate Hotel.

News headlines throughout 2005, 2006, and 2007 were also full of revelations about the Intelligence Community's secret activities and the ensuing political furor over their legality and publication. In November 2005, the *Washington Post* reported the existence of a top secret system of foreign CIA prisons or "black sites" that were being used to hold and interrogate some of the most important al Qaeda detainees.[132] One month later, the *New York Times* revealed that the National Security Agency had been wiretapping phone calls between parties in the United States and foreign countries, including American citizens suspected of al Qaeda connections—all without court warrants.[133] The NSA wiretapping program ignited a political firestorm about the program's legality, the security risks of revealing it, and whether White House, Justice Department, and intelligence officials had properly briefed members of Congress. Then in May 2006, *USA Today* reported that the National Security Agency had also secretly collected the domestic telephone records of millions of Americans and was mining the data to find clues of terrorist threats.[134] When General Michael Hayden appeared before the Senate Intelligence Committee for his CIA director confirmation hearings on May 18, scandal, not reform, was the main topic of conversation. As Committee Chairman Pat Roberts (R-KS) noted at the opening of the hearing, "the public debate in regard to your nomination has been dominated not by your record as a manager or your qualifications, the needs of the CIA, its strengths and its weaknesses and its future, but rather the debate is focused almost entirely on the presidentially authorized activities of another agency."[135] Finally, in March 2007 a Justice Department inspector general report found that the FBI had improperly used provisions of the PATRIOT Act to gather telephone, bank, and other information about American citizens. Bipartisan outrage erupted on Capitol Hill, with Democratic committee chairmen vowing to hold more hearings.[136]

Adaptation in Perspective

Some will argue that the assessment above is unduly harsh. The overwhelming consensus in Washington is that while much work remains, U.S. intelligence agencies are making progress. Scores of officials whose names are not known and whose work goes unheralded have dedicated their professional careers to one goal: getting the right information into the right hands to protect American lives. The steady refrain is that talented officials are working hard, and that we are safer now than before. As one FBI official remarked, "What bugs me the most is that the public believes the FBI is not an organization with truly dedicated people who want to make a difference. They are not here to make a lot of money. They do it for very altruistic reasons. The public often loses sight of that."[137]

Yes, tremendous effort has been expended, individuals have made extraordinary sacrifices, and improvements have been made. But some perspective is in order. Effort often does not translate into performance. And progress is not the same as success. The question is not whether the CIA and FBI are better equipped than they were on September 10, 2001—certainly a low standard. Nor is it whether the CIA and FBI have smart and dedicated officials; they always have. The question is whether these two agencies, and the rest of the U.S. Intelligence Community, have adapted to the point where they now stand a reasonable chance of preventing the next catastrophe. The evidence is not encouraging.

It is often said that change takes time. But it is now sixteen years since the end of the Cold War and the U.S. Intelligence Community is still struggling to develop the rudimentary building blocks to combat terrorism. History is filled with examples where more was accomplished in far less time. Twelve years after the Soviet Union stunned the world by launching Sputnik, the first satellite, the United States landed a man on the moon and won the space race. In 1945, just four years after Japan's surprise attack decimated much of the Pacific fleet at Pearl Harbor, the United States had built a fighting force that had crossed two oceans and defeated both Germany and Japan.[138] Within two years of the end of World War II, American leaders had helped create the United Nations and launched the Marshall Plan to rebuild Europe. And in 1787, it took less than one hundred working days to draft the U.S. Constitution.[139]

Yet here we are. Although al Qaeda has not attacked the U.S. homeland since 9/11, there is little evidence to suggest that effective intelligence is the reason. As one Congressional Intelligence Committee lawmaker noted in the fall of 2005, "We still stink at collecting. We still stink at analysis . . . all the problems we set out to correct are still there."[140]

CONCLUSION

This book's argument can be summed up in two words: Organization matters. The structures, cultures, and incentives of U.S. intelligence agencies critically influence what they do and how well they do it. Structures create capabilities and jurisdictions, determining who performs which tasks by what authority at what level of competence. Culture has an invisible but powerful hold, coloring how intelligence officials view the world and their role in it. Incentives unavoidably give greater weight to certain issues, jobs, and interests, encouraging some activities more than others. Individual leadership also plays a vital role in the policy process. Too often, however, discussion of foreign policy success and failure treats individuals as the only important factors, ignoring the powerful organizational forces in the background. Although organization alone cannot guarantee good policy outcomes, it can significantly affect what gets done, and how well. At the dawn of the Cold War, Senator Henry M. "Scoop" Jackson (D-WA) underscored the importance of getting the organizational basics right, noting, "Organization by itself cannot assure a strategy for victory in the cold war. But good organization can help, and poor organization can hurt."[141] Decades later, the 9/11 Commission, the Silberman-Robb Commission, and the House and Senate Intelligence Committees all confronted a radically different enemy but came to the same conclusion.

Criticizing U.S. intelligence agencies is nothing new. As early as 1948, the *New York Times* castigated a newly created CIA as "one of the weakest links in our national security."[142] The stakes, however, have never been higher. The spread of weapons of mass destruction, the information revolution, and the rise of transnational terrorist networks have changed the old rules and realities of international relations. For the first time in history, great power does not bring security. It is now the weak who threaten the strong. And it is intelligence, not military might, which provides the first and last line of defense. The United States' ability to protect itself hinges on whether U.S. intelligence agencies built for a different enemy at a different time can adapt. Many obstacles stand in the way. The crux of the problem lies in the enduring realities of American politics, and success requires finding ways to overcome them.

Intelligence Reform Catalog Methodology

THE INTELLIGENCE reform catalog was designed to include all major unclassified reports issued by government officials and outside experts examining U.S. intelligence and counterterrorism from the Cold's War end to 9/11. More specifically, I included:

> Any study that released its final report between January 1991 and September 2001.

> Reports issued by:
> * Presidential commissions
> * Congressional staff studies or investigations
> * Executive branch studies
> * Studies conducted by nonpartisan nongovernmental organizations (such as the Council on Foreign Relations)

> Reports covering any one of the following four subjects:
> * The CIA
> * The FBI
> * The U.S. Intelligence Community as a whole
> * U.S. counterterrorism capabilities

I began with fourteen major studies listed in the Congressional Joint Inquiry's October 3, 2002 staff statement, "Proposals for Reform within the Intelligence Community." These were:

> 1. 1995–96: Commission on the Roles and Capabilities of the U.S. Intelligence Community (Aspin-Brown Commission)
> 2. 1996: IC21: The Intelligence Community in the 21st Century (House Permanent Select Committee on Intelligence Staff Study)
> 3. 1997: Modernizing Intelligence: Structure and Change for the 21st Century (National Institute for Public Policy Study)
> 4. 1998: Intelligence Community Performance on the Indian Nuclear Test (Jeremiah Report)
> 5. 1999: The Rumsfeld Commission on the Ballistic Missile Threat
> 6. 2000: Countering the Changing Threat of International Terror-

ism, a report from the National Commission on Terrorism (Bremer Commission)

7. 2000: Report of the National Commission for the Review of the National Reconnaissance Office

8. 2000: National Imagery and Mapping Agency Commission Report

9. 2001: Road Map for National Security: Imperative for Change. The Phase III Report of the U.S. Commission on National Security/21st Century (Hart-Rudman Commission)

10. 2001: The Advisory Panel to Assess Domestic Response Capabilities to Terrorism Involving Weapons of Mass Destruction (Gilmore Commission)

11. 2001: Deutch Commission on Weapons of Mass Destruction

12. 2002: A Review of the Federal Bureau of Investigation Security Programs (Webster Commission)

13. 2002: House Permanent Select Committee on Intelligence Subcommittee on Terrorism Study

14. 2001–2002: Scowcroft Commission on U.S. Intelligence

I pared this list down from fourteen to seven based on three criteria:

1. *Date of final report*: The Review of the FBI's Security Programs (the Webster Commission) and the House Intelligence Subcommittee on Terrorism Study were excluded because their reports were released after September 11, 2001.

2. *Classification*: The 1998 Jeremiah Commission, the 1999 Rumsfeld Commission, and the 2001–2002 Scowcroft Commission were excluded because their final reports are classified. It should be noted, however, that these classified studies were highly critical of U.S. intelligence capabilities, suggesting that the catalog under-reports the extent of concern and awareness about U.S. intelligence deficiencies.

3. *Agency focus*: The 2000 Commission for the Review of the National Reconnaissance Office and the 2000 National Imagery and Mapping Agency Commission Report focused on two agencies that were outside the scope of the project.

Next, I identified additional studies by reviewing *The Encyclopedia of Government Advisory Organizations*, 16th ed. (New York: Gale Group, 2002) and conducting extensive interviews with intelligence officials, experts, and members and staff of the major studies already included in the catalog. These steps resulted in the addition of five reports to the catalog:

1. 1996: The Council on Foreign Relations Intelligence Task Force
2. 1996: The 20th Century Fund Task Force on the Future of U.S. Intelligence
3. 1993, 1995: The National Performance Review
4. 1998: FBI Strategic Plan
5. 2000: The Commission on the Advancement of Federal Law Enforcement (Webster Commission. Note: Two commissions were chaired by William Webster. The 2002 commission was excluded, while this one was included.)

Together, the twelve reports in the intelligence reform catalog issued 559 recommendations. Twenty of these recommendations were omitted because they suggested no actionable steps or focused narrowly on cost savings.

Implementation of the remaining 539 recommendations was determined by examining government documents and by interviewing principals and staff of the original studies as well as officials working in the affected agencies. Rather than making my own judgments about implementation, I solicited the judgments of others who were closer to the process and more inclined to overstate, rather than understate, progress.

Interviews were conducted between June 2003 and January 2005. Sources were asked to judge the implementation of each recommendation using four categories:

1. Fully implemented
2. Partially implemented
3. Not implemented
4. Don't know

At least two different sources were used to determine the implementation status of each recommendation. Where differences arose, I erred on the side of overstating implementation so that adaptation failure judgments would be conservative. For example, if one source believed a recommendation had been partially implemented, but a second source felt it had been fully implemented, the recommendation was listed as fully implemented. This process led to the exclusion of twenty-five recommendations from the catalog whose implementation could not be determined after discussions with three key sources. The final catalog included 514 reform recommendations.

* Notes *

ACKNOWLEDGMENTS

1. I am grateful to Diane Vaughan for coining this term in her article, "The Dark Side of Organizations: Mistake, Misconduct, and Disaster," in *Annual Review of Sociology* vol. 25 (Palo Alto: Annual Reviews, 1999): 271–305.

2. Patricia Sullivan, "Roberta M. Wohlstetter, Military Intelligence Expert," obituary, *Washington Post*, January 10, 2007, p. B7.

CHAPTER 1
AN ORGANIZATIONAL VIEW OF 9/11

1. General Brent Scowcroft, testimony before the House Permanent Select Committee on Intelligence (HPSCI) and Senate Select Committee on Intelligence (SSCI) Joint Inquiry, 107th Cong., 2nd sess., September 19, 2002.

2. Eleanor Hill, "The Intelligence Community's Knowledge of the September 11 Hijackers Prior to September 11, 2001," statement before the House Permanent Select Committee on Intelligence (HPSCI) and Senate Select Committee on Intelligence (SSCI) Joint Inquiry, 107th Cong., 2nd sess., September 20, 2002, p. 5. http://intelligence.senate.gov/0209hrg/020920/hill.pdf (accessed February 23, 2006).

3. George Tenet, testimony before the HPSCI, 107th Cong., 2nd sess., October 17, 2002.

4. Tenet issued the memo on December 4, 1998. Excerpts can be found in Eleanor Hill, "Joint Inquiry Staff Statement, Part I," SSCI and HPSCI hearing, 107th Cong., 2nd sess., September 18, 2002, p. 12.

5. George Tenet, "Worldwide Threats to U.S. National Security," testimony before the Senate Armed Services Committee, 106th Cong., 1st sess., February 2, 1999; George Tenet, "Annual Assessment of Security Threats against the United States," testimony before the Senate Select Committee on Intelligence, 106th Cong., 2nd sess., February 2, 2000; and George Tenet, "Worldwide Threats to National Security," testimony before the Senate Select Committee on Intelligence, 107th Cong., 1st sess., February 7, 2001.

6. *The 9/11 Commission Report: Final Report of the National Commission on Terrorist Attacks upon the United States* (hereafter referred to as *9/11 Commission Report*) (New York: W. W. Norton, 2004), pp. 254–63.

7. For most of the Cold War, the Intelligence Community consisted of the following thirteen agencies: the Central Intelligence Agency; the Defense Intelligence Agency; the Defense Mapping Agency (which was merged with other imagery units in the Pentagon and CIA into the National Imagery and Mapping Agency in 1996 and renamed the National Geospatial-Intelligence Agency in 2003); the National Reconnaissance Office, which builds and maintains spy satellites; the National Security Agency, which intercepts signals communications; the Federal Bureau of Investigation; and intelligence units in the Air Force, Army, Marine Corps, Navy, Energy Department, State Department, and Treasury Department. Today the Intelligence Community also includes the Drug Enforcement Administration, the Department of Homeland Security, and the Office of the Director of National Intelligence, bringing the total to sixteen major agencies. For an overview of the functions and history of various intelligence agencies, see the Intelligence Community home page, http://www.intelligence.gov/1-members.shtml (accessed July 7, 2006); and Jeffrey T. Richelson, *The U.S. Intelligence Community*, 4th ed. (Boulder, CO: Westview, 1999).

8. Hill, "The Intelligence Community's Knowledge of the September 11 Hijackers Prior to September 11, 2001," September 20, 2002, pp. 7–8. The Joint Inquiry unearthed one December 1999 memo providing general guidance about placing terrorists on the State Department's watch list, but the investigation found no routine or formal programs in place to ensure that adding names to the watch list received regular attention. Nor were there any consistent guidelines about thresholds for placing suspected terrorists on the watch list. As DCI Tenet testified, the al-Mihdhar episode "exposed a weakness in our internal training and an inconsistent understanding of watchlist thresholds." (Tenet testimony to SSCI and HPSCI, October 17, 2002). Moreover, several other intelligence officials told the Joint Inquiry that they had received no formal training on watchlisting. One CIA employee, for example, said he learned about watchlisting through "on-the-job training." *Joint Inquiry into Intelligence Community Activities before and after the Terrorist Attacks of September 11, 2001*, report of the U.S. Select Committee on Intelligence and U.S. House Permanent Select Committee on Intelligence, S. Report No. 107–351, H. Report No. 107–792, 107th Cong., 2nd sess., December 2002, p. 147 (hereafter referred to as *Joint Inquiry Report*). For a copy of the December 1999 watchlist memo, see *Joint Inquiry Report Appendix*, "CTC Watchlisting Guidance—December 1999."

9. Quoted in Hill, "The Intelligence Community's Knowledge of the September 11 Hijackers Prior to September 11, 2001," HPSCI and SSCI, September 20, 2002, p. 8.

10. Although widely reported and self-described as the "20th hijacker," Moussaoui's precise role is still unknown. For years, Moussaoui insisted that he was a member of al Qaeda, had some but limited knowledge of the September 11 plot, and was slated to participate in a second wave of terrorist attacks that never materialized. Moussaoui pleaded guilty to six counts of conspiring with al Qaeda in connection with 9/11, and his claims were corroborated by Khalid Sheikh Mohammed, the 9/11 mastermind who was taken into U.S. custody in 2003. At his sentencing trial, however, Moussaoui began inflating his role, first claiming and then denying that he was supposed to fly a fifth airplane into the White House on September 11, 2001, with convicted "shoe bomber" Richard Reid. Jurors failed to reach a unanimous decision, which was required for sentencing him to death, in part because three of them did not believe Moussaoui's later claims about being an integral part of plot. In May 2006, Moussaoui was ultimately sentenced to life in prison without the possibility of parole.

11. "Bin Ladin Determined to Strike in U.S.," *President's Daily Brief*, August 6, 2001, declassified April 10, 2004. For information about the mistaken claims of New York surveillance activities discussed in the PDB, see "Background Briefing Via Conference Call on the President's PDB of August 6, 2001," Office of the Press Secretary, The White House, April 10, 2004, available at www.whitehouse.gov/news/releases/2004/04/20040410–6.html (accessed September 17, 2004); "Fact Sheet: The August 6, 2001 PDB," Press release, Office of the Press Secretary, The White House, issued April 10, 2004, available at www.Whitehouse.gov/news/realeases/2004/04/print/20040410–5.html (accessed September 17, 2004); Matthew Cooper, Elaine Shannon, Viveca Novak, "Probing the Memo," *Time*, April 19, 2004, p. 19.

12. These two investigations produced a treasure trove of public research materials, including: declassified documents, interim staff reports, transcripts of public hearings with government officials and expert witnesses, and final reports. It is important to note, however, that the Joint Inquiry and 9/11 Commission did not cover the same ground, even when they discussed the same topics. For example, the Joint Inquiry noted, but the 9/11 Commission did not, that two of the 9/11 hijackers were living with an FBI informant in San Diego. The 9/11 Commission final report says, but Joint Inquiry materials do not, that one of these hijackers, Nawaf al-Hazmi, was listed in the San Diego telephone directory. And neither the Joint Inquiry final report nor the 9/11 Commission final report includes perhaps the most compelling piece of information about whether these two hijackers could have been caught: In a September 20, 2002, Joint Inquiry hearing, an FBI agent testified that on the night of 9/11, he gave Khalid al-Mihdhar's

name to the bureau's information technology center to see what a search of public records would uncover. A few hours later, the agent received al-Mihdhar's correct address in San Diego.

13. In 1996, the Commission on the Roles and Capabilities of the U.S. Intelligence Community (the Aspin-Brown Commission) reported that the National Foreign Intelligence Program (NFIP) comprised two-thirds of total intelligence spending. Given the 1997 declassified intelligence budget was $26.6 billion, the 1997 NFIP program would have been about $17.73 billion. The House Intelligence Committee noted in its unclassified Authorization Act Report for Fiscal Year 1998 that clandestine human intelligence (HUMINT) constituted "a single digit percentage" of the National Foreign Intelligence Program. (Intelligence Authorization Act for Fiscal Year 1998, 105 H. Rpt. 135 Part I, 105th Cong., 1st session, House Permanent Select Committee on Intelligence, June 18, 1997, p. 25). Conservatively estimating HUMINT's "single digit" share at 9 percent of NFIP funds provides an estimate of $1.6 billion in national clandestine human intelligence spending for fiscal year 1997. In August 1998, when a spy satellite blew up shortly after launch, news media widely reported its cost to be $1 billion, and the cost of the Titan 4A rocket that launched it at $400 million. See for example David Stout, "Air Force Rocket Explodes Just After Liftoff," *New York Times*, August 13, 1998, p. A16.

14. Interview, June 2005.

15. Quoted in *9/11 Commission Report*, p. 357.

16. *Joint Inquiry Report*, pp. 239–41.

17. Eleanor Hill, Joint Inquiry Staff Statement Part I, September 18, 2002, p. 13.

18. Federal Bureau of Investigation, *Draft FBI Strategic Plan: 1998–2003: Keeping Tomorrow Safe*, unclassified version, May 8, 1998 (hereafter referred to as *FBI Strategic Plan*).

19. "Law Enforcement, Counterterrorism, and Intelligence Collection in the United States Prior to September 11, *Staff Statement Number 9*, The 9/11 Commission, p. 4, issued April 13, 2004. Available at www.9–11commission.gov/hearings/hearing10.htm (accessed September 16, 2004).

20. For training specifics, see Alfred Cumming and Todd Masse, "FBI Intelligence Reform Since September 11, 2001: Issues and Options for Congress," Congressional Research Service RL 32336, August 4, 2004, pp. 14–15. http://www.fas.org/irp/crs/RL32336.pdf (accessed February 23, 2006).

21. *Joint Inquiry Report*, p. 340.

22. Ronald Kessler, *The Bureau: The Secret History of the FBI* (New York: St. Martin's, 2003), p. 348; interview with former FBI official, December 2004.

23. Quoted in Eric Lichtblau and Charles Piller, "Without a Clue: How the FBI lost its way," *Milwaukee Journal Sentinel*, August 11, 2002, p. 01J.

24. Interview with two officials who read the report, June 2004 and December 2004.

25. The classified reports were: *The Report of the Commission to Assess the Ballistic Missile Threat to the United States* (The Rumsfeld Commission), July 15, 1998, unclassified executive summary available at www.fas.org/irp/congress/2002_hr/100302hill.html (accessed January 30, 2006); *Report of the Intelligence Community Task Force on Personnel Reform*, July 1995 (The Jehn Study), unclassified summary in House Permanent Select Committee on Intelligence, *IC21: The Intelligence Community in the 21st Century*, Staff Study of the Permanent Select Committee on Intelligence, April 19, 1996, "Intelligence Community Management," Executive Summary, pp. 21–22; *The Intelligence Community Revolution Task Force Report* (June 1995), unclassified summary in the *Report of the Commission on Protecting and Reducing Government Secrecy* (The Moynihan Commission), Senate Document 105–102, 103rd Cong., 1997, chairman's forward.; *Intelligence Community Performance on the Indian Nuclear Test* (Jeremiah Report), June 2, 1998, unclassified news conference available at www.fas.org/irp/congress/2002_hr/100302hill.html (accessed January 30, 2006); Office of the Inspector General, U.S. Department of Justice, *The Handling of FBI Intelligence Information related to the Justice Department's Campaign Finance Investigation* (July 1999), unclassified executive summary available at www.usdoj.gov/oig/special/9907.htm (accessed January 30, 2006); Department of Defense, *U.S.S. Cole Commission Report* (January 9, 2001), unclassified executive summary available at www.defenselink.mil/pubs/cole20010109.htm (accessed January 30, 2006). Topics included an analysis of the CIA's failure to predict the Indian and Pakistani nuclear tests, an investigation into the al Qaeda bombing of the USS *Cole*, and two separate classified internal reviews recommending massive overhaul of intelligence personnel policies to, among other things, foster greater cooperation and coordination between agencies.

26. The unclassified studies consist of reports from commissions, governmental initiatives, and think tank task forces. The commission reports are: Commission on the Roles and Capabilities of the United States Intelligence Community (Aspin-Brown Commission), *Preparing for the 21st Century: An Appraisal of U.S. Intelligence* (Washington, DC:

GPO, 1996); Commission to Assess the Organization of the Federal Government to Combat the Proliferation of Weapons of Mass Destruction (Deutch commission), *Combating Proliferation of Weapons of Mass Destruction* (Washington, DC: GPO, 1999); Advisory Panel to Assess Domestic Response Capabilities for Terrorism Involving Weapons of Mass Destruction (1999 Gilmore Commission and 2000 Gilmore Commission), *First Annual Report to The President and The Congress: Assessing the Threat* (Washington, DC: GPO, 1999), and *Second Annual Report to The President and The Congress: Toward a National Strategy for Combating Terrorism* (Washington, DC: GPO, 2000); National Commission on Terrorism (Bremer Commission), *Countering the Changing Threat of International Terrorism* (Washington, DC: GPO, 2000); United States Commission on National Security/21st Century (Hart-Rudman Commission), *Road Map for National Security: Imperative for Change* (Washington, DC: GPO, 2001); Commission on the Advancement of Federal Law Enforcement (Webster Commission), *Law Enforcement in a New Century and a Changing World: Improving the Administration of Federal Law Enforcement* (Washington, DC: GPO, 2000). The governmental initiatives are: National Performance Review, "The Intelligence Community: Recommendations and Actions," in *From Red Tape to Results: Creating a Government that Works Better and Costs Less* (Washington, DC: U.S. GPO, September 1993); National Performance Review, *National Performance Review Phase II Initiatives: An Intelligence Community Report* (Washington, D.C.: U.S. GPO, 1995); House Permanent Select Committee on Intelligence, *IC21: The Intelligence Community in the 21st Century* (Washington, DC: U.S. GPO, 1996); and Federal Bureau of Investigation, *Draft FBI Strategic Plan: 1998–2003, Keeping Tomorrow Safe* (Washington, DC: U.S. GPO, 1998). The think tank task force reports are: Council on Foreign Relations Independent Task Force, *Making Intelligence Smarter: The Future of U.S. Intelligence* (New York: Council on Foreign Relations, 1996); Twentieth Century Fund Task Force on the Future of U.S. Intelligence, *In from the Cold: The Report of the Twentieth Century Fund Task Force on the Future of U.S. Intelligence* (New York: Twentieth Century Fund Press, 1996); and National Institute for Public Policy, *Modernizing Intelligence: Structure and Change for the 21st Century* (Fairfax, VA: National Institute for Public Policy, 2002).

27. For a discussion of how these reform recommendations were identified and analyzed, see appendix.

28. United States Commission on National Security/21st Century (Hart-Rudman Commission), "Phase III Report of the U.S. Commission on National Security/21st Century," *Road Map for National Security: Imperative for Change* (February 15, 2001), p. x. http://www.au.af.mil/au/awc/awcgate/nssg/phaseIIIfr.pdf (accessed February 23, 2006).

29. Richard Betts, "Fixing Intelligence," *Foreign Affairs* 81 (January–February 2002), p. 44.

30. For an example of Berger's charges, see Michael Elliott, "They Had a Plan," *Time Magazine Special Report*, August 12, 2002, p. 28. One year later, Albright told the *Los Angeles Times* editorial board in a taped conversation used for publication, "I try very hard to stay out of the [debate over who's to blame for 9/11]. . . . But when we did transition briefings, the Bush administration was not interested in what we were telling them about terrorism." Editors, "Sideline Diplomacy: Former Secretary Madeleine Albright on War, Peace, Terrorism," *Los Angeles Times*, November 2, 2003, home edition, p. M3.

31. See Condoleezza Rice, "9/11: For the Record," *Washington Post*, March 22, 2004, p. A21; Condoleezza Rice interview by Ed Bradley, *60 Minutes*, CBS News, March 28, 2004; James Rosen, "Cease-fire ends; blame game starts," *Minneapolis Star Tribune*, March 28, 2004, p. 1A.

32. See for example, David E. Rosenbaum, "Traces of Terror: The Critics; Bush Allies Direct Heaviest Fire Against Both F.B.I. and C.I.A.," *New York Times*, June 19, 2002, p. A19; Richard C. Shelby, "September 11 and the Imperative of Reform in the U.S. Intelligence Community," *Additional Views of Senator Richard C. Shelby, Vice Chairman, Senate Select Committee on Intelligence, Joint Inquiry Report*, December 10, 2002, p. 135.

33. Richard Clarke made his claims in an interview with Leslie Stahl on *60 Minutes*, a bestselling book, and nationally televised testimony before the 9/11 Commission. The Stahl interview aired on CBS News, March 21, 2004; The book is Richard A. Clarke, *Against All Enemies: Inside America's War on Terror* (New York: Free Press, 2004); Clarke's 9/11 Commission testimony was delivered on March 24, 2004 and can be found at: http://www.9–11commission.gov/archive/hearing8/9–11 Commission_Hearing_2004–03–24.pdf (accessed July 11, 2006).

34. Steve Coll, *Ghost Wars: The Secret History of the CIA, Afghanistan, and Bin Laden, from the Soviet Invasion to September 10, 2001*, reprint ed. (New York: Penguin, December 2004); Bill Gertz, *Breakdown: How America's Intelligence Failures Led to 9/11* (New York: Regnery, 2002); Ronald Kessler, *The CIA at War* (New York: St Martin's, 2003); Ronald Kessler, *The Bureau: The Secret History of the FBI* (New York: St. Martin's, 2003); Rich Lowry, *Legacy: Paying the Price of the Clinton Years* (New York: Regnery, 2003); John Miller, Chris Mitchell, and Michael Stone, *The Cell: Inside the 9/11 Plot and Why the FBI and CIA Failed to Stop It* (New York: Hyperion, 2003); Gerald L. Posner, *Why America Slept: The Failure to Prevent 9/11* (New York: Random House, 2003); James Risen, *State of War: The Secret History of the CIA and the Bush Administration* (New York: Free Press, 2006); Lawrence Wright, *The Looming Tower: Al-Qaeda and the Road to 9/11* (New York: Knopf, 2006).

35. Malcolm Gladwell, "Connecting the Dots: the Paradoxes of Intelligence Reform," *New Yorker*, March 10, 2003, pp. 83–89.

36. Gertz, pp. 21–27.

37. Miller et al., *The Cell*, p. 275.

38. Bob Woodward, *The Commanders: The Pentagon and the First Gulf War, 1989–1991*, rev. ed. (New York: Simon & Schuster, 2005), p. 34.

39. James Bamford, "War of Secrets: Eyes in the Sky, Ears to the Wall, and Still Wanting," *New York Times*, September 8, 2002, section 4, p. 5.

40. Amy B. Zegart, "Cloaks, Daggers, and Ivory Towers: Why Academics Don't Study U.S. Intelligence," in *Strategic Intelligence*, ed. Loch K. Johnson (Westport, CT: Praeger, 2006).

41. Sandy Berger, testimony before the 9/11 Commission eighth public hearing, March 24, 2004, p. 4, available at: http://www.9–11commission.gov/hearings/hearing8/berger_statement.pdf (accessed February 24, 2006).

42. Sandy Berger, testimony before the 9/11 Commission eighth public hearing (transcript), March 24, 2004, p. 73. http://www.9–11commission.gov/archive/hearing8/9–11Commission_Hearing_2004–03–24.pdf (accessed February 23, 2006).

43. *9/11 Commission Report*, p. 358.

44. *9/11 Commission Report*, pp. 358–59.

45. Sandy Berger, testimony before the 9/11 Commission eighth public hearing (transcript), March 24, 2004, p. 73. http://www.9–11commission.gov/archive/hearing8/9–11Commission_Hearing_2004–03–24.pdf (accessed February 23, 2006).

46. Prepared testimony of Samuel L. Berger before the National Commission on Terrorist Attacks Upon the United States (9/11 Commission), March 24, 2004, p. 4.

47. Richard Clarke, interview with Leslie Stahl, *60 Minutes*, CBS News, March 21, 2004.

48. Interview with Richard Clarke, *Larry King Live*, CNN, March 24, 2004.

49. Bush National Security Advisor Condoleezza Rice testified before the 9/11 Commission that she received the after-action report when she took office, and that the report concluded Ressam had been caught by chance. Condoleezza Rice, testimony before the 9/11 Commission ninth public hearing (transcript), April 8, 2004, p. 35. http://www.9–11commission.gov/archive/hearing9/9–11Commission_Hearing_2004–04–08.pdf (accessed February 23, 2006).

50. *9/11 Commission Report*, pp. 178–79.

51. Richard A. Clarke, *Against All Enemies: Inside America's War on Terror* (New York: Free Press, 2004), p. 212.

52. Trial testimony of Diana Dean, *United States v. Ressam*, No. CR99–666C, March 13, 2001, transcript, p. 124.

53. Lisa Myers, "Foiling Millennium Attack was Mostly Luck," NBC News, April 29, 2004.

54. Testimony by Condoleezza Rice, 9/11 Commision ninth public hearing, April 8, 2004, p. 17. http://www.9–11commission.gov/archive/hearing9/9–11Commission_Hearing_2004–04–08.pdf. Rice's testimony about the absence of a field alert was confirmed by other customs officials in an NBC news report. See Lisa Myers, "Foiling Millennium Attack was Mostly Luck," NBC News, April 29, 2004.

55. *9/11 Commission Report*, p. 179.

56. See, for example, Siobhan Gorman, "FBI Chief Struggling to Turn Rhetoric into Action," *National Journal*, August 23, 2004.

57. Interview, October 2005.

58. See for example Robert Mueller's testimony, "FBI Reorganization," House Appropriations Subcommittee for the Departments of Commerce, Justice, State and Judiciary, 107th Cong., 2nd sess., June 21, 2002; The Office of the Inspector General, Audit Division, U.S. Department of Justice, *The Federal Bureau of Investigation's Management of the Trilogy Information Technology Modernization Project*, February 2005, Audit Report 05–07, p. 1.

59. Interview, January 2007.

60. "FBI Trilogy Information Modernization Program," hearing of the Senate Appropriations Subcommittee on Commerce, Justice, State, and the Judiciary, 109th Cong., 1st sess., February 3, 2005.

61. The Office of the Inspector General, Audit Division, U.S. Department of Justice, *The Federal Bureau of Investigation's Management of the Trilogy Information Technology Modernization Project*, February 2005, Audit Report 05–07.

62. Interview, January 2007.

63. Roberta Wohlstetter, *Pearl Harbor: Warning and Decision* (Stanford, CA: Stanford University Press, 1962).

CHAPTER 2

CANARIES IN THE COAL MINE

1. U.S. Congress, House Permanent Select Committee on Intelligence and Senate Select Committee on Intelligence, "September 11 and the Imperative of Reform in the U.S. Intelligence Community: Additional Views of Senator Richard C. Shelby, Vice Chairman, Senate Select Committee on Intelligence," in *Joint Inquiry Report*, 107th Cong., 2nd sess., December 10, 2002, p. 3.

2. Interview, April 2002.

3. See for example Bill Gertz, *Breakdown: How America's Intelligence Failures Led to 9/11* (New York: Regnery, 2002); John Miller, Chris Mitchell, and Michael Stone, *The Cell: Inside the 9/11 Plot and Why the FBI and CIA Failed to Stop It* (New York: Hyperion, 2003); Gerald L. Posner, *Why America Slept: The Failure to Prevent 9/11* (New York: Random House, 2003).

4. Howard Aldrich, *Organizations Evolving* (London: Sage Publications, 1999), p. 164.

5. As Jim March wrote in 1981, "Organizations are continually changing, routinely, easily, and responsively. . . . What most reports on implementation indicate . . . is not that organizations are rigid and inflexible, but that they are impressively imaginative." March, "Footnotes on Organizational Change," *Administrative Science Quarterly* 26 (1981): 563.

6. Michael T. Hannan and John Freeman, "Structural Inertia and Organizational Change," *American Sociological Review* 49 (1984): 151.

7. James G. March, "Footnotes on Organizational Change," *Administrative Science Quarterly* 26 (1981): 563–77.

8. Samuel L. Berger, "Counterterrorism Policy," statement before the 9/11 Commission eighth public hearing, March 24, 2004. http:// www.9–11commission.gov/hearings/hearing8/berger_statement.pdf (accessed February 22, 2006). Former Director of Central Intelligence R. James Woolsey told senators at his February 1993 confirmation hearing, "In many ways, today's threats are harder to observe and understand than the one that was once presented by the USSR. . . . Yes, we have slain a large dragon, but we live now in a jungle filled with a bewildering variety of poisonous snakes, and in many ways the dragon was easier to keep track of." Testimony before the Senate Select Committee on Intelligence, 103rd Cong., 1st sess., February 2, 1993.

9. Robert Gates, quoted in John H. Hedley, "The Intelligence Community: Is it Broken? How to Fix It?" *Studies in Intelligence* 39, 5 (1996). http://www.cia.gov/csi/studies/96unclass/hedley.htm (accessed February 22, 2006).

10. According to The 9/11 Commission, national foreign intelligence program budgets declined every year between 1990 and 1996, and, with the exception of one large 1999 supplemental, remained basically flat between 1996 and 2000. See *9/11 Commission Report*, p. 93.

11. *Joint Inquiry Report*, p. 257.

12. J. Cofer Black, "9/11 Intelligence Investigation," testimony before the Joint Inquiry, 107th Cong., 2nd sess., September 26, 2002.

13. Eleanor Hill, "Joint Inquiry Staff Statement," testimony before the Joint Inquiry, 107th Cong., 2nd sess., September 18, 2002, p. 9.

14. *9/11 Commission Report*, p. 76.

15. Samuel L. Berger, "Counterterrorism Policy," testimony before the 9/11 Commission eighth public hearing (transcript), March 24, 2004, p. 69. http://www.9–11commission.gov/archive/hearing8/9–11Commission_Hearing_2004–03–24.pdf (accessed February 22, 2006).

16. George Tenet, "Worldwide Threat—Converging Dangers in a Post-9/11 World," testimony before the Senate Select Committee on Intelligence, 107th Cong., 2nd sess., February 6, 2002.

17. See in particular Thomas Powers, "The Trouble with the CIA," *New York Review of Books* 49 (Jan 2002): 17. http://www.nybooks.com/articles/15109 (accessed February 22, 2006).

18. Interview, April 2002.

19. George Tenet, "Activities of the Intelligence Community in Connection with the Attacks of September 11, 2001," testimony before the Joint Inquiry, 107th Cong., 2nd sess., October 17, 2002.

20. Louis J. Freeh, "On War and Terrorism," testimony before the 9/11 Commission tenth public hearing, April 13, 2004, p. 4. http://www.9–11commission.gov/hearings/hearing10/freeh_statement.pdf (accessed February 22, 2006).

21. Freeh, "On War and Terrorism," p. 8.

22. March 1981, p. 563.

23. Michael T. Hannan and John Freeman, "Structural Inertia and Organizational Change," *American Sociological Review* 49 (1984):151.

24. Interview, February 2004.

25. R. James Woolsey, "World Trouble Spots," testimony before the Senate Select Committee on Intelligence, 103rd Cong., 2nd sess., January 25, 1994; R. James Woolsey, "World Threat Assessment Brief," testimony before the Senate Select Committee on Intelligence, 104th Cong., 1st sess., January 10, 1995; John Deutch, "Worldwide Threats to U.S. National Security," testimony before the Senate Select Committee on Intelligence, 104th Cong., 2nd sess., February 22, 1996; George Tenet, "Worldwide Threats to National Security," testimony before the Senate Armed Services Committee, 105th Cong., 1st sess., February 6, 1997; George Tenet, "Worldwide Threats to National Security," testimony before the Senate Select Committee on Intelligence, 105th Cong., 2nd sess., January 28, 1998; George Tenet, "Worldwide Threats to U.S. National Security," testimony before the Senate Armed Services Committee, 106th Cong., 1st sess., February 2, 1999; George Tenet, "Annual Assessment of Security Threats against the United States," testimony before the Senate Select Committee on Intelligence, 106th Cong., 2nd sess., February 2, 2000; George Tenet, "Worldwide Threats to National Security," testimony before the Senate Select Committee on Intelligence, 107th Cong., 1st sess., February 7, 2001.

26. Eleanor Hill, "Joint Inquiry Staff Statement, Part I," statement to the Joint Inquiry, 107th Cong., 2nd sess., September 18, 2002.

27. Dale Watson, "9/11 Intelligence Investigations," testimony before the Joint Inquiry, 107th Cong., 2nd sess., September 26, 2002.

28. Freeh, "On War and Terrorism," p. 9.

29. Freeh, "On War and Terrorism," p. 9.

30. J. Cofer Black, statement before the 9/11 Commission tenth public hearing, April 13, 2004, p. 4. http://www.9–11commission.gov/hearings/hearing10/black_statement.pdf (accessed February 22, 2006).

31. Samuel L. Berger, "Events Surrounding the Terrorist Attacks of September 11, 2001," testimony before Panel II of a Joint Inquiry hearing, 107th Cong., 2nd sess., September 19, 2002.

32. For a translated text of the fatwa, see www.fas.org/irp/world/para/docs/980223-fatwa.htm (accessed June 23, 2005).

33. Hill, "Joint Inquiry Staff Statement, Part I," p. 9.

34. *9/11 Commission Report*, p. 70.

35. Hill, "Joint Inquiry Staff Statement, Part I," p. 12.

36. Ibid.

37. George Tenet, "Worldwide Threats to U.S. National Security," testimony before the Senate Armed Services Committee, 106th Cong., 1st sess., February 2, 1999.

38. George Tenet, "Annual Assessment of Security Threats against the United States," testimony before the Senate Select Committee on Intelligence, 106th Cong., 2nd sess., February 2, 2000.

39. George Tenet, "Worldwide Threats to National Security," testimony before the Senate Select Committee on Intelligence, 107th Cong., 1st sess., February 7, 2001.

40. Interview, April 2002.

41. The Joint Inquiry noted that "knowledge of the DCI's declaration appears to have been limited . . . many in the FBI had not heard of it. For example, the assistant director of the FBI's Counterterrorism Division testified to the Joint Inquiry that he 'was not specifically aware of that declaration of war.'" *Joint Inquiry Report*, p. 232.

42. Federal Bureau of Investigation, *Keeping Tomorrow Safe: Draft FBI Strategic Plan, 1998–2003*, unclassified version, May 8, 1998, p. 8.

43. Quoted by Louis Freeh, "On War and Terrorism," testimony before The 9/11 Commission, April 13, 2004.

44. Freeh, "On War and Terrorism," pp. 4–6.

45. R. James Woolsey, remarks (American Bar Association, Washington, DC, April 29, 1994).

46. William J. Clinton, "State of the Union Address," January 25, 1994, *Public Papers of the Presidents: William J. Clinton—1994*, vol. 1

(Washington, DC: GPO): 126–35; William J. Clinton, "State of the Union Address," January 24, 1995, *Public Papers of the Presidents: William J. Clinton—1995*, vol. 1 (Washington, DC: GPO): 75–86; William J. Clinton, "State of the Union Address," January 23, 1996, *Public Papers of the Presidents: William J. Clinton—1996*, vol. 1 (Washington, DC: GPO): 79–87; William J. Clinton, "State of the Union Address," February 4, 1997, *Public Papers of the Presidents: William J. Clinton—1997*, vol. 1 (Washington, DC: GPO): 109–17; William J. Clinton, "State of the Union Address," January 27, 1998, *Public Papers of the Presidents: William J. Clinton—1998*, vol. 1 (Washington, DC: GPO): 112–21; William J. Clinton, "State of the Union Address," January 19, 1999, *Public Papers of the Presidents: William J. Clinton—1999*, vol. 1 (Washington, DC: GPO): 62–71; William J. Clinton, "State of the Union Address," January 27, 2000, *Weekly Compilation of Presidential Documents* vol. 36, no. 4 (Washington, DC: GPO): 160–72.

47. William J. Clinton, "Remarks to the United Nations General Assembly in New York City," October 22, 1995, *Public Papers of the Presidents: William J. Clinton—1995*, vol. 2 (Washington, DC: GPO, 1995): 1654–57.

48. President William J. Clinton, "Remarks Announcing the Second Term National Security Team and an Exchange with Reporters," December 5, 1996, cited in *9/11 Commission Report*, p. 101.

49. John P. O'Neill, remarks (National Strategy Forum, Chicago, IL, June 11, 1997), collection of author.

50. National Defense Panel, *Transforming Defense: National Security in the 21st Century*, December 1, 1997. http://www.fas.org/man/docs/ndp/toc.htm (accessed February 22, 2006). William S. Cohen, U.S. Department of Defense, *Report of the Quadrennial Defense Review*, May 1997. http://www.defenselink.mil/pubs/qdr/ (accessed February 22, 2006).

51. John McWethy, John Miller, and Ted Koppel, "One of America's Most Dangerous Enemies," *Nightline*, ABC News, June 10, 1998.

52. President William J. Clinton, "Remarks to the opening session of the 53rd United Nations General Assembly," September 21, 1998, *Public Papers of the Presidents: William J. Clinton—1998*, vol. 2 (Washington, DC: GPO): 1629–33.

53. William S. Cohen, "Preparing for a Grave New World," *Washington Post*, July 26, 1999, p. A19.

54. George W. Bush, "Defense: A Period of Consequences" (speech, The Citadel, Charleston, SC, September 23, 1999); George W. Bush, "Foreign Policy: A Distinctly American Internationalism" (speech, the Ronald Reagan Library, Simi Valley, CA, November 19, 1999).

55. George W. Bush, "Foreign Policy: A Distinctly American Internationalism."

56. *9/11 Commission Report*, p. 198.

57. *Joint Inquiry Report*, p. 242.

58. *9/11 Commission Report*, p. 342. It bears noting the Commission remained skeptical about the full extent to which policymakers recognized the magnitude or imminence of the threat. The commission concluded that given the pace of the Clinton and Bush policy efforts, "we do not believe they fully understood just how many people al Qaeda might kill, and how soon it might do it. At some level that is hard to define, we believe the threat had not yet become compelling." *9/11 Commission Report*, pp. 342–43.

59. For a discussion of study selection criteria, see appendix. It is also worth noting that these studies err on understating awareness of the threat because they cover only unclassified reports. In addition, at least six classified reports were produced during the period that also urged reform of the U.S. Intelligence Community.

60. The commission reports are: Commission on the Roles and Capabilities of the United States Intelligence Community ("Aspin-Brown Commission"), *Preparing for the 21st Century: An Appraisal of U.S. Intelligence* (Washington, DC: GPO, 1996); National Commission on Terrorism ("Bremer Commission"), *Countering the Changing Threat of International Terrorism* (Washington, DC: GPO, 2000); Commission to Assess the Organization of the Federal Government to Combat the Proliferation of Weapons of Mass Destruction ("Deutch Commission"), *Combating Proliferation of Weapons of Mass Destruction* (Washington, DC: GPO, 1999); Advisory Panel to Assess Domestic Response Capabilities for Terrorism Involving Weapons of Mass Destruction ("1999 Gilmore Commission" and "2000 Gilmore Commission"), *First Annual Report to The President and The Congress: Assessing the Threat* (Washington, DC: GPO, 1999), and *Second Annual Report to The President and The Congress: Toward a National Strategy for Combating Terrorism* (Washington, DC: GPO, 2000); United States Commission on National Security/21st Century ("Hart-Rudman Commission"), *Road Map for National Security: Imperative for Change* (Washington, DC: GPO, 2001); Commission on the Advancement of Federal Law Enforcement ("Webster Commission"), *Law Enforcement in a New Century and a Changing World: Improving the Administration of Federal Law Enforcement* (Washington, DC: GPO, 2000).

61. Council on Foreign Relations, *Making Intelligence Smarter: The Future of U.S. Intelligence* ("CFR Report") (New York: CFR, 1996); National Institute for Public Policy, *Modernizing Intelligence: Structure and Change for the 21st Century* ("Odom Report") (Fairfax, VA: NIPP, 2002); Twenti-

eth Century Fund, *In From the Cold: The Report of the Twentieth Century Fund Task Force on the Future of U.S. Intelligence* ("TCF Report") (New York: Twentieth Century Fund Press, 1996).

62. *Draft FBI Strategic Plan*; National Performance Review, "The Intelligence Community: Recommendations and Actions," in *From Red Tape to Results: Creating a Government that Works Better and Costs Less* ("National Performance Review 1993") (Washington, DC: GPO, September 1993), and *National Performance Review Phase II Initiatives: An Intelligence Community Report* ("National Performance Review 1995") (Washington, DC: GPO, 1995); House Permanent Select Committee on Intelligence, *IC21: The Intelligence Community in the 21st Century* ("IC21") (Washington, DC: GPO, 1996).

63. "An Act to deter terrorism, provide justice for victims, provide for an effective death penalty, and for other purposes (Antiterrorism and Effective Death Penalty Act of 1996)." (PL 104–132, April 24, 1996). United States Statutes at Large 110 (1996): 1213–319.

64. Hart-Rudman Commission, *Road Map for National Security: Imperative for Change*, Phase III Report, January 31, 2001, p. 83.

65. Council on Foreign Relations, *Making Intelligence Smarter: The Future of U.S. Intelligence, Report of an Independent Task Force* (New York: Council on Foreign Relations, 1996), p. 1.

66. House Permanent Select Committee on Intelligence Staff Study, *IC21: The Intelligence Community in the 21st Century*, chapter 1, "Overview and Summary" (Washington: GPO, 1996), p. 5. http://www.access.gpo.gov/congress/house/intel/ic21/ic21_toc.html (accessed February 22, 2006).

67. *IC21*, chapter 1, "Overview and Summary," p. 7.

68. Ibid., p. 26.

69. Ibid., p. 28.

70. National Terrorism Commission, *Countering the Changing Threat of International Terrorism: Report of the National Commission on Terrorism*, June 7, 2000, p. iv. http://www.access.gpo.gov/nct/index.html (accessed February 22, 2006).

71. *Report of the National Commission on Terrorism*, p. 13.

72. Gilmore Commission recommendations are from the panel's 1999 and 2000 reports. The commission issued two reports after the September 11, 2001, terrorist attacks that were not included in this analysis.

73. Amy Zegart, "Blue Ribbons, Black Boxes: Toward a Better Understanding of Presidential Commissions," *Presidential Studies Quarterly*, 35 (June 2004), p. 366. Although The 9/11 Commission and the more recent Commission on the Intelligence Capabilities of the United

States Regarding Weapons of Mass Destruction (the Silberman-Robb Commission) appear to fit the stereotyped mold—they were reluctantly created by the president to quell public demands for action—most national security oriented commissions are not so visible and are not intended to deflect political heat from the president by moving issues off his agenda. Instead, an analysis of all commissions created from 1981 to 2001 (668 in total) found that 61 percent of all foreign policy commissions served a different purpose: these "information commissions" were created out of the public eye, targeted senior policymakers themselves rather than the general public, and were designed to provide new ideas, new facts, or new analysis about foreign policy issues looming on the horizon. By contrast only 32 percent of all domestic policy commissions in the same period fell into this information commission category.

74. For example, the National Performance Review recommended that the Foreign Broadcast Information Service reexamine its mission for a post–Cold War threat environment, and the FBI's 1998 Strategic Plan suggested the FBI explore the feasibility of instituting a capability to exchange unclassified investigative material to others in the law enforcement and Intelligence Community.

75. Council on Foreign Relations, *Making Intelligence Smarter*, p. 25.

76. *9/11 Commission Report*, p. 86.

77. The two exceptions were the Webster and Bremer Commissions.

78. National Performance Review, "INTEL02: Enhance Community Responsiveness to Customers," *The Intelligence Community: Recommendations and Actions*, September 1993. http://govinfo.library.unt.edu/npr/library/reports/intel.html (accessed February 22, 2006).

79. *IC21*, "Overview and Summary," p. 26.

80. Hart-Rudman Commission, *Road Map for National Security*, p. 82.

81. These were the Webster and Deutch Commissions.

82. The Bremer and Gilmore Commissions recommended abolishing the guidelines. The Council on Foreign Relations task force and the Hart-Rudman Commission urged the CIA to review the guidelines and make recruiting clandestine assets one of the Intelligence Community's top priorities. For effects of the "scrub order," see Seymour M. Hersh, "Annals of National Security: What Went Wrong," *New Yorker*, December 8, 2001. http://www.newyorker.com/fact/content/?011008fa_FACT (accessed February 22, 2006).

83 The National Performance Review, *The Intelligence Community: Recommendations and Actions*.

84. In a 2004 report, the House Intelligence Committee revealed that it had repeatedly criticized the CIA's human intelligence efforts and

recommended corrective action in classified annexes to its annual authorization bills years before September 11. House Permanent Select Committee on Intelligence, *Intelligence Authorization Act for FY 2005*, H. Report 108–558, 108th Cong., 2nd sess., June 21, 2004, p. 24.

85. National Institute for Public Policy, *Modernizing Intelligence*, pp. 85–98.

86. *IC21*, "Intelligence Community Management," p. 21.

87. The Hart-Rudman Commission had a broader focus, advocating a massive new educational initiative to improve the scientific and mathematics base for future national security needs.

88. Commission on the Roles and Capabilities of the United States Intelligence Community ("Aspin-Brown Commission"), "Chapter 9: The Need to 'Right-Size' and Rebuild the Community" in *Preparing for the 21st Century: An Appraisal of U.S. Intelligence* (Washington, DC: GPO, 1996), pp. 2–7.

89. The two exceptions were the Gilmore and Hart-Rudman Commissions.

90. *Joint Inquiry Report*, p. 43.

91. The 9/11 Commission, "The Performance of the Intelligence Community," *Staff Statement Number 11*, April 14, 2004, p. 12.

92. *9/11 Commission Report*, p. 357; *Joint Inquiry Report*, pp. 236–37.

93. *Joint Inquiry Report*, p. 49.

94. The 9/11 Commission, "The Performance of the Intelligence Community," April 14, 2004, p. 9.

95. *Joint Inquiry Report*, p. 49.

96. *9/11 Commission Report*, p. 90.

97. *Joint Inquiry Report*, p. 265.

98. The House Intelligence Committee noted in its unclassified Authorization Act Report for Fiscal Year 1998 that clandestine human intelligence constituted "a single digit percentage" of the National Foreign Intelligence Program budget and had declined in real dollar terms in the mid-1990s. Intelligence Authorization Act for Fiscal Year 1998, 105 H. Rpt. 135 part I, 105th cong., 1st sess., House Permanent Select Committee on Intelligence, June 18, 1997, p. 25.

99. Interview, June 2004.

100. Editors, "Intelligence Gaps: America's Spy Network Needs a Auick Fix," *San Diego Union Tribune*, April 22, 2002, p. B6.

101. Powers, "The Trouble with the CIA."

102. *Joint Inquiry Report*, p. xvi.

103. Interview, January 2004.

104. *Joint Inquiry Report*, p. xv.

CHAPTER 3
CROSSING AN ACADEMIC NO-MAN'S LAND

1. Understanding the evolution or deficiencies of U.S. national security agencies has never been central to political science. For decades, international relations theory has concentrated on relations between states, not what goes on inside them. To be sure, a number of international relations theorists do study inside-the-state variables (Graham Allison, *Essence of Decision: Explaining the Cuban Missile Crisis*: [Boston: Little, Brown, 1971]; Morton H. Halperin, *Bureaucratic Politics and Foreign Policy* [Washington, DC: Brookings Institution Press, 1974]; James D. Fearon, "Domestic Political Audiences and the Escalation of International Disputes," in *American Political Science Review* 88, 3 [September 1994]: 557–992; Kenneth A. Schultz, "Domestic Opposition and Signaling in International Crises," in *American Political Science Review* 92 [1998]: 829–44). However, the main intellectual currents of international relations scholarship flow elsewhere. The most popular recent arguments, for example, are Joseph Nye's work on American "soft power" and Samuel Huntington's "Clash of Civilizations." Both gaze beyond national borders at how American values and conflicts between civilizations shape international dynamics rather than looking within them, at how a country's national security agencies respond or fail to respond to changing threats. (Joseph S. Nye, Jr., *Soft Power: The Means to Success in World Politics* [New York: Public Affairs, 2004]; Samuel P. Huntington, *The Clash of Civilizations and the Remaking of the World Order* [New York: Simon & Schuster, 1996]).

In American politics, research on the bureaucracy has focused almost exclusively on American domestic policy agencies. In the 1970s and 1980s, capture theory examined U.S. domestic regulatory agencies like the Interstate Commerce Commission and argued that private industry designed and operated government agencies for its own benefit (George J. Stigler, "The Theory of Economic Regulation," *Bell Journal of Economics and Management Science* 2 [1971]: 3–21; Sam Peltzman, "Toward a More General Theory of Regulation," *Journal of Law and Economics* 19 [1976]: 211–40; Gary Becker, "A Theory of Competition Among Pressure Groups for Influence," *Quarterly Journal of Economics* 98 [1983]: 371–400). More recently, new institutionalists have used transaction cost economics to explain bureaucratic design and behavior, but have applied these new ideas to the same old agencies (Weingast and Moran 1983; Dan B. Wood, "Principles, Bureaucrats, and Responsiveness in Clean Air Enforcement," *American Political Science Review* 82 [1988]: 213–34; Mathew D. McCubbins, Roger G. Noll, and Barry R. Weingast, "Administrative Procedures as Instruments of Political Control," in *Journal of Law, Economics, and Organization* 3 [1987]: 243–77; Moe 1989; Lawrence S. Rothenberg, *Regulation, Organizations, and Politics: Motor Freight Policy at the Interstate Commerce Commission* [Ann Arbor: University of Michigan Press, 1994]). The study of U.S. national security agencies remains an undertilled field.

Although a number of historians and political scientists have reinvigorated the historical study of the American state in recent years, as Daniel Carpenter writes, this work still concentrates on the creation of agencies rather than their transformation. Carpenter, *The Forging of Bureaucratic Autonomy: Reputations, Networks, and Policy Innovation in Executive Agencies, 1862–1928* (Princeton, NJ: Princeton University Press, 2001), p. 11.

Intelligence agencies have received a particularly short shrift. Even after 9/11 and the Iraq War, with intelligence issues capturing headlines and policymaker attention, professors at America's best universities have continued to teach and write about nearly everything except U.S. intelligence agencies. For example, only four of the top twenty-five U.S. universities ranked by *U.S. News & World Report* in 2006 offered any undergraduate courses on the U.S. Intelligence Community. More, in fact, offered courses on the history of rock and roll, giving undergraduates a better chance of learning about the hit band U2 than the spy plane by the same name. ("Best National Universities," *U.S. News & World Report* 139, 7 [August 29, 2005]: 80; analysis of online university course catalogs conducted March 24–31, 2006). Between 2001 and 2006, the top three scholarly journals in political science, the *American Political Science Review*, the *American Journal of Political Science*, and the *Journal of Politics*, published 750 research articles. Only one article examined intelligence issues. The other 99.9 percent discussed other topics. (Based on analysis of article abstracts from January 2001 though May 2006). For more on journal rankings, see James C. Garrand and Micheal W. Giles, "Journals in the Discipline: A Report on a New Survey of American Political Scientists," *PS: Political Science and Politics* (April 2003): 293–308.

2. Notable examples of such cross-disciplinary work are: Scott D. Sagan, *The Limits of Safety* (Princeton, NJ: Princeton University Press, 1993); Charles Perrow, *Normal Accidents: Living with High-Risk Technologies* (Princeton, NJ: Princeton University Press, 1999); Diane Vaughan, *The Challenger Launch Decision: Risky Technology, Culture, and Deviance at NASA* (Chicago: University of Chicago Press, 1996); and Lynn Eden, *Whole World on Fire: Organizations, Knowledge, and Nuclear Weapons Devastation* (Ithaca, NY: Cornell University Press, 2003).

3. Intraorganizational variables pose many problems for political scientists. Chief among them: factors like culture and norms are inher-

ently difficult to measure; require historical research rather than the quantitative methods that most political scientists use; fit uneasily with rational actor models; and tend to explain persistence rather than major change over time. For a discipline dominated by rational choice explanations of major developments such as the causes of war, intraorganizational factors are inherently messy and unattractive.

4. One important and large exception is the neo-institutionalism school in sociology, which argues that organizations are not just the products of individual rational decision-making, but are influenced in important ways by broader "institutional environments" such as organizational sector and higher-level structure. See, for example, John W. Meyer and Brian Rowan, "Institutionalized Organizations: Formal Structure as Myth and Ceremony," *American Journal of Sociology* 83: 340–63 (1977); Walter W. Powell and Paul J. DiMaggio, eds., *The New Institutionalism in Organizational Analysis* (Chicago: University of Chicago Press, 1991); W. Richard Scott, "Reflections on a Half-Century of Organizational Sociology," *Annual Review of Sociology* vol. 30 (August 2004): 1–21.

5. In James March's words, the field has served as "a kind of Switzerland of ideas." James G. March, *The Pursuit of Organizational Intelligence* (London: Blackwell, 1999), p. 43.

6. Glenn R. Carroll, "Organizational Ecology," in *Annual Review of Sociology* vol. 10 (Palo Alto: Annual Reviews, 1984); Michael T. Hannan and John Henry Freeman, "The Population Ecology of Organizations," *American Journal of Sociology* 82, 5 (March 1977): 929–64; Michael T. Hannan and John Henry Freeman, "Structural Inertia and Organizational Change," *American Sociological Review* 49, 2 (April 1984): 149–64; Michael T. Hannan and John Henry Freeman, *Organizational Ecology* (Cambridge: Harvard University Press, 1989).

7. Joel A.C. Baum and Jitendra V. Singh, *Evolutionary Dynamics of Organizations* (Oxford: Oxford University Press, 1994); Howard Aldrich, *Organizations Evolving* (London: Sage, 1999).

8. Barbara Levitt and James G. March, "Organizational Learning," *Annual Review of Sociology,* vol. 14 (1988): 319–340; Richard M. Cyert and James G. March, *A Behavioral Theory of the Firm* (London: Blackwell, 1963); Mary Ann Glynn, Theresa K. Lant, and Frances J. Milliken, "Mapping Learning Processes in Organizations: A Multi-Level Framework Linking Learning and Organizing, "in *Advances in Managerial Cognition and Organizational Information Processing* vol. 5 (Greenwich, CT: JAI Press, 1994): 43–83; Anne S. Miner and Stephen J. Mezias, "Ugly Duckling No More: Pasts and Futures of Organizational Learning Research," *Organization Science* 7, 1 (January–February 1996): 88–

99; James G. March, "Exploration and Exploitation in Organizational Learning," *Organization Science* vol. 2, no. 1 (February 1991): 71–87.

9. David Osborne and Ted Gaebler, *Reinventing Government: How the Entrepreneurial Spirit is Transforming the Public Sector* (New York: Penguin, 1993); David Osborne and Peter Plastrik, *Banishing Bureaucracy: The Five Strategies for Reinventing Government* (New York: Penguin, 1998); James Q. Wilson, *Bureaucracy: What Government Agencies Do and Why They Do It* (New York: Basic Books, 2000). For more on differences between public and private sectors, see Joel D. Aberbach and Bert A. Rockman, *In the Web of Politics: Three Decades of the U.S. Federal Executive* (Washington, DC: Brookings Institution Press, 2000); Terry M. Moe, "The New Economics of Organization," in *American Journal of Political Science* 28 (1984): 739–77; Moe, "The Politics of Structural Choice: Toward a Theory of Public Bureaucracy," in *Organization Theory: From Chester Barnard to the Present and Beyond*, ed. Oliver E. Williamson (New York: Oxford University Press, 1990).

10. For James G. March, one key lies in whether an organization can properly balance exploration, or the search for new ways of doing things, with what he calls exploitation, the ability to harness these new ideas and stop doing things the old way (March 1991). Howard Aldrich, by contrast, sees adaptation as a deadly four-stage Darwinian process where organizations must develop variations, select the right ones, replicate them effectively, and compete for scarce resources as the organizations around them also change (Aldrich 1999). Michael Hannan and John Henry Freeman believe that adaptation almost never occurs within organizations. Instead, it takes place between them, through the death of unfit firms and their replacement by newer, fitter entrants in a process of natural selection (Hannan and Freeman 1977; 1984; and 1989).

11. Aldrich 1999, p. 262.

12. Proprietary data based on surveys from 1979 to 1999 provided by Zagat.

13. For a useful examination of the decline of Bethlehem Steel, see Carol J. Loomis, "The Sinking of Bethlehem Steel," *Fortune*, April 5, 2004, p. 174.

14. U.S. Census Bureau, *Statistical Abstract of the United States: 2003* (Washington, DC: Government Printing Ofice, 2003), p. 506. Firm birth rate figures based on 1999–2000 annual data.

15. In the 1950s, Robert Merton argued that organizations have difficulty meeting even stable goals because workers tend to focus their efforts on building and maintaining the organization rather than advancing broad organizational aims. Robert K. Merton, *Social Theory and Social Structure*, 2nd ed., (Glencoe, IL: Free Press, 1957). Ironically, the

very devices used to enhance an organization's reliability such as the creation of standard operating procedures also diminish its ability to achieve organizational goals. Hannan and Freeman take this thinking further, arguing that organizational structures, which are crucial to developing reliability and accountability, often become so accepted by workers that they assume moral and political importance (Hannan and Freeman 1984), p. 154. With employees viewing proposed changes in moral terms ("this is wrong!") rather than technical terms ("this is not efficient!"), organizational changes stand little chance. Even James March, who views organizational adaptation with greater optimism, admits that organizations often get lulled into keeping existing routines and technologies rather than adopting new alternatives out of a sense of comfort from past experience (Levitt and March 1988).

16. Cyert and March, p. xi.

17. In his 1999 book about organizational evolution, *Organizations Evolving*, Howard Aldrich criticizes the selection bias of organization theory. Notably, though, he is troubled by the inordinate attention paid to large publicly traded corporations instead of smaller, privately held businesses. Aldrich's idea of broadening organization theory is to include different kinds of businesses, not political organizations (Aldrich 1999).

18. For more on difference between private and public sector, see James Q. Wilson, *Bureaucracy: What Government Agencies Do and Why They Do It* (New York: Basic Books, 2000); Terry M. Moe, "The Politics of Structural Choice: Toward a Theory of Public Bureaucracy," in Oliver E. Williamson, ed., *Organization Theory: From Chester Barnard to the Present and Beyond* (Oxford: Oxford University Press, 1990), pp. 116–53; Terry M. Moe, "The New Economics of Organization," *American Journal of Political Science* vol. 28 (November 1984): 739–77.

19. See in particular Hannan and Freeman 1977 and 1984 for an overview of this approach.

20. Anthony Downs, *Inside Bureaucracy* (Boston: Little, Brown 1967); Arthur Stinchcombe, "Social Structures and Organizations, "in *Handbook of Organizations*, ed. James G. March (Chicago: Rand McNally, 1965), pp. 142–93; Herbert Kaufman, *Are Government Organizations Immortal?* (Washington, D.C.: Brookings, 1976); Theodore J. Lowi, *The End of Liberalism: The Second Republic of the United States* (New York: Norton, 1979). Note that David Lewis finds surprising mortality in his data set of agencies from 1946 to 1997. David E. Lewis, *Presidents and the Politics of Agency Design: Political Insulation in the United States Government Bureaucracy, 1946–1997* (Stanford: Stanford University Press, 2003).

21. Kaufman 1976, p. 34. Kaufman's study found 148 of 175 organizations in existence in 1923 were also in existence in 1973. Moreover, he found that in 27 cases of agency "death," activities were transferred to other units rather than being discontinued (p. 64). The durability of

agencies has more recently come into question. See David E. Lewis 2003; Daniel P. Carpenter, *The Forging of Bureaucratic Autonomy: Reputations, Networks and Policy Innovation in Executive Agencies, 1862–1928* (Princeton: Princeton University Press, 2000).

22. Howard E. Aldrich, *Organizations and Environments* (Englewood Cliffs, NJ: Prentice-Hall, 1979), p. 36.

23. Lewis 2003, p. 174.

24. U.S. Census Bureau, *Statistical Abstract of the United States: 2003* (Washington, DC: Government Printing Office, 2003), p. 506. Analysis based on firm birth rates of 1999–2000.

25. Aldrich writes, "Ecologists assume that the most important processes to study are population demographics, patterns of foundings, transformations, and disbandings. These events constitute the dependent variables in most ecological analyses" (Aldrich 1999), p. 43.

26. Charles Perrow, *Complex Organizations: A Critical Essay*, 3rd ed. (New York: McGraw-Hill, 1986), p. 213.

27. For important exceptions, see Peter J. Katzenstein, ed., *The Culture of National Security: Norms and Identity in World Politics* (New York: Columbia University Press, 1996); Elizabeth Kier, *Imagining War: French and British Military Doctrine between the Wars* (Princeton: Princeton University Press, 1999); and Scott D. Sagan, *The Limits of Safety: Organizations, Accidents, and Nuclear Weapons* (Princeton: Princeton University Press, 1995).

28. Mathew D. McCubbins "The Legislative Design of Regulatory Structure," *American Journal of Political Science* 29 (1985): 721–48; Barry Weingast and Mark Moran, "Bureaucratic Discretion or Congressional Control? Regulatory Policymaking by the Federal Trade Commission," *Journal of Political Economy* vol. 91 (1983): 775–800.

29. Sharyn O'Halloran and David Epstein make this distinction between *ex ante* and ongoing oversight mechanisms. David Epstein and Sharyn O'Halloran, "Administrative Procedures, Information, and Agency Discretion," *American Journal of Political Science* 38 (1994): 697–722. For major work on *ex ante* controls, see Murray J. Horn, *The Political Economy of Public Administration: Institutional Choice in the Public Sector* (New York: Cambridge University Press, 1995); Mathew D. McCubbins and Thomas Schwartz, "Congressional Oversight Overlooked: Policy Patrol Versus Fire Alarm," *American Journal of Political Science* vol. 32 (1984): 165–77; Mathew D. McCubbins, Roger Noll, and Barry Weingast, "Administrative Procedures as Instruments of Political Control," *Journal of Law, Economics, and Organization* vol. 3 (1987): 243–77; Mathew D. McCubbins, Roger Noll, and Barry Weingast, "Structure and Process, Politics and Policy: Administrative Arrangements and the Political Control of Agencies," *Virginia Law Review* vol. 75 (1989): 431–82. For work on ongoing controls, see Randall Calvert, Mark Moran,

and Barry Weingast, "Congressional Influence Over Policy Making: The Case of the FTC," in *Congress: Structure and Policy*, ed. Mathew McCubbins and Terry Sulivan (Cambridge: Cambridge University Press, 1987); Jerry L. Mashaw, "Explaining Administrative Process: Normative, Positive, and Critical Stories of Legal Development," *Journal of Law, Economics, and Organization* vol. 6 (1990): 272–98; Randall Calvert, Mathew McCubbins, and Barry Weingast, "A Theory of Political Control and Agency Discretion," *American Journal of Political Science* vol. 33 (1989): 588–611. For a discussion of how legislators choose between different options, see Kathleen Bawn, "Political Control Versus Expertise: Congressional Choices about Administrative Procedures," *American Political Science Review* vol. 89 (1995): 62–73; David Epstein and Sharyn O'Halloran, *Delegating Powers* (New York: Cambridge University Press, 1999).

30. Mathew D. McCubbins, "The Legislative Design of Regulatory Structure," *American Journal of political Science* vol. 29, no. 4 (1985): 728.

31. Terry M. Moe, "An Assessment of the Positive Theory of 'Congressional Dominance,'" *Legislative Studies Quarterly* vol. 12, no. 4 (1987): 475–520.

32. Epstein and O'Halloran 1999, p. 29.

33. I do not mean to suggest that all agency heads are so well-intentioned and interested in maximizing organizational performance. Instead, the device is a heuristic, used to tease out the ways in which agencies can be reformed and the forces that are likely to block reforms from succeeding.

34. It is important to note that this claim is vigorously debated. For an alternative view, see James G. March and Johan P. Olsen, *Ambiguity and Choice in Organizations* (Bergen, Norway: Universitetsforlaget, 1976). Moreover, explanations of adaptation failure vary widely, as well.

35. This view is commonly referred to as the Carnegie School of organization theory. See Herbert A. Simon, *Administrative Behavior: A Study of Decision-Making Processes in Administrative Organizations*, 3rd ed. (New York: Free Press, 1976); James G. March and Herbert A. Simon, *Organizations* (New York: Wiley, 1958); Cyert and March 1963.

36. Simon 1976.

37. For a rich discussion of structural secrecy, see Vaughan 1996.

38. Janet Reno, testimony before the 9/11 Commission tenth public hearing (transcript), April 13, 2004, p. 62. http://www.0–11commission.gov/archive/hearing10/9–11Commission_Hearing_2004–04–13.pdf (accessed February 11, 2006).

39. *Joint Inquiry Report*, p. 25.

40. Major work arguing that administrative agencies become more durable as they get older includes: Anthony Downs, *Inside Bureaucracy*

(Boston: Little, Brown, 1967); Herbert Kaufman, *Are Government Organizations Immortal?* (Washington, DC: Brookings, 1976); Theodore J. Lowi, *The End of Liberalism: The Second Republic of the United States* (New York: Norton, 1979); David E. Lewis, *Presidents and the Politics of Agency Design: Political Insulation in the United States Government Bureaucracy, 1946–1997* (Stanford: Stanford University Press, 2003). A great deal of work suggests government agencies are like firms and other organizations in this regard. See, in particular, Arthur L. Stinchcombe, "Social Structures and Organizations," in *Handbook of Organizations*, ed. James G. March (Chicago: Rand McNally, 1965).

41. For more on efforts to motivate employees, see Thomas J. Peters and Robert H. Waterman, Jr., *In Search of Excellence: Lessons from America's Best-Run Companies* (New York: Warner Books, 1982).

42. In a seminal article, Hannan and Freeman (1984) discuss this idea with respect to firms, noting that the very characteristics that give an organization stability and reliability reduce the probability of change.

43. Charles Perrow 1986, p. 26.

44. Rosabeth Moss Kanter, *Men and Women of the Corporation* (New York: Basic Books, 1977); G. Stasser, L. A. Taylor, and C. Hanna, "Information Sampling in a Structured and Unstructured Discussion of Three- and Six-person Groups," *Journal of Personality and Social Psychology* 57, 1 (January): 67–78; Donald T. Campbell, "Variation and Selective Retention in Socio-Cultural Evolution," *General Systems* 14 (1969): 69–85; Irving L. Janis, "Escalation of the Vietnam War: How Could it Happen?" from *Groupthink: Psychological Studies of Policy Decisions and Fiascoes*, 2nd. ed. (New York: Houghton Mifflin, 1982).

45. Meyer and Zucker 1989; Jeffrey Pfeffer and Gerald Salancik, *The External Control of Organizations* (New York: Harper & Row, 1978); Hussein Leblebici, Gerald Salancik, Anne Copay, and Tom King, "Institutional Change and the Transformation of Interorganizational Fields: An Organizational History of the U.S. Radio Broadcasting Industry," in *Administrative Science Quarterly* 36: 333–63.

46. Mathew McCubbins and Thomas Schwartz, "Congressional Oversight Overlooked: Police Patrols Versus Fire Alarms," in McCubbins and Sullivan, eds., *Congress: Structure and Policy* (Cambridge University Press, 1987), pp. 426–40; Barry Weingast and Mark Moran, "Bureaucratic Discretion or Congressional Control? Regulatory Policymaking by the Federal Trade Commission," in *Journal of Political Economy* 91 (1983): 765–800; Mathew D. McCubbins, "The Legislative Design of Regulatory Structure," in *American Journal of Political Science* 29 (1985): 721–48; David Epstein and Sharyn O'Halloran, *Delegating Powers* (Cambridge: Cambridge University Press, 1999).

47. HPSCI, Report, together with Minority Views on the Intelligence Authorization Act for Fiscal Year 2005 (Report 108–558), 108th Cong., 2nd sess., June 21, 2004, p. 24.

48. Terry M. Moe, "The Politics of Bureaucratic Structure," in *Can the Government Govern?* Ed. John E. Chubb and Paul E. Peterson (Washington, DC: Brookings Institution Press, 1989); Amy B. Zegart, *Flawed by Design: The Evolution of the CIA, JCS, and NSC* (Stanford: Stanford University Press, 1999).

49. For more on the differences between public and private sector managers, see Wilson 2000.

50. Interview, July 2004.

51. Terry M. Moe, "The Politicized Presidency," in *The New Direction in American Politics*. Ed. John E. Chubb and Paul E. Peterson (Washington: Brookings, 1985).

52. Richard E. Neustadt, *Presidential Power* (New York: Wiley, 1960).

53. For an historical overview of intelligence reform efforts, see Richard A. Best, Jr., *CRS Report RL32500: Proposals for Intelligence Reorganization, 1949–2004* (Washington, DC: 2004).

54. David Mayhew, *Congress: The Electoral Connection* (New Haven: Yale University Press, 1974).

55. Intelligence committee term limits were originally established in the 1970s to prevent lawmakers from cozying up to intelligence agencies. In 2004, the Senate abolished term limits for the Senate Select Committee on Intelligence. The House Permanent Select Committee on Intelligence, however, still has them for all members except the chairman and ranking minority member.

56. Amy Zegart, *Flawed by Design: The Evolution of the CIA, JCS, and NSC* (Stanford: Stanford University Press, 1999).

57. Moe 1989, p. 326.

58. Zegart 1999.

59. Ibid.

60. Philip Zelikow, remarks at the Pacific Council on International Policy, Los Angeles, CA, October 18, 2004. Ordinarily, comments made at PCIP events are off the record. In this case, however, Zelikow agreed to be attributed by name for this particular comment.

CHAPTER 4
FIGHTING OSAMA

1. Quoted in David E. Kaplan, Kevin Whitelaw, and Monica M. Ekman, "Mission Impossible: The inside story of how a band of reformers tried—and failed—to change America's spy agencies," *U.S. News & World Report*, August 2, 2004, p. 40.

2. Before the National Security Act of 1947, the U.S. military was split between two different cabinet departments, the Departments of War and Navy, with no common superior short of the president. The War Department consisted of the Army ground and air forces, while the Navy oversaw the Navy, the Marine Corps, and its own aviation unit. Note that there was no separate Department of the Air Force. In fact, the autonomy of the U.S. air forces proved to be a major issue in the National Security Act debates.

3. *New York Times*, October 20, 1945, p. 3.

4. Thomas F. Troy, *Donovan and the CIA: A History of the Establishment of the Central Intelligence Agency* (Frederick, MD: University Publications of America, 1981), p. 278.

5. For a detailed account of the CIA's origins, see Zegart, *Flawed by Design*, 1999, pp. 163–84.

6. *United States Statutes at Large*, vol. 61, Part I (Washington, DC: GPO, 1948) PL 253, p. 498.

7. Ibid.

8. The number of agencies comes from the Intelligence Authorization Act of 1993, which explicitly defined the United States Intelligence Community for first time. Public Law 102–496, 102nd Cong., 2nd sess., October 24, 1992, Title VII, "Intelligence Organization Act of 1992."

9. In 1996, mapping and imagery intelligence activities in the Pentagon and CIA were consolidated into new National Imagery and Mapping Agency (NIMA). In 2003, the Defense Authorization Bill changed the agency's name again to its current version, the National Geospatial-Intelligence Agency.

10. The four other agencies were: the FBI, the State Department's Bureau of Intelligence and Research, and intelligence units in the departments of Energy and Treasury. "Intelligence Authorization Act for Fiscal Year 1993," Public Law 102–496, 102nd Cong., 2nd sess., October 24, 1992, Section VII, "Intelligence Organization Act of 1992."

11. Interview, December 2004.

12. Brent Scowcroft, testimony before the HPSCI and SSCI Joint Inquiry, "Panel II of a Joint Hearing: Events Surrounding the Terrorist Attacks of September 11, 2001," 107th Cong., 2nd. sess., September 19, 2002, p. 4.

13. Interview, March 2004.

14. See for example, PBS *Frontline* interviews with former CIA clandestine service officers Gary Berntsen and Gary Schroen. Berntsen interview conducted January 20, 2006, edited transcript available at: http://www.pbs.org/wgbh/pages/frontline/darkside/interviews/berntsen.html (accessed July 12, 2006); Schroen interview conducted January 20, 2006, edited transcript available at: http://www.pbs.org/

wgbh/pages/frontline/darkside/interviews/schroen.html (accessed July 12, 2006).

15. *9/11 Commission Report*, p. 268.

16. Interview, July 2004.

17. Interview, March 2004.

18. Interview, July 2004.

19. Interview, February 2004.

20. Interview, September 2004.

21. *9/11 Commission Report*, p. 91.

22. Brent Scowcroft, testimony before the HPSCI and SSCI Joint Inquiry, "Events Surrounding the Terrorist Attacks of September 11, 2001," 107th Cong., 2nd sess., September 19, 2002.

23. Interview, March 2004.

24. See for example, Amy Borrus, "Should the CIA start spying for corporate America?" *Business Week*, October 14, 1991, p. 96.

25. William G. Hyland, op-ed, [no title] *New York Times*, May 20, 1991, p. A15.

26. Quoted in Don Oberdorfer, "Shift to domestic concerns urged: US foreign policy experts point to major problems at home," *Washington Post*, July 19, 1991, p. A19. William Colby, who served as the CIA's spy chief during the 1970s, even made a television commercial in which he sounded more like a local politician than a former CIA Director. "The Cold War is over, and the military threat is far less," he declared. "Now it is time to cut our military spending by 50 percent and invest that money in our schools, health care and our economy." Quoted in Elaine Sciolino, "CIA casting about for new missions," *New York Times*, February 4, 1992, p. A1.

27. Elizabeth Kolbert, "The 1992 Campaign: Campaign Watch; Clinton's Big Moment is Short on Telegenics," *New York Times*, July 18, 1992, p. 10.

28. Word count of text President Clinton's speech delivered July 16, 1992. A full text of the speech can be found at the The American Presidency Project at University of California, Santa Barbara, http://www.presidency.ucsb.edu/shownomination.php?convid=7 (accessed July 6, 2006).

29. *9/11 Commission Report*, p. 93; George Tenet, testimony before the 9/11 Commission eighth public hearing, March 24, 2004, p. 24.

30. George Tenet, testimony before the 9/11 Commission tenth public hearing, April 14, 2004, p. 1.

31. Woolsey quote from interview with PBS *Frontline*, date not listed, "The Dark Side: Analysis: The CIA—History and Performance," http://www.pbs.org/wgbh/pages/frontline/darkside/themes/cia.html (accessed June 22, 2006).

32. R. James Woolsey, testimony before the Senate Select Committee on Intelligence, "Nomination to become Director of Central Intelligence," 103rd Cong., 1st sess., February 2, 1993.

33. R. James Woolsey, hearing of the Senate Governmental Affairs Committee, "Reorganizing America's Intelligence Community: A View from the Inside," 108th Cong., 2nd sess., August 16, 2004, p. 26.

34. The joke has been widely reported, and was cited by Woolsey himself in an interview with PBS *Frontline*, date not listed, "The Dark Side: Analysis: The CIA—History and Performance," http://www.pbs.org/wgbh/pages/frontline/darkside/themes/cia.html (accessed June 22, 2006).

35. *National Security Review* 29, November 15, 1991, declassified text available online at http://www. fas.org/irp/offdocs/nsr/, p. 2 (accessed December 15, 2005).

36. Robert Gates, testimony before the House and Senate Intelligence Committees (joint hearing), "Intelligence Reorganization," April 1, 1992; Mark Lowenthal, *U.S. Intelligence: Evolution and Anatomy*, 2nd ed., (Washington, DC: Center for Strategic and International Studies, 1992, p. 96; John Prados, "Woolsey and the CIA," *Bulletin of the Atomic Scientists* 49, 6 (July—August 1993): 33–38.

37. For details, see the *9/11 Commission Report*, pp. 346–48. The Gates internal studies did lead to substantial change in one area: strengthening the relationship between civilian and military intelligence. The benefits of this change, however, are hotly debated. Supporters claim the marriage between intelligence and the military has revolutionized American warfare, enabling more devastating capabilities with greater accuracy and lower U.S. casualties. Critics argue that these gains have come at a high price, draining resources and capabilities from strategic intelligence collection and analysis that are vital for warning against surprise attack and enabling policymakers to make good decisions about the use of force.

38. Interview, December 2004.

39. For details, see David Boren, Joint Hearing of the House and Senate Select Committees on Intelligence, "Intelligence Reorganization,"102nd Cong., 2nd sess., April 1, 1992. See also Frank J. Smist, Jr., *Congress overseas the United States Intelligence Community*, 2nd ed. (Knoxville, TN: University of Tennessee Press, 1994), p. 286; Pamela Fessler, "Chairmen Boren, McCurdy Urge Leaner, Revamped Operations," *Congressional Quarterly Weekly Report* vol. 50, no. 6 (February 8, 1992): 316–17.

40. Letter from Secretary of Defense Richard Cheney to Representative Les Aspin, March 17, 1992, full text available at http://www.fas.org/irp/congress/1992-cr/cheney1992.pdf (accessed January 18, 2005).

41. John Deutch, "The Intelligence Community," *NPR Best Kept Secrets of the Government Report*, 1996, from www.fas.org/irp/offdocs/npr/vp96_intell.htm, p. 2.

42. Aspin-Brown Commission 1996, chapter 9, p. 6.

43. For more, see Aspin-Brown chapter 9.

44. Interview, December 2004.

45. House Permanent Select Committee on Intelligence, FY 1995 Authorization Report, 103rd Cong., 2nd sess., 103 H. Rpt. 541, Part I, June 9, 1994.

46. *9/11 Commission Report*, p. 90, citing information provided by James Pavitt in an interview, January 8, 2004.

47. John Walcott, "Mission impossible?" *Washington Post*, December 8, 1996, p. C1.

48. David Wise, "The Path to 9/11," *Vanity Fair*, November 2004, p. 326.

49. Ibid. John Millis, who served as a former intelligence operations officer and chief staffer of the House Permanent Select Committee on Intelligence, rated John Deutch the first, second, and third worst DCI in history. Vernon Loeb, "Back Channels: The Intelligence Community; in House of Mirrors, a Bad Reflection," *Washington Post*, February 18, 2000, p. A 21.

50. George Tenet, testimony before the HPSCI and SSCI Joint Inquiry, "Activities of the Intelligence Community in Connection with the Attacks of September 11, 2001," 107th Cong., 2nd sess., October 17, 2002, p. 22; interview with former senior intelligence official, March 2004; interview with former clandestine officer Robert Baer, November 2004.

51. Senate Select Committee on Intelligence, "An assessment of the Aldrich H. Ames espionage case and its implications for U.S. intelligence," November 1, 1994, Part I, available at http://www.fas.org/irp/congress/1994_rpt/ssci_ames.htm (accessed February 27, 2006).

52. *U.S. Statutes at Large* (Washington, DC: GPO, 1995) PL 359, pp. 3457–59.

53. "The Brown Commission and the Future of Intelligence; A Roundtable Discussion," *Studies in Intelligence* 39, 5 (1996), Center for the Study of Intelligence, Central Intelligence Agency, p. 9.

54. Larry Combest, quoted in Tim Weiner, "Proposal would reorganize U.S. intelligence agencies," *New York Times*, March 5, 1996, p. A20.

55. Larry Combest quoted in Walter Pincus, "Untangling the spy network's webs," *Washington Post*, March 5, 1996, p. A13.

56. *Congress and the Nation* vol. IX (1997) (Washington, DC: Congressional Quarterly Press): 246.

57. Walter Pincus, "Panels continue impasse on intelligence," *Washington Post*, June 7, 1996, p. A21. White also delivered strong testimony opposing the House bill in hearings held by the House National Security Committee, "Intelligence Community Reform," 104th Cong., 2nd sess., July 11, 1996.

58. Richard A. Best, Jr., "Proposals for Intelligence Reorganization, 1949–2004," *Congressional Research Service Report*, September 24, 2004, CRS RL 32500, p. 37.

59. *Joint Inquiry Report*, p. 230.

60. David Wise, "The path to 9/11," *Vanity Fair*, November 2004, p. 326.

61. *9/11 Commission Report*, p. 109.

62. Eleanor Hill, Joint Inquiry Staff Statement, "Hearing on the Intelligence Community's Response to Past Terrorist Attacks against the United States from February 1993 to September 2001," hearing of the House and Senate Intelligence Committees, 107th Cong., 2nd sess., October 8, 2002, p. 12.

63. *9/11 Commission Report*, p. 109.

64. Eleanor Hill, Joint Inquiry Staff Statement, "Hearing on the Intelligence Community's Response to Past Terrorist Attacks Against the United States from February 1993 to September 2001," House and Senate Intelligence Committees hearing, 107th Cong., 2nd. sess., October 8, 2002, p. 12.

65. No author, "CIA, FBI and Pentagon team to fight terrorism," daily briefing, September 19, 2000, available at http://www.govexec.com/dailyfed/0900/091900nj.htm.

66. Eleanor Hill, Joint Inquiry Staff Statement, October 8, 2002, p. 12.

67. *9/11 Commission Report*, p. 109.

68. Interview, December 2004.

69. James L. Pavitt, testimony before the 9/11 Commission tenth public hearing (transcript), April 14, 2004, p. 93. http://www.9–11commission.gov/archive/hearing10/9–11Commission_Hearing_2004–04–14.pdf (accessed February 24, 2006).

70. *Joint Inquiry Report*, p. 233.

71. Eleanor Hill, Joint Inquiry Staff Statement, Part I, September 18, 2002, p. 13.

72. Interview, August 2004.

73. The House and Senate Intelligence Committees' Joint Inquiry concluded, "In interviews, many persons on the National Security Council staff and at CTC [the CIA's Counterterrorist Center] pointed to the August 1998 bombings of two U.S. embassies in East Africa as the moment when they recognized that bin Ladin was waging war against the United States." (*Joint Inquiry Report*, p. 230).

74. These were the Deutch Commission, the Bremer Commission, the Gilmore Commission, and the Hart-Rudman Commission.

75. Director of Central Intelligence George Tenet was no stranger to legislative reform efforts, having served as staff director of the Senate Intelligence Committee back in 1992, when Chairman Boren first advocated the idea of a massive, post–Cold War intelligence overhaul.

76. Quoted in *Joint Inquiry Report*, p. 231.

77. David E. Kaplan, Kevin Whitelaw, and Monica M. Ekman, "Mission Impossible: The inside story of how a band of reformers tried—and failed—to change America's spy agencies," *U.S. News & World Report*, August 2, 2004, pp. 32–45.

78. "DCI's Strategic Intent for the United States Intelligence Community," unclassified version, mimeograph in collection of author, no date provided. Note: 9/11 Commission staff member Kevin Scheid testified before the Commission on April 14, 2004 that the DCI's Strategic Intent was issued in 1998. See The 9/11 Commission, "The Performance of the Intelligence Community," *Staff Statement Number 11*, April 14, 2004, p. 12. http://www.9–11commission.gov/staff_statements/staff_statement_11.pdf (accessed February 24, 2006).

79. Many key FBI and defense officials were unaware of the director's declaration of war until after the September 11 attacks. Eleanor Hill, Joint Inquiry Staff Statement, Part I, September 18, 2002, p. 12; *Joint Inquiry Report*, p. 236. Many inside Tenet's own agency did not appear to give his declaration of war much attention.

80. *9/11 Commission Report*, p. 357.

81. Interview, July 2004.

82. *Joint Inquiry Report*, p. 236.

83. Interviews with two intelligence officials, March 2004; December 2004.

84. David E. Kaplan, Kevin Whitelaw, and Monica M. Ekman, "Mission Impossible," pp. 32–45.

85. In its Fiscal Year 2001 Authorization Act report, the House Intelligence Committee reported that it was "frustrated" by the "funereal" pace of progress in electronic collaboration, and revealed that Director Tenet had "stated flatly" in "startling testimony" that electronic collaboration was being blocked by the parochial interests of intelligence agencies. House Report 106–620, "Intelligence Authorization Act for Fiscal Year 2001," 106th Cong., 2nd sess., pp. 17–18 (available at http://frwebgate.access.gpo.gov/cgi-bin/getdoc.cgi?dbname=106_cong_reports&docid=f:hr620.106.pdf). See also David E. Kaplan, Kevin Whitelaw, and Monica M. Ekman, "Mission Impossible," pp. 32–45.

86. Quoted in David E. Kaplan, Kevin Whitelaw, and Monica M. Ekman, "Mission Impossible," p. 40.

87. Interview with intelligence official, December 2004.

88. Ibid.

89. David E. Kaplan, Kevin Whitelaw, and Monica M. Ekman, "Mission Impossible," pp. 32–45; interview with intelligence official, December 2004.

90. Interview, February 2004.

91. As the 9/11 Commission noted, strategic analysis "is more than a news report." Whereas tactical analysis examines a specific operation in a specific situation, strategic analysis seeks to provide a 50,000-foot view of future threats, looking "beyond the particular to see patterns, notice gaps, or assemble a larger picture on a wider timeframe." 9/11 Commission, *Staff Statement Number 11*, "The Performance of the Intelligence Community," April 14, 2004, p. 3.

92. 9/11 Commission, *Staff Statement Number 11*, April 14, 2004, p. 3.

93. Graham Allison and Philip Zelikow, *Essence of Decision: Explaining the Cuban Missile Crisis*, 2nd ed. (New York: Longman, 1999), pp. 207–14.

94. Interview, December 2004.

95. *Joint Inquiry Report*, pp. 336–41; 9/11 Commission, *Staff Statement Number 11*, April 14, 2004, p. 5.

96. *9/11 Commission Report*, p. 342.

97. Ibid.

98. 9/11 Commission, *Staff Statement Number 11*, April 14, 2004, p. 4.

99. Ibid.

100. Ibid.

101. Although the National Intelligence Council included personnel from other agencies, it reported to the director of central intelligence, was housed in the CIA headquarters building, and was historically dominated by the CIA.

102. Interview, June 2005.

103. *9/11 Commission Report*, p. 341.

104. The 1997 NIE's omission of al Qaeda's involvement in the Somalia "Black Hawk down" incident was the subject of one of the most testy exchanges in the 9/11 Commission's public hearings. Former Senator Robert Kerrey, one of the commissioners, began drilling Director of Central Intelligence George Tenet. "Why? Why was it not in the update? Why didn't the president of the United States and the key policymakers get this information?" he asked. When Tenet replied that important information is not always included in the national intelligence estimate, Kerrey became irate. "The NIE is a foundational document that lots of people use," he shot back. "Now I've got to tell you, I think if the president of the United States of America had come and said that Osama bin Laden and Al Qaida is responsible for shooting

down a Black Hawk helicopter in 1993, I believe that speech would have galvanized the United States of America against bin Laden. . . . I think [it] would have given you permission to do operations that you didn't have permission to do. [It] would have changed the whole dynamic." Bob Kerrey, 9/11 Commission tenth public hearing (transcript), April 14, 2004, p. 25. http://www.9–11commission.gov/archive/hearing10/9–11Commission_Hearing_2004–04–14.pdf (accessed February 24, 2006).

105. *9/11 Commission Report*, pp. 341–42.

106. Ibid., pp. 341–43.

107. George Tenet, "Worldwide Threats to U.S. National Security," testimony before the Senate Armed Services Committee, 106th Cong., 1st sess., February 2, 1999.

108. Interview, June 2005.

109. Interview with two former intelligence officials, March 2004 and October 2005.

110. Interview, March 2004.

111. *9/11 Commission Report*, p.142, *Joint Inquiry Report*, pp. 237–40.

112. *Joint Inquiry Report*, pp. 237–38.

113. According to Tenet, between 1999 and 2001, the CIA's human agent base against al Qaeda increased 50 percent and included more than 70 sources and subsources, 25 of whom operated inside Afghanistan. Testimony of George J. Tenet before the 9/11 Commission tenth public hearing (transcript) April 14, 2004, p. 3. http://www.9–11commission.gov/archive/hearing10/9–11Commission_Hearing_2004–04–14.pdf (accessed February 24, 2006).

114. *9/11 Commission Report*, pp. 126–43. For a detailed discussion of covert options against bin Laden and the dispute between the CIA and White House about whether those options sanctioned assassination, see *9/11 Commission Report*, pp. 126–43.

115. *Joint Inquiry Report*, pp. 385–88; George Tenet, testimony before the 9/11 Commission tenth public hearing (transcript), April 14, 2004, p. 5. http://www.9–11commission.gov/archive/hearing10/9–11 Commission_Hearing_2004–04–14.pdf (accessed February 24, 2006).

116. Senator Mike DeWine, "Additional Comments," *Joint Inquiry Report*, p. 11. Several former clandestine officials attributed the growth of this risk aversion to the natural aging of the CIA. As one remarked, "I think that all organizations reach a point in time where the internal culture becomes so strong and becomes so set in its place, that the dynamism that was there at the beginning, and I think characterized the agency in the early years . . . just starts to concretize." Interview, December 2004.

117. George Tenet, testimony before the 9/11 Commission tenth public hearing (transcript), April 14, 2004, p. 18. http://www.9–11commission.gov/archive/hearing10/9–11Commission_Hearing_2004–04–14.pdf (accessed February 24, 2006).

118. James L. Pavitt, testimony before the 9/11 Commission tenth public hearing (transcript), April 14, 2004, p. 92. http://www.9–11commission.gov/archive/hearing10/9–11Commission_Hearing_2004–04–14.pdf (accessed February 24, 2006.

119. *Joint Inquiry Report*, p. xvii.

120. Robert Bryant, John Hamre, John Lawn, John MacGaffin, Howard Shapiro, and Jeffrey Smith, "America Needs More Spies," *Economist* July 10, 2003, pp. 30–31.

121. Mark Lowenthal, remarks at the Regional Intelligence Conference, Center for the Study of Intelligence and the University of Southern California, Los Angeles, CA, February 2, 2006.

122. Cofer Black, testimony before HPSCI and SSCI Joint Inquiry hearing, "9/11 Intelligence Investigation," 107th Cong., 2nd sess., September 26, 2002.

123. Interviews with three former intelligence officials, December 2004.

124. *Joint Inquiry Report*, p. 342.

125. *9/11 Commission Staff Statement, Number 11*, p. 3.

126. *9/11 Commission Report*, p. 342.

127. *Joint Inquiry Report*, pp. 339–40.

128. Ibid.

129. Interview, March 2004.

130. Interview, June 2004.

131. *Joint Inquiry Report*, p. 387.

132. Interview, June 2005.

133. See Reuel Marc Gerecht, "The Counterterrorist Myth," *Atlantic Monthly*, July—August 2001, pp. 38–42.

134. Interview, December 2004.

135. Interviews with three former clandestine officials, December 2004.

136. Interview, December 2004.

137. John Walcott and Brian Duffy, "The CIA's Darkest Secrets," *U.S. News & World Report*, July 4, 1994, p. 46.

138. Edward G. Shirley, pseudonym for Reuel Marc Gerecht, "Can't Anybody Here Play this Game?" *Atlantic Monthly*, February 1998, p. 48.

139. Ibid. Interviews with four former clandestine officials, December 2004 and November 2006.

140. Interview, November 2004.

141. Interview, November 2004.

142. Interview, June 2004.

143. Interview, December 2004.

144. Interview, December 2004.

145. Interview, December 2004.

146. President George H. W. Bush issued 166 executive orders, President Bill Clinton issued 364, and President George W. Bush issued 25 before September 11, 2001. Data from the National Archives online, http://www.archives.gov/federal-register/executive-orders/disposition.html (accessed July 12, 2006).

147. President George H. W. Bush used two types of national security documents, National Security Reviews (NSRs) and National Security Directives (NSDs). According to Bush presidential library records, 30 NSRs and 79 NSDs were issued during the four years of his administration. (http://bushlibrary.tamu.edu/research/reviews.html (accessed July 12, 2006). President Clinton used different names, calling review directives Presidential Review Directives, or PRDs, and Presidential Decision Directives, or PDDs. Clinton issued an estimated 72 PRDs and 71 PDDs. (PRD numbers from the Federation of American Scientists, http://www.fas.org/irp/offdocs/direct.htm. [accessed July 12, 2006]. PDD numbers from Harold C. Relyea, "Presidential Directives: Background and Overview," *Congressional Research Service Report* 98–611 GOV, updated January 7, 2005, p. 11). President George W. Bush appears to have consolidated review and decision directives into a single document, the National Security Presidential Directive. Between his inauguration and September 11, 2001, Bush issued between five and seven of these directives. (Bush estimates from Federation of American Scientists, http://www.fas.org/irp/offdocs/nspd/index.html [accessed July 12, 2006]).

148. For an overview about the names and purposes of national security directives, see Harold C. Relyea, "Presidential Directives: Background and Overview," *Congressional Research Service Report* 98–611 GOV, updated January 7, 2005, pp. 8–12.

149. National Security Review 29, "Intelligence Capabilities: 1992–2005," November 15, 1991. Text available at http://www.fas.org/irp/offdocs/nsr/nsr29.pdf (accessed July 12, 2006).

150. Presidential Decision Directive 35, "Intelligence Requirements," March 2, 1995. For public statements by the White House discussing the content of PDD-35, see http://www.fas.org/irp/offdocs/pdd35.htm (accessed July 12, 2006).

151. *Joint Inquiry Report*, p. 48.

152. Ibid., pp. 48–49.

153. Ibid., William J. Clinton, "Remarks on the 50th Anniversary of the Central Intelligence Agency," Langley, Virginia, September 16, 1997, *Public Papers of the Presidents: William J. Clinton—1997* vol. 2 (Washington, DC: GPO): 1169–71.

154. Interview, June 2005.

155. Presidential Decision Directive 39, "U.S. Policy on Counterterrorism," June 21, 1995. An unclassified and redacted version can be found at http://www.fas.org/irp/offdocs/pdd39.htm (accessed July 12, 2006).

156. These were Presidential Decision Directives 62 and 63. See *Joint Inquiry Report*, pp. 234–35; *9/11 Commission Report*, pp. 101–102; "Fact Sheet: Combating Terrorism: Presidential Directive 62," Office of the Press Secretary, The White House, released May 22, 1998, available at http://www.fas.org/irp/offdocs/pdd-62.htm (accessed July 12, 2006); Text of PDD-63, "Critical Infrastructure Protection," and "Fact Sheet: Protecting America's Critical Infrastructures: PDD 63," Office of the Press Secretary, The White House, released May 22, 1998, available at http://www.fas.org/irp/offdocs/pdd/pdd-63.htm (accessed July 12, 2006).

157. *Joint Inquiry Report*, p. 235.

158. Ibid., pp. 234–35.

159. Richard Clarke, *Against All Enemies: Inside America's War on Terror* (New York: Free Press, 2004), p. 170.

160. These were the Gilmore Commission, the Bremer Commission, the Deutch Commission, and the Hart-Rudman Commission.

161. National Security Presidential Directive-5, "Review of U.S. Intelligence," issued May 9, 2001.

162. Interview, April 2002.

CHAPTER 5

SIGNALS FOUND AND LOST

1. Interview, December 2004.

2. Quoted in *9/11 Commission Report*, p. 353.

3. "Three 9/11 Hijackers: Identification, Watchlisting, and Tracking," *Staff Statement Number 2*, The 9/11 Commission, January 26, 2004, www.9–11commission.gov/hearings/hearing7.htm (accessed February 28, 2006), pp. 1–5; *9/11 Commission Report*, pp. 353–57. The analysis in this chapter and in chapter 7 relies on publicly available government documents (such materials from the 9/11 Commission), which are considered the most authoritative official accounts and the most accessible sources for scholars interested in conducting future research on the subject. General readers interested in more details should see Lawrence Wright, *The Looming Tower*.

4. "Three 9/11 Hijackers: Identification, Watchlisting, and Tracking," *Staff Statement Number 2*, The 9/11 Commission, January 26, 2004, www.9–11commission.gov/hearings/hearing7.htm, p. 6.

5. "Three 9/11 Hijackers: Identification, Watchlisting, and Tracking," *Staff Statement Number 2*, The 9/11 Commission, January 26, 2004, www.9–11commission.gov/hearings/hearing7.htm; *Joint Inquiry Report*, pp. 143–52, *9/11 Commission Report*, pp. 353–57.

6. *9/11 Commission Report*, p. 268.

7. Interview, December 2004.

8. Interview, March 2004.

9. Cofer Black, quoted in *9/11 Commission Report*, p. 356.

10. George Tenet, from *Joint Inquiry Report*, p. 149.

11. *Joint Inquiry Report*, p. 152.

12. *9/11 Commission Report*, p. 267.

13. *Joint Inquiry Report*, pp. 157–68.

14. *9/11 Commission Report*, p. 221.

15. Eleanor Hill, testimony before the HPSCI and SSCI Joint Inquiry, "The Malaysia Hijacking and September 11th," 107th Cong., 2nd sess., September 20, 2002, p. 8.

16. *Joint Inquiry Report*, p. 148.

17. Unidentified FBI agent, testimony before the HPSCI and SSCI Joint Inquiry, "The Malaysia Hijackers and September 11th," 107th Cong., 2nd sess., September 20, 2002.

18. *9/11 Commission Report*, p. 242.

19. On May 8, 2001, al-Hazmi met with Ahmed al-Ghamdi, one of the hijackers on United Airlines Flight 175, which struck the World Trade Center's South Tower. A few weeks later, al-Hazmi was living with several other operatives in Paterson, New Jersey. These included other members of his own team, which crashed American Airlines Flight 77 into Pentagon, as well as Abdul Aziz al Omari, who was part of the team that flew American Airlines Flight 11 into the World Trade Center's North Tower. *9/11 Commission Report*, p. 230.

20. Quoted in *Joint Inquiry Report*, p. 19.

21. Ibid.

22. Although legal restrictions known as "the wall" limited the exchange of information between intelligence and criminal investigations, these restrictions applied to a narrow range of circumstances; no legal barriers prevented officials from divulging what they knew in these instances. Eleanor Hill, "The Intelligence Community's Knowledge of the September 11 Hijackers Prior to September 11, 2001," Staff Statement for House and Senate Intelligence Committees, 107th Cong., 2nd sess., September 20, 2002; *Joint Inquiry Report*, pp. 363–67. For a more thorough discussion of the wall, see Janet Reno, "Testimony of Janet Reno, Former Attorney General of the United States before the National Commission on Terrorist Attacks Upon the United States," 9/11 Commission tenth public hearing, April 13, 2004, available at

www.9–11commission.gov/hearings/hearing10/htm (accessed February 28, 2006).

23. *Joint Inquiry Report*, p. 367.

24. *9/11 Commission Report*, p. 268.

25. Ibid., pp. 267–68, 355.

26. *Joint Inquiry Report*, p. 150; Eleanor Hill, "The Intelligence Community's Knowledge of the September 11 Hijackers Prior to September 11, 2001," HPSCI and SSCI Joint Inquiry, September 20, 2002, p. 9.

27. *Joint Inquiry Report*, pp. 150–51.

28. Unidentified FBI agent, testimony before the HPSCI and SSCI Joint Inquiry, "The Malaysia Hijackers and September 11th," September 20, 2002.

29. *Joint Inquiry Report*, pp. 30–31.

30. *9/11 Commission Report*, pp. 276–77.

31. "Bin Ladin Determined to Strike in U.S.," *President's Daily Brief*, August 6, 2001, declassified April 10, 2004.

32. *9/11 Commission Report*, p. 260.

33. Specific word counts are: 383 words for historical intelligence, 83 devoted to current intelligence. Word count does not include title or portions redacted in declassification.

34. "Bin Ladin Determined to Strike in U.S.," *President's Daily Brief*, August 6, 2001, declassified April 10, 2004.

35. *9/11 Commission Report*, p. 260.

36. Condoleezza Rice, testimony before the 9/11 Commission ninth public hearing (transcript), April 8, 2004, p. 24. http://www.9–11commission.gov/archive/hearing9/9–11Commission_Hearing_2004–04–08.pdf (accessed March 1, 2006).

37. The third piece of intelligence noted "CIA and the FBI are investigating a call to our Embassy in the UAE in May saying that a group of bin Laden supporters was in the US planning attacks with explosives." Although the Bush White House issued a fact sheet stating that no information confirmed the connection between this call and the September 11 attacks, the fact sheet stopped short of dismissing the possibility or issuing a definitive judgment on the matter. "Fact Sheet: The August 6, 2001 PDB," Press release, Office of the Press Secretary, The White House, issued April 10, 2004, available at www.whitehouse.gov/news/realeases/2004/04/print/20040410–5.html (accessed September 17, 2004).

38. "Bin Ladin Determined to Strike in U.S.," *President's Daily Brief*, August 6, 2001, declassified April 10, 2004. For information about the mistaken claims of New York surveillance activities discussed in the PDB, see "Background Briefing Via Conference Call on the President's PDB of August 6, 2001," Office of the Press Secretary, The White

House, April 10, 2004, available at www.whitehouse.gov/news/releases/2004/04/20040410–6.html (accessed September 17, 2004); "Fact Sheet: The August 6, 2001 PDB," press release, Office of the Press Secretary, The White House, issued April 10, 2004, available at www .Whitehouse.gov/news/releases/2004/04/print/20040410–5.html (accessed September 17, 2004); Matthew Cooper, Elaine Shannon, and Viveca Novak, "Probing the Memo," *Time*, April 19, 2004, p. 19.

39. Notably, senior FBI officials, including Acting Director Thomas Pickard and Counterterrorism Chief Dale Watson, knew nothing about Moussaoui's case.

40. *9/11 Commission Report*, p. 259.

41. 9/11 Commission, *Staff Statement Number 11*, pp. 11–12.

42. 9/11 Commission tenth public hearing (transcript) April 14, 2004, p. 57. http://www.9–11commission.gov/archive/hearing10/9–11Commission_Hearing_2004–04–14.pdf (accessed March 1, 2006); 9/11 Commission, "Threats and Responses in 2001," *Staff Statement Number 10*, April 13, 2004, p. 5. http://www.9–11commission.gov/staff_statements/staff_statement_10.pdf (accessed March 1, 2006).

43. *9/11 Commission Report*, p. 275.

44. George Tenet, submitted testimony before the 9/11 Commission tenth public hearing, April 14, 2004, p. 5. http://www .9–11commission.gov/hearings/hearing10/tenet_statement.pdf (accessed March 1, 2006).

45. *9/11 Commission Report*, p. 265.

46. Janet Reno, "Testimony of Janet Reno, Former Attorney General of the United States before the National Commission on Terrorist Attacks Upon the United States," April 13, 2004, p. 6.

47. Interview, March 2004.

48. Interview, March 2004.

49. Interview, December 2004.

50. 9/11 Commission, *Staff Statement Number 11*, p. 4.

51. *9/11 Commission Report*, p. 254.

52. *9/11 Commission Report*, pp. 341–43.

53. Roberta Wohlstetter, *Pearl Harbor: Warning and Decision* (Stanford, CA: Stanford University Press, 1962).

54. Bruce Berkowitz, "Spying in the Post-September 11 World," *Hoover Digest* 4 (2003).

55. National Security Agency Director Lt. General Michael Hayden, quoted in James Bamford, "War of Secrets: Eyes in the Sky, Ears to the Wall, and Still Wanting," *New York Times*, September 8, 2002, section 4, p. 5.

56. James Bamford, "War of Secrets: Eyes in the Sky, Ears to the Wall, and Still Wanting," *New York Times*, September 8, 2002, section 4, p. 5.

57. John Diamond, "Terror group's messengers steer clear of NSA," *USA Today,* October 18, 2002, p. 12A.

58. Dale Watson, testimony before HPSCI and SSCI Joint Inquiry, 107th Cong., 2nd sess., September 26, 2002.

59. "Three 9/11 Hijackers: Identification, Watchlisting, and Tracking," *Staff Statement Number. 2,* 9/11 Commission seventh public hearing, January 26, 2004, p. 3.

60. 9/11 Commission, *Staff Statement Number 2,* p. 2.

61. Quotes from Intelligence Community communications of June 28, 2001 and July 10, 2001, reprinted in *Joint Inquiry Report,* p. 7.

62. *9/11 Commission Report,* p. 259.

63. For details about steps the U.S. government took in the summer of 2001, see *9/11 Commission Report,* pp. 256–65.

64. As 9/11 Commission staff concluded, "there was no comprehensive collection strategy to pull together human sources, imagery, signals intelligence, and open sources. (9/11 Commission, *Staff Statement Number 11,* p. 9).

CHAPTER 6
REAL MEN DON'T TYPE

1. Interview, January 2005.

2. The Federal Bureau of Investigation, "Origins, 1908–1910," *FBI History,* http://www.fbi.gov/libref/historic/history/text.htm#origins (accessed December 12, 2005). For jurisdiction see the U.S. Code, which authorizes the attorney general to "appoint officials to detect . . . crimes against the United States." U.S. Code 28 (1966) § 533.

3. In 1940, President Roosevelt signed an order creating a "Special Intelligence Service" within the FBI. During the war, more than 340 SIS agents and staff worked undercover in Latin America collecting intelligence about Axis spy and sabotage activities. The SIS was disbanded after the war, and its responsibilities assumed by the newly created CIA. For more see http://www.fbi.gov/page2/june05/history062405.htm (accessed November 8, 2006).

4. "Threats and responses in 2001," *9/11 Commission, Staff Statement Number 10,* April 13, 2004, p. 5.

5. There are three exceptions. The FBI's three largest offices, which are located in Los Angeles, New York City, and Washington, D.C., are run by assistant directors-in-charge (ADICs), with program-oriented SACs reporting to them. See Todd Masse and William Krouse, "The FBI: Past, Present, and Future," *Congressional Research Service Report RL 32095,* October 2, 2003, pp. 13–14.

6. The Federal Bureau of Investigation, "Early Days (1910–1021)," *FBI History*, http://www.fbi.gov/libref/historic/history/text.htm #early (accessed January 12, 2005).

7. Ronald Kessler, *The Bureau: The Secret History of the FBI* (New York: St. Martin's, 2003), pp. 21–26; Todd Masse and William Krouse, "The FBI: Past, Present, and Future," *Congressional Research Service Report* RL32095, October 2, 2003; Federal Bureau of Investigation, *History of the FBI*, available at http://www.fbi.gov/libref/historic/history/text.htm#origins (accessed July 13, 2006).

8. Interview with former FBI official, October 2005.

9. For more about FBI field office autonomy before the September 11, 2001, terrorist attacks, see *9/11 Commission Report*, p. 74.

10. Richard Thornburgh, "FBI Reorganization," statement before the House Appropriations Subcommittee on Commerce, Justice, State, and the Judiciary, 108th Cong., 1st sess., June 18, 2003, p. 2. http://www.napawash.org/resources/testimony/FBITestimony%2006-18-03.pdf (accessed February 10, 2006).

11. Federal Bureau of Investigation, *The FBI's Counterterrorism Program Since September 2001: Report to the National Commission on Terrorist Attacks upon the United States*, April 14, 2004, p. 20.

12. Kessler, *The Bureau*, p. 218. The plaque quoted Elbert Hubbard: "If you work for a man, in heaven's name work for him; speak well of him and stand by the institution he represents . . . if you [criticize the institution], the first high wind that comes along will blow you away, and probably you will never know why."

13. Ibid., p. 24.

14. Interview, June 2004.

15. Louis J. Freeh, with Howard Means, *My FBI: Bringing Down the Mafia, Investigating Bill Clinton, and Fighting the War on Terror* (New York: St. Martin's Press, 2005), p. viii.

16. *Joint Inquiry Report*, p. 259.

17. Freeh, *My FBI*, p. 289.

18. Kessler, *The Bureau*, pp. 44–46.

19. Ibid., p. 44

20. Ibid.

21. Quoted in Eric Lichtblau and Charles Piller, "Without a Clue: How the FBI Lost Its Way," *Milwaukee Journal Sentinel*, Aug. 11, 2002, all edition, p. 01J.

22. The Commission on the Intelligence Capabilities of the United States Regarding Weapons of Mass Destruction (the Silberman-Robb Commission), "Report to the President of the United States," (Washington, DC: GPO, March 31, 2005), p. 455 (hereafter *Silberman-Robb*

Commission Report). http://www.wmd.gov/report/wmd_report.pdf (accessed February 15, 2006), p. 453.

23. Alfred Cumming and Todd Masse, "FBI Intelligence Reform Since September 11, 2001: Issues and Options for Congress," *Congressional Research Service Report No. RL 32336*, April 6, 2004, available at www. Fas.org/irp/crs/RL32336.html (accessed February 27, 2006), pp. 14–15.

24. The Silberman-Robb Commission, for example, found that in 2005, only nine of the fifty-six heads of field offices came from divisions other than the Criminal Division. Silberman-Robb Commission, p. 453. See also "Law Enforcement, Counterterrorism, and Intelligence Collection in the United States Prior to 9/11," *9/11 Commission Staff Statement Number 9*, April 13, 2004, p. 8.

25. Interview, December 2004.

26. *Joint Inquiry Report*, pp. 331–39; *Silberman-Robb Commission Report*, p. 455; "Law Enforcement, Counterterrorism, and Intelligence Collection in the United States Prior to 9/11," *9/11 Commission Staff Statement Number 9*, April 13, 2004, p. 9; "Reforming Law Enforcement, Counterterrorism, and Intelligence Collection in the United States," *9/11 Commission, Staff Statement Number 12*, April 14, 2004, p. 6.

27. Alfred Cumming and Todd Masse, "FBI Intelligence Reform Since September 11, 2001: Issues and Options for Congress," *Congressional Research Service Report No. RL 32336*, April 6, 2004, available at www. Fas.org/irp/crs/RL32336.html (accessed February 27, 2006), p. 13.

28. Ibid.

29. Office of the Inspector General, U.S. Department of Justice, "A Review of the FBI's Handling of Intelligence Information Related to the Spetember 11 Attacks," November 2004, redacted, declassified, and released publicly June 2005 [hereafter *OIG Report*], pp. 89–91.

30. "Law Enforcement, Counterterrorism, and Intelligence Collection in the United States Prior to 9/11," *9/11 Commission Staff Statement Number 9*, April 13, 2004, p. 9.

31. Louis Freeh, "Fiscal Year 2002 Appropriations," hearing of the House Appropriations Subcommittee on Commerce, Justice, State, and the Judiciary hearing, 107th Cong., 1st sess., May 17, 2001.

32. Federal Bureau of Investigation, "The FBI's Counterterrorism Program Since September 2001," *Report to the National Commission on Terrorist Attacks Upon the United States*, April 14, 2004, p. 51.

33. Shane Harris, "Rebooting the Bureau," govexec.com, August 1, 2002.

34. Several FBI officials who were sent Kenneth Williams's Phoenix memo, for example, told Congressional investigators that they never

received the electronic communication. See Eleanor Hill "The FBI's Handling of the Phoenix Electronic Communication and Investigation of Zacarias Moussaoui Prior to September 11, 2001," statement before the HPSCI and SSCI Joint Inquiry, 107th Cong., 2nd sess., September 24, 2002, supplemented October 17, 2002. See also *Joint Inquiry Report*, pp. 331–32.

35. Eleanor Hill, "The FBI's Handling of the Phoenix Electronic Communication and Investigation of Zacarias Moussaoui Prior to September 11, 2001," statement before the HPSCI and SSCI Joint Inquiry, 107th Cong., 2nd sess., September 24, 2002, p. 5.

36. Dale Watson, statement before the HPSCI and SSCI Joint Inquiry, 107th Cong., 2nd sess., September 26, 2002, p. 5. http://intelligence .senate.gov/0209hrg/020926/watson.pdf (accessed January 23, 2006). The Justice Department Inspector General's office found that staffing remained at this level "for much of the 1990s." *OIG Report*, p. 12.

37. Federal Bureau of Investigation, "The End of the Cold War (1989–1993)," *History of the FBI*, http://www.fbi.gov/libref/historic/history/text.htm#coldwar (accessed February 10, 2006).

38. Ibid.

39. *Joint Inquiry Report*, pp. 4–5.

40. Janet Reno, statement before the 9/11 Commission tenth public hearing, April 13, 2004, p. 4. http://www.9-11commission.gov/hearings/hearing10/reno_statement.pdf (accessed January 23, 2006). The act was the Violent Crime Control and Law Enforcement Act of 1994, Public Law 103-322, 103nd Cong., 2nd sess. (September 13, 1994).

41. The Communications Assistance to Law Enforcement Act (CALEA), Public Law 103-414, 103rd Cong., 2nd sess. (October 7, 1994).

42. Louis Freeh, "Fiscal Year 1995 Commerce, Justice, State Appropriations," prepared statement before the Senate Appropriations Subcommittee on Commerce, Justice, and State, the Judiciary, and Related Agencies, 103rd Cong., 2nd sess., April 14, 1994.

43. Louis Freeh, "FY 1996 budget," statement before the House Appropriations Subcommittee on Commerce, Justice, State and the Judiciary, 104th Cong., 1st sess., March 9, 1995. In fact, Freeh uttered the word "terrorism" only twice during his remarks at the 1995 budget hearing, both times referring to it as one issue in a long list of FBI activities.

44. Thornburgh, "FBI Reorganization," p. 4.

45. Whether the FBI had used devices that might have ignited the fire was debated for years. The issue, however, seemed to be resolved in July 2000, when an independent inquiry led by former Senator John Danforth concluded that federal officials had no part in setting the blaze. Danforth did find, however, that Justice Department employees had hidden the fact that the FBI had fired exploding tear gas canisters

near the compound during the siege. See John Danforth, "Interim Report to the Deputy Attorney General Concerning the 1993 Confrontation at the Mt. Carmel Complex, Waco, Texas," July 21, 2000, available at http://www.cesnur.org/testi/DanforthRpt.pdf (accessed November 17, 2005).

46. The Gallup poll was conducted in conjunction with CNN and *USA Today* between April 21 and 24, 1995, and can be found at http://brain.gallup.com/documents/questionnaire.aspx?STUDY=CNN5001018, question 28b (accessed November 21, 2005); the Pew poll was conducted August 17–20, 1995 and released on August 24, 1995. "Support for Independent Candidate in '96 is Up," The Pew Research Center for the People and the Press, available at http://people-press.org/reports/display.php3?Page ID=412 (accessed November 22, 2005).

47. The 9/11 Commission, "Law Enforcement, Counterterrorism, and Intelligence Collection in the United States Prior to 9/11," *Staff Statement Number 9*, April 13, 2004, p. 3. http://www.9-11commission.gov/staff_statements/staff_statement_9.pdf (accessed January 23, 2006). It is worth noting two serious criticisms of the FBI's legal attaché program. First, in interviews, two government officials familiar with the program argued that the impetus for legal attaché expansion was not terrorism, but organized crime. (Interviews, October 2005). See also Jim McGee, "The Rise of the FBI," *Washington Post Magazine*, July 20, 1997, p. W10. As one former FBI official put it, "Louis Freeh made it very clear that this was about crime. He did NOT want the FBI becoming an intel agency." (Interview, October 2005). Second, the Congressional Joint Inquiry found evidence that the legat program was not particularly effective because headquarters staffing and budgets for the offices were insufficient, because most FBI agents did not understand the program to use it effectively, and because legat offices covered jurisdictions that were too broad to establish personal relationships with key foreign law enforcement officials. (*Joint Inquiry Report*, p. 278).

48. Louis Freeh, statement before the HPSCI and SSCI Joint Inquiry, October 8, 2002, p. 18. http://intelligence.senate.gov/0210hrg/021008/freeh.pdf (accessed February 11, 2006). Specific figures of legats in 2001 from Freeh's statement; number of legats in 1996 from Freeh's statement before House Appropriations Subcommittee on the Departments of Commerce, Justice, and State, the Judiciary, and Related Agencies, Hearing on International Law Enforcement Programs of the Department of Justice, 106th Cong., 1st sess., May 1, 1996; locations of legats from *Joint Inquiry Report*, p. 271.

49. Interview, December 2004.

50. Interview, December 2004.

51. Interviews with two former FBI officials, December 2004.

52. Interview, December 2004.

53. Federal Bureau of Investigation, *Keeping Tomorrow Safe: Draft FBI Strategic Plan, 1998–2003*, unclassified version, May 8, 1998, p. 7.

54. *Draft FBI Strategic Plan*, p. 30.

55. Ibid., pp. 30–35. "The development of an appreciation for intelligence will undoubtedly require a significant culture change for FBI managers," the report noted, p. 33.

56. Interview, December 2004.

57. *Draft FBI Strategic Plan*, pp. 36–41.

58. Ibid., p. 36.

59. Ibid., pp. 2–3.

60. Ibid., p. 36.

61. Louis Freeh, statement before the 9/11 Commission tenth public hearing, April 13, 2004, p. 7. http://www.9-11commission.gov/hearings/hearing10/freeh_statement.pdf (accessed January 28, 2006).

62. Alfred Cumming and Todd Masse, "Appendix 5: Past Efforts to Reform FBI Intelligence," in "FBI Intelligence Reform Since September 11, 2001: Issues and Options for Congress," *Congressional Research Service Report No. RL 32336*, August 4, 2004, p. 53. http://www.fas.org/irp/crs/RL32336.pdf (accessed January 25, 2006); The 9/11 Commission, *Staff Statement Number 9*, pp. 5–6.

63. Freeh, statement before the 9/11 Commission tenth public hearing, April 13, 2004, p. 7. http://www.9-11commission.gov/hearings/hearing10/frech_statement.pdf.

64. The 9/11 Commission, *Staff Statement Number 9*, p. 6.

65. Interview, June 2004.

66. Interviews with three former FBI officials, August 2004, June 2004, and December 2004.

67. *9/11 Commission Report*, p. 76.

68. Interview, December 2004.

69. The 9/11 Commission, *Staff Statement Number 9*, p. 4.

70. Based on data from fiscal year 2000, the last full fiscal year before September 11. See U.S. Department of Justice, Office of the Inspector General, "Federal Bureau of Investigation Casework and Human Resource Allocation," Executive Summary, Report No. 03-37, redacted and unclassified, September 2003, pp. 3–4. www.usdoj.gov/oig/reports/FBI/a0337/exec.htm (accessed January 29, 2006).

71. *Joint Inquiry Report*, pp. 244, 263.

72. The 9/11 Commission, *Staff Statement Number 9*, p. 4.

73. Ibid.

74. U.S. Department of Justice, Office of the Inspector General, "Federal Bureau of Investigation Casework and Human Resource Alloca-

tion," Executive Summary, Report No. 03-37, redacted and unclassified, September 2003. www.usdoj.gov/oig/reports/FBI/a0337/exec.htm (accessed January 29, 2006).

75. *Joint Inquiry Report*, p. 244.

76. Quoted in *Joint Inquiry Report*, p. 38.

77. *9/11 Commission Report*, p. 265.

78. The 9/11 Commission, *Staff Statement Number 9*, p. 7.

79. *Joint Inquiry Report*, p. 249.

80. The 9/11 Commission, "Reforming Law Enforcement, Counterterrorism, and Intelligence Collection in the United States," *Staff Statement Number 12*, April 14, 2004, pp. 5–6. http://www.9-11commission.gov/staff_statements/staff_statement_12.pdf (accessed January 26, 2006). See also *Joint Inquiry Report*, pp. 337–38.

81. Ibid., p. 266.

82. Ibid., pp. 266–67.

83. U.S. Department of Justice, Office of the Inspector General, "A Review of the Federal Bureau of Investigation's Counterterrorism Program: Threat Assessment, Strategic Planning, and Resource Management," Executive Summary, Report Number 02-38, redacted and unclassified, September 2002. www.fas.org/irp/agency/doj/oig/fbi02sum.html (accessed January 28, 2006).

84. Quoted in *Joint Inquiry Report*, p. 345.

85. Ibid., p. 340.

86. U.S. Department of Justice, Office of the Inspector General, "A Review of the Federal Bureau of Investigation's Counterterrorism Program: Threat Assessment, Strategic Planning, and Resource Management," Executive Summary, Report Number 02-38, redacted and unclassified, September 2002. www.fas.org/irp/agency/doj/oig/fbi02sum.html (accessed January 28, 2006).

87. Federal Bureau of Investigation Directorate of Intelligence, Office of Intelligence On-Site Review of Field Intelligence Groups, September 10, 2004, p. 6, cited in *Silberman-Robb Commission Report*. The Commission on the Intelligence Capabilities of the United States Regarding Weapons of Mass Destruction (the Silberman-Robb Commission), "Report to the President of the United States," (Washington, DC: GPO, March 31, 2005), p. 455. http://www.wmd.gov/report/wmd_report.pdf (accessed February 15, 2006).

88. *Silberman-Robb Commission Report*, p. 454.

89. 9/11 Public Discourse Project, "Remarks by Chairman Thomas H. Kean and Vice Chair Lee. H. Hamilton," *Final Report of the 9/11 Public Discourse Project*, December 5, 2005, p. 4. http://www.9-11pdp.org/press/2005-12-05_statement.pdf (accessed January 31, 2006).

90. Interview, December 2004. A former FBI official offered a similar assessment nearly two years later, noting in November 2006 that the FBI's entire intelligence system is still "let's get this asset to help with this case."

91. House Appropriations Subcommittee on Commerce, Justice, State, and Justice, "Fiscal Year 2002 Appropriations For FBI And DEA" hearing, 107th Cong., 1st sess., May 16, 2001.

92. Janet Reno, statement before the 9/11 Commission tenth public hearing, April 13, 2004, p. 7. http://www.9-11commission.gov/ hearings/hearing10/reno_statement.pdf (accessed January 27, 2006).

93. Budget figures for ACS from Representative Harold Rogers, House Appropriations Subcommittee on Commerce, Justice, State, and the Judiciary, "Fiscal Year 2002 Appropriations For FBI And DEA" hearing, 107th Cong., 1st sess., May 16, 2001.

94. Federal Bureau of Investigation, *Report to the National Commission on Terrorist Attacks Upon the United States: The FBI's Counterterrorism Program Since September 11, 2001*, April 14, 2004, p. 51. http://www.fbi .gov/publications/commission/9-11commissionrep.pdf (accessed February 3, 2006); Kessler, *The Bureau*, p. 454; Shane Harris, "Rebooting the Bureau," *Government Executive*, August 1, 2002, pp. 33–37.

95. Kessler, *The Bureau*, p. 522.

96. Thomas J. Pickard, statement before the 9/11 Commission tenth public hearing, April 13, 2004, 6. http://www.9-11commission.gov/ hearings/hearing10/pickard_statement.pdf (accessed January 30, 2006).

97. Kessler, *The Bureau*, p. 348; interview with former FBI official, December 2004; Wright, *The Looming Tower*, p. 237. Wright notes, "The bureau was technologically crippled even before Freeh arrived, but by the time he left not even church groups would accept the vintage FBI computers as donations."

98. Janet Reno, testimony before the 9/11 Commission tenth public hearing (transcript), April 13, 2004, p. 74. http://www.9-11 commission.gov/archive/hearing10/9-11Commission_Hearing_2004 -04-13.pdf(accessed February 11, 2006).

99. Memo quoted by Timothy Roemer, 9/11 Commission tenth public hearing (transcript), April 13, 2004, p. 60. http://www.9-11commission .gov/archive/hearing10/9-11Commission_Hearing_2004-04-13.pdf (accessed February 11, 2006).

100. Ibid.

101. Ibid.

102. Reno, the 9/11 Commission tenth public hearing (transcript), April 13, 2004, p. 52.

103. Louis Freeh, "Fiscal Year 2002 Appropriations for FBI And DEA," testimony before the House Appropriations Subcommittee on Commerce, Justice, State, and the Judiciary hearing, 107th Cong., 1st sess., May 16, 2001.

104. U.S. Department of Justice, Office of the Inspector General, Audit Division, "The Federal Bureau of Investigation's Management of the Trilogy Information Technology Management Project," Audit Report 05-07 (February 2005), p. 1.

105. Robert Dies, "Reforming FBI Management: the Views From Inside and Out," testimony before the Senate Judiciary Committee, 107th Cong., 1st sess., July 18, 2001; Kessler, *The Bureau*, pp. 454–55.

106. Harris, "Rebooting the Bureau."

107. U.S. Department of Justice, "The Federal Bureau of Investigation's Management of the Trilogy Information Technology Management Project," p. 2. See also hearing of the HPSCI and SSCI Joint Inquiry, morning session, "Events Surrounding September 11th," 107th Cong., 2nd sess., September 24, 2002.

108. United States General Accounting Office, "FBI Transformation: FBI Continues to Make Progress in Its Efforts to Transform and Address Priorities," GAO-04-578T (Washington, DC: March 2004), p. 14; U.S. Department of Justice, "The Federal Bureau of Investigation's Management of the Trilogy Information Technology Management Project," p. 33.

109. Interview, June 2005. Emphasis original.

110. See for example Robert S. Mueller III, testimony before the House Appropriations Subcommittee for the Departments of Commerce, Justice, and State, the Judiciary, and Related Agencies, 107th Cong., 2nd sess., June 21, 2002.

111. U.S. Department of Justice, "The Federal Bureau of Investigation's Management of the Trilogy Information Technology Modernization Project," pp. 27–30; Senate Appropriations Subcommitee on Commerce, Justice, and State, the Judiciary, and Related Agencies, "FBI Information Technology Modernization," hearing, 109th Cong., 1st sess., February 3, 2005; Jonathan Krim, "FBI Rejects Its New Case File Software: Database Project Has Cost Nearly $170 Million," *The Washington Post*, January 14, 2005, final edition, p. A05.

112. Senate Appropriations Subcommittee on Commerce, Justice, and State, the Judiciary, and Related Agencies, "FBI Information Technology Modernization," hearing, 109th Cong., 1st sess., February 3, 2005.

113. *Joint Inquiry Report*, p. 335; The 9/11 Commission, *Staff Statement Number 12*, p. 6.

114. Legal guidelines known collectively as "the wall," intended to prevent the misuse of government power, prohibited intelligence agents from passing some information to the criminal side of the Justice Department. However, these guidelines were almost universally misinterpreted and misapplied to restrict nearly all information sharing between criminal and intelligence agents inside the FBI. For more on "the wall," see *9/11 Commission Report*, pp. 78–80; Reno, statement before The 9/11 Commission tenth public hearing, April 13, 2004.

115. *Joint Inquiry Report*, p. 25.

116. The Phoenix memo reached some officials in the New York field office and was forwarded to the Portland Office, which took no action. No other field offices received it. In fact, FBI Director Mueller explicitly told the Joint Inquiry: "the Phoenix memo should have been disseminated to all field offices and to our sister agencies, and it should have triggered a broader analytical approach." (*Joint Inquiry Report*, p. 330). The Moussaoui investigation was known by a handful of headquarters officials and some agents in the bureau's Oklahoma City field office who had been dispatched to the Airman Flight School, which Moussaoui had previously attended. See Eleanor Hill, "The FBI's Handling of the Phoenix Electronic Communication and Investigation of Zacarias Moussaoui Prior to September 11, 2001," statement before the HPSCI and SSCI Joint Inquiry, 107th Cong., 2nd sess., September 24, 2002.

117. Thomas Pickard, testimony before the 9/11 Commission tenth public hearing (transcript), April 13, 2004, pp. 117, 136, 153. http://www.9-11commission.gov/archive/hearing10/9-11Commission_Hearing_2004-04-13.pdf (accessed February 14, 2006).

118. This was partly a matter of procedure and technology, as well. Different agencies inside the U.S. Intelligence Community used different classification levels for the same information and incompatible computer systems.

119. *Joint Inquiry Report*, pp. 80–81.

120. The 9/11 Commission, *Staff Statement Number 12*, p. 7.

121. *Joint Inquiry Report*, p. 80; "Threats and Responses," *9/11 Commission Staff Statement Number 10*, April 13, 2004, p. 9.

122. Kenneth J. Williams, Phoenix Memo, July 10, 2001, in appendix 2, "Phoenix EC," United States Department of Justice, Office of the Inspector General, *A Review of the FBI's Handling of Intelligence Information Related to the September 11 Attacks*, November 2004, redacted and unclassified June 2005, p. 10. http://www.fas.org/irp/agency/doj/oig/fbi-911/ (accessed February 7, 2006).

123. Interview, December 2004.

124. Interview, June 2004.

125. The 9/11 Commission, "Threats and Responses in 2001," *Staff Statement Number 10*, April 13, 2004, p. 5. http://www.9-11 commission.gov/staff_statements/staff_statement_10.pdf (accessed January 24, 2006).

126. U.S. Department of Justice, Office of the Inspector General, "A Review of the Federal Bureau of Investigation's Counterterrorism Program: Threat Assessment, Strategic Planning, and Resource Management," September 2002, executive summary.

127. *9/11 Commission Report*, p. 76.

128. The 9/11 Commission, *Staff Statement Number 9*, p. 6.

129. Interviews with two former FBI officials, June 2004 and December 2004.

130. Interview with three former FBI officials, June 2004, August 2004, and December 2004.

131. The 9/11 Commission, *Staff Statement Number 9*, p. 6.

132. Interview, August 2004.

133. Presidential Decision Directives 62 and 63 were issued May 22, 1998. These documents are classified, but unclassified summaries are available. Office of the Press Secretary, The White House, "Fact Sheet: Combating Terrorism: Presidential Decision Directive 62," May 22, 1998, http://www.fas.org/irp/offdocs/pdd-62.htm (accessed February 6, 2006); Office of the Press Secretary, the White House, "Fact Sheet: Protecting America's Critical Infrastructures: PDD 63," May 22, 1998, http://www.fas.org/irp/offdocs/pdd-63.htm (accessed February 6, 2006). See also *Joint Inquiry Report*, p. 217.

134. Quoted in John Yang, "House Pares, Then Passes, Crime, Terrorism Measure; Clinton Calls It Too Weak to be Effective," *The Washington Post*, March 15, 1996, p. A04.

135. President William Clinton, "President's Statement on Anti-terrorism Bill Signing," April 24, 1996, Clinton Presidential Materials Project (National Archives). http://clinton6.nara.gov/1996/04/1996-04-24-president-statement-on-antiterrorism-bill-signing.html (accessed February 3, 2006).

136. President William Clinton, "U.S. Policy on Counterterrorism," Presidential Decision Directive 39, June 21, 1995, redacted and declassified January 24, 1999. http://www.fas.org/irp/offdocs/pdd39.htm (accessed February 15, 2005). The directive established four main program areas: reducing vulnerabilities, deterring terrorist attack, response, and preventing terrorists from acquiring weapons of mass destruction.

137. "U.S. Policy on Counterterrorism," Presidential Decision Directive 39. The directive explicitly states, "The Director, Central Intelligence shall lead the efforts of the Intelligence Community to reduce

U.S. vulnerabilities to international terrorism through an aggressive program of foreign intelligence collection, analysis, counterintelligence and covert action." (Presidential Decision Directive 39, p. 3). By contrast, the directive discusses the FBI's prevention role in this section using vague terms that conflate prevention and response, noting only, "The Director, FBI, as head of the investigative agency for terrorism, shall reduce vulnerabilities by an expanded program of counterterrorism." (Presidential Decision Directive 39, p. 2). Compare this treatment to discussion of the FBI's role in responding to terrorist attacks. "This directive validates and reaffirms existing lead agency responsibilities for all facets of the United States counterterrorism effort. Lead agencies are those that have the most direct role in and responsibility for implementation of U.S. counterterrorism policy," the directive notes, just before designating the FBI the lead agency for responding to terrorist incidents inside the United States. (Presidential Decision Directive 39, pp. 6–7).

138. *Joint Inquiry Report*, p. 235.

139. Freeh, *My FBI*, pp. 244–46, 255–56.

140. Ibid., pp. 255–56.

141. *Joint Inquiry Report*, p. 235; *9/11 Commission Report*, pp. 201–03.

142. *9/11 Commission Report*, pp. 204, 209–10.

143. Ibid., p. 209.

144. Based on Lexis-Nexis word count total and text analysis of the following hearings: Senate Appropriations Subcommittee on Commerce, Justice, State and Judiciary, "FY 98 Appropriations," 105th Cong., 1st sess., April 10, 1997; "FY '99 Budget Request for Counterterrorism,"105th Cong., 2nd sess., March 31, 1998; "Fiscal Year 2000 Budget Requests for the FBI and Drug Enforcement Administration," 106th Cong., 1st sess., March 24, 1999; "FY 2001 Budget for the FBI, DEA and INS," 106th Cong., 2nd sess., March 7, 2000; "Fiscal Year 2002 Appropriations for the FBI, DEA, INS," 107th Cong., 1st sess., May 17, 2001; House Appropriations Subcommittee on Commerce, Justice, State and the Judiciary, "FY 1998 Commerce, Justice, State Appropriations," hearing, 105th Cong., 1st sess., March 5, 1997; "FY 1999 Commerce, Justice, State Appropriations," hearing, 105th Cong., 2nd sess., March 5, 1998; "FY 2000 Commerce, Justice, State Appropriations," hearing, 106th Cong., 1st sess., March 17, 1999; "FY 2001 Commerce, Justice, State Appropriations," hearing, 106th Cong., 2nd sess., March 16, 2000; "Fiscal Year 2002 Appropriations for FBI and DEA," hearing, 107th Cong., 1st sess., May 16, 2001.

145. Senate Appropriations Subcommittee on Commerce, Justice, State and the Judiciary, "FY 2000 Budget Requests for the FBI and Drug Enforcement Administration," 106th cong., 1st sess., March 24, 1999.

146. For congressional attention to terrorism, see also *9/11 Commission Report*, pp. 106–107.

147. Figures based on qualitative analysis of hearings listed in *Congressional Information Service Index—Abstracts of Congressional Publications* (Washington, DC: Congressional Information Service), 1993, 1994, 1995, 1996, 1997, 1998, 1999, 2000, 2001, and 2002.

148. The Act, which expanded federal jurisdiction and stiffened penalties for some terrorism crimes, was attacked by liberals and conservatives alike and widely criticized as a politically motivated and toothless response to the Oklahoma City bombing. More significant than what the bill enacted is what provisions it excluded. Congress scuttled roving wiretap authority, which would have enabled agents to track a suspect using multiple phones; and refused to grant the FBI the same access to hotel, phone, and other records in terrorism cases that used car dealers had. Louis Freeh, statement before The 9/11 Commission tenth public hearing, April 13, 2004, p. 15. http://www.9-11commission.gov/hearings/hearing10/freeh_statement.pdf (accessed January 26, 2006).

149. Rep. Charles Schumer (D-NY), quoted in "Anti-terrorism Law Expected to Pass This Week," *Pittsburgh Post-Gazette*, April 16, 1996, sooner edition, p. A-6.

150. Senate Judiciary Committee, "Nomination for Director of Federal Bureau of Investigations," hearing, 107th Cong., 1st sess., July 30, 2001.

151. Senate Judiciary Committee, "Nomination for Director of Federal Bureau of Investigations," hearing 107th Cong., 1st sess., July 31, 2001.

152. Senate Judiciary Committee, "Nomination for Director of Federal Bureau of Investigations," hearing, 107th Cong., 1st sess., July 30, 2001.

153. Based on textual analysis of Senate Judiciary Committee hearings, "Nomination for Director of Federal Bureau of Investigations," 107th Cong., 1st sess., July 30–31, 2001.

154. *9/11 Commission Report*, pp. 106–107. Open hearings, as the name suggests, are open to the public and transcribed for the public record. Closed hearings, by contrast, involve the discussion of sensitive or classified information and are closed to the public.

155. Interview, October 2005.

156. Interview, October 2005.

157. *9/11 Commission Report*, p. 107.

158. Ibid., p. 106.

159. *Joint Inquiry Report*, p. 244.

160. *Silberman-Robb Commission Report*, p. 453; The 9/11 Commission, *Staff Statement Number 9*, p. 8; Alfred Cumming and Todd Masse, "Intelligence Reform Implementation at the Federal Bureau of Investigation: Issues and Options for Congress," *Congressional Research Service Report No. RL33033*, August 16, 2005, p. 38. http://www.fas.org/sgp/crs/intel/RL33033.pdf (accessed January 25, 2006).

161. *Joint Inquiry Report*, p. 57.

162. Federal Bureau of Investigation, *Report to the National Commission on Terrorist Attacks Upon the United States: The FBI's Counterterrorism Program Since September 11, 2001*, April 14, 2004, p. 20. http://www.fbi.gov/publications/commission/9-11commissionrep.pdf (accessed February 3, 2006).

163. Gebhardt memo quoted in Stuart Taylor, "Spying on Terrorists: Will the FBI Ever Be Up To the Job?" *National Journal* 35, 2 (January 13, 2003): 80–81.

164. For training specifics, see Alfred Cumming and Todd Masse, "FBI Intelligence Reform Since September 11, 2001: Issues and Options for Congress," pp. 14–15.

165. Ibid., pp. 13 and 28.

166. There are two levels of awards: Distinguished Service Awards, which are awarded to no more than 1 percent of career executives a year and grant winners 35 percent of their base pay; and Meritorious Executive Awards, which are given to no more than 5 percent of career executives a year and provide 20 percent bonuses.

167. Interview, April 2005.

168. Based on textual analysis of Presidential Rank Award citations in annual FBI awards service programs, 1992–2001.

169. Interview, December 2004.

170. For more, see General Accounting Office, "FBI Intelligence Investigations: Coordination Within Justice on Counterintelligence Criminal Matters is Limited," Report to the Ranking Minority Member, Committee on Governmental Affairs, U.S. Senate, GAO 01–780 (Washington, DC: July 2001).

171. Jamie S. Gorelick, "Instructions on Separation of Certain Foreign Counterintelligence and Criminal Investigations," memo to Mary Jo White, Louis Freeh, and Jo Ann Harris, day unspecified, 1995, declassified April 10, 2004, p. 2.

172. Indeed, the former head of the FBI's international terrorism division told congressional investigators that Reno leaned toward closing down intelligence surveillance if she believed it would hinder a criminal case. Eleanor Hill, "Hearing on the Intelligence Community's Response to Past Terrorist Attacks Against the United States from February 1993 to September 2001," Joint Inquiry Staff Statement, Oct.

8, 2002, p. 18. http://www.fas.org/irp/congress/2002_hr/100802hill .pdf (accessed February 15, 2006).

173. See John Ashcroft, statement before the 9/11 Commission tenth public hearing, April 13, 2004. http://www.9-11commission.gov/ hearings/hearing10/ashcroft_statement.pdf (accessed January 31, 2006).

174. These were: the Gilmore commission, the Aspin-Brown commission, the Bremer commission, the Council on Foreign Relations report, the Deutch Commission, the Hart-Rudman Commission, and the House Intelligence Committee staff study, IC21.

175. Interview, April 2002.

176. Interview, October 2005.

177. Senate Judiciary Committee, "Nomination for Director of Federal Bureau of Investigation," 107th Cong., 1st sess., July 30–31, 2001.

CHAPTER 7
EVIDENCE TEAMS AT THE READY

1. Eleanor Hill, staff statement, "The Intelligence Community's Knowledge of the September 11 Hijackers Prior to September 11, 2001, HPSCI and SSCI Joint Inquiry hearing, 107th Cong., 2nd. sess., September 20, 2002, pp. 13–14.

2. The same agent authored the August 29, 2001 e-mail to FBI headquarters warning that "Someday someone will die . . . and . . . the public will not understand why we were not more effective and throwing every resource we had" at counterterrorism. The agent was not identified by name because of his continuing involvement in sensitive counterterrorism activities. The *OIG Report* refers to him as a New York Office FBI agent named "Scott." At his appearance before the House and Senate Intelligence Committees' Joint hearing on September 20, 2002, the agent was shielded by a screen to protect his identity. In his testimony, however, the agent noted that he had served in the military between 1985 and 1993, and joined the FBI in 1995, where he was assigned to the New York Field Office's Joint Terrorism Task Force. His assignments included the TWA Flight 800 investigation and the 1998 African Embassy bombings investigation. In 1999, he joined the New York Field Office's Osama bin Laden case squad. Between October 2000 and September 11, 2001, he was investigating the bombing of the USS *Cole*. HPSCI and SSCI Joint Inquiry hearing, 107th Cong., 2nd. sess., September 20, 2002. In 2006, Lawrence Wright identified the agent as Steven Bongardt. Wright, *The Looming Tower*, pp. 341 and 353–54.

3. Testimony by FBI agent before HPSCI and SSCI Joint Inquiry "Panel II: The Malaysia Hijackers and September 11th," 107th Cong., 2nd sess., September 20, 2002. Note: the agent's identify was not revealed during these hearings because of his ongoing involvement in sensitive counterterrorism investigations.

4. Office of the Inspector General, U.S. Department of Justice, *A Review of the FBI's Handling of Intelligence Information Related to the September 11 Attacks*, November 2004, redacted and unclassified June 2005 (hereafter *OIG Report*), p. 248.

5. *Joint Inquiry Report*, pp. 157–68. According to the *OIG Report*, al-Mihdhar stayed at the informant's residence from May to June 10, 2000, and al-Hazmi lived in the informant's residence from May to December 10, 2000. *OIG Report*, pp. 248, 252.

6. *Joint Inquiry Report*, pp. 27–28, 168–80; *OIG Report*, pp. 248–49.

7. Ibid., p. 115.

8. Ibid., p. 15.

9. *9/11 Commission Report*, p. 270.

10. FBI agents request assistance or information by sending documents that are called "leads." In order to prioritize work, leads are typically assigned one of three precedence levels: "Immediate," "Priority," and "Routine." According to the FBI's investigative manual, "immediate" precedence should be used "when the addressee(s) must take prompt action or have an urgent need for the information." Priority precedence should be used when information is needed within twenty-four hours. Routine precedence, by contrast, has no timeframe associated with it and is supposed to be used when information is needed in the normal course of business. *OIG Report*, pp. 56–57.

11. *OIG Report*, pp. 345–46; *9/11 Commission Report*, pp. 271–72.

12. For details about the FBI's search for al-Mihdhar and al-Hazmi, see *OIG Report*, pp. 295–304.

13. "Law Enforcement, Counterterrorism, and Intelligence Collection in the United States Prior to 9/11," *9/11 Commission Staff Statement Number. 9*, April 13, 2004, p. 1.

14. *OIG Report*, pp. 295–96.

15. Ibid., p. 296.

16. Ibid., pp. 345–56.

17. Ibid., pp. 297–301.

18. *9/11 Commission Report*, p. 271.

19. Janet Reno testimony to 9/11 Commission tenth public hearing, April 13, 2004, p. 5. Available at http://www.9-11commission.gov/hearings/hearing10/reno_statement.pdf (accessed February 27, 2006).

20. *OIG Report*, p. 345.

21. Ibid., p. 346.

22. Ibid., p. 301. The agent had graduated from the FBI academy in June, 2000, and after serving brief stints on a number of different squads, was assigned to the bin Laden unit in July of 2001.

23. Eleanor Hill, "The FBI's Handling of the Phoenix Electronic Communiation and Investigation of Zacarias Moussaoui Prior to September 11, 2001," staff statement before HPSCI and SSCI Joint Inquiry, September 24, 2002, supplemented October 17, 2002.

24. The memo went to the unit chief of the Radical Fundamentalist Unit, an analyst in the Radical Fundamentalist Unit, the acting unit chief of the Osama bin Laden unit, and three analysts in the Osama bin Laden Unit. *OIG Report*, p. 65.

25. Ibid., p. 65.

26. Kenneth J. Williams, Phoenix Memo, July 10, 2001, in appendix 2, "Phoenix EC," United States Department of Justice, Office of Inspector General, *A Review of the FBI's Handling of Intelligence Information Related to the September 11 Attacks*, November 2004, redacted and unclassified June 2005, p. 1.

27. *Joint Inquiry Report*, p. 326.

28. Kenneth J. Williams, Phoenix Memo, July 10, 2001, p. 2; *Joint Inquiry Report*, p. 326.

29. Interview, January 2007.

30. *Joint Inquiry Report*, p. xiii.

31. Ibid., p. 80; "Threats and Responses in 2001," *9/11 Commission Staff Statement Number 10*, April 13, 2004, p. 9.

32. "Threats and Responses in 2001," *9/11 Commission Staff Statement Number 10*, April 13, 2004, p. 9; *Joint Inquiry Report*, p. 80.

33. Quote in *Joint Inquiry Report*, p. 330.

34. Ibid., pp. 28, 332; Eleanor Hill, "The FBI's Handling of the Phoenix Electronic Communication and Investigation of Zacarias Moussaoui Prior to September 11, 2001," staff statement before HPSCI and SSCI Joint Inquiry, September 24, 2002, supplemented October 17, 2002. See also the testimony of Agent Williams before the SSCI and HPSCI Joint Inquiry hearing, 107th Cong., 2nd sess., September 24, 2002.

35. *United States v Zacarias Moussaoui*, Crim. No. 1:01cr455 (E.D. Virginia 2005), available at: http://i.cnn.net/cnn/2005/images/04/23/moussaoui.plea.transcript.pdf (accessed February 28, 2006). Although Moussaoui has admitted, and other evidence confirms, his participation in al Qaeda and connection to other operatives in the 9/11 plot, it remains unclear whether Moussaoui was intended to be part of the original hijackings on September 11 or participate in a second round of attacks. See *9/11 Commission Report*, pp. 245–47.

36. Joint Inquiry staff statement, "The FBI's Handling of the Phoenix Electronic Communication and Investigation of Zacarias Moussaoui Prior to September 11, 2001," HPSCI and SSCI Joint Inquiry hearing, 107th Cong., 2nd. sess., September 24, 2004, as supplemented October 17, 2002; *Joint Inquiry Report*, pp. 316–17. It should be noted that popular reports claimed Moussaoui was not interested in taking off or landing. The Joint Inquiry found the opposite to be true.

37. Quote from August 18, 2001 memorandum from FBI Minneapolis Field office to FBI Headquarters, in *Joint Inquiry Report*, p. 319.

38. For details about FISA, see "FBI Intelligence Investigations: Coordination within Justice on Counterintelligence Criminal Matters is Limited," U.S. General Accounting Office, Report Number GAO-01–780, July 16, 2001.

39. For evidence of the connection in Moussaoui's belongings, see *Joint Inquiry Report*, p. 324. For connections between Moussaoui and Binalshibh, see *9/11 Commission Report*, pp. 161, 225, 243–50.

40. FBI lawyers working on the Moussaoui warrant told the Congressional Joint Inquiry that they were unaware of the Phoenix memo, and that inclusion of the memo would have made a stronger case for their warrant. See Joint Inquiry staff statement, "The FBI's Handling of the Phoenix Electronic Communication and Investigation of Zacarias Moussaoui Prior to September 11, 2001," HPSCI and SSCI Joint Inquiry, September 24, 2002, 107th Cong., 2nd. sess., supplemented October 17, 2002, p. 15.

41. Millennium terrorist Ahmed Ressam was cooperating with U.S. government officials at the time and subsequently identified Moussaoui as someone who had gone to one of al Qaeda's Afghan training camps. See *9/11 Commission Report*, pp. 276–77. The chief of the FBI's radical fundamentalist unit admitted to Congress that "[t]he photograph was not shown before 9/11 and it should have been," *Joint Inquiry Report*, p. 324.

42. Quote in *9/11 Commission Report*, p. 258.

43. Ibid., p. 264.

44. Ibid., p. 259.

45. Ibid., p. 265. For specifics of Pickard's telephone calls, see 9/11 Commission tenth public hearing, "Law Enforcement and the Intelligence Community, April 13, 2004, transcript available at http://www.9–11commission.gov/archive/hearing10/9–11Commission_Hearing_2004–04–13.pdf (accessed February 27, 2006), pp. 84, 110–12.

46. *9/11 Commission Report*, p. 265.

47. Ibid., p. 275. The Moussaoui investigation was known only to some agents in the bureau's Oklahoma City field office who had been dispatched to Airman Flight School, which Moussaoui had previously

attended. See Eleanor Hill, Staff Statement, "The FBI's Handling of the Phoenix Electronic Communication and Investigation of Zacarias Moussaoui Prior to September 11, 2001," HPSCI and SSCI Joint Inquiry hearing, 107th Cong., 2nd. sess., September 24, 2004, as supplemented October 17, 2002.

48. *Joint Inquiry Report*, p. 27.

49. Ibid.

50. Ibid.

51. The imam is named in the *9/11 Commission Report*, p. 221.

52. *Joint Inquiry Report*, p. 28. The 9/11 Commission reached no definitive conclusions about the relationship between al-Hazmi and the imam, but believes that their rendezvous in Virginia "may not have been coincidental" (p. 221).

53. Joint Inquiry Staff Statement, "The FBI's Handling of the Phoenix Electronic Communication and Investigation of Zacarias Moussaoui Prior to September 11, 2001," September 24, 2002, supplemented October 17, 2002, p. 8; Morning session of HPSCI, SSCI Joint Inquiry hearing, "Events Surrounding September 11," 107th Cong., 2nd sess., September 24, 2002.

54. *Joint Inquiry Report*, p. 25.

55. The Phoenix memo reached some officials in the New York field office and was forwarded to the Portland Office, which took no action. No other field offices received it. The Moussaoui investigation was known by a handful of headquarters officials and some agents in the bureau's Oklahoma City field office who had been dispatched to Airman Flight School, which Moussaoui had previously attended. See Eleanor Hill, Staff Statement, "The FBI's Handling of the Phoenix Electronic Communication and Investigation of Zacarias Moussaoui Prior to September 11, 2001," Joint Inquiry hearing, 107th Cong., 2nd. sess., September 24, 2002, supplemented October 17, 2002.

56. *OIG Report*, pp. 303–304.

57. Unnamed Minneapolis agent, afternoon session of HPSCI and SSCI Joint Inquiry hearing, "Events Surrounding September 11th," 107th Cong., 2nd sess., September 24, 2002.

58. Quoted in *Joint Inquiry Report*, p. 330.

59. Quote from FBI tactical analyst, *OIG Report*, p. 66.

60. *Joint Inquiry Report*, pp. 266–67.

61. Ibid., p. 335.

62. Quoted in *Joint Inquiry Report*, p. 61.

63. Ibid., p. 57; Eleanor Hill testimony, morning session of a HPSCI and SSCI Joint Inquiry hearing, "events surrounding September 11th," 107th Cong., 2nd sess., September 24, 2002.

64. Ibid., pp. 56–58.

CHAPTER 8

THE MORE THINGS CHANGE...

1. Interview, November 2006.

2. Interview, March 2007.

3. Interview, February 2006.

4. Adam Clymer, "A Nation Challenged: The Political Parties; Disaster Forges a Spirit of Cooperation in a Usually Contentious Congress," *New York Times*, September 20, 2001, p. B3.

5. Interviews with four congressional staffers, April 2002 and October 2005.

6. The PATRIOT Act included three provisions that President Clinton had tried, but failed, to pass in the mid-1990s: "roving wiretaps," which enabled the FBI to obtain a single court warrant for multiple telephone and communications devices used by a single terrorism suspect rather than requiring separate court orders for each device; expanded FBI access to telephone and other records in terrorism cases; and lower restrictions governing the FBI's use of "pen registers" or "trap and trace" devices to monitor the identities of those sending and receiving communications in terrorism cases. For a discussion of the statutory changes President Clinton sought but never won, see President William Clinton, "President's Statement on Antiterrorism Bill Signing," April 24, 1996, Clinton Materials Project (National Archives). http://clinton6.nara.gov/1996/04/1996–04–24-president-statement-on -antiterrorism-bill-signing.html (accessed February 3, 2006); *Congress and the Nation*, vol. IX (1993–96) (Washington, DC: Congressional Quarterly Press), pp. 727–33. For an analysis of the provisions of the PATRIOT Act, see Charles Doyle, "The USA Patriot Act: A Legal Analysis," *Congressional Research Service Report RL 31377*, April 15, 2002.

7. Interview, October 2005.

8. Interview, July 2006.

9. In the House, 357 representatives voted in favor of the PATRIOT Act, while 66 voted against it.

10. Interview, July 2006.

11. Walter Pincus, "Rumsfeld Casts Doubt On Intelligence Reform: Changes Suggested by Presidential Panel," *Washington Post*, April 9, 2002, p. A17; interview with former government official, November 2005. This report was the first of two classified reviews of U.S. intelligence led by Scowcroft.

12. Walter Pincus, "Rumsfeld Casts Doubt On Intelligence Reform: Changes Suggested by Presidential Panel," *Washington Post*, April 9, 2002, p. A17.

13. In 2003 the National Imagery and Mapping Agency was renamed the National Geospatial-Intelligence Agency.

14. Walter Pincus, "Rumsfeld Casts Doubt On Intelligence Reform: Changes Suggested by Presidential Panel," *Washington Post*, April 9, 2002, p. A17.

15. Interview, November 2005.

16. Spencer Ackerman, "Small Change," *New Republic*, December 13, 2004, p. 12; interview with government official, October 2005; interview with former government official, November 2005.

17. Spencer Ackerman, "Small Change," *New Republic*, December 13, 2004, p. 12.

18. "Remarks by the President in Address to the Nation," June 6, 2002, Office of the Press Secretary, the White House, available at http://www.whitehouse.gov/news/releases/2002/06/20020606-8.html (accessed July 18, 2006).

19. President George W. Bush, "A Bill to Establish a Department of Homeland Security," "submitted to Congress June 18, 2002, available at http://www.whitehouse.gov/news/releases/2002/06/20020618-5.html (accessed July 19, 2006).

20. See for example, Government Accountability Office, *Department of Homeland Security: A Comprehensive and Sustained Approach Needed to Achieve Management Integration*, GAO 05–139, March 16, 2005.

21. Amelia Gruber, "Squeezing Services," *Government Executive Magazine*, March 1, 2005, available at http://www.govexec.com/features/0305–01/0305–01sls4.htm (accessed July 18, 2006).

22. Todd Datz, "From the Ground Up," *CSO Magazine*, March 1, 2004.

23. Quoted in Michael Crowley, "Bush's Disastrous Homeland Security Department," *New Republic*, March 15, 2004, p. 17.

24. Susan B. Glasser and Michael Grunwald, "Department's Mission was Undermined from Start," *Washington Post*, December 22, 2005, p. A01.

25. *The Homeland Security Act of 2002*, Public Law 107–296, 107th Cong., 2nd sess., November 25, 2002.

26. Quoted in Susan B. Glasser and Michael Grunwald, "Department's Mission was Undermined from Start," *Washington Post*, December 22, 2005, p. A01.

27. "Consolidating Intelligence Analysis: A Review of the President's Proposal to Create a Terrorist Threat Integration Center," Senate Committee on Homeland Security and Governmental Affairs, 108th Cong., 1st sess., February 14, 2003 and February 26, 2003.

28. Press release, "Senator Collins Receives Answers on Terrorist Threat Integration Center: Satisfied with Response, but Concerned by

its Delay," April 20, 2004, Senate Committee on Homeland Security and Governmental Affairs.

29. Task Force on National Security in the Information Age, Markle Foundation, *Creating a Trusted Network for Homeland Security: Second Report of the Markle Foundation Task Force*, December 2003, p. 3.

30. Richard A. Falkenrath, "The 9/11 Commission Report: A Review Essay," *International Security* 29, 3 (Winter 2004–05): 172.

31. Joby Warrick, Joe Stephens, Mary Pat Flaherty, and James V. Grimaldi, "FBI Agents Ill-Equipped to Predict Terror Acts," *Washington Post*, September 24, 2001, p. A01.

32. Editorial, "The Spy Puzzle," *New York Times*, November 4, 2001, p. 12.

33. These were: "Joint Inquiry Staff Statement, Part I," HPSCI and SSCI hearing, 107th Cong., 2nd sess., September 18, 2002; "The Intelligence Community's Knowledge of the September 11 Hijackers Prior to September 11, 2001," 107th Cong., 2nd sess., September 20, 2002; "The FBI's Handling of the Phoenix Electronic Communication and Investigation of Zacarias Moussaoui Prior to September 11, 2001," HPSCI and SSCI hearing, 107th Cong., 2nd sess., September 24, 2002; "Counterterrorism Information Sharing with Other Federal Agencies and with State and Local Governments and the Private Sector," HPSCI and SSCI hearing, 107th Cong., 2nd sess., October 1, 2002; "Joint Inquiry Staff Statement: Proposals for Reform within the Intelligence Community," HPSCI and SSCI hearing, 107th Cong., 2nd sess., October 3, 2002; "Joint Inquiry Staff Statement: Hearing on the Intelligence Community's Response to Past Terrorist Attacks Against the United States from February 1993 to September 2001," HPSCI and SSCI hearing, 107th Cong., 2nd sess., October 8, 2002; "Joint Inquiry Staff Statement," HPSCI and SSCI hearing, 107th Cong., 2nd sess., October 17, 2002. The staff statements were submitted in open hearings which also featured testimony by senior government officials, key intelligence personnel, and outside experts.

34. Eleanor Hill, "Joint Inquiry Staff Statement, Part I," HPSCI and SSCI hearing, 107th Cong., 2nd sess., September 18, 2002.

35. Interview, April 2002.

36. TTIC later became the National Counterterrorism Center.

37. Senate Select Committee on Intelligence, *U.S. Intelligence Community's Prewar Intelligence Assessments on Iraq*, 108th Cong., 2nd sess., July 9, 2004.

38. Senate Select Committee on Intelligence, *U.S. Intelligence Community's Prewar Intelligence Assessments on Iraq*, 108th Cong., 2nd sess., July 9, 2004.

39. Analysis from based on full text LexisNexis searches of ABC, CBS, NBC, CNN, Fox News, MSNBC, CNBC, and *The News Hour with Jim Lehrer* between July 22, 2004 and December 10, 2004.

40. Interview, November 2005.

41. Quote in Philip Shenon and Douglas Jehl, "House Proposal Puts Less Power in New Spy Post," *New York Times*, September 25, 2004, p. A1.

42. Interview, October 2005.

43. Interview, October 2005. See also comments made by Representative Jane Harman and Senator Pat Roberts, *Fox News Sunday*, November 21, 2004.

44. Representative Jane Harman, Intelligence Reauthorization News conference with members of the House Permanent Select Committee on Intelligence, March 30, 2006. Harman went on to say that she believed the law had overcome Pentagon objections and provided adequate statutory budget authority to the DNI, but needed more vigorous leadership to be effective.

45. Myers's letter can be found in Intelligence Reform and Terrorism Prevention Act of 2004 Conference Report, *Congressional Record* S11939-S12010, appendix. Available at www.fas.org/irp/congress/2004_cr/s120804.html (accessed February 22, 2006).

46. Letter from Richard Cheney to Senator Les Aspin, March 17, 1992, available at http://www.fas.org/irp/congress/1992_cr/cheney1992.pdf (accessed February 16, 2006); letter from Deputy Secretary of Defense John White to Senate Armed Services Committee Chairman Strom Thurmond (R-SC), April 29, 1996, described in Walter Pincus, "Panels continue impasse on intelligence," *Washington Post*, June 7, 1996, p. A21.

47. Pat Roberts, *Fox News Sunday*, November 21, 2004.

48. Quoted in Walter Pincus, "Intelligence Bill Clears Congress," *Washington Post*, December 9, 2004, p. A4.

49. Interview, October 2005.

50. Interviews with four officials, October 2005 and November 2005. See also Mary Curtius, "Intelligence Reform Looks Like a Lame Duck for Now," *Los Angeles Times*, November 12, 2004, p. A24; Charles Babington and Mike Allen, "White House View of Stalled Bill in Doubt," *Washington Post*, November 24, 2004, p. A4; Michael Isikoff and Eleanor Clift, "Intel Reform: Did Bush Push Hard?" *Newsweek*, December 6, 2004, p. 6; Julie Hirschfield Davis, "Intelligence Reform in Limbo," *Baltimore Sun*, November 23, 2004, p. 1A; Elisabeth Bumiller and Philip Shenon, "Bush Urged to Get Pentagon In Step on Intelligence Bill," *New York Times*, November 23, 2004, p. A20.

51. Interview, November 2005.

52. Interview, May 2004.

53. Interview, November 2005.

54. Letter from the Honorable Laurence H. Silbmeran and The Honorable Charles S. Robb to the president, March 31, 2005, reprinted in *Silberman-Robb Commission Report*, preface.

55. *Silberman-Robb Commission Report*, p. 6.

56. *9/11 Commission Report*, p. 93.

57. Walter Pincus, "Some Lawmakers Doubt DNI has Taken Intelligence Reigns," *Washington Post*, February 2, 2006, p. A09; interview with Congressional Intelligence Committee member, October 2005; interview with former CIA official, February 2006. See also Richard A. Posner, *Countering Terrorism* (Oxford: Rowman & Littlefield, 2006); Scott Shane, "In New Job, Spymaster Draws Bipartisan Criticism," *New York Times*, April 20, 2006, p. A1; John Lehman, "Are We Any Safer?" *Proceedings of the U.S. Naval Institute*, September 2006.

58. Senate Select Committee on Intelligence, "Progress Made on Intelligence Reform," 110th Cong., 1st sess., January 23, 2007.

59. John Gannon, written testimony submitted to the Senate Judiciary Committee, hearing on FBI oversight, 109th Cong., 2nd. sess., May 2, 2006.

60. Eric Schmitt, "Clash Foreseen Between CIA and Pentagon," *New York Times*, May 10, 2006, p. A1.

61. Barton Gellman and Dafna Linzer, "Pushing the Limits of Wartime Powers," *Washington Post*, December 18, 2005, p. A01.

62. Walter Pincus, "Pentagon's Intelligence Authority Widens; Fact Sheet Details Secretive Agency's Growth from Focus on Policy to Counterterrorism," *Washington Post*, December 19, 2005, p. A10.

63. Quote in Walter Pincus, "Pentagon's Pentagon's Intelligence Authority Widens; Fact Sheet Details Secretive Agency's Growth from Focus on Policy to Counterterrorism," *Washington Post*, December 19, 2005, p. A10.

64. Eric Schmitt, "Clash Foreseen between CIA and Pentagon," *New York Times*, May 10, 2006, p. A1.

65. Jane Harman, Remarks at the Second Annual Rand/Terrorism Early Warning Group Conference, Santa Monica, CA, October 19, 2006. Secretary Rumsfeld announced his resignation on November 8, one day after Democrats regained control of both the House and Senate in the 2006 midterm elections.

66. Interview, July 2005.

67. Interviews with six current and former intelligence officials, October 2005, November 2005, and February 2006.

68. Interview, May, 2006.

69. Interview, February 2006.

70. Quote in Scott Shane, "Year into Revamped Spying, Troubles and Some Progress," *New York Times*, February 28, 2006, p. A12.

71. House Permanent Select Committee on Intelligence, Intelligence Authorization Act for Fiscal Year 2007, 109th Cong., 2nd sess., April 6, 2006, Report 109–411.

72. Quote from *Fox News Sunday*, April 23, 2006.

73. Ibid.

74. Press release, office of Senator Jay Rockefeller, January 4, 2007, available online at http://www.senate.gov/~rockefeller/news/2007/pr010407a.html (accessed March 9, 2007).

75. Admiral John Scott Redd, Director, National Counterterrorism Center, "Statement for the Record," Senate Foreign Relations Committee hearing, 109th Cong., 2nd sess., June 13, 2006.

76. Michael Isikoff and Daniel Klaidman, "Look Who's Not Talking—Still," *Newsweek*, April 4, 2005, p. 30.

77. Interview, March 2007.

78. Michael Isikoff and Daniel Klaidman, "Look Who's Not Talking-Still," *Newsweek*, April 4, 2005, p. 30.

79. Senator Mike DeWine, Hearing on the Nomination of General Michael Hayden to be the director of CIA, SSCI, 109th Cong., 2nd sess., May 18, 2006. See also comments on NCTC by former Acting CIA Director John McLaughlin, Council on Foreign Relations Meeting, "Intelligence Support to the Military," Washington, DC, April 4, 2006; Helen Fessenden, "The Limits of Intelligence Reform," *Foreign Affairs* 84, 6 (November—December 2005), pp. 106–20.

80. *Silberman-Robb Commission Report*, p. 320.

81. Ibid. pp. 320–21. Information sharing with state and local agencies is worse. See Richard Falkenrath, "Prepared Statement of Testimony before the Senate Committee on Homeland Security and Governmental Affairs, 109th Cong., 2nd sess., September 12, 2006.

82. Shane Harris and Greta Wodele, "Bureaucracy Hinders 9/11 Commission Recommendations," *National Journal*, January 13, 2006.

83. *Final Report on 9/11 Commission Recommendations*, 9/11 Public Discourse Project, December 5, 2005, available at www.9-11.pdp.org (accessed December 5, 2005), p. 3.

84. Zoe Baird and James Barksdale, chairmen, Markle Foundation Task Force on National Security in the Information Age, *Mobilizing Information to Prevent Terrorism: Accelerating Development of a Trusted Information Sharing Environment*, July 2006, p. 7.

85. Ibid., p. 1.

86. Testimony of Major General Dale Meyerrose, associate director of National Intelligence and chief information officer, Senate Select

Committee on Intelligence, "Progress Made on Intelligence Reform," 110th Cong., 1st sess., January 23, 2007.

87. *Silberman-Robb Commission Report*, p. 5.

88. Ibid.

89. Ibid.

90. Testimony of Michael Hayden, Senate Select Committee on Intelligence, "Hearing on the Confirmation of General Michael B. Hayden to become Director of the Central Intelligence Agency," 109th Cong., 2nd sess., May 18, 2006.

91. Quoted in Tim Weiner, "Langley, We Have a Problem," *New York Times*, May 14, 2006, Week in Review, section 4, p. 1.

92. Quoted in Tim Weiner, "Langley, We Have a Problem," *New York Times*, May 14, 2006, Week in Review, section 4, p. 1.

93. Office of the Press Secretary, the White House, "Memorandum for the Director of Central Intelligence," November 23, 2004, available at www.whitehouse.gov/news/releases/2004/11/print/20041123–5.html (accessed February 8, 2006). See also hearing of the House Select Committee on Homeland Security, Subcommittee on Intelligence, Information Sharing, and Terrorism Risk Assessment, 109th Cong., 2nd sess., May 10, 2006; U.S. Government Accountability Office, "Information Sharing: The Federal Government Needs to Establish Policies and Processes for Sharing Terrorism-Related and Sensitive but Unclassified Information," GAO-06–385, March 17, 2006.

94. Mark Mazzetti, "CIA Making Rapid Strides for Regrowth," *New York Times*, May 17, 2006, p. A1.

95. Interviews with four former clandestine officials, December 2004 and June 2005; interview with member of Congressional Intelligence Committee, October 2005; Siobhan Gorman, "Fewer Better Spies Key to Intelligence Reform, Former Official Says," *National Journal*, March 18, 2005.

96. Quoted in Siobhan Gorman, "Fewer Better Spies Key to Intelligence Reform, Former Official Says," *National Journal*, March 18, 2005.

97. Interview, December 2004.

99. Interview, December 2004.

99. Quoted in Siobhan Gorman, "Fewer Better Spies Key to Intelligence Reform, Former Official Says," *National Journal*, March 18, 2005.

100. Federal Bureau of Investigation, "The FBI Workforce by the Numbers," www.fib.gov/page2/aug04/workforce082504.htm (accessed February 10, 2006).

101. Testimony of Director Robert Mueller, House Appropriations Subcommittee on Science, State, Justice and Commerce and Related Agencies, 109th Cong., 1st sess., September 14, 2005.

102. Interview with FBI official, October 2006; interview with former CIA official, November 2006.

103. The National Security Branch was created in September 2005. For more see the FBI's Web site at http://www.fbi.gov/hq/nsb/nsb_faq.htm (accessed July 25, 2006).

104. Interview, October 2006. Six other current FBI officials expressed similar views in interviews conducted during the fall of 2006.

105. Chitra Ragavan, "Fixing the FBI," *U.S. News and World Report*, March 28, 2005, pp. 19–30; *Silberman-Robb Commission Report*, pp. 451–57; hearing of the House Appropriations Subcommittee on Science, State, Justice and Commerce and Related Agencies, 109th Cong., 1st sess., September 14, 2005.

106. *Silberman-Robb Commission Report*, p. 453.

107. In early 2007, the bureau added three more weeks of national security training to its eighteen-week new agent training program. Interview with senior law enforcement official, March 2007; testimony of John S. Pistole, deputy director of the FBI, Senate Select Committee on Intelligence, "Intelligence Reform," 110th Cong., 1st sess., January 25, 2007.

108. Office of the Inspector General, Audit Division, U.S. Department of Justice, *The Federal Bureau of Investigation's Efforts to Hire, Train, and Retain Intelligence Analysts*, Audit Report 05–20, May 2005, p. 116.

109. Ibid., p. 64.

110. Ibid., pp. x–xi, *Silberman-Robb Commission Report*, p. 455; hearing of the House Appropriations Subcommittee on Science, State, Justice and Commerce and Related Agencies, 109th Cong., 1st sess., September 14, 2005; testimony of Glenn A. Fine, Inspector General, U.S. Department of Justice, Senate Judiciary Committee hearing, "FBI Oversight," 109th Cong., 2nd sess., May 2, 2006.

111. Office of the Inspector General, Audit Division, U.S. Department of Justice, *The Federal Bureau of Investigation's Efforts to Hire, Train, and Retain Intelligence Analysts*, Audit Report 05–20, May 2005, p. 86.

112. Ibid., p. xi.

113. Quote in testimony by Todd Masse, House Appropriations Subcommittee on Science, State, Justice and Commerce and Related Agencies, 109th Cong., 1st sess., September 14, 2005.

114. For an excellent discussion of the differences between law enforcement and intelligence cultures, see Richard A. Posner, *Countering Terrorism* (Oxford: Rowman & Littlefield, 2006), chapter 5.

115. Quoted in Jeff Stein, "FBI Under the Gun," *CQ Weekly*, May 1, 2006, p. 1152.

116. Interview, October 2006.

117. Interview, January 2007.

118. Available at http://www.fbi.gov/aboutus/faqs/faqsone.htm (accessed March 8, 2007).

119. Interview with Robert Mueller, January 2007; interview with Wayne Murphy, February 2007; interview with two FBI special agents, October 2006.

120. Interview, February 2007.

121. Interview, October 2006.

122. Interview, October 2006.

123. Testimony before the Senate Select Committee on Intelligence, "Intelligence Reform," 110th Cong., 1st sess., January 25, 2007.

124. U.S. Department of Justice, "The Federal Bureau of Investigation's Management of the Trilogy Information Technology Modernization Project," pp. 27–30; Senate Appropriations Subcommitee on Commerce, Justice, and State, the Judiciary, and Related Agencies, "FBI Information Technology Modernization," hearing, 109th Cong., 1st sess., February 3, 2005; Jonathan Krim, "FBI Rejects Its New Case File Software: Database Project Has Cost Nearly $170 Million," *The Washington Post*, January 14, 2005, p. A05.

125. Glenn A. Fine, Inspector General, United States Department of Justice, testimony before the Senate Judiciary Committee, "FBI Oversight," 109th Cong., 2nd sess., May 2, 2006.

126. Interview, January 2007.

127. *Silberman-Robb Commission Report*, p. 454.

128. *Final Report on 9/11 Commission Recommendations*, 9/11 Public Discourse Project, December 5, 2005, available at www.9–11.pdp.org (accessed December 5, 2005), p. 3.

129. John Gannon, written testimony submitted to the Senate Judiciary Committee, hearing on "FBI Oversight," 109th Cong., 2nd. sess., May 2, 2006.

130. Ibid.

131. Goss was effectively demoted three months later when Congress passed the Intelligence Reform and Terrorism Prevention Act, which established the director of national intelligence.

132. Dana Priest, "CIA Holds Terror Suspects in Secret Prisons," *Washington Post*, November 2, 2005, p. A1.

133. James Risen and Eric Lichtblau, "Bush Lets U.S. Spy on Callers without Courts," *New York Times*, December 16, 2005, p. A1.

134. Leslie Cauley, "NSA has massive database of Americans' phone calls," *USA Today*, May 11, 2006, p. 1A. Note: significant details of this original report were subsequently recanted, although the program was verified by additional sources in other reports. See Frank Ahrens and Howard Kurtz, "USA Today Takes Back Some of NSA Phone-Record

Report," *Washington Post*, July 1, 2006, p. A02. The call records do not include contents of the conversations.

135. Senator Pat Roberts, hearing on the nomination of General Michael Hayden to be director of the CIA, Senate Select Committee on Intelligence, 109th Cong., 2nd. sess., May 18, 2006.

136. Quoted in David Stout, "F.B.I. Head Admits Mistakes in Use of Security Act," *New York Times*, March 10, 2007, p. A1.

137. Interview, October 2006.

138. The Silberman-Robb Commission first made this comparison, p. 452.

139. National Archives, "Constitution of the United States: Questions and Answers," http://www.archives.gov/national-archives -experience/charters/constitution_q_and_a.html (accessed July 25, 2006).

140. Interview, October 2005.

141. Henry M. Jackson, "How Shall We Forge a Strategy for Survival?" Address before the National War College (April 16, 1959), in Karl F. Inderfurth and Loch K. Johnson, eds., *Decisions of the Highest Order: Perspectives on the National Security Council* (Pacific Grove, CA: Brooks/Cole, 1988), pp. 78–81.

142. Hanson W. Baldwin, "Intelligence—I; One of the Weakest Links in Our Security, Survey Shows—Omissions, Duplications," *New York Times*, July 20, 1948, p. 6.

* References *

9/11 Commission. 2003. "9/11 Commission Fourth Public Hearing: Intelligence and the War on Terrorism." The National Commission on Terrorist Attacks Upon the United States (The 9/11 Commission). http://www.9–11commission.gov/archive/hearing4/9–11Commission_Hearing_2003–10–14.pdf, October 14.

———. 2003. "9/11 Commission Sixth Public Hearing: Security and Liberty." http://www.9–11commission.gov/archive/hearing6/9–11Commission_Hearing_2003–12–08.pdf, December 8.

———. 2004. "9/11 Commission Seventh Public Hearing: Borders, Transportation, and Managing Risk." http://www.9–11commission.gov/archive/hearing7/9–11Commission_Hearing_2004–01–26.pdf and http://www.9–11commission.gov/archive/hearing7/9–11Commission_Hearing_2004–01–27.pdf, January 26–27.

———. 2004. *9/11 Commission Staff Statement Number 1: Entry of the 9/11 Hijackers into the United States.* Http://www.9–11commission.gov/staff_statements/staff_statement_1.pdf, January 26.

———. 2004. *9/11 Commission Staff Statement Number 2: Three 9/11 Hijackers: Identification, Watchlisting, and Tracking.* http://www.9–11commission.gov/staff_statements/staff_statement_2.pdf, January 26.

———. 2004. "9/11 Commission Eighth Public Hearing: Counterterrorism Policy." http://www.9–11commission.gov/archive/hearing8/9–11Commission_Hearing_2004–03–23.pdf and http://www.9–11commission.gov/archive/hearing8/9–11Commission_Hearing_2004–03–24.pdf, March 23–24.

———. 2004. *9/11 Commission Staff Statement Number 5: Diplomacy.* http://www.9–11commission.gov/staff_statements/staff_statement_5.pdf, March 23.

———. 2004. *9/11 Commission Staff Statement Number 6: The Military.* http://www.9–11commission.gov/staff_statements/staff_statement_6.pdf, March 23.

———. 2004. *9/11 Commission Staff Statement Number 7: Intelligence Policy.* http://www.9–11commission.gov/staff_statements/staff_statement_7.pdf, March 24.

———. 2004. *9/11 Commission Staff Statement Number 8: National Policy Coordination.* Http://www.9–11commission.gov/staff_statements/staff_statement_8.pdf, March 24.

9/11 Commission. 2004. "9/11 Commission Ninth Public Hearing: Testimony from Dr. Condoleezza Rice." http://www.9–11commission.gov/archive/hearing9/9–11Commission_Hearing_2004–04–08.pdf, April 8.

———. 2004. *9/11 Commission Staff Statement Number 9: Law Enforcement, Counterterrorism, and Intelligence Collection in the United States Prior to 9/11.* Http://www.9–11commission.gov/staff_statements/staff_statement_9.pdf, April 13.

———. 2004. *9/11 Commission Staff Statement Number 10: Threats and Responses in 2001.* Http://www.9–11commission.gov/staff_statements/staff_statement_10.pdf, April 13.

———. 2004. "9/11 Commission Tenth Public Hearing: Law Enforcement and the Intelligence Community." Http://www.9–11commission.gov/archive/hearing10/911Commission_Hearing_2004–04–13.pdf, April 13–14.

———. 2004. *9/11 Commission Staff Statement Number 11: The Performance of the Intelligence Community.* Http://www.9–11commission.gov/staff_statements/staff_statement_11.pdf, April 14.

———. 2004. *9/11 Commission Staff Statement Number 12: Reforming Law Enforcement, Counterterrorism, and Intelligence Collection in the United States.* Http://www.9–11commission.gov/staff_statements/staff_statement_12.pdf, April 14.

———. 2004. *9/11 Commission Staff Statement Number 15: Overview of the Enemy.* Http://www.9–11commission.gov/staff_statements/staff_statement_15.pdf, June 16.

———. 2004. *9/11 Commission Staff Statement Number 16: Outline of the 9/11 Plot.* Http://www.9–11commission.gov/staff_statements/staff_statement_16.pdf, June 16.

———. 2004. "9/11 Commission Twelfth Public Hearing: The 9/11 Plot and National Crisis Management." Http://www.9–11commission.gov/archive/hearing12/9–11Commission_Hearing_2004–06–16.pdf and http://www.9–11commission.gov/archive/hearing12/9–11Commission_Hearing_2004–06–17.pdf, June 16–17.

———. 2004. *The 9/11 Commission Report: Final Report of the National Commission on Terrorist Attacks Upon the United States,* authorized edition. New York: W. W. Norton.

9/11 Public Discourse Project. 2005. *Final Report of the 9/11 Public Discourse Project,* http://www.9–11pdp.org/press/2005–12–05_statement.pdf, December 5.

Aberbach, Joel D., and Bert A. Rockman. 2000. *In the Web of Politics: Three Decades of the U.S. Federal Executive.* Washington, DC: Brookings Institution Press.

Ackerman, Spencer. 2004. "Small Change," *New Republic,* December 13.

Ackerman, Spencer, and John B. Judis. 2003. "The Operator," *New Republic*, September 22.

Advisory Panel to Assess Domestic Response Capabilities for Terrorism Involving Weapons of Mass Destruction [Gilmore Commission]. 1999. *First Annual Report to the President and the Congress: Assessing the Threat.* Washington, DC: Government Printing Office, December 15.

———. 2000. *Second Annual Report to the President and the Congress: Toward a National Strategy for Combating Terrorism.* Washington, DC: Government Printing Office, December 15.

———. 2001. *Third Annual Report to the President and the Congress: For Ray Downey:* Washington, DC: Government Printing Office, December 15.

———. 2002. *Fourth Annual Report to the President and the Congress: IV: Implementing the National Strategy.* Washington, DC: Government Printing Office, December 15.

———. 2003. *Fifth Annual Report to the President and the Congress: Forging America's New Normalcy: Security our Homeland, Preserving our Liberty.* Washington, DC: Government Printing Office, December 15.

Ahrens, Frank, and Howard Kurtz. 2006. "*USA Today* Takes Back Some of NSA Phone-Record Report," *Washington Post*, July 1, p. A02.

Aldrich, Howard. 1979. *Organizations and Environments*. Englewood Cliffs, NJ: Prentice-Hall.

———. 1999. *Organizations Evolving*. London: Sage Publications.

Allison, Graham. 1971. *Essence of Decision: Explaining the Cuban Missile Crisis*. Boston: Little, Brown.

———. 2004. *Nuclear Terrorism: The Ultimate Preventable Catastrophe*. New York: Henry Holt.

Antiterrorism and Effective Death Penalty Act of 1996. Public Law 104–132, April 24, 1996. *United States Statutes at Large* 110 (1996): 1213–319.

Andrew, Christopher. 1995. *For the President's Eyes Only: Secret Intelligence and the American Presidency from Washington to Bush*. New York: HarperCollins.

Anonymous [Michael Scheurer]. 2004. *Imperial Hubris: Why the West is Losing the War on Terror*. Washington, DC: Brassey's, Inc.

Aspin, Les, and Harold Brown, chairmen. 1996. "Report of the Commission on the Roles and Capabilities of the United States Intelligence Community" (Aspin-Brown Commission Report), http://www.access.gpo.gov/int/report.html.

Babington, Charles, and Mike Allen. 2004. "White House View of Stalled Bill in Doubt," *Washington Post*, November 24, p. A4.

Baer, Robert. 2002. *See No Evil: The True Story of a Ground Soldier in the CIA's War on Terrorism*. New York: Crown Publishing Group.

Baird, Zoe, and James Barksdale, chairmen of the Markle Foundation Task Force on National Security in the Information Age. 2002. *Protecting America's Freedom in the Information Age*, October.

———. 2006. *Mobilizing Information to Prevent Terrorism: Accelerating Development of a Trusted Information Sharing Environment*, July.

Baldwin, Hanson W. 1948. "Intelligence—I; One of the Weakest Links in Our Security, Survey Shows—Omissions, Duplications," *New York Times*, July 20, p. 6.

Bamford, James. 1982. *The Puzzle Palace*. New York: Houghton Mifflin.

———. 2001. *Body of Secrets: Anatomy of the Ultra-Secret National Security Agency*. New York: Doubleday.

———. 2002. "War of Secrets: Eyes in the Sky, Ears to the Wall, and Still Wanting," *New York Times*, September 8, section 4, p. 5.

Barry, John, with Tom Morganthau. 1991. "Remaking the CIA," *Newsweek*, May 27, p. 18.

Barry, John, Michael Hirsh, and Michael Isikoff. 2004. "The Roots of Torture," *Newsweek*, May 24, 2004, p. 26.

Baum, Joel A. C., and Jitendra V. Singh. 1994. *Evolutionary Dynamics of Organizations*. Oxford: Oxford University Press.

Bawn, Kathleen. 1995. "Political Control Versus Expertise: Congressional Choices About Administrative Procedures." *American Political Science Review* 89 (March): 62–73.

Becker, Gary. 1983. "A Theory of Competition Among Pressure Groups for Influence." *Quarterly Journal of Economics* 98: 329–47.

Berkowitz, Bruce D. 1996. "U.S. Intelligence at a Crossroads: Agendas for Reform." *Orbis* 40, 4 (Fall): 653–64.

———. 2003. "Spying in the Post-September 11 World." *Hoover Digest* 4: 14–21.

Berkowitz, Bruce D., and Allan E. Goodman. 2000. *Best Truth: Intelligence in the Information Age*. New Haven, CT: Yale University Press.

Berkowitz, Peter, ed. 2005. *The Future of American Intelligence*. Stanford, CA: Hoover Institution Press.

Best, Richard A., Jr. 2004. "Homeland Security: Intelligence Support." *Congressional Research Service Report RS21283*, updated February 23.

———. 2004. "Proposals for Intelligence Reorganization, 1949–2004." *Congressional Research Service Report RL 32500*, updated September 24.

———. 2004. "Intelligence Issues for Congress." *Congressional Research Service Report IB10012*, updated December 9.

Betts, Richard K. 1978. "Analysis, War, and Decision: Why Intelligence Failures are Inevitable." *World Politics* 31, 1: 61–89.

———. 2002. "Fixing Intelligence." *Foreign Affairs* 81 (January—February): 43–59.

Boren, David. 1992. "The Intelligence Community: How Crucial." *Foreign Affairs* 71, 3 (Summer): 52–62.

Borrus, Amy. 1991. "Should the CIA start spying for corporate America?" *Business Week*, October 14.

Brown, Harold, chairman. 1996. Commission on the Roles and Capabilities of the United States Intelligence Community (Aspin-Brown Commission). *The Need for Policy Guidance,* www.gpo.gov/su_docs/dpos/epubs/int/int007.html.

Bryant, Robert, John Hamre, John Lawn, John MacGaffin, Howard Shapiro, and Jeffrey Smith. 2003. "America Needs More Spies," *Economist*, July 10, pp. 30–31.

Bumiller, Elisabeth and Philip Shenon. 2004. "Bush Urged to Get Pentagon In Step on Intelligence Bill," *New York Times*, November 23, p. A20.

Bush, George H. W. 1991. "State of the Union Address." The American Presidency Project, University of California, Santa Barbara. Http://www.presidency.ucsb.edu/index.php, January 21.

———. 1991. National Security Review 29, "Intelligence Capabilities: 1992–2005." November 15, http://www.fas.org/irp/offdocs/nsr/nsr29.pdf.

———. 1992. "State of the Union Address." *Public Papers of the Presidents: George Bush—1992*. Vol. 1 (January 28). Washington, DC: Government Printing Office: 156–63.

Bush, George W. 1999. "Defense: A Period of Consequences," speech, The Citadel, Charleston, SC, September 23.

———. 1999. "Foreign Policy: A Distinctly American Internationalism," speech, the Ronald Reagan Presidential Library, Simi Valley, CA, November 19.

———. 2001. "State of the Union Address." February 27. *Weekly Compilation of Presidential Documents* vol. 37, no. 9 (Week ending Friday, March 2, 2001). Washington, DC: Government Printing Office: 351–357.

———. 2002. "A Bill to Establish a Department of Homeland Security," http://www.whitehouse.gov/news/releases/2002/06/20020618-5.html, June 18.

———. 2004. "Executive Order 13353: Establishing the President's Board on Safeguarding Americans' Civil Liberties." *Federal Register* 69, 169 (August 27): 53583–87.

———. 2004. "Executive Order 13354: National Counterterrorism Center." *Federal Register* 69, 169 (August 27): 53589–92.

———. 2004. "Executive Order 13355: Strengthened Management of the Intelligence Community." *Federal Register* 69, 169 (August 27): 53593–97.

Bush, George W. 2004. "Executive Order 13356: Strengthening the Sharing of Terrorism Information to Protect Americans." *Federal Register* 69, 169 (August 27): 53599–602.

————. 2004. "Strengthening Central Intelligence Agency Capabilities," memorandum for the Director of Central Intelligence, released by the Office of the Press Secretary, the White House, November 23.

Calabresi, Massimo, and Romesh Ratnesar. 2002. "Can We Stop the Next Attack?" *Time*, March 11, p. 24.

Calvert, Randall L., Matthew D. McCubbins, and Barry R. Weingast. 1980. "A Theory of Political Control and Agency Discretion." *American Journal of Political Science* 33 (August): 588–611.

Calvert, Randall, Mark Moran, and Barry R. Weingast. 1987. "Congressional Influence Over Policy Making: The Case of the FTC." In *Congress: Structure and Policy*, ed. by Matthew McCubbins and Terry Sullivan. Cambridge: Cambridge University Press.

Campbell, Donald T. 1969. "Variation and Selective Retention in Socio-Cultural Evolution." *General Systems* 14: 69–85.

Campbell, Kurt M., and Michèle Flournoy. 2001. *To Prevail: An American Strategy for the Campaign against Terrorism*. Washington, DC: The Center for Strategic and International Studies Press.

Carpenter, Daniel P. 2001. *The Forging of Bureaucratic Autonomy: Reputations, Networks and Policy Innovation in Executive Agencies, 1862–1928*. Princeton: Princeton University Press.

Carroll, Glenn R. 1984. "Organizational Ecology." *Annual Review of Sociology* 10: 71–93.

Cauley, Leslie. 2006. "NSA has massive database of Americans' phone calls," *USA Today*, May 11, p. 1A.

Center for the Study of Intelligence, Central Intelligence Agency. 1996. "The Brown Commission and the Future of Intelligence; A Roundtable Discussion." *Studies in Intelligence* 39, 5.

Central Intelligence Agency. 1999. "DCI's Strategic Intent," unclassified version of "Strategic Intent for the Intelligence Community."

————. 2001. "Strategic Investment Plan for Intelligence Community Analysis." Http://www.cia.gov/cia/reports/unclass_sip/cover.jpg, February.

Cheney, Richard. 1992. Letter to Representative Les Aspin. Http://www.fas.org/irp/congress/1992-cr/cheney1992.pdf, March 17.

Clarke, Richard A. 2004. *Against All Enemies: Inside America's War on Terror*. New York: Free Press.

————. 2004. *60 Minutes*, interview by Leslie Stahl, CBS News, March 21.

————. 2004. "*Larry King Live*: Interview with Richard Clarke," CNN, March 24.

Clinton, William J. 1993. "State of the Union Address." February 17. *Weekly Compilation of Presidential Documents* 29, 7 (Week ending Friday, February 19, 1993). Washington, DC: Government Printing Office, 215–24.

———. 1994. "State of the Union Address." *Public Papers of the Presidents: William J. Clinton—1994.* Vol. 1 (January 25). Washington, DC: Government Printing Office, 126–35.

———. 1995. "State of the Union Address." *Public Papers of the Presidents: William J. Clinton—1995.* Vol. 1 (January 24). Washington, DC: Government Printing Office, 75–86.

———. 1995. Presidential Decision Directive 39, "U.S. Policy on Counterterrorism." June 21, http://www.fas.org/irp/offdocs/pdd39.htm.

———. 1995. "Remarks to the United Nations General Assembly in New York City." *Public Papers of the Presidents: William J. Clinton— 1995.* vol. 2 (October 22). Washington, DC: Government Printing Office, 1654–57.

———. 1996. "State of the Union Address." *Public Papers of the Presidents: William J. Clinton—1996.* Vol. 1 (January 23). Washington, DC: Government Printing Office, 79–87.

———. 1996. "President's Statement on Antiterrorism Bill Signing." April 24. *Weekly Compilation of Presidential Documents* vol. 32, no. 17 (Week ending Friday April 26, 1996). Washington, DC: Government Printing Office, 719–721.

———. 1997. "State of the Union Address." *Public Papers of the Presidents: William J. Clinton—1997.* Vol. 1 (February 4). Washington, DC: Government Printing Office, 109–17.

———. 1997. "Remarks by the President at the 50th Anniversary of the Central Intelligence Agency." *Public Papers of the Presidents: William J. Clinton—1997.* Vol. 2 (September 16). Washington, DC: Government Printing Office, 1169–71.

———. 1998. "State of the Union Address." *Public Papers of the Presidents: William J. Clinton—1998.* Vol. 1 (January 27). Washington, DC: Government Printing Office, 112–21.

———. 1998. "Remarks to the opening session of the 53rd United Nations General Assembly." United Nations, New York, September 21. *Weekly Compilation of Presidential Documents* 34, 39 (Week Ending Friday, September 25). Washington, DC: Government Printing Office, 1848–51.

———. 1999. "State of the Union Address." *Public Papers of the Presidents: William J. Clinton—1999.* Vol. 1 (January 19). Washington, DC: Government Printing Office, 62–71.

Clinton, William J. 2000. "State of the Union Address." January 27. *Weekly Compilation of Presidential Documents* vol. 36, no. 4 (Week ending Friday, January 28, 2000). Washington, DC: Government Printing Office, 160–72.

Cohen, William S. 1997. *Report of the Quadrennial Defense Review.* U.S. Department of Defense. http://www.defenselink.mil/pubs/qdr/ , May.

———. 1999. "Preparing for a Grave New World," op-ed, *Washington Post*, July 26, p. A19.

Coll, Steve C. 2004. *Ghost Wars: The Secret History of the CIA, Afghanistan, and Bin Laden, from the Soviet Invasion to September 10, 2001,* reprint ed. New York: Penguin.

Combest, Larry. 1996. "IC21: The Intelligence Community in the 21st Century, the Intelligence Community Act of 1996: Statement by Chairman Larry Combest." U.S. House of Representatives, Permanent Select Committee on Intelligence. 104th Cong., 2nd sess., March 4.

Commission on Protecting and Reducing Government Secrecy (Moynihan Commission). 1997. *Report of the Commission on Protecting and Reducing Government Secrecy.* Senate Document 105–2, 103rd Cong., 2nd sess.

Commission on the Advancement of Federal Law Enforcement (Webster Commission). 2000. *Law Enforcement in a New Century and a Changing World: Improving the Administration of Federal Law Enforcement.* Washington, DC: Government Printing Office.

Commission on the Intelligence Capabilities of the United States Regarding Weapons of Mass Destruction (Silberman-Robb Commission). 2005. *Report to the President of the United States.* Washington, DC: Government Printing Office.

Commission on the Roles and Capabilities of the United States Intelligence Community (Aspin-Brown Commission). 1996. *Preparing for the 21st Century: An Appraisal of U.S. Intelligence.* Washington, DC: Government Printing Office.

Commission to Assess the Organization of the Federal Government to Combat the Proliferation of Weapons of Mass Destruction (Deutch Commission). 1999. *Combating Proliferation of Weapons of Mass Destruction.* Washington, DC: Government Printing Office.

Conan, Neal. 2005. "The NSA and Domestic Surveillance," Talk of the Nation, National Public Radio, December 19.

Congressional Quarterly. 1981. *Congress and the Nation, 1977–1980,* vol. V. Washington, DC: Congressional Quarterly Press.

———. 1985. *Congress and the Nation, 1981–1984,* vol. VI. Washington, DC: Congressional Quarterly Press.

Congressional Quarterly. 1990. *Congress and the Nation, 1985–1988*, vol. VII. Washington, DC: Congressional Quarterly Press.

———. 1992. "The New CIA: Does the Agency Have a Role in the Post-Cold War Era?" *CQ Researcher* 2, 46: 1073–96, December 11.

———. 1993. *Congress and the Nation, 1989–1992*, vol. VIII. Washington, DC: Congressional Quarterly Press.

———. 1998. *Congress and the Nation, 1993–1996*, vol. IX. Washington, DC: Congressional Quarterly Press.

———. 2002. *Congress and the Nation, 1997–2000*, vol. X. Washington, DC: Congressional Quarterly Press.

———. 2006. *Congress and the Nation, 2001–2004*, vol. XI. Washington, DC: Congressional Quarterly Press.

Cooper, Mary H. 1996. "Reforming the CIA." *CQ Researcher*, February 2, pp. 99–119.

Cooper, Matthew, Elaine Shannon, and Viveca Novak. 2004. "Probing the Memo," *Time*, April 19, p. 19.

Council on Foreign Relations. 1996. *Making Intelligence Smarter: The Future of U.S. Intelligence*. New York: Council on Foreign Relations.

———. 2004. "The Central Intelligence Agency." Meeting featuring Walter Pincus, R. James Woolsey, William H. Webster, and Stansfield Turner. New York, May 12.

———. 2006. "Intelligence Support to the Military." Meeting featuring Jane Harman, John McLaughlin, Elizabeth Sherwood-Randall. Washington, DC, April 4.

Crowley, Michael. 2004. "Bush's Disastrous Homeland Security Department," *New Republic*, March 15, p. 17.

Cumming, Alfred, and Todd Masse. 2004. "FBI Intelligence Reform Since September 11, 2001: Issues and Options for Congress." *Congressional Research Service Report RL 32336*, August 4.

———. 2005. "Intelligence Reform Implementation at the Federal Bureau of Investigation: Issues and Options for Congress." *Congressional Research Service Report RL33033*, August 16.

Curtius, Mary. 2004. "Intelligence Reform Looks Like a Lame Duck for Now," *Los Angeles Times*, November 12, p. A24.

Cyert, Richard M., and James G. March. 1963. *A Behavioral Theory of the Firm*. London: Blackwell Publishers.

Danforth, John. 2000. "Interim Report to the Deputy Attorney General Concerning the 1993 Confrontation at the Mt. Carmel Complex, Waco, Texas," http://www.cesnur.org/testi/DanforthRpt.pdf, July 21.

Darling, Arthur B. 1990. *The Central Intelligence Agency: An Instrument of Government, to 1950*. University Park, PA: Pennsylvania State University Press.

Datz, Todd. 2004. "From the Ground Up," *CSO Magazine*, March 1.

Davis, Julie Hirschfield. 2004. "Intelligence Reform in Limbo," *Baltimore Sun*, November 23, p. 1A.

Davis, Lynn E., Gregory F. Treverton, Daniel Byman, Sara Daly, and William Rosenau. 2004. "Coordinating the War on Terror." Rand Occasional Paper. Santa Monica, CA: Rand.

Dean, Diana. 2001. "Trial testimony of Diana Dean," *United States v. Ressam*, no. CR99–666C, March 13.

Decker, Raymond J. 2001. "Combating Terrorism: Comments on Counterterrorism Leadership and National Strategy." Testimony before the House Committee on Governmental Reform, Subcommittee on National Security, Veterans Affairs, and International Relations, U.S. Government Accountability Office, GAO-01–556T, March 27.

Derthick, Martha. 1990. *Agency Under Stress: The Social Security Administration in American Government*. Washington, DC: Brookings Institution Press.

Deutch, John. 1996. "Worldwide Threats to U.S. National Security," testimony before the Senate Select Committee on Intelligence, 104th Cong., 2nd sess., February 22.

———. 1996. "The Intelligence Community," *NPR Best Kept Secrets of the Government Report*, www.fas.org/irp/offdocs/npr/vp96_intell.htm.

DeWine, Mike. 2006. "Hearing on the Nomination of General Michael Hayden to be the Director of CIA," U.S. Senate Select Committee on Intelligence, 109th Cong., 2nd sess., May 18.

Diamond, John. 2002. "Terror group's messengers steer clear of NSA," *USA Today*, October 18, p. 12A.

Dies, Robert. 2001. "Reforming FBI Management: the Views From Inside and Out," testimony before the Senate Judiciary Committee, 107th Cong., 1st sess., July 18.

Doherty, Caroll J. 1996. "Spy Agency Overhaul Drive Loses Momentum," *Congressional Quarterly*, August 24.

Downs, Anthony. 1967. *Inside Bureaucracy*. Upper Saddle River, NJ: Scott Foresman & Co.

Doyle, Charles. 2002. "The USA Patriot Act: A Legal Analysis," *Congressional Research Service Report*, RL 31377, April 15.

Duffy, Michael. 2003. "Could It Happen Again?" *Time Magazine*, August 4, p. 22.

Eden, Lynn. 2003. *Whole World on Fire: Organizations, Knowledge, and Nuclear Weapons Devastation*. Ithaca, NY: Cornell University Press.

Eggen, Dan. 2004. "Bush Gives CIA Director More Power," *Washington Post*, August 28, p. A1.

Eisendrath, Craig, ed. 2000. *National Insecurity: U.S. Intelligence After the Cold War*. Philadelphia: Temple University Press.

Ekstrand, Laurie E., and Randolph C. Hite. 2004. "FBI Transformation: FBI Continues to Make Progress in its Efforts to Transform and Address Priorities." Testimony before the Senate Appropriations Committee, Subcommittee on Commerce, Justice, State, and the Judiciary. Government Accountability Office, GAO-04–578T, March 23.

Elliott, Michael. 2002. "They Had a Plan," *Time Magazine Special Report*, August 12, p. 28.

Ensor, David. 2005. "Intelligence Chief: U.S. Safer Since 9/11," CNN, December 2.

Epstein, David, and Sharyn O'Halloran. 1994. "Administrative Procedures, Information, and Agency Discretion." *American Journal of Political Science* 38 (August): 697–722.

Epstein, David, Sharyn O'Halloran, Randall Calvert, and Thrainn Eggertsson. 1999. *Delegating Powers*. New York: Cambridge University Press.

Falkenrath, Richard A. 2005. "The 9/11 Commission Report: A Review Essay." *International Security* 29, 3 (Winter 2004–2005): 170–90.

———. 2006. "Prepared Statement of Testimony. Senate Committee on Homeland Security and Governmental Affairs, 109th Cong. 2nd sess., September 12.

Fearon, James D. 1994. "Domestic Political Audiences and the Escalation of International Disputes." *American Political Science Review* 88 (September): 577–92.

Federal Bureau of Investigation. 1998. *Draft FBI Strategic Plan: 1998–2003, Keeping Tomorrow Safe*. Unclassified version, May. Washington, DC: Government Printing Office.

———. 2004. "The FBI Workforce by the Numbers," www.fbi.gov/page2/aug04/workforce082504.htm, August 25.

———. 2004. *Report to the National Commission on Terrorist Attacks Upon the United States: The FBI's Counterterrorism Program Since September 11, 2001,* http://www.fbi.gov/publications/commission/9–11commissionrep.pdf, April 14.

———. 2006. "The End of the Cold War (1989–1993)," *History of the FBI*, http://www.fbi.gov/libref/historic/history/text.htm#coldwar.

———. 2006. "Origins, 1908–1910," *FBI History*, http://www.fbi.gov/libref/historic/history/text.htm#origins.

Fessenden, Helen. 2006. "The Limits of Intelligence Reform," *Foreign Affairs* 84, 6: 106–20.

Fessler, Pamela. 1992. "Chairmen Boren, McCurdy Urge Leaner, Revamped Operations." *Congressional Quarterly Weekly Report* 50, 6 (February 8): 316–17.

Fine, Glenn A, inspector general, U.S. Department of Justice. 2002. "Homeland Security: Tracking International Students in Higher Education—Progress and Issues since 9–11," testimony before the House Committee on Education and the Workforce, Subcommittee on 21st Century Competitiveness, Subcommittee on Select Education, 107th Cong., 2nd sess., September 24.

Fine, Glenn A. 2002. "The OIG's Audit of Aspects of the Federal Bureau of Investigation's Counterterrorism Program,"testimony before the Senate Judiciary Committee, Subcommittee on Technology, Terrorism, and Government Information, 107th Cong., 2nd sess., October 9.

———. 2006. "FBI Oversight," testimony before the Senate Judiciary Committee hearing, 109th Cong., 2nd sess., May 2.

Finnemore, Martha, and Kathryn Sikkink. 1998. "International Norm Dynamics and Political Chance." *International Organization* 52 (Autumn): 887–917.

Frank, Thomas. 2002. "Push is On to Overhaul FBI," *Newsday*, December 29, p. A8.

Freeh, Louis J. 1995. "FY 1996 budget," statement before the House Appropriations Subcommittee on Commerce, Justice, State and the Judiciary, 104th Cong., 1st sess., March 9.

———. 1995. "Fiscal Year 1995 Commerce, Justice, State Appropriations," prepared statement before the Senate Appropriations Subcommittee on Commerce, Justice, and State, the Judiciary, and Related Agencies, 103d Cong., 2nd sess., April 14.

———. 2001. "Fiscal Year 2002 Appropriations," hearing of the House Appropriations Subcommittee on Commerce, Justice, State, and the Judiciary, 107th Cong., 1st sess., May 17.

———. 2004. "On War and Terrorism," testimony before The 9/11 Commission, tenth public hearing, http://www.9–11 commission.gov/hearings/hearing10/freeh_statement.pdf, April 13.

Freeh, Louis J., and Howard Means. 2005. *My FBI: Bringing Down the Mafia, Investigating Bill Clinton, and Fighting the War on Terror.* New York: St. Martin's Press.

Freeman, John Henry, and Michael T. Hannan. 1977. "The Population Ecology of Organizations." *American Journal of Sociology* 82 (March): 929–64.

———. 1984. "Structural Inertia and Organizational Change." *American Sociological Review* 49 (April): 149–64.

———. 1989. *Organizational Ecology.* Cambridge, MA: Harvard University Press.

Friel, Brian. 2001. "Behind the Badge," Govexec.com, December 1.

Gannon, John. 2006. Written testimony submitted to the Senate Judiciary Committee, hearing on "FBI Oversight," 109th Cong., 2nd sess., May 2.

Gates, Robert. 1992. Testimony before the House and Senate Intelligence Committees (joint hearing), "Intelligence Reorganization," 102nd Cong., 2nd sess., April 1.

Gebicke, Mark F. 1999. "Combating Terrorism: Observations on Growth in Federal Programs." Testimony before the House Committee on Transportation and Infrastructure, Subcommittee on Oversight, Investigations, and Emergency Management, Government Accountability Office T-NSIAD99–181, June 9.

Gellman, Barton, and Dafna Linzer. 2005. "Pushing the Limits of Wartime Powers," *Washington Post*, December 18, p. A01.

George, Roger Z., and Robert D. Kline, eds. 2005. *Intelligence and the National Security Strategist: Enduring Issues and Challenges.* Washington, DC: National Defense University Press.

Gerecht, Reuel Marc. 2001. "The Counterterrorist Myth," *Atlantic Monthly*, July–August, pp. 38–42.

———. 2004. "The Sorry State of the CIA." American Enterprise Institute for Public Policy Research, July.

Gertz, Bill. 2002. *Breakdown: How America's Intelligence Failures Led to 9/11.* New York: Regnery, 2002.

Gladwell, Malcolm. 2003. "Connecting the Dots: the Paradoxes of Intelligence Reform," *New Yorker*, March 10, pp. 83–89.

Glasser, Susan B., and Michael Grunwald. 2005. "Department's Mission was Undermined from Start," *Washington Post*, December 22, p. A01.

Glynn, Mary Ann, Theresa K. Lant, and Frances J. Milliken. 1994. "Mapping Learning Processes in Organizations: A Multi-Level Framework Linking Learning and Organizing," in *Advances in Managerial Cognition and Organizational Information Processing*, vol. 5. Greenwich, CT: JAI Press.

Gorelick, Jamie S. 1995. "Instructions on Separation of Certain Foreign Counterintelligence and Criminal Investigations," memo to Mary Jo White, Louis Freeh, and Jo Ann Harris, day unspecified.

Gorman, Siobhan. 2003. "Worlds Apart: Since 9/11, the FBI and CIA Need Each Other, but They Can Barely Communicate. Can This Relationship Be Saved?" *National Journal*, August 2.

———. 2004. "FBI Chief Struggling to Turn Rhetoric into Action," *National Journal*, August 23.

———. 2005. "Fewer Better Spies Key to Intelligence Reform, Former Official Says," *National Journal*, March 18.

———. 2006. "Lingering Mistrust between Pentagon, CIA Fuels Concerns," *Baltimore Sun*, May 9, p. 1A.

Gorman, Siobhan, and Sydney J. Freedberg, Jr. 2004. "National Security: Carter and Turner on Intelligence Reform," *National Journal*, October 9.

Graham, Bob, with Jeff Nussbaum. 2004. *Intelligence Matters: The CIA, the FBI, Saudi Arabia, and the Failure of America's War on Terror*. New York: Random House.

Gray, Jerry. 1996. "FBI Chief Pleads for Anti-Terror Firepower," *New York Times*, August 2, p. A12.

———. 1996. "Republicans Weaken House Bill on Combating Terrorism," *New York Times*, August 3, p. A7.

Griffin, Rodman D. 1992. "The New CIA: The Issues." *Congressional Quarterly Researcher* 2, 46 (December): 1073–96.

Gruber, Amelia. 2005. "Squeezing Services," *Government Executive Magazine*, http://www.govexec.com/features/0305–01/0305–01sls4 .htm, March 1.

Halperin, Morton H. 1974. *Bureaucratic Politics and Foreign Policy*. Washington, DC: Brookings Institution Press.

Hammond, Thomas H. 2005. "Why is the Intelligence Community so Difficult to Redesign?" Paper presented at the Annual Conference of the Midwest Political Science Association. Chicago, IL.

Harman, Jane, and Pat Roberts. 2004. *Fox News Sunday*, November 21.

Harris, John F. 1996. "Clinton Signs 'Mighty Blow,' Against Terrorism," *Washington Post*, April 25, p. A4.

Harris, Shane. 2002. "Come Together," www.govexec.com, March 1.

———. 2002. "Rebooting the Bureau," www.govexec.com, August 1.

———. 2002. "FBI Technology Shortcomings Hamper Sniper Investigation," www.govexec.com, October 23.

Harris, Shane, and Drew Clark. 2003. "FBI Chief Seeks New Powers; Rebuffs Critics," www.govexec.com, February 11.

Hedley, John H. 1996. "The Intelligence Community: Is it Broken? How to Fix It?" *Studies in Intelligence* 39, 5, http://www.cia.gov/csi/ studies/96unclass/hedley.htm.

Hersh, Seymour M. 2001. "Annals of National Security: What Went Wrong." *New Yorker*, October 8, p. 34.

Heymann, Philip B. 1998. *Terrorism and America: A Commonsense Strategy for a Democratic Society*. Cambridge, MA: MIT Press.

Hill, Eleanor. 2002. "Joint Inquiry Staff Statement, Part I." House Permanent Select Committee on Intelligence and Senate Select Committee on Intelligence, *Joint Inquiry into Intelligence Community Activities Before and After the Terrorist Attacks of September 11, 2001*, 107th Cong., 2nd sess., September 18.

———. 2002. "Joint Inquiry Staff Statement: The Intelligence Community's Knowledge of the September 11 Hijackers Prior to September 11, 2001." House Permanent Select Committee on Intelligence and

Senate Select Committee on Intelligence, *Joint Inquiry into Intelligence Community Activities Before and After the Terrorist Attacks of September 11, 2001,* 107th Cong., 2nd sess., September 20.

Hill, Eleanor. 2002. "Joint Inquiry Staff Statement: Counterterrorism Information Sharing with Other Federal Agencies and with State and Local Governments and the Private Sector." House Permanent Select Committee on Intelligence and Senate Select Committee on Intelligence, *Joint Inquiry into Intelligence Community Activities Before and After the Terrorist Attacks of September 11, 2001,* 107th Cong., 2nd sess., October 1.

———. 2002. "Joint Inquiry Staff Statement: Proposals for Reform within the Intelligence Community." House Permanent Select Committee on Intelligence and Senate Select Committee on Intelligence, *Joint Inquiry into Intelligence Community Activities Before and After the Terrorist Attacks of September 11, 2001,* 107th Cong., 2nd sess., October 3.

———. 2002. "Joint Inquiry Staff Statement: Hearings on the Intelligence Community's Response to Past Terrorist Attacks Against the United States from February 1993 to September 2001." House Permanent Select Committee on Intelligence and Senate Select Committee on Intelligence, *Joint Inquiry into Intelligence Community Activities Before and After the Terrorist Attacks of September 11, 2001,* 107th Cong., 2nd sess., October 8.

———. 2002. "Joint Inquiry Staff Statement: The FBI's Handling of the Phoenix Electronic Communication and Investigation of Zacarias Moussaoui Prior to September 11, 2001." House Permanent Select Committee on Intelligence and Senate Select Committee on Intelligence, *Joint Inquiry into Intelligence Community Activities Before and After the Terrorist Attacks of September 11, 2001,* 107th Cong., 2nd sess., September 24, supplemented October 17.

———. 2002. "Joint Inquiry Staff Statement." House Permanent Select Committee on Intelligence and Senate Select Committee on Intelligence, *Joint Inquiry into Intelligence Community Activities Before and After the Terrorist Attacks of September 11, 2001,* 107th Cong., 2nd sess., October 17.

Hoekstra, Peter, and Jane Harman. 2006. "News Conference with Members of the House Select Committee on Intelligence," March 30.

———. 2006. "Interview on Fox News Sunday," April 23.

Hoge, James F., Jr., and Gideon Rose, eds. 2001. *How Did This Happen? Terrorism and the New War.* New York: Public Affairs.

Horn, Murray J. 1995. *The Political Economy of Public Administration: Institutional Choice in the Public Sector.* New York: Cambridge University Press.

Howell, William G., and David E. Lewis. 2002. "Agencies by Presidential Design." *Journal of Politics* 64, 4: 1095–14.

Hulnick, Arthur S. 1999. *Fixing the Spy Machine: Preparing American Intelligence for the Twenty-first Century.* Westport, CT: Praeger.

Huntington, Samuel P. 1996. *The Clash of Civilizations and the Remaking of the World Order.* New York: Simon & Schuster.

Hyland, William G. 1991. Untitled. *New York Times,* May 20, p. A15.

Inderurth, Karl F., and Loch K. Johnson, eds. 1988. *Decisions of the Highest Order: Perspectives on the National Security Council.* Pacific Grove, CA: Brooks/Cole.

Intelligence Authorization Act for Fiscal Year 1993. 1992. Public Law 102–496, 102nd Cong., 2nd sess., October 24.

Intelligence Community Performance on the Indian Nuclear Test (Jeremiah Report). June 2, 1998. Unclassified news conference at http://www.fas.org/irp/congress/2002_hr/100302hill.html, June 2.

Intelligence Community Revolution Task Force. June 1995. *Report of the Intelligence Community Revolution Task Force.* Unclassified summary in *Report of the Commission on Protecting and Reducing Government Secrecy* (Moynihan Commission), 1997. Senate Doc. 105–2, 103rd Cong., 2nd sess., June.

Intelligence Community Task Force on Personnel Reform (Jehn Study). July 1995. *Report of the Intelligence Community Task Force on Personnel Reform.* Unclassified summary in "Executive Summary," House Permanent Select Committee on Intelligence, *IC21: The Intelligence Community in the 21st Century,* 104th Cong., 2nd sess., April 19, 1996, pp. 21–22.

Intelligence Reform and Terrorism Prevention Act of 2004 Conference Report, Congressional Record S11939- 12010, appendix, www.fas.org/irp/congress/2004_cr/s120804.html.

Isikoff, Michael, and Eleanor Clift. 2004. "Intel Reform: Did Bush Push Hard?" *Newsweek,* December 6, p. 6.

Isikoff, Michael, and Daniel Klaidman. 2005. "Look Who's Not Talking—Still," *Newsweek,* April 4, p. 30.

Janis, Irving L. 1982. "Escalation of the Vietnam War: How Could it Happen?" from *Groupthink: Psychological Studies of Policy Decisions and Fiascoes,* 2nd ed. New York: Houghton Mifflin.

Jeffreys-Jones, Rhodri. 1989. *The CIA & American Democracy.* New Haven, CT: Yale University Press.

———. 2002. *Cloak and Dollar: A History of American Secret Intelligence.* New Haven, CT: Yale University Press.

Jeffreys-Jones, Rhodri, and Christopher Andrew, eds. 1997. *Eternal Vigilance? 50 Years of the CIA* London: Frank Cass.

Jehl, Douglas. 2004. "A Trusted Troubleshooter, and Overseer of Intelligence Efforts at the Defense Department," *New York Times*, May 12, p. A14.

Jehl, Douglas, and Eric Schmitt. 2004. "Pentagon Seeks to Expand Role in Intelligence," *New York Times*, December 19, p. A1.

Johnson, Loch K. 1996. *Secret Agencies: U.S. Intelligence in a Hostile World*. New Haven, CT: Yale University Press.

———. 2002. *Bombs Bugs, Drugs, and Thugs: Intelligence and America's Search for Security*. New York: New York University Press.

———. 2004. "The Aspin-Brown Intelligence Inquiry: Behind the Closed Doors of a Blue Ribbon Commission." *Studies in Intelligence* 48, 3.

———, ed. 2006. *Strategic Intelligence* (5 volumes). Westport, CT: Praeger.

Johnson, Loch K., and James J. Wirtz, eds. 2004. *Strategic Intelligence: Windows into a Secret World*. Los Angeles: Roxbury Press.

Joint Security Commission. 1994. Redefining Security: A Report to the Secretary of Defense and the Director of Central Intelligence. Washington, DC: Government Printing Office, February 28.

Kaplan, David E., Kevin Whitelaw, and Monica M. Ekman. 2004. "Mission Impossible: The inside story of how a band of reformers tried— and failed—to change America's spy agencies," *U.S. News & World Report*, August 2, p. 40.

Kanter, Rosabeth Moss. 1977. *Men and Women of the Corporation*. New York: Basic Books.

Katzenstein, Peter, ed. 1996. *The Culture of National Security: Norms and Identity in World Politics*, New York: Columbia University Press.

Kaufman, Herbert. 1976. *Are Government Organizations Immortal?* Washington, DC: Brookings Institution Press.

Kean, Thomas H., and Lee H. Hamilton, with Benjamin Rhodes. 2006. *Without Precedent: The Inside Story of the 9/11 Commission*. New York: Alfred A. Knopf.

Kessler, Ronald. 2003. *The Bureau: The Secret History of the FBI*. New York: St. Martin's.

———. 2003. *The CIA at War*. New York: St Martin's.

Kier, Elizabeth. 1999. *Imagining War: French and British Military Doctrine between the Wars*. Princeton: Princeton University Press.

Kindsvater, Larry C. 2003. "The Need to Reorganize the Intelligence Community." *Studies in Intelligence* 47, 1: 33–37.

Kitfield, James. 2000. "CIA, FBI, and Pentagon Team to Fight Terrorism," *National Journal*, September 16.

Klein, Joe. 2001. "Closework: Why We Couldn't See What was Right in Front of Us." *New Yorker*, October 10.

Kolbert, Elizabeth. 1992. "The 1992 Campaign: Campaign Watch; Clinton's Big Moment is Short on Telegenics," *New York Times*, July 18, p. 10.

Korb, Lawrence J. 2003. *A New National Security Strategy in an Age of Terrorists, Tyrants, and Weapons of Mass Destruction*. New York: Council on Foreign Relations.

Krim, Jonathan. 2005. "FBI Rejects Its New Case File Software: Database Project Has Cost Nearly $170 Million," *Washington Post*, January 14, p. A05.

Labaton, Stephen. 1996. "House Kills Sweeping Provisions in Counterterrorism Legislation," *New York Times*, March 14, p. A1.

Leblebici, Hussein, Gerald Salancik, Anne Copay, and Tom King. 1983. "Institutional Change and the Transformation of Interorganizational Fields: An Organizational History of the U.S. Radio Broadcasting Industry." *Administrative Science Quarterly* 36: 333–63.

Lehman, John. 2006. "Are We Any Safer?" Proceedings of the U.S. Naval Institute (September).

Levitt, Barbara, and James G. March. 1988. "Organizational Learning." *Annual Review of Sociology* 14: 319–40.

Lewis, David E. 2003. *Presidents and the Politics of Agency Design: Political Insulation in the United States Government Bureaucracy, 1946–1997*. Stanford, CA: Stanford University Press.

Lichtblau, Eric, and Charles Piller. 2002. "Without a Clue: How the FBI lost its way," *Milwaukee Journal Sentinel*, August 11, p. 01J.

Linzer, Dafna, and Charles R. Babcock. 2006. "Ousted CIA No. 3 is Target of Raids," *Washington Post*, March 13, p. A1.

Loeb, Vernon. 2000. "Back Channels: The Intelligence Community; in House of Mirrors, a Bad Reflection," *Washington Post*, February 18, p. A 21.

Loomis, Carol J. 2004. "The Sinking of Bethlehem Steel." *Fortune*, April 5, p. 174.

Los Angeles Times. 2003. Editorial. "Sideline Diplomacy: Former Secretary Madeleine Albright on War, Peace, Terrorism," November 2, home edition, p. M3.

Lowenthal, Mark M. 1992. *U.S. Intelligence: Evolution and Anatomy*, 2nd ed. Washington, DC: Center for Strategic and International Studies.
———. 2006. *Intelligence: From Secrets to Policy*, 3rd ed. Washington, DC: Congressional Quarterly Press.

Lowi, Theodore J. 1979. *The End of Liberalism: The Second Republic of the United States*. New York: W. W. Norton.

Lowry, Rich. 2003. *Legacy: Paying the Price of the Clinton Years*. New York: Regnery.

March, James G. 1981. "Footnotes to Organizational Change." *Administrative Science Quarterly* 26 (December): 563–77.

———. 1991. "Exploration and Exploitation in Organizational Learning." *Organizational Science* 2: 71–87.

———. 1999. *The Pursuit of Organizational Intelligence*. Malden, MA: Blackwell.

March, James G., and Herbert A. Simon. 1958. *Organizations*. New York: John Wiley & Sons.

March, James G., and Johan P. Olsen. 1976. *Ambiguity and Choice in Organizations*. Bergen, Norway: Universitetsforlaget.

———. 1999. "Institutional Perspectives on Political Institutions." In *The Pursuit of Organizational Intelligence*, ed. by James G. March. Oxford: Blackwell Publishers.

Mashaw, Jerry L. 1990. "Explaining Administrative Process: Normative, Positive, and Critical Stories of Legal Development." *Journal of Law, Economics, and Organization* 6: 272–98.

Masse, Todd and William Krouse. 2003. "The FBI: Past, Present, and Future." *Congressional Research Service Report RL 32095*, October 2.

Mayhew, David. 1974. *Congress: The Electoral Connection*. New Haven, CT: Yale University Press.

Mazzetti, Mark. 2006. "CIA Making Rapid Strides for Regrowth," *New York Times*, May 17, p. A1.

McCubbins, Matthew D. 1985. "The Legislative Design of Regulatory Structure." *American Journal of Political Science* 29 (November): 721–48.

McCubbins, Matthew D., Roger G. Noll, and Barry R. Weingast. 1987. "Administrative Procedures as Instruments of Political Control." *Journal of Law, Economics, and Organization* 3: 243–77.

———. 1989. "Structure and Process, Politics and Policy: Administrative Arrangements and the Political Control of Agencies." *Virginia Law Review* 75: 431–82.

McCubbins, Matthew D., and Thomas Schwartz. 1984. "Congressional Oversight Overlooked: Policy Patrol Versus Fire Alarm." *American Journal of Political Science* 28 (February): 165–79.

McGee, Jim. 1997. "The Rise of the FBI," *Washington Post Magazine*, July 20, p. W10.

McGee, Jim, and Brian Duffy. 1996. "Someone to Watch Over Us," *Washington Post*, June 23, p. W9.

McGroddy, James C., and Herbert S. Lin, eds. 2004. *A Review of the FBI's Trilogy Information Modernization Program*. Committee on the FBI's Trilogy Information Technology Modernization Program, Computer Science and Telecommunications Board, Division on Engineering and Physical Sciences, National Research Council of the National Academies. Washington, DC: The National Academies Press.

McLaughlin, John. 2006. "Intelligence Support to the Military," Address at Council on Foreign Relations Meeting, Washington, DC, April 4.

McWethy, John, John Miller, and Ted Koppel. 1998. "One of America's Most Dangerous Enemies," *Nightline*, ABC News, June 10.

Merton, Robert K. 1957. *Social Theory and Social Structure*, 2nd ed. Glencoe, IL: Free Press.

Meyer, John W., and Brian Rowan. 1977. "Institutionalized Organizations: Formal Structure as Myth and Ceremony." *American Journal of Sociology* 83:340–63.

Meyer, Marshall W., and Lynne G. Zucker. 1989. *Permanently Failing Organizations*. Newbury Park, CA: Sage Publications.

Mezias, Stephen J., and Anne S. Miner. 1996. "Ugly Duckling No More: Pasts and Futures of Organizational Learning Research." *Organizational Science* 7 (January–February): 88–99.

Miller, Greg. 2006. "Hayden Defends Spying by NSA," *Los Angeles Times*, May 19, p. A1.

Miller, John, Chris Mitchell, and Michael Stone. 2003. *The Cell: Inside the 9/11 Plot and Why the FBI and CIA Failed to Stop It*. New York: Hyperion.

Moe, Terry M. 1984. "The New Economics of Organization." *American Journal of Political Science* 28 (November): 739–77.

———. 1985. "The Politicized Presidency." In *The New Direction in American Politics*, ed. John E. Chubb and Paul E. Peterson. Washington, DC: Brookings Institution Press.

———. 1987. "An Assessment of the Positive Theory of 'Congressional Dominance.'" *Legislative Studies Quarterly* 12 (November): 475–520.

———. 1989. "The Politics of Bureaucratic Structure." In *Can the Government Govern?*, ed. John E. Chubb and Paul E. Peterson. Washington, DC: Brookings Institution Press.

———. 1990. "The Politics of Structural Choice: Toward a Theory of Public Bureaucracy." In *Organization Theory, From Chester Barnard to the Present and Beyond*, ed. Oliver E. Williamson. New York: Oxford University Press.

Moran, Michael. 2004. "The Intelligence Wars," MSNBC Special Report, August 19.

Mueller, Robert. 2002. "FBI Reorganization," testimony before the House Appropriations Subcommittee for the Departments of Commerce, Justice, State and Judiciary, 107th Cong., 2nd sess., June 21.

Myers, Lisa. 2004. "Foiling Millennium Attack was Mostly Luck," NBC News, April 29.

Naftali, Timothy. 2005. *Blind Spot: The Secret History of American Counterterrorism*. New York: Basic Books.

National Archives. "Constitution of the United States: Questions and Answers," http://www.archives.gov/national-archives-experience/charters/constitution_q_and_a.html.

National Commission on Terrorism (Bremer Commission). 2000. *Countering the Changing Threat of International Terrorism*. Washington, DC: Government Printing Office.

National Defense Panel. 1997. *Transforming Defense: National Security in the 21st Century*, http://www.fas.org/man/docs/ndp/toc.htm, December 1.

National Institute for Public Policy. 2002. *Modernizing Intelligence: Structure and Change for the 21st Century*. Fairfax, VA: National Institute for Public Policy.

National Performance Review. 1993. *From Red Tape to Results: Creating a Government that Works Better and Costs Less*. Washington, DC: Government Printing Office.

———. 1993. "INTEL02: Enhance Community Responsiveness to Customers," *The Intelligence Community: Recommendations and Actions*, http://govinfo.library.unt.edu/npr/library/reports/intel.html.

———. 1995. *National Performance Review Phase II Initiatives: An Intelligence Community Report*. Washington, DC: Government Printing Office.

Neustadt, Richard E. 1960. *Presidential Power*. New York: John Wiley & Sons.

New, William. 2003. "Bipartisan Group of Senators Bashes FBI, Files Oversight Bill, "National Journal's Technology Daily, February 25.

New York Times. 2001. "The Spy Puzzle." Editorial. November 4, p. 12.

Nye, Joseph S., Jr. 2004. *Soft Power: The Means to Success in World Politics*. New York: Public Affairs.

Oberdorfer, Don. 1991. "Shift to domestic concerns urged: US foreign policy experts point to major problems at home," *Washington Post*, July 19, p. A19.

Office of the Press Secretary, the White House. 1995. "Fact Sheet on Omnibus Counterterrorism Act," February 10.

———. 1995. "Text of Clinton Letter to Congress on Counterterrorism Act of 1995," February 10.

———. 1998. "Fact Sheet: Combating Terrorism: Presidential Decision Directive 62," http://www.fas.org/irp/offdocs/pdd-62.htm, May 22.

———. 1998. "Text of Presidential Decision Directive 63, "Critical Infrastructure, Protection," http://www.fas.org/irp/offdocs/pdd/pdd-63.htm, May 22.

Office of the Press Secretary, the White House. 1998. "Fact Sheet: Protecting America's Critical Infrastructures: PDD 63," http://www.fas.org/irp/offdocs/pdd/pdd-63.htm, May 22.

———. 2002 "Remarks by the President in Address to the Nation," http://www.whitehouse.gov/news/releases/2002/06/20020606–8.html, June 6.

———. 2003. "Fact Sheet: Strengthening Intelligence to Better Protect America," www.whitehouse.gov/news/releases/2003/01/20030128–12.html, January 28.

———. 2004. "Background Briefing Via Conference Call on the President's PDB of August 6, 2001," www.whitehouse.gov/news/releases/2004/04/20040410–6.html, April 10.

———. 2004. "Memorandum for the Director of Central Intelligence," www.whitehouse.gov/news/releases/2004/11/print/20041123–5.html, November 23.

Office of the Inspector General, U.S. Department of Justice. 1999. *The Handling of FBI Intelligence Information related to the Justice Department's Campaign Finance Investigation.* Special Report, July.

———. 2002. *An Investigation of the Belated Production of Documents in the Oklahoma City Bombing Case.* Special Report, March 19.

———. 2002. *A Review of the Federal Bureau of Investigation's Counterterrorism Program: Threat Assessment, Strategic Planning, and Resource Management.* Audit Report 02–38 (Executive Summary Declassified and Redacted), September.

———. 2003. *Federal Bureau of Investigation Casework and Human Resource Allocation.* Audit Report 03–37, September.

———. 2003. *The Federal Bureau of Investigation's Implementation of Information Technology Recommendations.* Audit Report 03–36, September.

———. 2003. *The Federal Bureau of Investigation's Efforts to Improve the Sharing of Intelligence and Other Information.* Audit Report 04–10, December.

———. 2004. *The Federal Bureau of Investigation's Foreign Language Program—Translation of Counterterrorism and Counterintelligence Foreign Language Material* (Unclassified/Redacted Executive Summary). Audit Report 04–25, July.

———. 2005. *The Federal Bureau of Investigation's Management of the Trilogy Information Technology Modernization Project.* Audit Report 05–07, February.

———. 2005. *The Federal Bureau of Investigation's Efforts to Hire, Train, and Retain Intelligence Analysts.* Audit Report 05–20, May.

———. 2005 [unclassified]. *A Review of the FBI's Handling of Intelligence Information Related to the September 11 Attacks,* June.

O'Neill, John P. 1997. Remarks at National Strategy Forum, Chicago, IL, June 11, collection of author.

Osborne, David, and Peter Plastrik. 1998. *Banishing Bureaucracy: The Five Strategies for Reinventing Government*. New York: Penguin.

Osborne, David, and Ted Gaebler. 1993. *Reinventing Government: How the Entrepreneurial Spirit is Transforming the Public Sector*. New York: Penguin.

Peltzman, Sam. 1976. "Toward a More General Theory of Regulation." *Journal of Law and Economics* 19 (August): 211–40.

Perrow, Charles. 1986. *Complex Organizations: A Critical Essay*, 3rd ed. New York: McGraw-Hill.

———. 1999. *Normal Accidents: Living with High-Risk Technologies*. Princeton, NJ: Princeton University Press.

Peters, Thomas J., and Robert H. Waterman, Jr. 1982. *In Search of Excellence: Lessons from America's Best-Run Companies*. New York: Warner Books.

Pfeffer, Jeffrey, and Gerald Salancik. 1978. *The External Control of Organizations*. New York: Harper & Row.

Pillar, Paul R. 2001. *Terrorism and U.S. Foreign Policy*. Washington, DC: Brookings Institution Press.

Pincus, Walter. 1996. "Untangling the spy network's webs," *Washington Post*, March 5, p. A13.

———. 1996. "Panels continue impasse on intelligence," *Washington Post*, June 7, p. A21.

———. 2002. "Rumsfeld Casts Doubt On Intelligence Reform. Changes Suggested by Presidential Panel," *Washington Post*, April 9, p. A17.

———. 2004. "Intelligence Bill Clears Congress," *Washington Post*, December 9, p. A4.

———. 2005. "Pentagon's Intelligence Authority Widens; Fact Sheet Details Secretive Agency's Growth from Focus on Policy to Counterterrorism," *Washington Post*, December 19, p. A10.

———. 2006. "Some Lawmakers Doubt DNI has Taken Intelligence Reigns," *Washington Post*, February 2, p. A09.

———. 2006. "FBI Role in Terror Probe Questioned: Lawyers Point to Fine Line between Sting and Entrapment," *Washington Post*, September 2, p. A1.

Pittsburgh Post-Gazette. 1996. "Anti-terrorism Law Expected to Pass This Week," April 16, sooner edition, p. A-6.

Posner, Gerald L. 2003. *Why America Slept: The Failure to Prevent 9/11*. New York: Random House.

Posner, Richard A. 2004. "The 9/11 Report: A Dissent," *New York Times Book Review*, August 29, p. 1.

Posner, Richard A. 2005. *Preventing Surprise Attacks: Intelligence Reform in the Wake of 9/11.* Oxford: Rowman & Littlefield.

———. 2006. *Uncertain Shield: The U.S. Intelligence System in the Throes of Reform.* Oxford: Rowman & Littlefield.

———. 2006 *Countering Terrorism.* Oxford: Rowman & Littlefield, 2006.

Powell, Walter W., and Paul J. DiMaggio. 1991. *The New Institutionalism in Organizational Analysis.* Chicago: The University of Chicago Press.

Powers, Thomas. 2002. "The Trouble with the CIA." *New York Review of Books* 49, http://www.nybooks.com/articles/15109, January 17.

———. 2002. *Intelligence Wars: American Secret History from Hitler to Al-Qaeda.* New York: New York Review Books.

Prados, John. 1993. "Woolsey and the CIA," *Bulletin of the Atomic Scientists* 49, 6: 33–38.

Priest, Dana. 2005. "CIA Holds Terror Suspects in Secret Prisons," *Washington Post*, November 2, p. A1.

Public Broadcasting Corporation (PBS). 2002. "The Man Who Knew," October 3.

———. 2006. "The Dark Side," June 20.

Purdum, Todd S. 1996. "Clinton Proposes Harsher Measures Against Terrorism," *New York Times*, July 29, p. A1.

Ragavan, Chitra. 2005. "Fixing the FBI," *U.S. News and World Report*, March 28.

Ranelagh, John. 1986. *The Agency: The Rise and Decline of the CIA.* New York: Simon & Schuster.

Ransom, Harry Howe. 1970. *The Intelligence Establishment.* Cambridge, MA: Harvard University Press.

Redd, John Scott (director, National Counterterrorism Center). 2006. "Statement for the Record," Senate Foreign Relations Committee hearing, 109th Cong., 2nd sess., June 13.

Reno, Janet. 1995. "Procedures for Contacts Between the FBI and the Criminal Division Concerning Foreign Intelligence and Foreign Counterintelligence Investigations." Memo to assistant attorney general, FBI director, Counsel for Intelligence Policy, and United States Attorneys, July 19.

Rice, Condoleezza. 2004. "9/11: For the Record," *Washington Post*, March 22, p. A21.

———. 2004. *60 Minutes*, CBS News, interview by Ed Bradley, March 28.

Richelson, Jeffrey T. 1999. *The U.S. Intelligence Community*, 4th ed. Boulder, CO: Westview.

Ripley, Randall B., and James M. Lindsay, eds. 1997. *U.S. Foreign Policy After the Cold War.* Pittsburgh, PA: University of Pittsburgh Press.

Risen, James. 2006. *State of War: The Secret History of the CIA and the Bush Administration*. New York: Free Press.

Risen, James, and David Johnston. 2002. "FBI Report Found Agency Not Ready to Counter Terror," *New York Times*, June 1, p. A1.

Risen, James, and Eric Lichtblau. 2005. "Bush Lets U.S. Spy on Callers Without Courts," *New York Times*, December 16, p. A1.

Roberts, Pat. 2004. *Fox News Sunday*, November 21.

Rosen, James. 2004. "Cease-fire ends; blame game starts," *Minneapolis Star Tribune*, March 28, p. 1A.

Rosen, Jeffrey. 1996. "Shell Game," *New Republic*, May 13, p. 6.

Rosenbaum, David E. 2002. "Traces of Terror: The Critics; Bush Allies Direct Heaviest Fire against both F.B.I. and C.I.A." *New York Times*, June 19, p. A19.

Rothenberg, Lawrence S. 1994. *Regulation, Organizations, and Politics: Motor Freight Policy at the Interstate Commerce Commission*. Ann Arbor, MI: University of Michigan Press.

Sagan, Scott D. 1993. *The Limits of Safety: Organizations, Accidents, and Nuclear Weapons*. Princeton, NJ: Princeton University Press.

San Diego Union Tribune. 2004. "Intelligence gaps: America's spy network needs a quick fix." Editorial. April 22, p. B6.

Scalingi, Paula L. 1992. "U.S. Intelligence in an Age of Uncertainty: Refocusing to Meet the Challenge." *The Washington Quarterly* 15 (Winter): 144.

Schlosser, Julie, and Ellen Florian. 2004. "The biggest moneymakers! The best investments! The hall-of-famers and the one-hit-wonders! The triumphs, the failures, the milestones! Fifty years of . . . Amazing Facts!" *Fortune,* April 5, p. 152.

Schmitt, Eric. 2006. "Clash Foreseen between CIA and Pentagon," *New York Times*, May 10, p.A1.

Schultz, Kenneth A. 1998. "Domestic Opposition and Signaling in International Crises." *American Political Science Review* 92 (December): 829–44.

Sciolino, Elaine. 1992. "CIA casting about for new missions," *New York Times*, February 4, p. A1.

Scott, W. Richard. 2004. "Reflections on a Half-Century of Organizational Sociology." *Annual Review of Sociology* 30 (August) 1–21.

Serwer, Andy. 2002. "Breaking Records—For Bankruptcies; Chapter 11 is the hottest fad in business. But that's not even the half of it," *Fortune*, July 22, p. 213.

Shane, Scott. 2006. "Year into Revamped Spying, Troubles and Some Progress," *New York Times*, February 28, p. A12.

Shane, Scott. 2006. "In New Job, Spymaster Draws Bipartisan Criticism," *New York Times*, April 20, p. A1.

Shane, Scott, and Lowell Bergman. 2006. "FBI Struggling to Reinvent Itself to Fight Terror," *New York Times*, October 10, p. A1.

Shelby, Richard C. 2002. "September 11 and the Imperative of Reform in the U.S. Intelligence Community," *Additional Views of Senator Richard C. Shelby, Vice Chairman, Senate Select Committee on Intelligence, Joint Inquiry Report*, 107th Cong., 2nd sess., December 10.

Shenon, Philip, and Douglas Jehl. 2004. "House Proposal Puts Less Power in New Spy Post," *New York Times*, September 25, p. A1.

Shenon, Philip, and Neil A. Lewis. 2006. "Tracing Terror Plots, British Watch, Then Pounce," *New York Times*, August 13, p. A1.

Shirley, Edward G. (Reuel Marc Gerecht). 1998. "Can't Anybody Here Play This Game?" *Atlantic Monthly* 281, February, pp. 45–61.

Simon, Herbert A. 1976. *Administrative Behavior: A Study of Decision-Making Processes in Administrative Organizations*, 3rd ed. New York: Free Press.

Sims, Jennifer E., and Burton Gerber, eds. 2005. *Transforming U.S. Intelligence*. Washington, DC: Georgetown University Press.

Singh, Jitendra V., ed. 1990. *Organizational Evolution: New Directions*. Newbury Park, CA: Sage Publications.

Smist, Frank J., Jr. 1994. *Congress overseas the United States Intelligence Community*, 2nd ed. Knoxville, TN.: University of Tennessee Press.

Smith, R. Jeffrey. 1996. "Gingrich Hits FBI for Handling of Files," *Washington Post*, August 5, p. A7.

Snider, L. Britt. 2005. "A Different Angle on the Aspin-Brown Commission." *Studies in Intelligence* 49, 1.

Specter, Arlen. 1996. "The Intelligence Organization Act of 1996." *Congressional Record*. 104th Cong., 2nd sess., March 6.

Stasser, Garold, Laurie A. Taylor, and Coleen Hanna. 1989. "Information Sampling in a Structured and Unstructured Discussion of Three- and Six-person Groups." *Journal of Personality and Social Psychology*, 57, 1 (July): 67–78.

Stein, Jeff. 2006. "FBI Under the Gun," *CQ Weekly*, May 1, p. 1152.

Stigler, George J. 1971. "The Theory of Economics Regulation." *Bell Journal of Economics and Management Science* 2: 3–21.

Stinchcombe, Arthur L. 1965. "Social Structures and Organizations." In *Handbook of Organizations*, ed. James G. March. Chicago: Rand McNally.

Stout, David. 1998. "Force Rocket Explodes Just After Liftoff," *New York Times*, August 13, p. A16.

Suskind, Ron. 2006. *The One Percent Doctrine*. New York: Simon & Schuster.

Talbott, Strobe, and Nayan Chanda, eds. 2001. *The Age of Terror: America and the World After September 11*. New York: Basic Books.

Taylor, Stuart. 2004. "Spying on Terrorists: Will the FBI Ever Be Up To the Job?" *National Journal*, 35, 2: 80–81.

Tenet, George. 1997. "Worldwide Threats to National Security," testimony before the Senate Armed Services Committee, 105th Cong., 1st sess., February 6.

———. 1998. "Worldwide Threats to National Security," testimony before the Senate Select Committee on Intelligence, 105th Cong., 2nd sess., January 28.

———. 1999. "Worldwide Threats to U.S. National Security," testimony before the Senate Armed Services Committee, 106th Cong., 1st sess. February 2, 1999.

———. 2000. "Annual Assessment of Security Threats against the United States," testimony before the Senate Select Committee on Intelligence, 106th Cong., 2nd sess., February 2.

———. 2001. "Worldwide Threats to National Security," testimony before the Senate Select Committee on Intelligence, 107th Cong., 1st sess., February 7.

———. 2002. Testimony before the HPSCI and SSCI, "Activities of the Intelligence Community in Connection with the Attacks of September 11, 2001," 107th Cong., 2nd sess., October 17.

Economist. 2002. "Special report: Time for a rethink—America's Intelligence Services," April 18, pp. 23–25.

———. 2005. "Can Spies be Made Better?" Special Report, March 19.

The Gallup Organization. 1995. CNN/USA Today Poll on Trust in Government, April 21–24, http://brain.gallup.com/documents/questionnaire.aspx?STUDY=cnn5001018.

The Homeland Security Act of 2002. 2002. Public Law 107–296, 107th Cong., 2nd sess., November 25.

The Pew Research Center for the People and the Press. 1995. "Other Important Findings and Analysis," August 17–20, http://people-press.org/reports/display.php3?PageID=412.

The Report of the Commission to Assess the Ballistic Missile Threat to the United States (Rumsfeld Commission), July 15, 1998, unclassified executive summary available at www.fas.org/irp/congress/2002_hr/100302hill.html (accessed January 30, 2006).

Thomas, Evan. 1995. *The Very Best Men: Four Who Dared: The Early Years of the CIA*. New York: Simon & Schuster.

Thornburgh, Richard. 2003. "FBI Reorganization," statement before the House Appropriations Subcommittee on Commerce, Justice, State, and the Judiciary, 108th Cong., 1st sess., June 18, p. 2. http://www.napawash.org/resources/testimony/FBITestimony%2006–18–03.pdf (accessed February 10, 2006).

Treverton, Gregory F. 1987. *Covert Action: The Limits of Intervention in the Postwar World.* New York: Basic Books.

———. 2002. "Set Up to Fail," govexec.com, September 1.

———. 2003. *Reshaping National Intelligence for an Age of Information.* Cambridge, UK: Cambridge University Press.

———. 2006. *Toward a Theory of Intelligence: Workshop Report 2006.* Santa Monica, CA: Rand.

Troy, Thomas F. 1981. *Donovan and the CIA: A History of the Establishment of the Central Intelligence Agency.* Frederick, MD: University Publications of America.

Turner, Michael A. 1995. "CIA-FBI Non-Cooperation: Cultural Trait or Bureaucratic Inertia?" *International Journal of Intelligence and Counterintelligence* 8, 3 (Fall): 259–73.

Twentieth Century Fund Task Force on the Future of U.S. Intelligence. 1996. *In from the Cold: The Report of the Twentieth Century Fund Task Force on the Future of U.S. Intelligence.* New York: Twentieth Century Fund Press.

United States Statutes at Large. 1948. Vol. 61, Part 1: 495–510. *National Security Act of 1947.* Public Law 80–253, July 26, 1947.

———. 1997. Vol. 110, Part 5: 3461–87. *Intelligence Authorization Act for Fiscal Year 1997.* Public Law 104–293, October 11, 1996.

———. 2002. Vol. 115, Part 1: 272–402. *USA PATRIOT Act.* Public Law 107–56, October 26, 2001.

———. 2003. Vol. 116, Part 3: 2135–2321. *Homeland Security Act of 2002.* Public Law 107–296, November 25, 2002.

United States Statutes at Large. 2005. Vol. 118, Part 4: 3638–872. *Intelligence Reform and Terrorism Prevention Act of 2004.* Public Law 108–458, December 17, 2004.

United States v Zacarias Moussaoui, Crim. No. 1:01cr455 (E.D. Virginia 2005), http://i.cnn.net/cnn/2005/images/04/23/moussaoui.plea.transcript.pdf.

U.S. Census Bureau. 2003. *Statistical Abstract of the United States: 2003.* Washington, DC: Government Printing Office.

———. 1999. *New World Coming: American Security in the 21st Century.* Phase I Report, http://www.au.af.mil/au/awc/awcgate/nssg/nwc.pdf, September 15.

U.S. Commission on National Security/21st Century (Hart-Rudman Commission). 2000. *Seeking a National Strategy: A Concert for Preserv-*

ing Security and Promoting Freedom. Phase II Report, http://www.au.-af.mil/au/awc/awcgate/nssg/phaseII.pdf, April 15.

U.S. Commission on National Security/21st Century (Hart-Rudman Commission). 2001. *Road Map for National Security: Imperative for Change*. Phase III Report, http://www.au.af.mil/au/awc/awcgate/nssg/phaseIIIfr.pdf, February 15.

————. 2001. *Road Map for National Security: Addendum on Structure and Process Analyses*, Volumes I-VII, April 15.

U.S. Department of Defense. 2001. *U.S.S. Cole Commission Report*. Unclassified executive summary, http://www.defenselink.mil/pubs/cole20010109.htm, January 9.

U.S. Department of State. 1999. Accountability Review Boards. Report of the Accountability Review Boards: Bombings of the U.S. Embassies in Nairobi, Kenya and Dar es Salaam, Tanzania on August 7, 1998. Http://www.state.gov/www.regions/africa/board_overview.html.

U.S. Government Accountability Office. 1997. *Combating Terrorism: Federal Agencies' Efforts to Implement National Policy and Strategy*. Report to Congressional Requesters, September.

————. 2001. *FBI Intelligence Investigations: Coordination within Justice on Counterintelligence Criminal Matters is Limited*. Report to Ranking Minority Member, Senate Committee on Governmental Affairs, GAO-01–780, July 16.

————. 2005. *Department of Homeland Security: A Comprehensive and Sustained Approach Needed to Achieve Management Integration*. Report to Congressional Requesters, GAO 05–139, March 16.

————. 2006. *Information Sharing: The Federal Government Needs to Establish Policies and Processes for Sharing Terrorism-Related and Sensitive but Unclassified Information*. Report to Congressional Requesters, GAO-06–385, March 17.

U.S. House. 1991. Permanent Select Committee on Intelligence. *FY 1992 Intelligence Authorization Act Report*. 102nd Cong., 1st sess., 102 H. Rept. 65, Part I, May 15.

————. 1992. Permanent Select Committee on Intelligence. *FY 1993 Intelligence Authorization Act Report*. 102nd Cong., 2nd sess., 102 H. Rpt. 544, Part I, June 2.

————. 1993. Permanent Select Committee on Intelligence. *FY 1994 Intelligence Authorization Act Report*. 103rd Cong., 1st sess., 103 H. Rpt. 162, June 29.

————. 1994. Permanent Select Committee on Intelligence. *FY 1995 Intelligence Authorization Act Report*. 103rd Cong., 2nd sess., 103 H. Rpt. 541, Part I, June 9.

————. 1995. Judiciary Committee. *Hearing on Terrorism*, 104th Cong., 1st sess., April 6.

U.S. House. 1995. Permanent Select Committee on Intelligence. *FY 1996 Intelligence Authorization Act Report.* H. Rpt. 104- 138 Part I, 104th Cong., 1st sess., June 14.

———. 1996. Permanent Select Committee on Intelligence. *IC21: The Intelligence Community in the 21st Century.* 104th Cong., 2nd sess., http://ww.gpo.gov/congress/house/intel/ic21/.

———. 1996. Appropriations Subcommittee on the Departments of Commerce, Justice, and State, the Judiciary, and Related Agencies. *Hearing on International Law Enforcement Programs of the Department of Justice.* 104th Cong., 1st sess., May 1.

———. 1996. Permanent Select Committee on Intelligence. *FY 1997 Intelligence Authorization Act Report.* 104th Cong., 2nd sess., H. Rpt. 104–832, May 15.

———. 1996. National Security Committee. *Hearing on Intelligence Community Reform.* 104th Cong., 2nd sess., July 11.

———. 1997. Judiciary Subcommittee on Crime. *Hearing on FBI.* 105th Cong., 1st sess., June 5.

———. 1997. Permanent Select Committee on Intelligence. *FY 1998 Intelligence Authorization Act Report.* H. Rpt. 105–135 Part I, 105th Cong., 1st sess., June 18.

———. 1998. Permanent Select Committee on Intelligence. *FY 1999 Intelligence Authorization Act Report.* H. Rpt. 105–508, 105th Cong., 2nd sess., May 5.

———. 1999. Permanent Select Committee on Intelligence. *FY 2000 Intelligence Authorization Act Report.* H. Rpt. 106–130 Part I, 106th Cong., 1st sess., May 7.

———. 1999. Appropriations Subcommittee on Commerce, Justice, State and the Judiciary. *Hearing on FY 2000 Commerce, Justice, State Appropriations.* 106th Cong., 1st sess., March 17.

———. 2000. Appropriations Subcommittee on Commerce, Justice, State, the Judiciary, and Related Agencies. *Hearing on the Fiscal Year 2001 Budget.* 106th Cong., 2nd sess., March 16.

———. 2000. Permanent Select Committee on Intelligence. *FY 2001 Intelligence Authorization Act Report.* H. Rpt. 106–620, 106th Cong., 2nd sess., May 16.

———. 2001. Appropriations Subcommittee on Commerce, Justice, State, and Justice. *Hearing on Fiscal Year 2002 Appropriations For FBI And DEA.* 107th Cong., 1st sess., May 16.

———. 2002. Appropriations Subcommittee on Commerce, Justice, State, and Justice. *Hearing on FBI Reorganization.* 107th Cong., 2nd sess., June 21.

———. 2004. Appropriations Subcommittee on the Departments of Commerce, Justice, State, the Judiciary, and Related Agencies. *Hearing on FBI Transformation.* 108th Cong., 2nd sess., June 3.

U.S. House. 2004. Committee on Armed Services. *Hearings on U.S. Intelligence Reform.* 108th Cong., 2nd sess., August 10, 11.

———. 2004. Committee on Government Reform. *Hearing on Moving from "Need to Know" to "Need to Share": A Review of the 9/11 Commission's Recommendations.* 108th Cong., 2nd sess., August 3.

———. 2004. Committee on the Judiciary. *Hearing on Anti-Terrorism Intelligence Tools Improvement Act of 2003.* 108th Cong., 2nd sess., May 18.

———. 2004. Committee on the Judiciary. *Hearing on Privacy and Civil Liberties in the Hands of the Government Post-September 11, 2001.* 108th Cong., 2nd sess., August 20.

———. 2004. Committee on the Judiciary. *Hearing on the Recommendations of the 9/11 Commission.* 108th Cong., 2nd sess., August 23.

———. 2004. Permanent Select Committee on Intelligence. *Intelligence Authorization Act for FY 2005,* H. Report 108–558, 108th Cong., 2nd sess., June 21.

———. 2004. Permanent Select Committee on Intelligence. *Hearing on the 9/11 Commission Report.* 108th Cong., 2nd sess., August 11.

———. 2004. Select Committee on Homeland Security. *Hearing on Information Sharing After September 11.* 108th Cong., 2nd sess., June 24.

———. 2004. Select Committee on Homeland Security. *Hearing on 9/11 Commission.* 108th Cong., 2nd sess., August 17.

———. 2005. Committee on Appropriations Surveys and Investigations Staff. *A Report to the Committee on Appropriations on the Federal Bureau of Investigation's Implementation of Virtual Case File.* 109th Cong., 1st sess., April.

———. 2006. Permanent Select Committee on Intelligence. *Intelligence Authorization Act for Fiscal Year 2007.* H.Rpt. 109–411, 109th Cong., 2nd sess., April 6.

———. 2006. Select Committee on Homeland Security, Subcommittee on Intelligence, Information Sharing, and Terrorism Risk Assessment. *Hearing on Protection of Privacy in the Department of Homeland Security Intelligence Enterprise.* 109th Cong., 2nd sess., May 10.

U.S. House and Senate. 1992. Committees on Intelligence. *Hearings on Intelligence Reorganization.* 102nd Cong., 2nd sess., April 1.

———. 2002. House Permanent Select Committee on Intelligence and Senate Select Committee on Intelligence. *Public hearings of the Joint Inquiry into Intelligence Community Activities Before and After the Terrorist Attacks of September 11, 2001.* 107th Cong., 2nd sess., September 18–20, 24, and 26.

———. 2002. House Permanent Select Committee on Intelligence and Senate Select Committee on Intelligence. *Public hearings of the Joint Inquiry into Intelligence Community Activities Before and After the Ter-*

rorist Attacks of September 11, 2001. 107th Cong., 2nd sess., October 1, 3, 8, and 17.

U.S. House and Senate. 2002. Joint Inquiry into Intelligence Community Activities Before and After the Terrorist Attacks of September 11, 2001. *Report of the U.S. Senate Select Committee on Intelligence and the U.S. House Permanent Select Committee on Intelligence (Joint Inquiry Final Report).* 107th Cong., 2nd sess., December.

———. 2004. "Intelligence Reform and Terrorism Prevention Act of 2004 Conference Report," *Congressional Record*, 108th Cong., 2nd sess., December 8: S11939–S12010.

U.S. Office of Management and Budget, the Executive Office of the President. 2004. "Historical Tables: Budget of the United States Government, Fiscal Year 2005. Washington, DC: Government Printing Office, www.whitehouse.gov/omb/budget/fy2005.

U.S. Senate. 1993. Select Committee on Intelligence. *Hearing on the Nomination of R. James Woolsey to become Director of Central Intelligence.* 103rd Cong., 1st sess., February 2.

———. 1994. Judiciary Subcommittee on Technology and the Law. *Hearing on Digital Telephony and Law Enforcement Access to Advanced Telecommunications Technologies and Services.* 103rd Cong., 2nd sess., March 18.

———. 1994. Select Committee on Intelligence. *Hearing on Counterintelligence.* 103rd Cong., 2nd sess., May 3.

———. 1994. Select Committee on Intelligence. *An assessment of the Aldrich H. Ames espionage case and its implications for U.S. intelligence,* http://www.fas.org/irp/congress/1994_rpt/ssci_ames.htm, November 1.

———. 1995. Committee on the Judiciary. *Hearing on Terrorism.* 104th Cong., 1st sess., April 27.

———. 1998. Committee on the Judiciary. *Hearing on Counterterrorism Strategy.* 105th Cong., 2nd sess., September 3.

———. 1999. Appropriations Subcommittee of Commerce, Justice, State, and the Judiciary. *Hearing on Counterterrorism.* 106th Cong., 1st sess., February 4.

———. 2001. Committee on the Judiciary. *Hearing on Reforming FBI Management: The Views from Inside and Out.* 107th Cong., 1st sess., July 18.

———. 2001. Committee on the Judiciary. *Hearing on the Nomination for Director of Federal Bureau of Investigation.* 107th Cong., 1st sess., July 30.

———. 2002. Committee on the Judiciary. *Hearings on Reforming the FBI in the 21st Century.* 107th Cong., 2nd sess., March 21, April 9, and May 8.

———. 2002. Committee on the Judiciary. *Hearing on Counterterrorism.* 107th Cong., 2nd sess., June 6.

U.S. Senate. 2002. Committee on the Judiciary. *Hearing on FBI Computers: 1992 Hardware—2002 Problems.* 107th Cong., 2nd sess., July 16.

———. 2003. Committee on Homeland Security and Governmental Affairs. *Hearing on Consolidating Intelligence Analysis: A Review of the President's Proposal to Create a Terrorist Threat Integration Center.* 108th Cong., 1st sess., February 14 and 26.

———. 2003. Committee on the Judiciary. *Hearing on The War Against Terrorism: Working Together to Protect America.* 108th Cong., 1st sess., March 4.

———. 2004. Committee on Armed Services. *Hearing on Implications for the Department of Defense and Military Operations of Proposals to Reorganize the U.S. Intelligence Community.* 108th Cong., 2nd sess., August 16 and 17.

———. 2004. Committee on Governmental Affairs. *Hearing on the Recommendations of the 9/11 Commission.* 108th Cong., 2nd sess., July 30.

———. 2004. Committee on Governmental Affairs. *Hearing on Assessing America's Counterterrorism Capabilities.* 108th Cong., 2nd sess., August 3.

———. 2004. Committee on Governmental Affairs. *Hearing on Reorganizing America's Intelligence Community: A View from the Inside.* 108th Cong., 2nd sess., August 16.

———. U.S. Senate. 2004. Committee on Governmental Affairs. *Hearing on Voicing the Need for Reform: The Families of 9/11.* 108th Cong., 2nd sess., August 17.

———. 2004. Committee on Governmental Affairs. *Hearing on Building an Agile Intelligence Community to Fight Terrorism and Emerging Threats.* 108th Cong., 2nd sess., September 8.

———. 2004. Committee on Governmental Affairs. *Hearing on Ensuring the U.S. Intelligence Community Supports Homeland Defense and Departmental Needs.* 108th Cong., 2nd sess., September 13.

———. 2004. Committee on Governmental Affairs. *Hearing on 9/11 Commission Human Capital Recommendations.* 108th Cong., 2nd sess., September 14.

———. 2004. Committee on the Judiciary. *Hearing on FBI Oversight: Terrorism and Other Topics.* 108th Cong., 2nd sess., May 20.

———. 2004. Committee on the Judiciary. *Hearing on Department of Justice Oversight: Terrorism and Other Topics.* 108th Cong., 2nd sess., June 8.

U.S. Senate. 2004. Select Committee on Intelligence. *U.S. Intelligence Community's Prewar Intelligence Assessments on Iraq*, S. Rpt. 108–301, 108th Cong., 2nd sess., July 9.

———. 2004. Select Committee on Intelligence. *Hearing on Intelligence Reform.* 108th Cong., 2nd sess., July 20.

———. 2004. Select Committee on Intelligence. *Hearing on Intelligence Reform.* 108th Cong., 2nd sess. August 18.

U.S. Senate. 2004. Select Committee on Intelligence. *Hearing on Reform of the U.S. Intelligence Community.* 108th Cong., 2nd sess., September 7.

―――. 2004. Select Committee on Intelligence. *Hearing on the Nomination of Porter Goss to be Director of Central Intelligence.* 108th Cong., 2nd sess., September 14.

―――. 2005. Appropriations Subcommittee on Commerce, Justice, State, the Judiciary, and Related Agencies. *Hearing on FBI Information Technology Modernization.* 109th Cong., 1st sess., February 3.

―――. 2005. Appropriations Subcommittee on Commerce, Justice, State, and the Judiciary. *Hearing on the Fiscal Year 2006 Appropriations for the Department of Justice.* 109th Cong., 1st sess., May 24.

―――. 2006. Select Committee on Intelligence. *Hearing on the Confirmation of General Michael B. Hayden to become Director of the Central Intelligence Agency.* 109th Cong., 2nd sess., May 18.

―――. 2007. Select Committee on Intelligence. *Hearing on Progress Made on Intelligence Reform.* 110th Cong., 1st sess., January 23 and 25.

Vaughan, Diane. 1996. *The Challenger Launch Decision: Risk Technology, Culture, and Deviance at NASA.* Chicago: University of Chicago Press.

―――. 1999. "The Dark Side of Organizations: Mistake, Misconduct, and Disaster." *Annual Review of Sociology* 25:271–305.

Vest, Jason. 2006. "Thin Ranks," www.govexec.com, January 1.

Walcott, John. 1996. "Mission Impossible?" *Washington Post*, December 8, p. C1.

Walcott, John, and Brian Duffy. 1994. "The CIA's Darkest Secrets," *U.S. News & World Report*, July 4, p. 46.

Warner, Michael. 2001. *Central Intelligence: Origin and Evolution.* Washington, DC: Center for the Study of Intelligence, Central Intelligence Agency.

Warrick, Joby, Joe Stephens, Mary Pat Flaherty, and James V. Grimaldi. 2001. "FBI Agents Ill-Equipped to Predict Terror Acts," *Washington Post*, September 24, p. A01.

Weiner, Tim. 1996. "Proposal Would Reorganize U.S. Intelligence Agencies," *New York Times*, March 5, p. A20.

―――. 2006. "Langley, We Have a Problem," *New York Times*, May 14, Week in Review, section 4, p. 1.

Weingast, Barry, and Mark Moran. 1983. "Bureaucratic Discretion or Congressional Control? Regulatory Policymaking by the Federal Trade Commission." *Journal of Political Economy* 91 (October): 765–800.

Weymouth, Lally. 1996. "Odd Alliances in the War on Terrorism," op-ed, *Washington Post*, August 14, p. A21.

White, John P. 1996. Testimony before the House National Security Committee, *Hearing on Intelligence Community Reform*, 104th Cong., 2nd sess., July 11.

Whoriskey, Peter, and Dan Eggen. 2006. "Terror Suspects Had No Explosives and Few Contacts," *Washington Post*, June 24, p. A3.

Wilson, James Q. 2000. *Bureaucracy: What Government Agencies Do and Why They Do It*. New York: Basic Books.

Wohlstetter, Roberta. 1962. *Pearl Harbor: Warning and Decision*. Stanford, CA: Stanford University Press.

Woolsey, R. James. 1994. "World Trouble Spots," testimony before the Senate Select Committee on Intelligence, 103rd Cong., 2nd sess., January 25.

———. 1995. "World Threat Assessment Brief," testimony before the Senate Select Committee on Intelligence, 104th Cong., 1st sess., January 10.

———. 2004. "Remarks at American Bar Association." Washington, DC, April 29.

Wood, Dan B. 1988. "Principles, Bureaucrats, and Responsiveness in Clean Air Enforcement." *American Political Science Review* 82: 213–34.

Woodward, Bob. 2002. *Bush At War*. New York: Simon & Schuster.

———. 2004. *Plan of Attack*. New York: Simon & Schuster.

———. 2005. *The Commanders: The Pentagon and the First Gulf War, 1989–1991*, rev. ed. New York: Simon & Schuster.

———. 2006. *State of Denial: Bush at War, Part III*. New York: Simon & Schuster.

Wright, Lawrence. 2006. *The Looming Tower: Al-Qaeda and the Road to 9/11*. New York: Knopf.

Yang, John. 1996. "House Pares, Then Passes, Crime, Terrorism Measure; Clinton Calls It Too Weak to be Effective," *Washington Post*, March 15, p. A04.

———. 1996. "House Approves Anti-Terrorism Measure," *Washington Post*, August 3, p. A9.

Zegart, Amy B. 1999. *Flawed by Design: The Evolution of the CIA, JCS, and NSC*. Stanford: Stanford University Press.

———. 2004. "Blue Ribbons, Black Boxes: Toward a Better Understanding of Presidential Commissions," *Presidential Studies Quarterly* 35, 2 (June): 366–93.

———. 2006. "Cloaks, Daggers, and Ivory Towers: Why Academics Don't Study U.S. Intelligence." In *Strategic Intelligence*, ed. Loch K. Johnson. Westport, CT: Praeger.

Zeman, Ned, David Wise, David Rose, and Bryan Burrough. 2004. "The Path to 9/11," *Vanity Fair*, Special investigation, November.

✳ *Index* ✳